NO NEED FOR TENCHI!™

CHEF OF IRON

STORY AND ART BY
HITOSHI OKUDA

CONTENTS

This volume contains NO NEED FOR TENCHI! PART EIGHT in its entirety.

**STORY AND ART BY
HITOSHI OKUDA**

**ENGLISH ADAPTATION BY
FRED BURKE**

Translation/Lillian Olsen
Touch-Up Art & Lettering/Dan Nakrosis
Cover Design/Hidemi Sahara
Editor/Jason Thompson

Managing Editor/Annette Roman
Editor-in-Chief/Hyoe Narita
Publisher/Seiji Horibuchi

Printed in Canada

Published by Viz Communications, Inc.
P.O. Box 77010 • San Francisco, CA 94107

10 9 8 7 6 5 4 3 2 1
First printing, July 2000

Vizit us at our World Wide Web site at **www.vizkids.com**!

<u>NO NEED FOR TENCHI! GRAPHIC NOVELS TO DATE</u>
NO NEED FOR TENCHI!
SWORD PLAY
MAGICAL GIRL PRETTY SAMMY
SAMURAI SPACE OPERA
UNREAL GENIUS
DREAM A LITTLE SCHEME
TENCHI IN LOVE
CHEF OF IRON

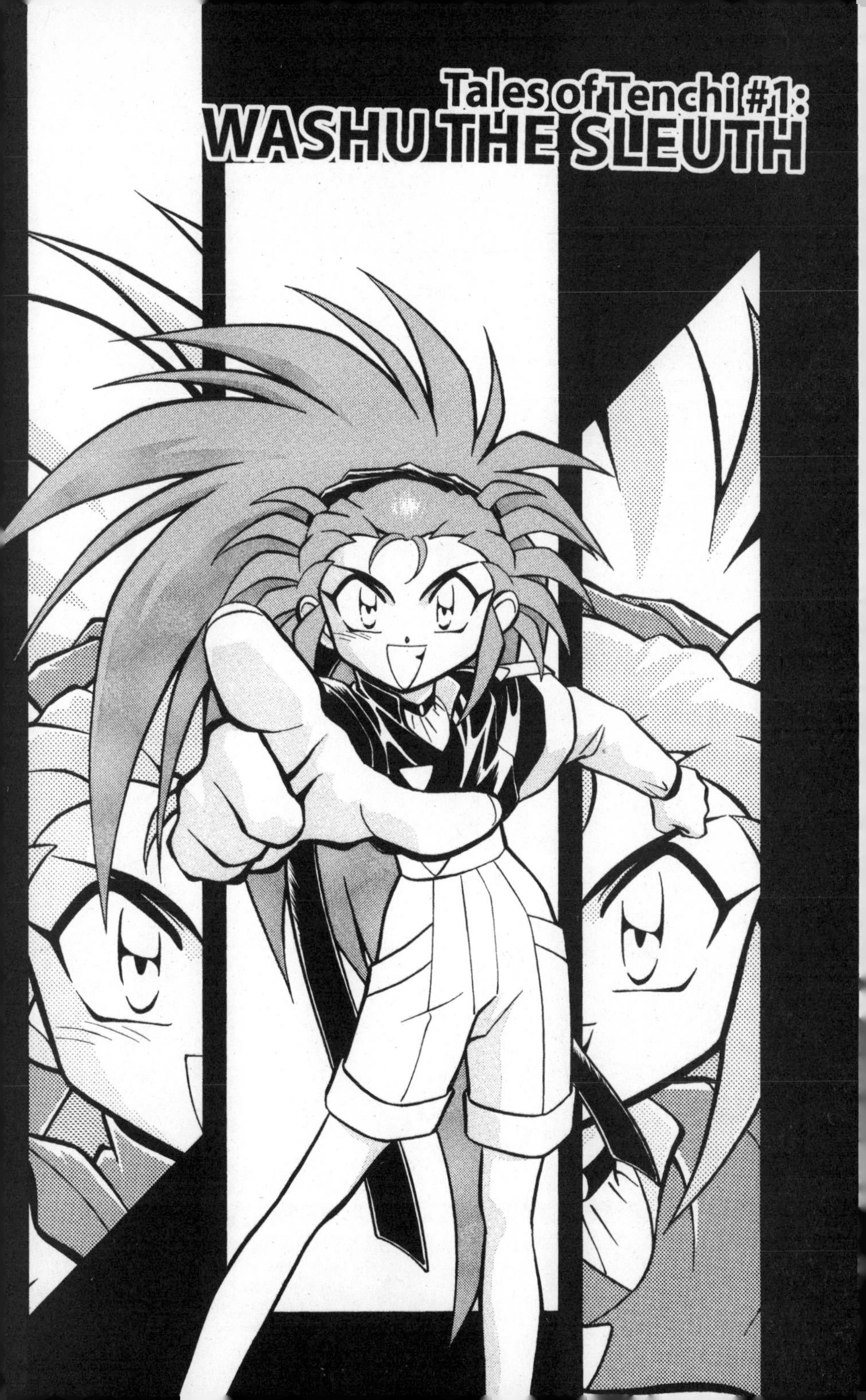
Tales of Tenchi #1:
WASHU THE SLEUTH

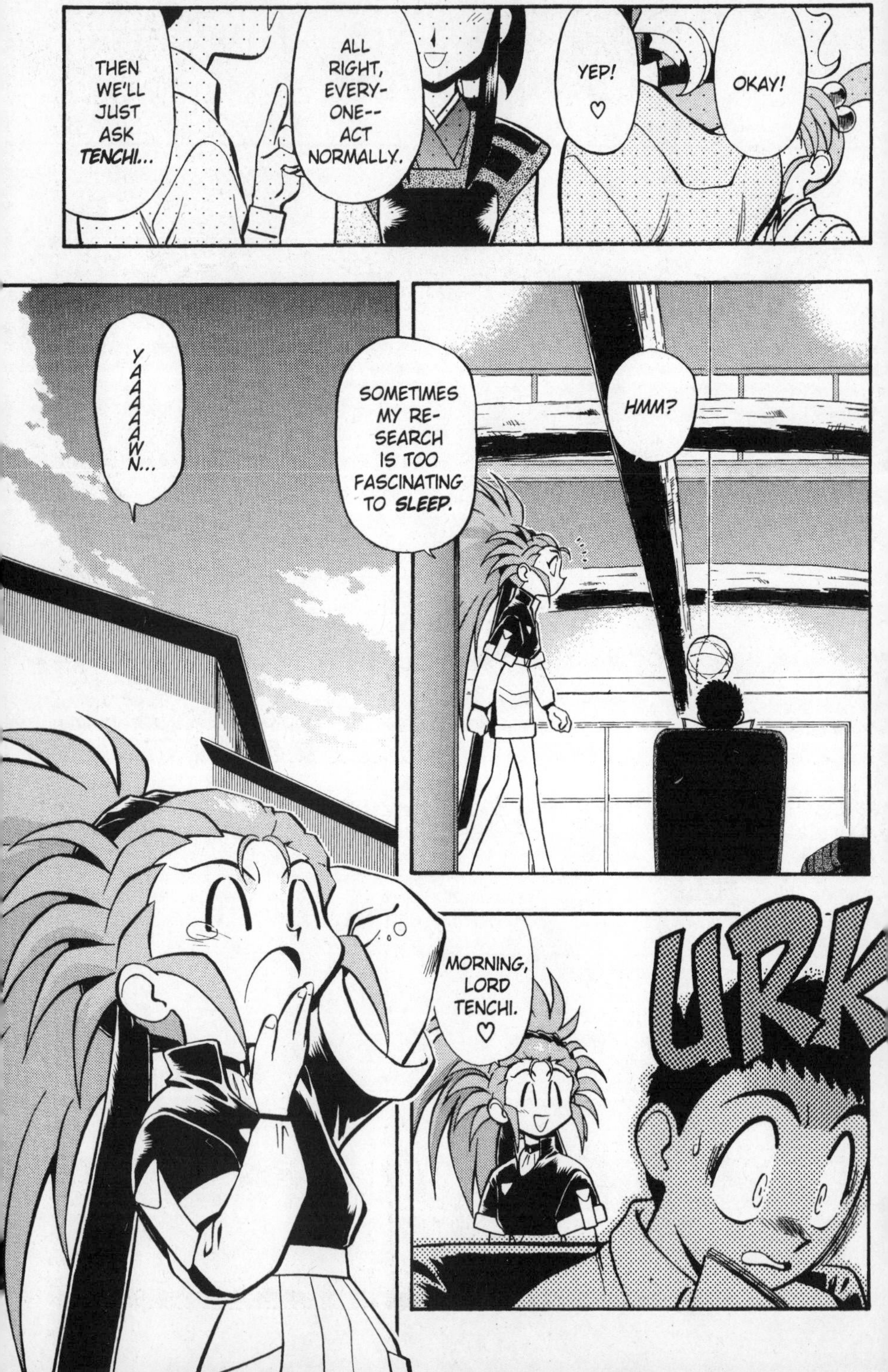
THEN WE'LL JUST ASK TENCHI...
ALL RIGHT, EVERY-ONE-- ACT NORMALLY.
YEP! ♡
OKAY!
YAAAAAAWN...
SOMETIMES MY RE-SEARCH IS TOO FASCINATING TO SLEEP.
HMM?
MORNING, LORD TENCHI. ♡
URK

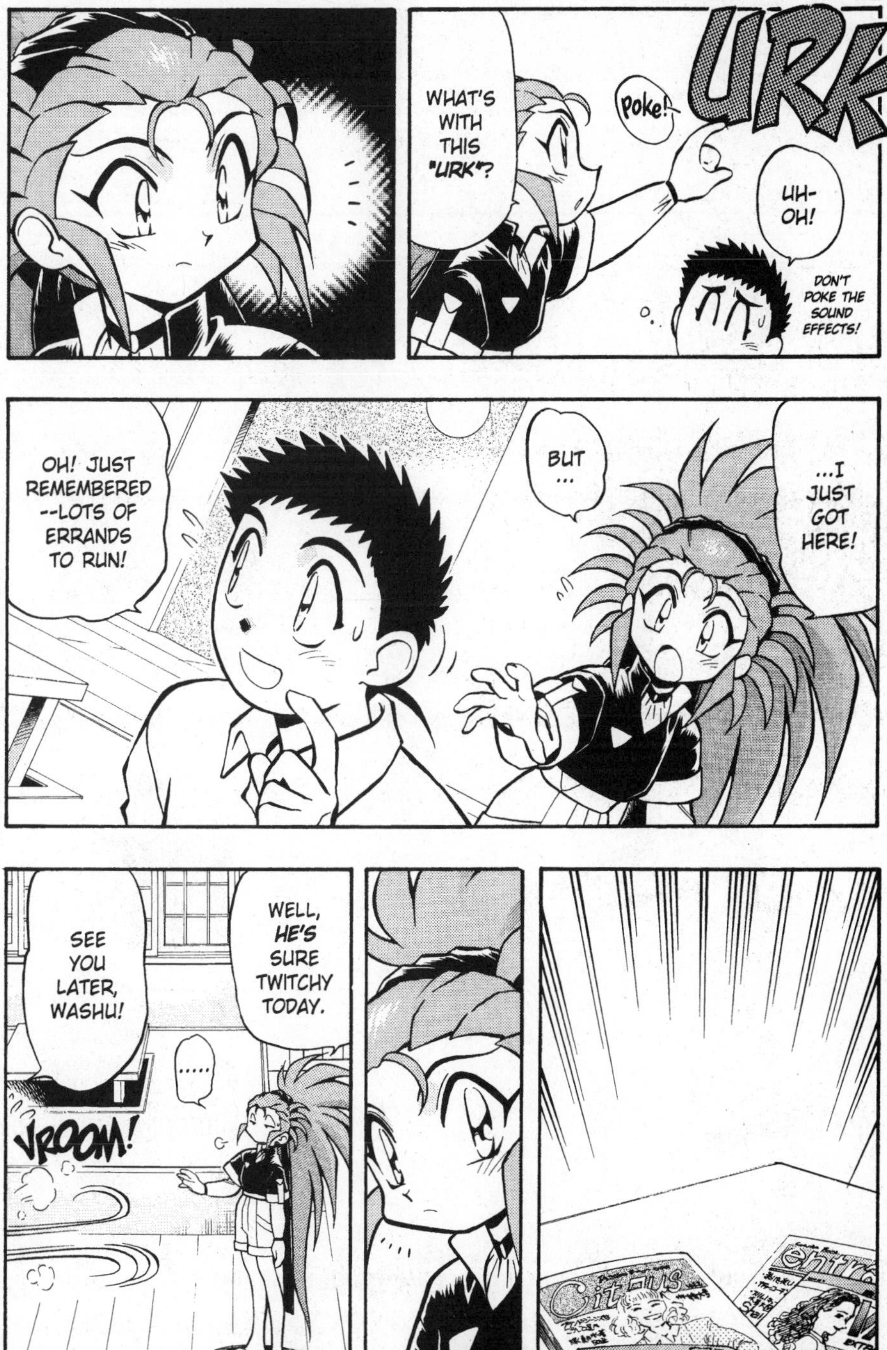
WHAT'S WITH THIS "URK"?
Poke!
URK
UH-OH!
DON'T POKE THE SOUND EFFECTS!
OH! JUST REMEMBERED --LOTS OF ERRANDS TO RUN!
BUT ...
...I JUST GOT HERE!
SEE YOU LATER, WASHU!
WELL, HE'S SURE TWITCHY TODAY.
......
VROOM!
Bianca
July

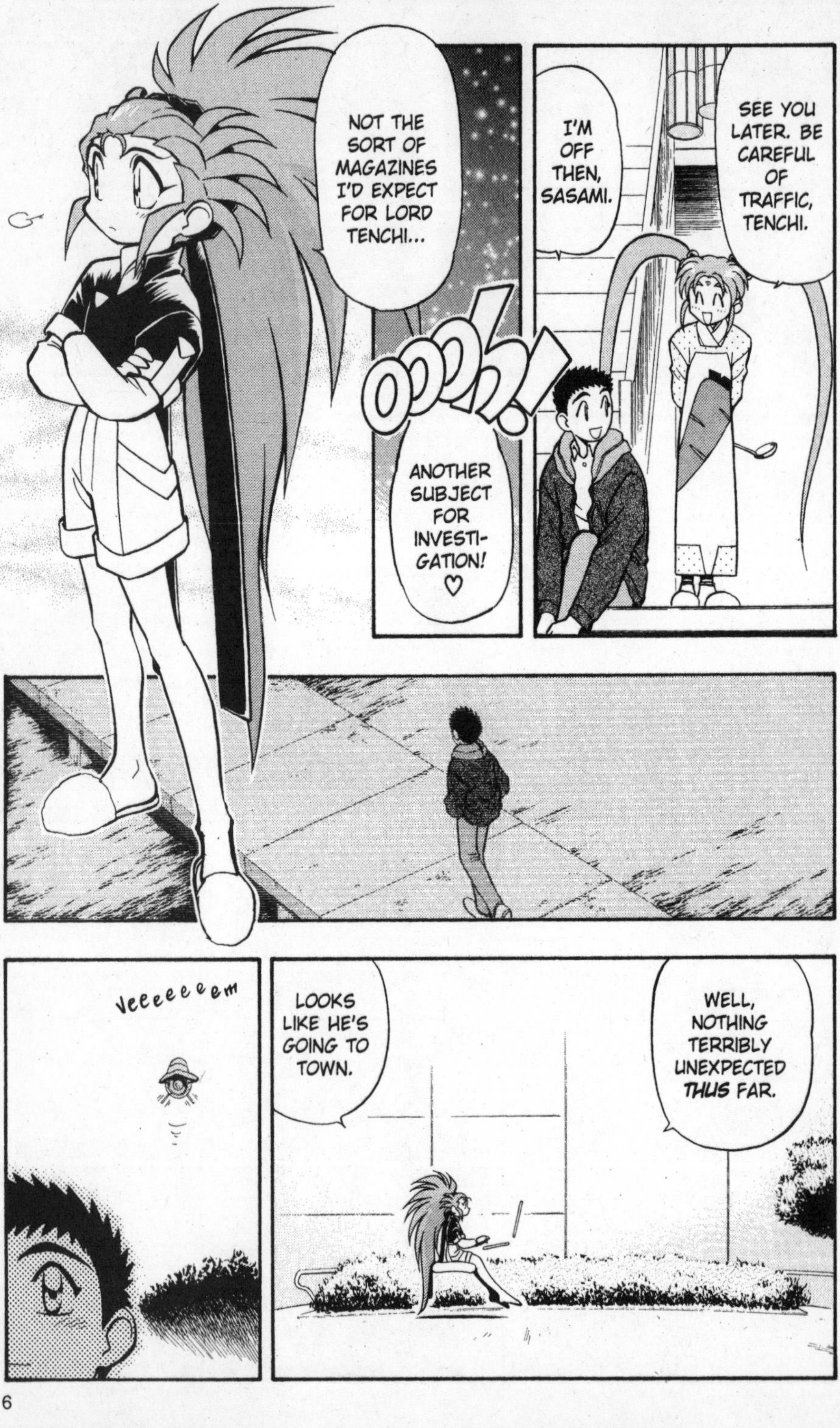

NOT THE SORT OF MAGAZINES I'D EXPECT FOR LORD TENCHI...
OOOH!
ANOTHER SUBJECT FOR INVESTI-GATION! ♡
I'M OFF THEN, SASAMI.
SEE YOU LATER. BE CAREFUL OF TRAFFIC, TENCHI.
Veeeeeeem
LOOKS LIKE HE'S GOING TO TOWN.
WELL, NOTHING TERRIBLY UNEXPECTED *THUS* FAR.

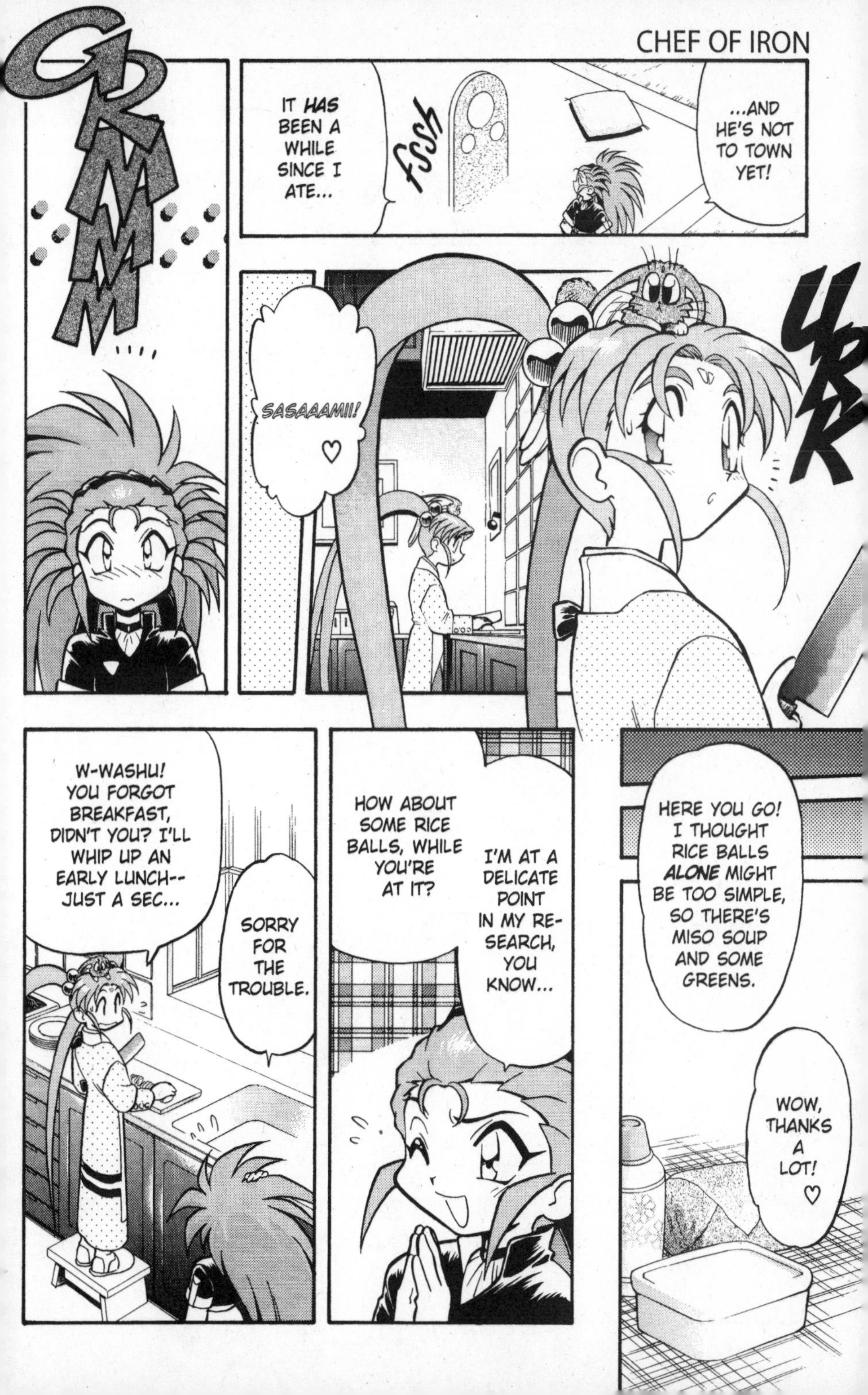
GRMMM
IT HAS BEEN A WHILE SINCE I ATE...
fssh
...AND HE'S NOT TO TOWN YET!
SASAAAMII! ♡
URK
W-WASHU! YOU FORGOT BREAKFAST, DIDN'T YOU? I'LL WHIP UP AN EARLY LUNCH--JUST A SEC...
SORRY FOR THE TROUBLE.
HOW ABOUT SOME RICE BALLS, WHILE YOU'RE AT IT?
I'M AT A DELICATE POINT IN MY RE-SEARCH, YOU KNOW...
HERE YOU GO! I THOUGHT RICE BALLS ALONE MIGHT BE TOO SIMPLE, SO THERE'S MISO SOUP AND SOME GREENS.
WOW, THANKS A LOT! ♡

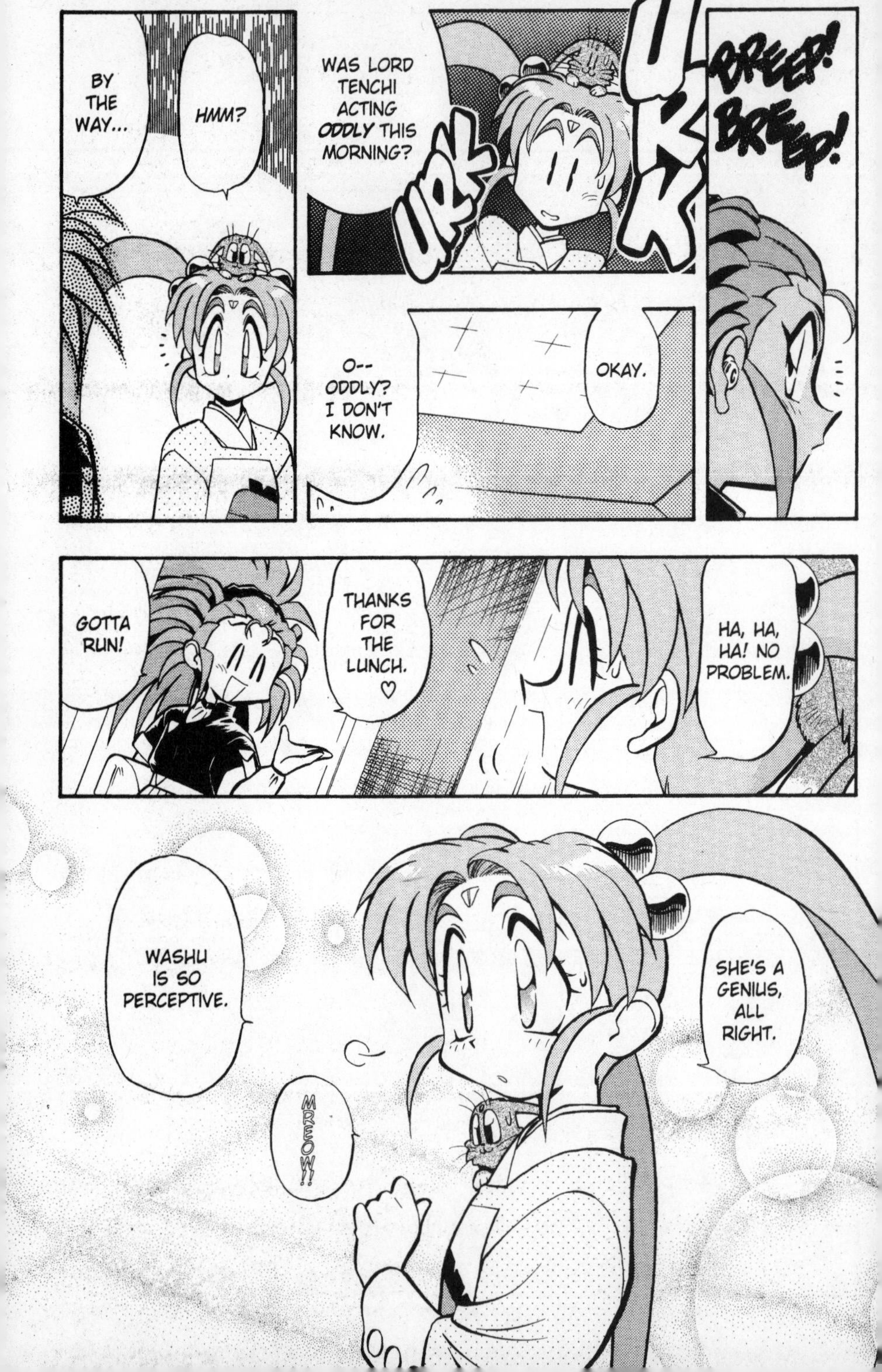
BY THE WAY...
HMM?
WAS LORD TENCHI ACTING ODDLY THIS MORNING?
URK
U K K
BREEP! BREEP!
O-- ODDLY? I DON'T KNOW.
OKAY.
GOTTA RUN!
THANKS FOR THE LUNCH. ♡
HA, HA, HA! NO PROBLEM.
WASHU IS SO PERCEPTIVE.
SHE'S A GENIUS, ALL RIGHT.
MREOW!!

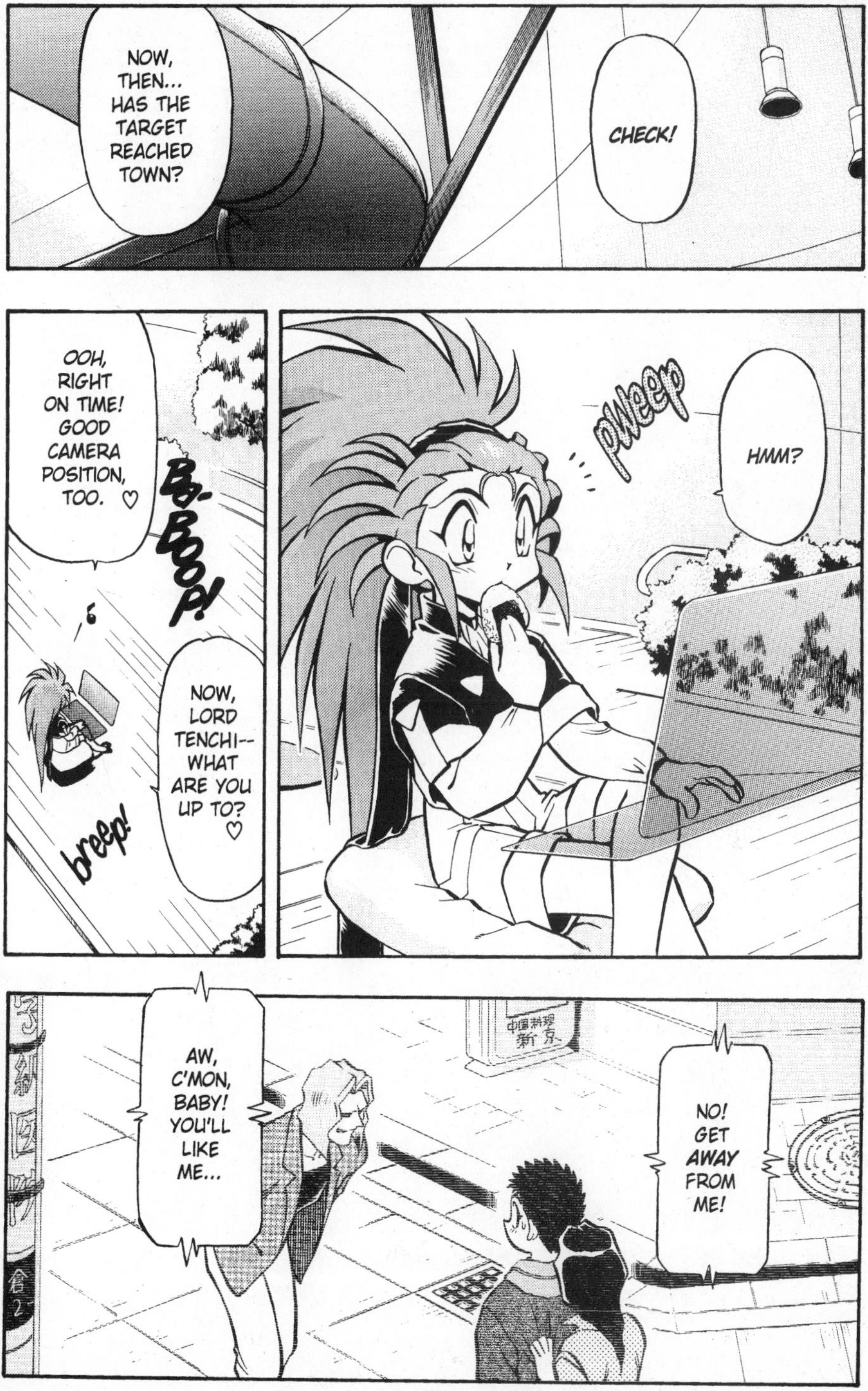
NOW, THEN... HAS THE TARGET REACHED TOWN?
CHECK!
OOH, RIGHT ON TIME! GOOD CAMERA POSITION, TOO. ♡
BA-BOOP!
NOW, LORD TENCHI-- WHAT ARE YOU UP TO? ♡
breep!
pweep
HMM?
AW, C'MON, BABY! YOU'LL LIKE ME...
NO! GET AWAY FROM ME!

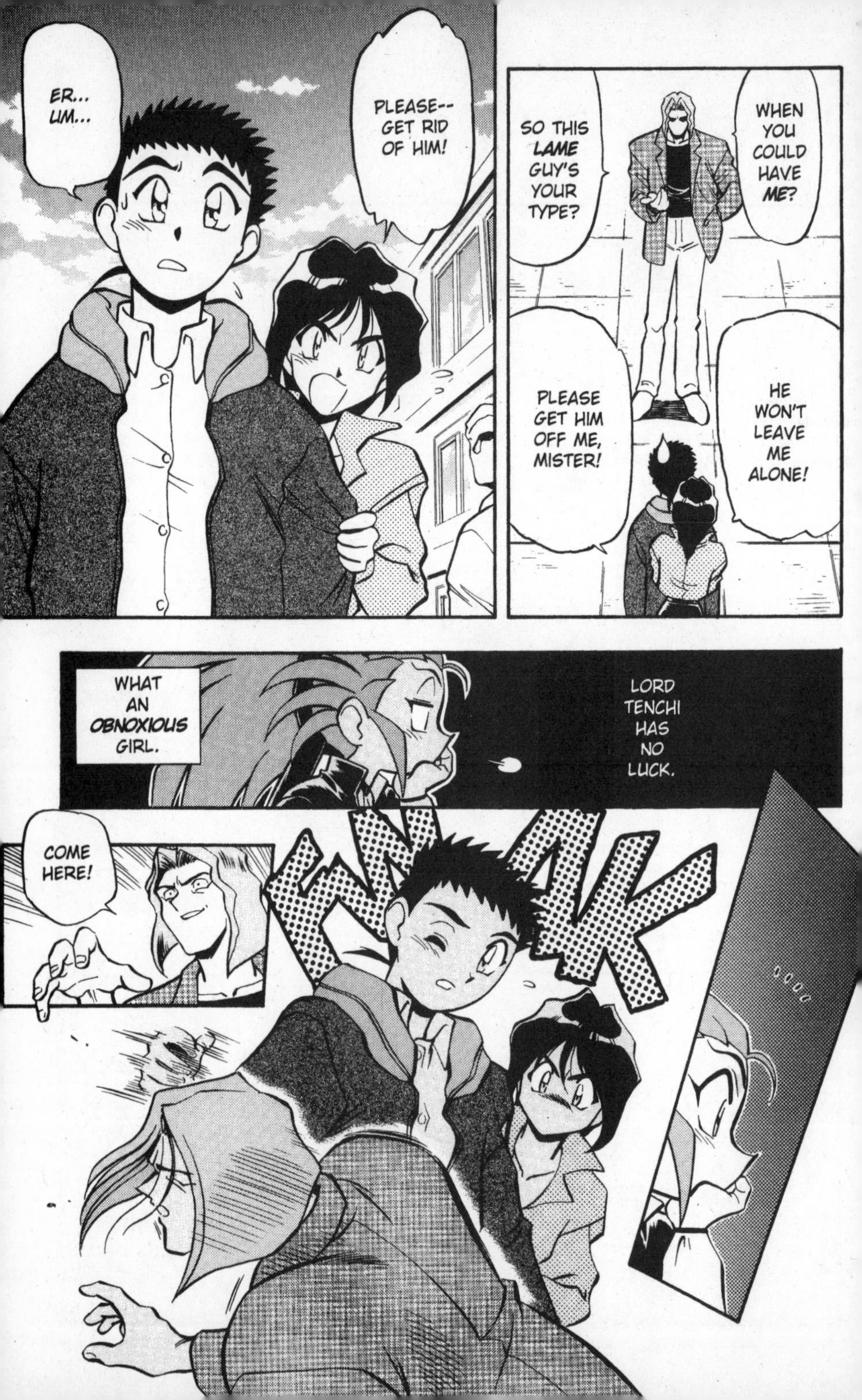
ER... UM...
PLEASE-- GET RID OF HIM!
SO THIS *LAME* GUY'S YOUR TYPE?
WHEN YOU COULD HAVE *ME?*
PLEASE GET HIM OFF ME, MISTER!
HE WON'T LEAVE ME ALONE!
WHAT AN *OBNOXIOUS* GIRL.
LORD TENCHI HAS NO LUCK.
COME HERE!
WHAK

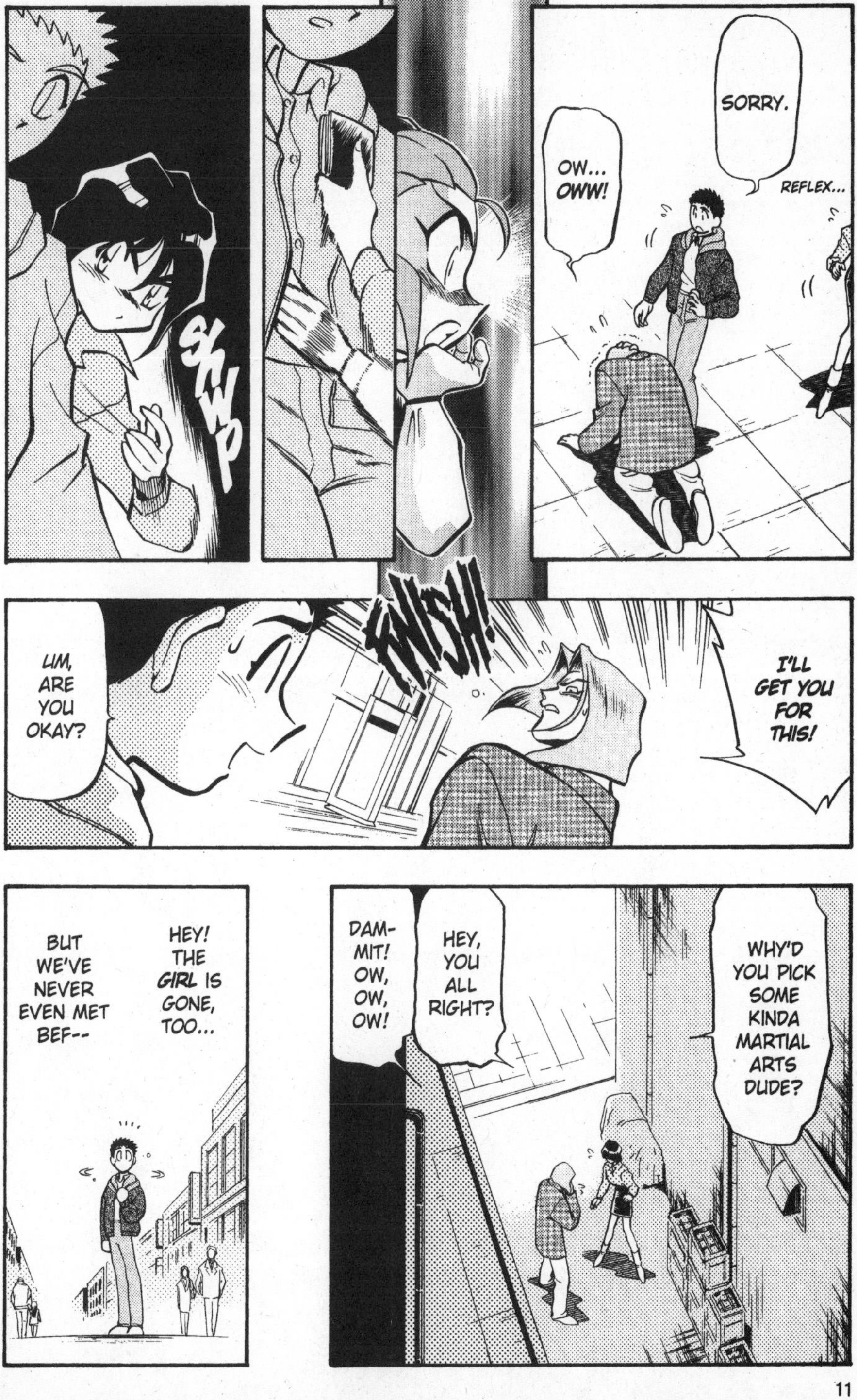
SHWMP
SORRY.
OW... OWW!
REFLEX...
UM, ARE YOU OKAY?
FWISH!
I'LL GET YOU FOR THIS!
BUT WE'VE NEVER EVEN MET BEF--
HEY! THE GIRL IS GONE, TOO...
DAM-MIT! OW, OW, OW!
HEY, YOU ALL RIGHT?
WHY'D YOU PICK SOME KINDA MARTIAL ARTS DUDE?

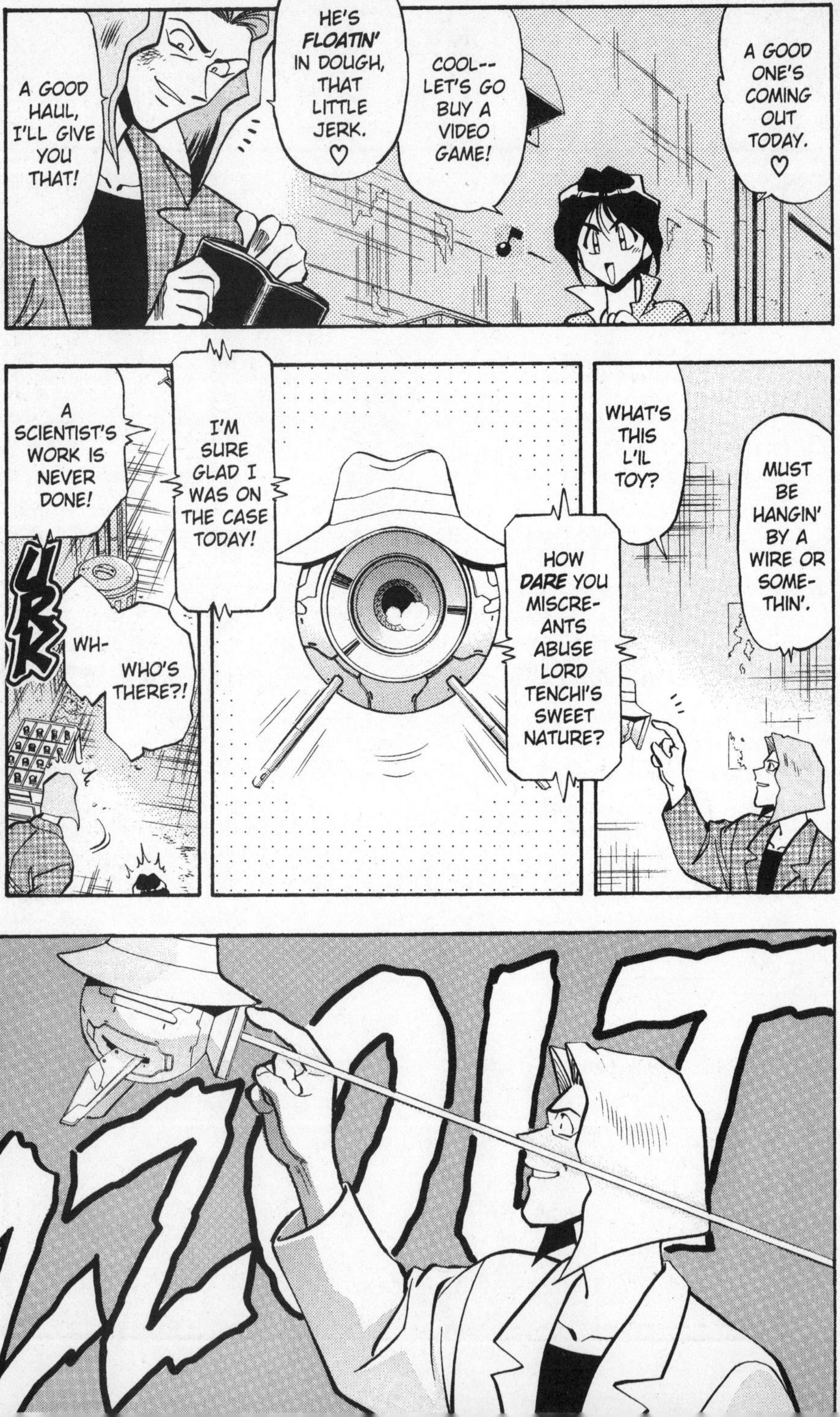
A GOOD HAUL, I'LL GIVE YOU THAT!
HE'S FLOATIN' IN DOUGH, THAT LITTLE JERK. ♡
COOL-- LET'S GO BUY A VIDEO GAME!
A GOOD ONE'S COMING OUT TODAY. ♡
A SCIENTIST'S WORK IS NEVER DONE!
URK
WH-
WHO'S THERE?!
I'M SURE GLAD I WAS ON THE CASE TODAY!
HOW DARE YOU MISCREANTS ABUSE LORD TENCHI'S SWEET NATURE?
WHAT'S THIS L'IL TOY?
MUST BE HANGIN' BY A WIRE OR SOMETHIN'.
ZZOLT

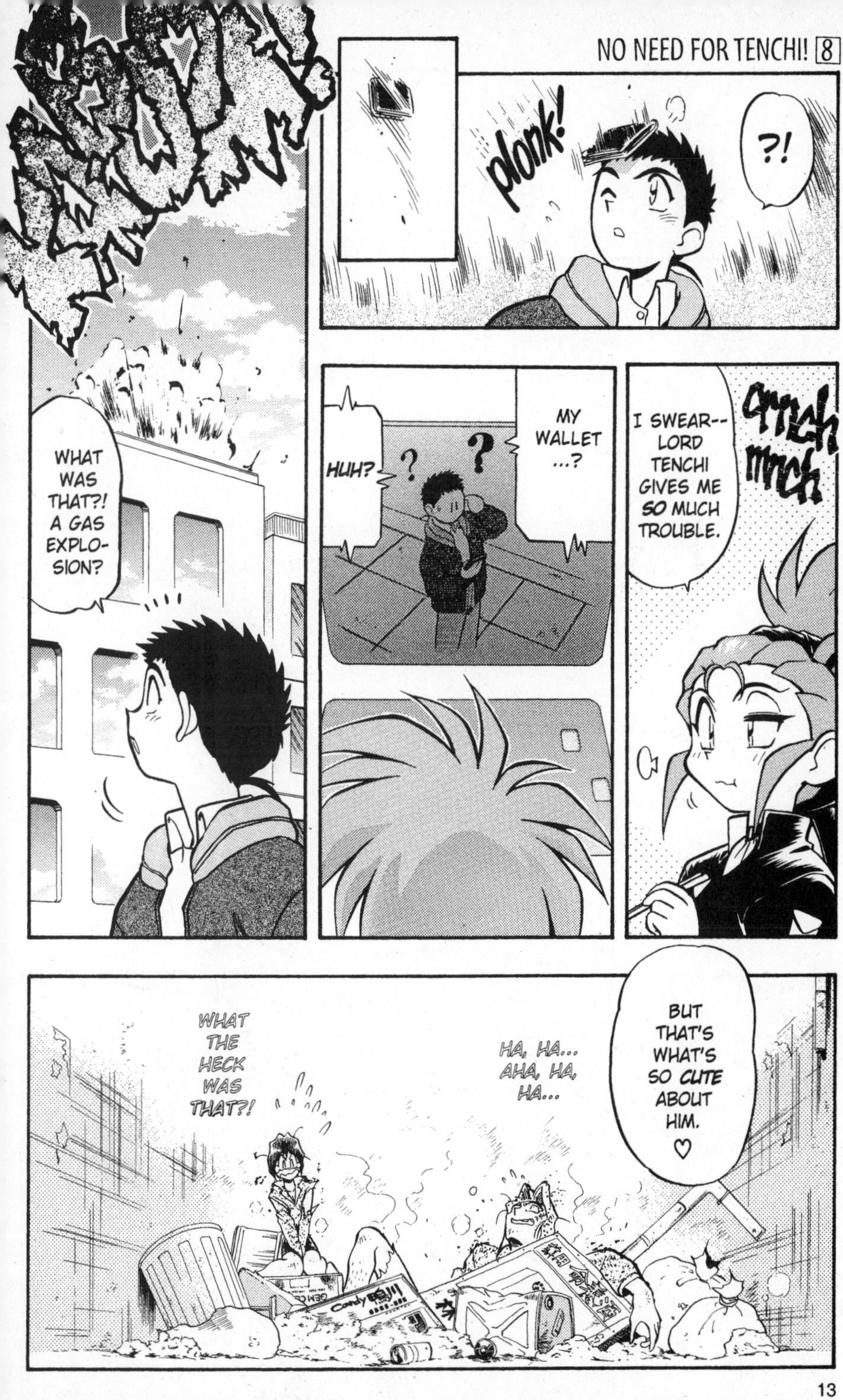
WHAT WAS THAT?! A GAS EXPLOSION?
plonk!
?!
HUH?
MY WALLET ...?
I SWEAR-- LORD TENCHI GIVES ME SO MUCH TROUBLE.
crnch mnch
WHAT THE HECK WAS THAT?!
HA, HA... AHA, HA, HA...
BUT THAT'S WHAT'S SO CUTE ABOUT HIM. ♡

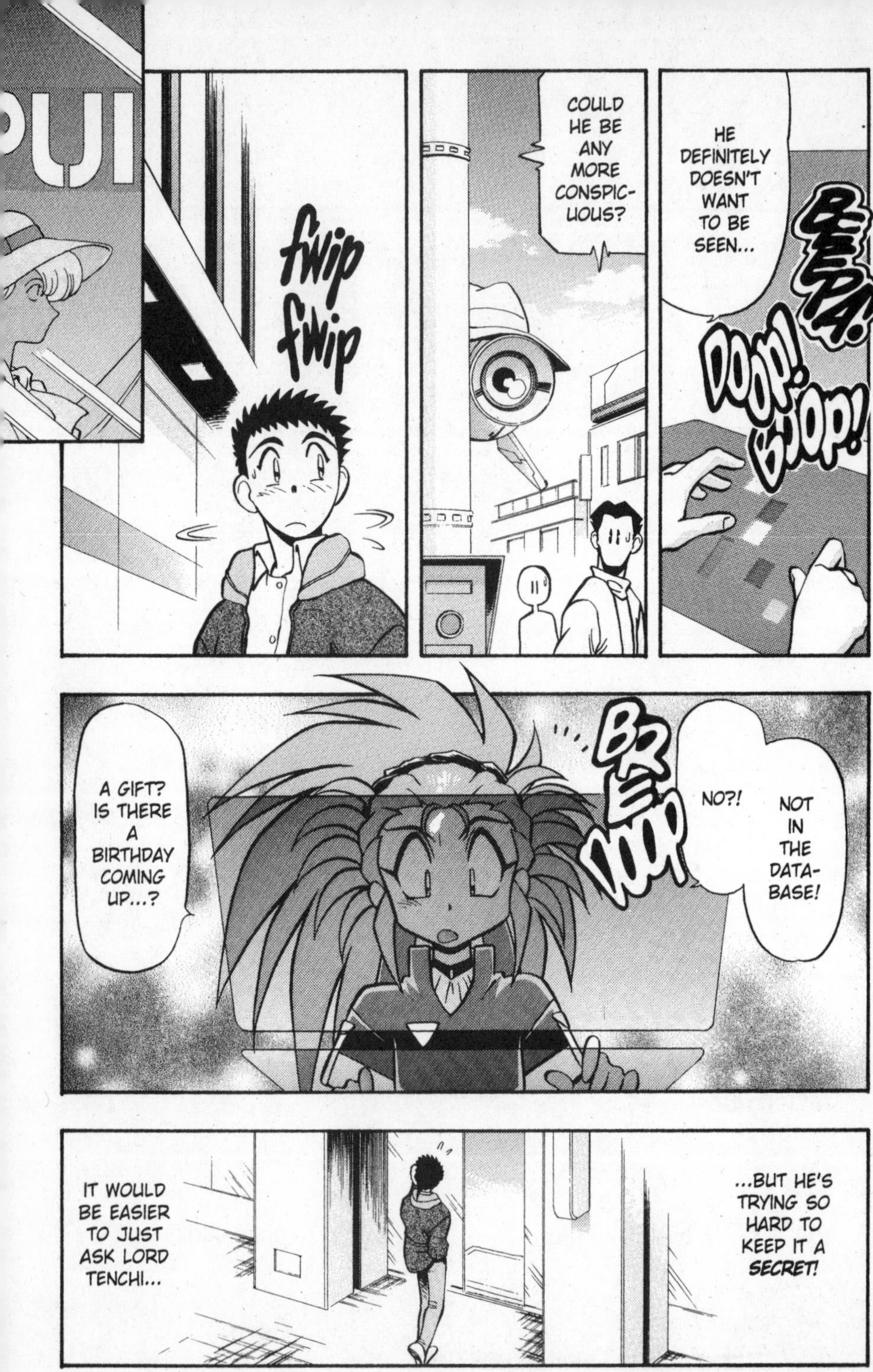
PUI
fwip fwip
COULD HE BE ANY MORE CONSPICUOUS?
HE DEFINITELY DOESN'T WANT TO BE SEEN...
BEEPA!
DOOP! BOOP!
A GIFT? IS THERE A BIRTHDAY COMING UP...?
BZZEE VOOP
NO?!
NOT IN THE DATABASE!
IT WOULD BE EASIER TO JUST ASK LORD TENCHI...
...BUT HE'S TRYING SO HARD TO KEEP IT A **SECRET**!

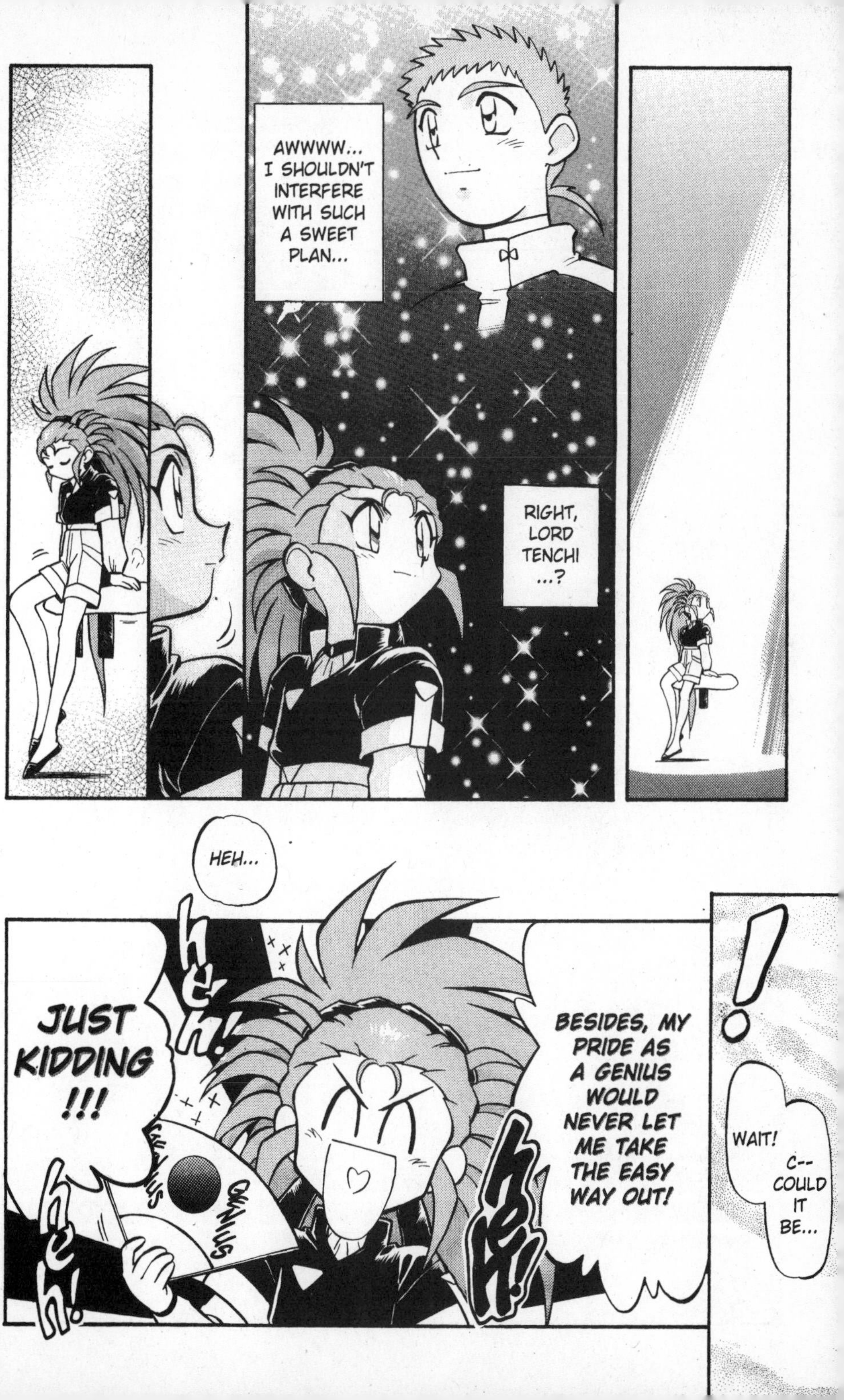
AWWWW... I SHOULDN'T INTERFERE WITH SUCH A SWEET PLAN...
RIGHT, LORD TENCHI ...?
HEH...
heh!
JUST KIDDING !!!
GENIUS
GENIUS
heh!
BESIDES, MY PRIDE AS A GENIUS WOULD NEVER LET ME TAKE THE EASY WAY OUT!
heh!
!
WAIT!
C-- COULD IT BE...

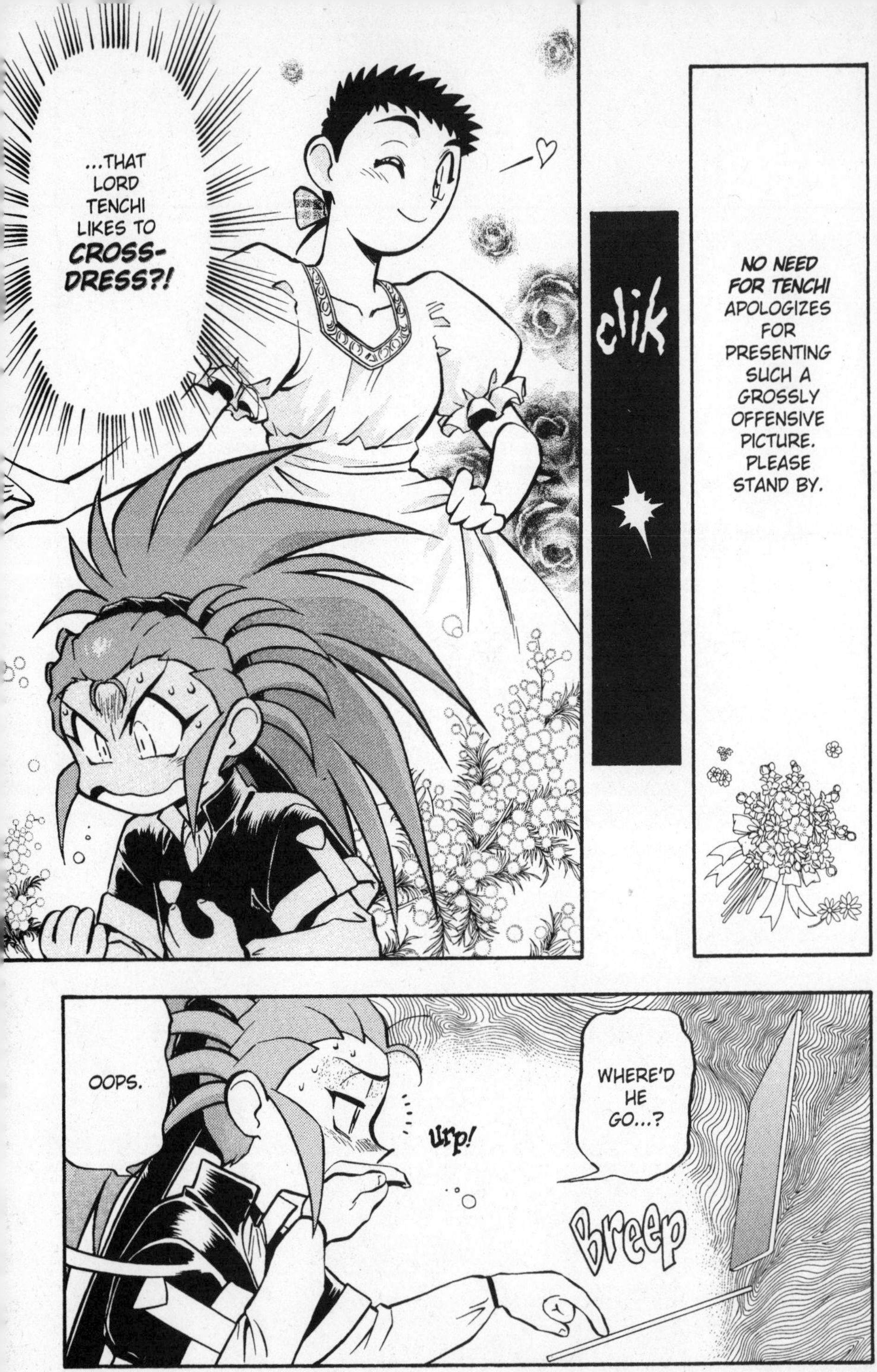
...THAT LORD TENCHI LIKES TO CROSS-DRESS?!
clik
NO NEED FOR TENCHI APOLOGIZES FOR PRESENTING SUCH A GROSSLY OFFENSIVE PICTURE. PLEASE STAND BY.
OOPS.
Urp!
WHERE'D HE GO...?
Breep

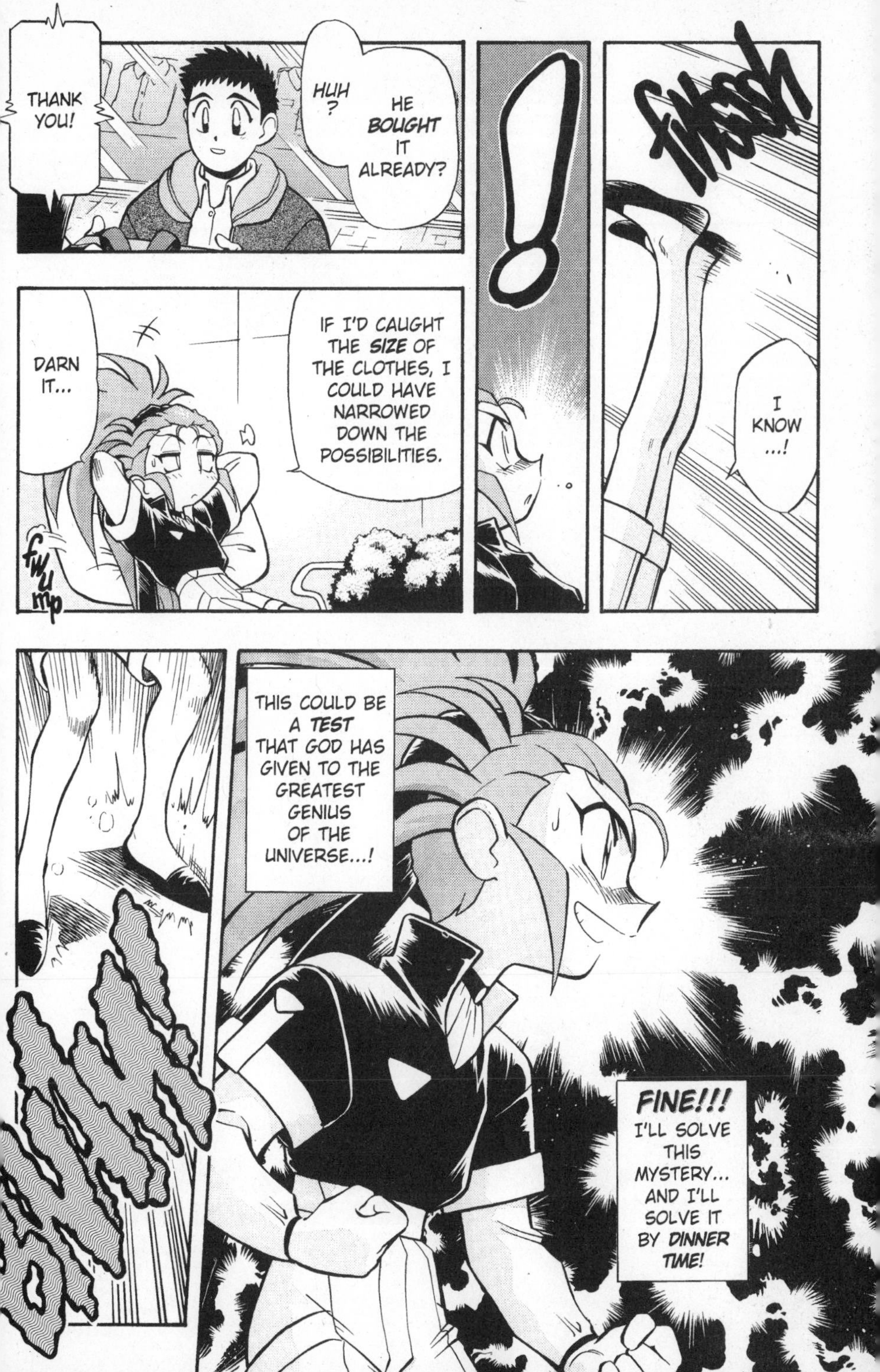
THANK YOU!
HUH?
HE BOUGHT IT ALREADY?
DARN IT...
IF I'D CAUGHT THE SIZE OF THE CLOTHES, I COULD HAVE NARROWED DOWN THE POSSIBILITIES.
fwump
!
I KNOW ...!
THIS COULD BE A TEST THAT GOD HAS GIVEN TO THE GREATEST GENIUS OF THE UNIVERSE...!
FINE!!! I'LL SOLVE THIS MYSTERY... AND I'LL SOLVE IT BY DINNER TIME!

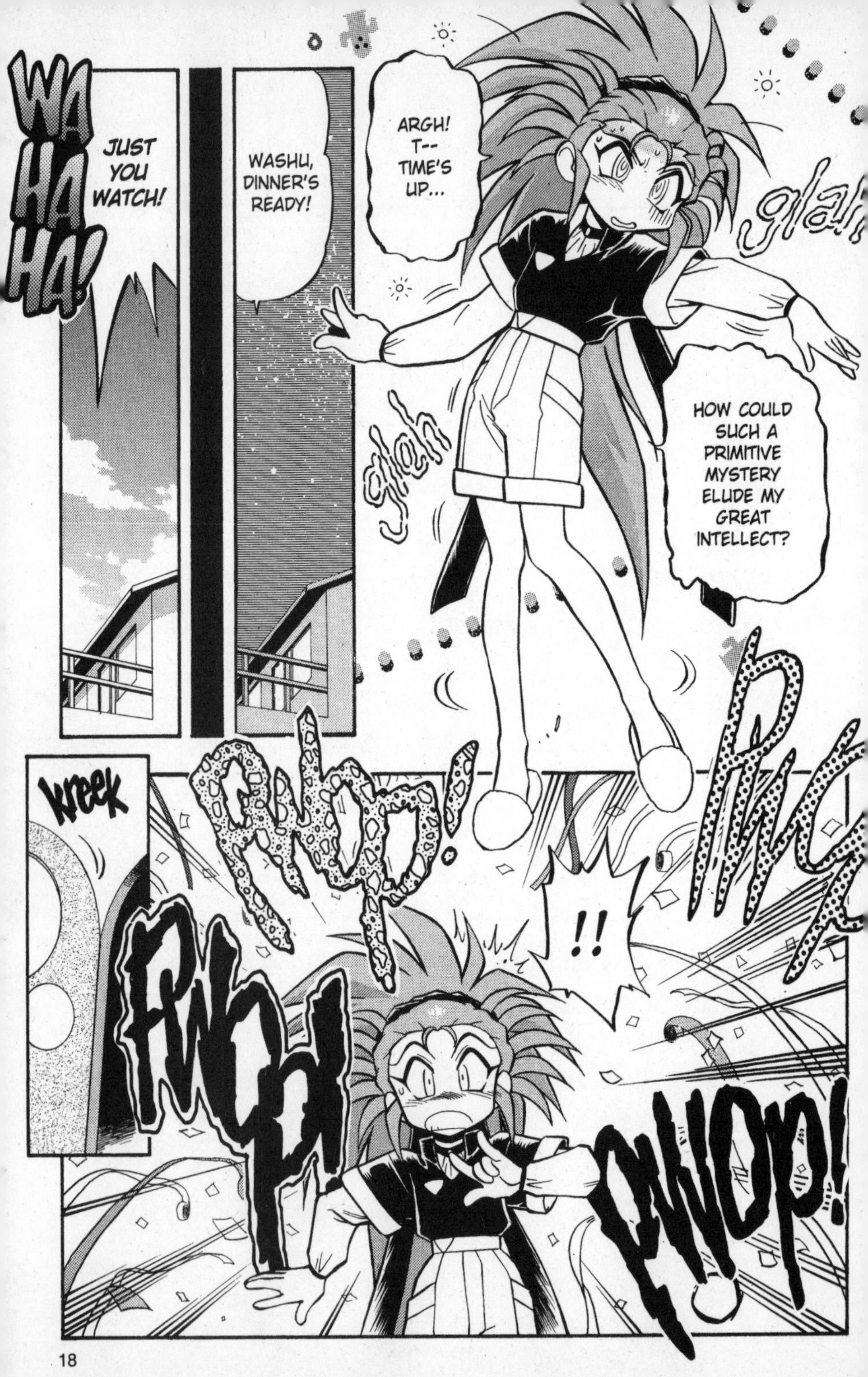
WA HA HA!
JUST YOU WATCH!
WASHU, DINNER'S READY!
ARGH! T-- TIME'S UP...
glah
glah
HOW COULD SUCH A PRIMITIVE MYSTERY ELUDE MY GREAT INTELLECT?
kreek
PWOP!
PWOP
!!
PWOP!

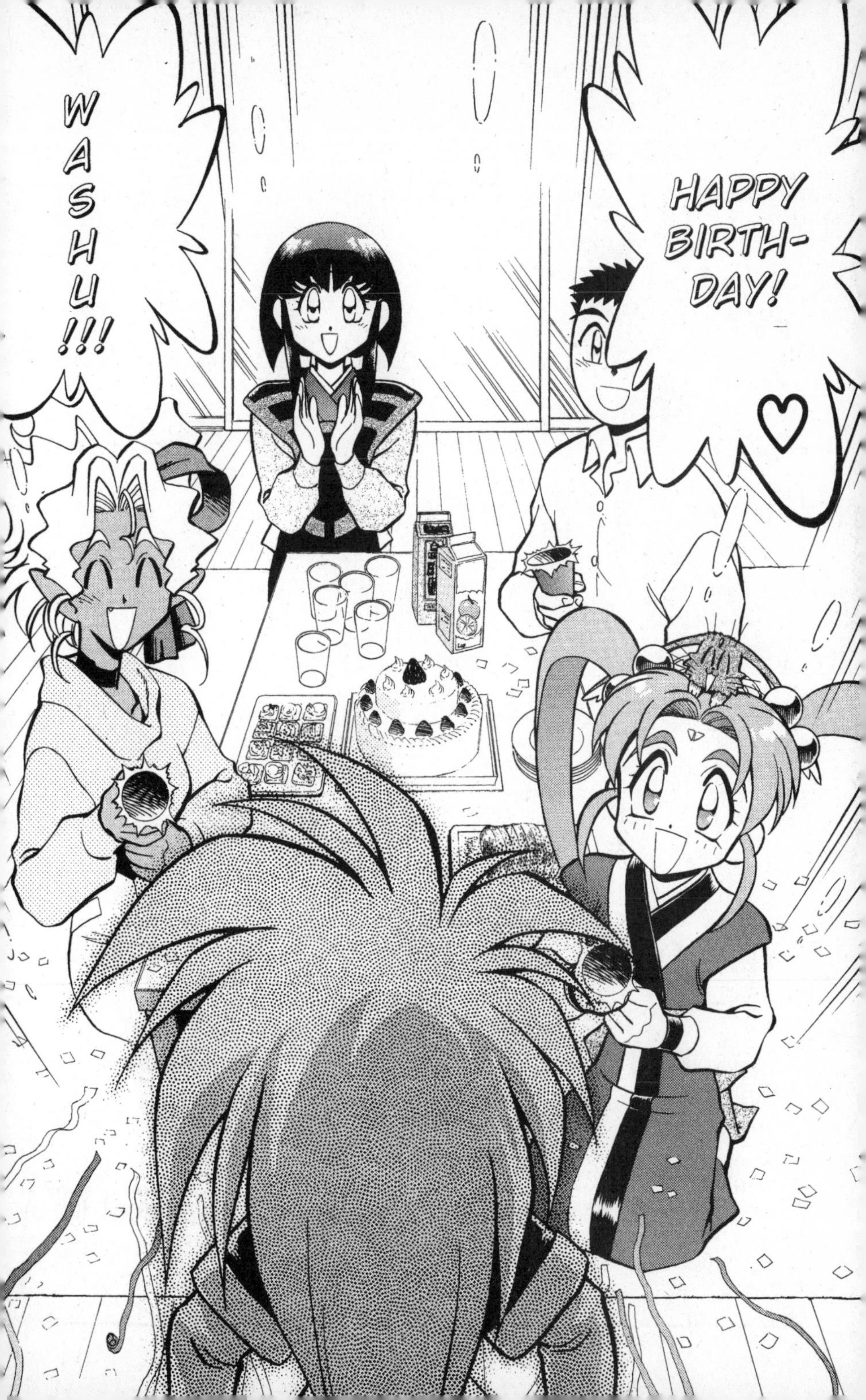
WASHU!!!
HAPPY BIRTH-DAY!

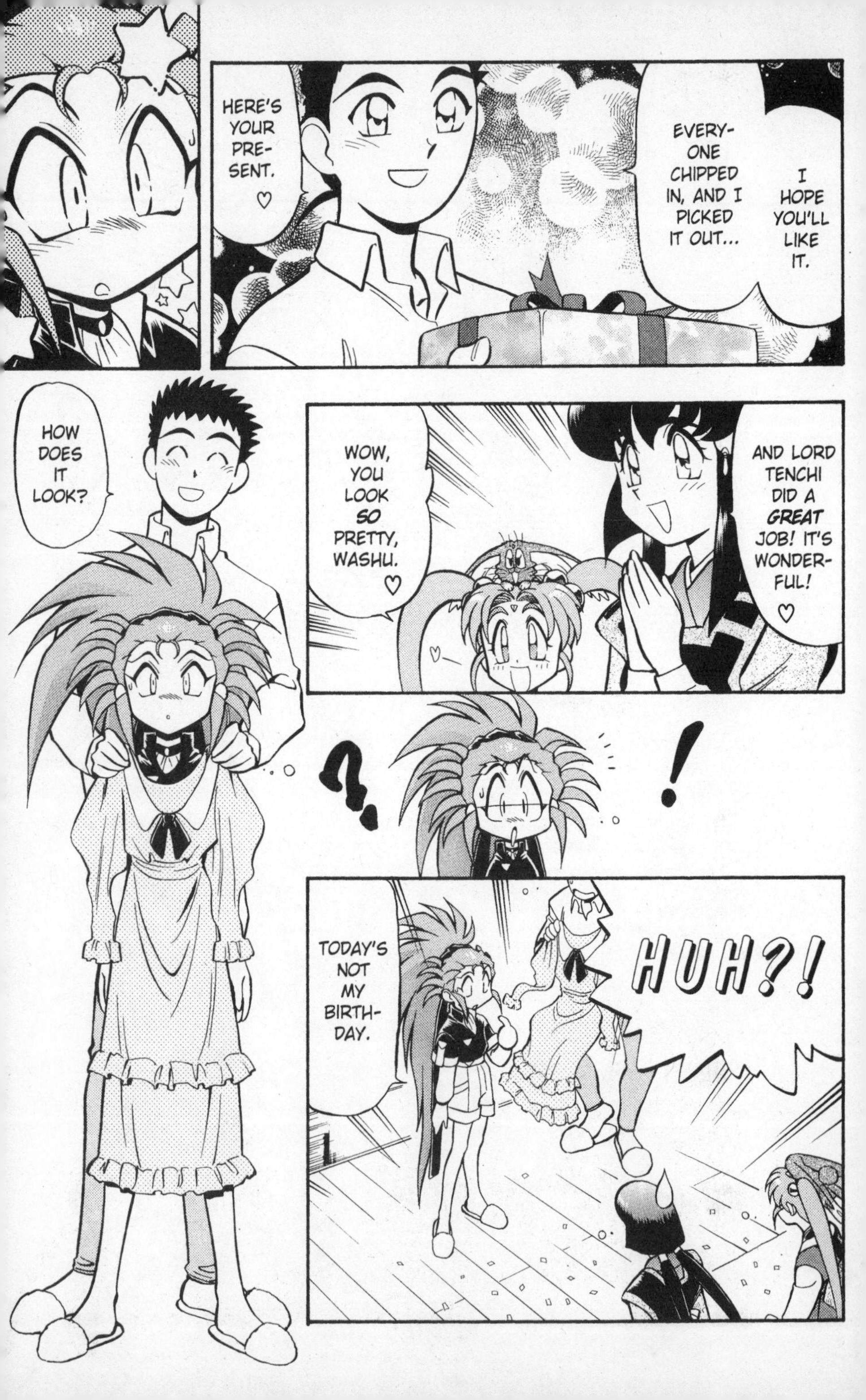
HERE'S YOUR PRESENT. ♡
EVERYONE CHIPPED IN, AND I PICKED IT OUT...
I HOPE YOU'LL LIKE IT.
HOW DOES IT LOOK?
WOW, YOU LOOK SO PRETTY, WASHU. ♡
AND LORD TENCHI DID A GREAT JOB! IT'S WONDERFUL! ♡
?
!
TODAY'S NOT MY BIRTHDAY.
HUH?!

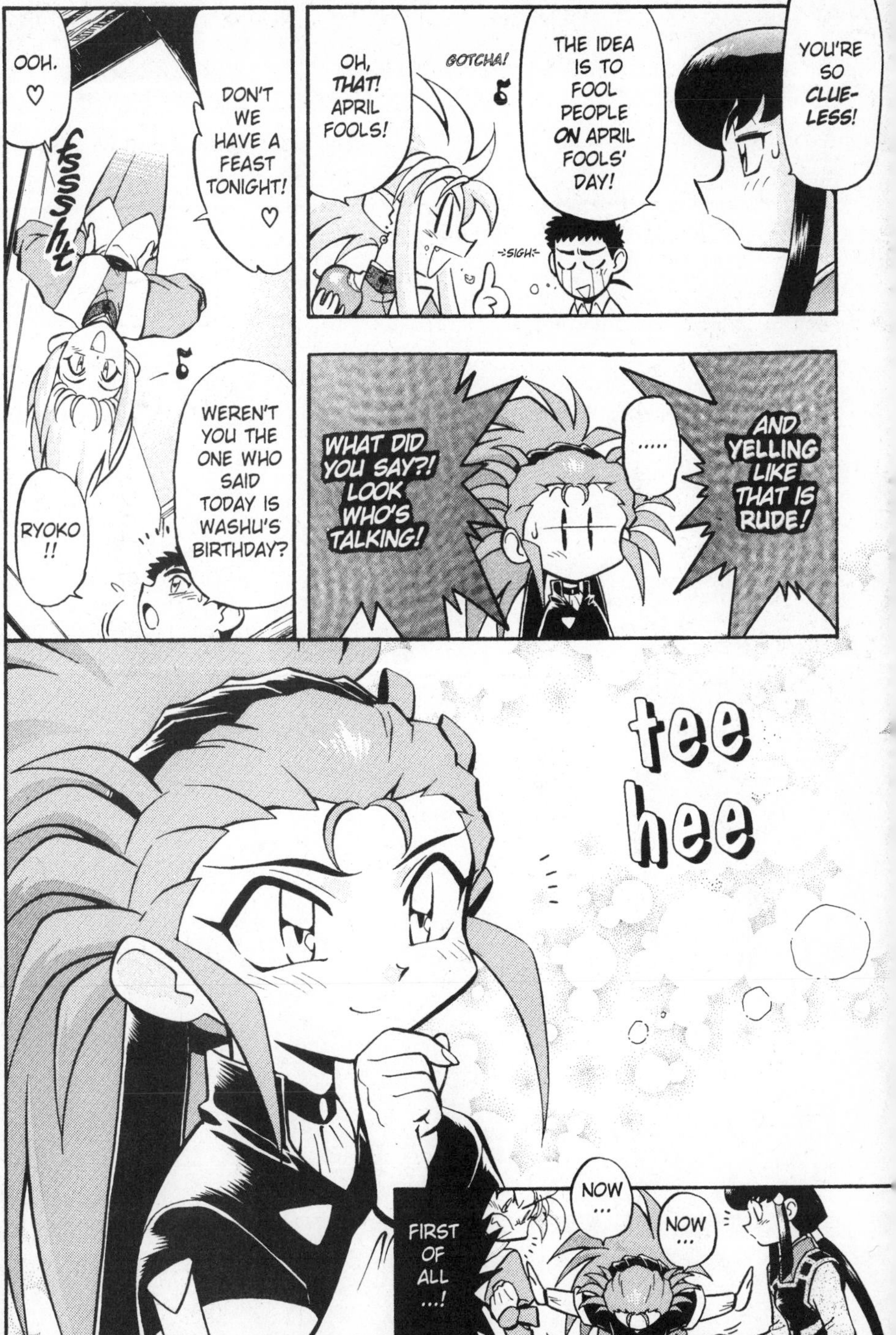
OOH. ♡
DON'T WE HAVE A FEAST TONIGHT! ♡
FSSSHT
WEREN'T YOU THE ONE WHO SAID TODAY IS WASHU'S BIRTHDAY?
RYOKO!!
OH, THAT! APRIL FOOLS!
GOTCHA!
THE IDEA IS TO FOOL PEOPLE ON APRIL FOOLS' DAY!
SIGH
YOU'RE SO CLUELESS!
WHAT DID YOU SAY?! LOOK WHO'S TALKING!
......
AND YELLING LIKE THAT IS RUDE!
tee hee
FIRST OF ALL ...!
NOW ...
NOW ...

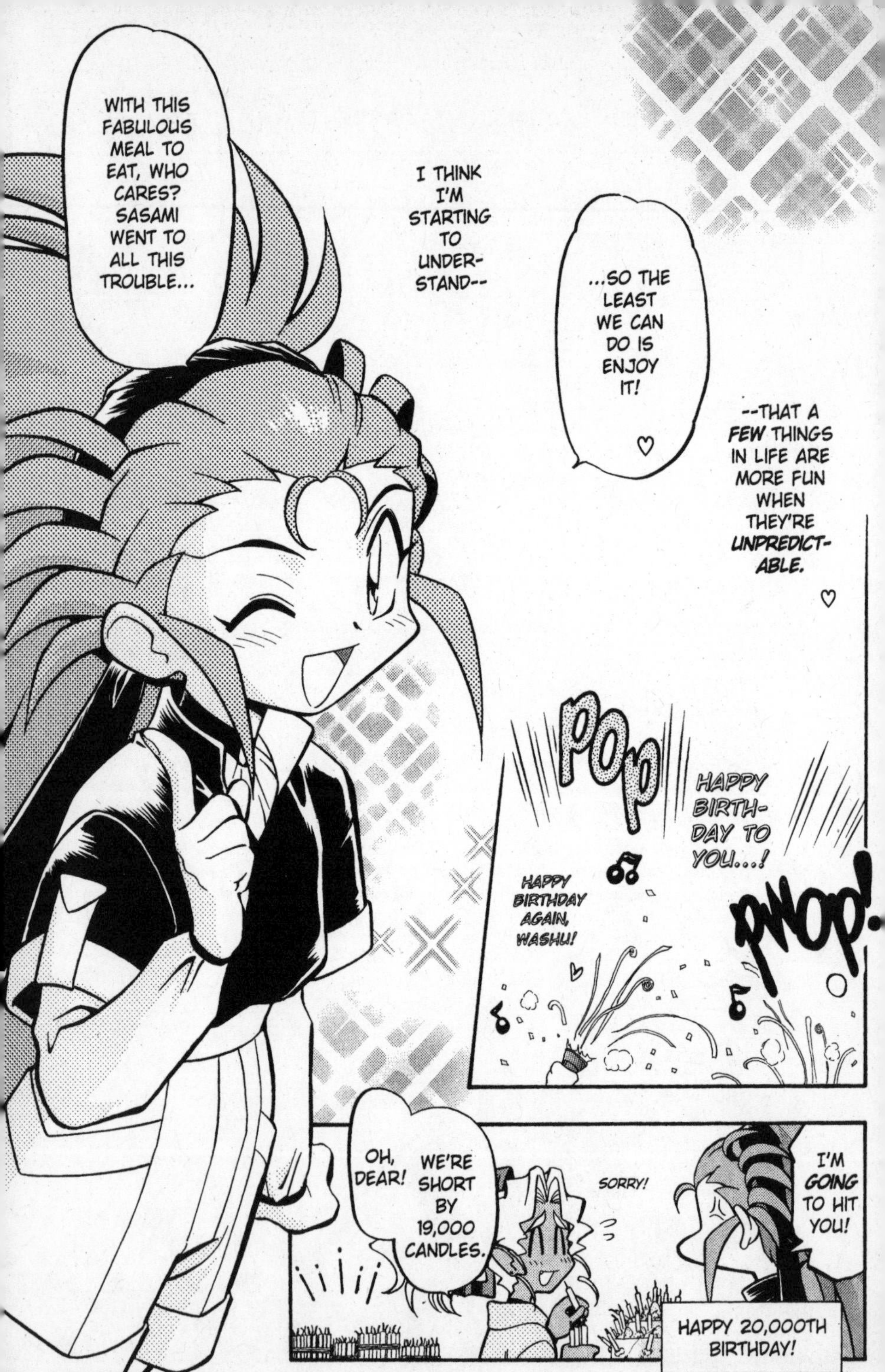
WITH THIS FABULOUS MEAL TO EAT, WHO CARES? SASAMI WENT TO ALL THIS TROUBLE...
I THINK I'M STARTING TO UNDER-STAND--
...SO THE LEAST WE CAN DO IS ENJOY IT! ♡
--THAT A FEW THINGS IN LIFE ARE MORE FUN WHEN THEY'RE UNPREDICT-ABLE. ♡
POP
HAPPY BIRTHDAY AGAIN, WASHU!
HAPPY BIRTH-DAY TO YOU...!
PWOP!
OH, DEAR!
WE'RE SHORT BY 19,000 CANDLES.
SORRY!
I'M GOING TO HIT YOU!
HAPPY 20,000TH BIRTHDAY!

Tales of Tenchi #2: POWERLESS

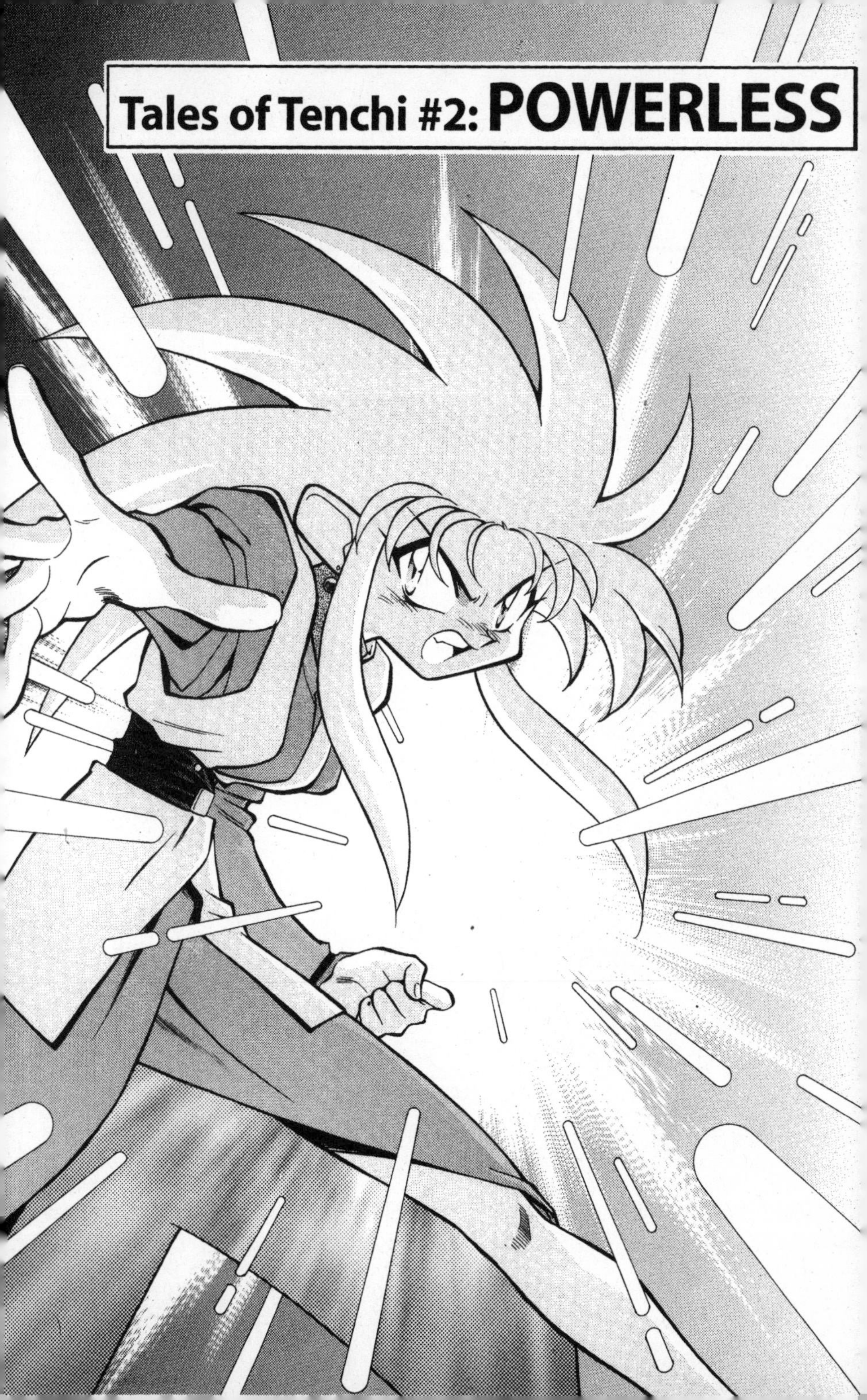

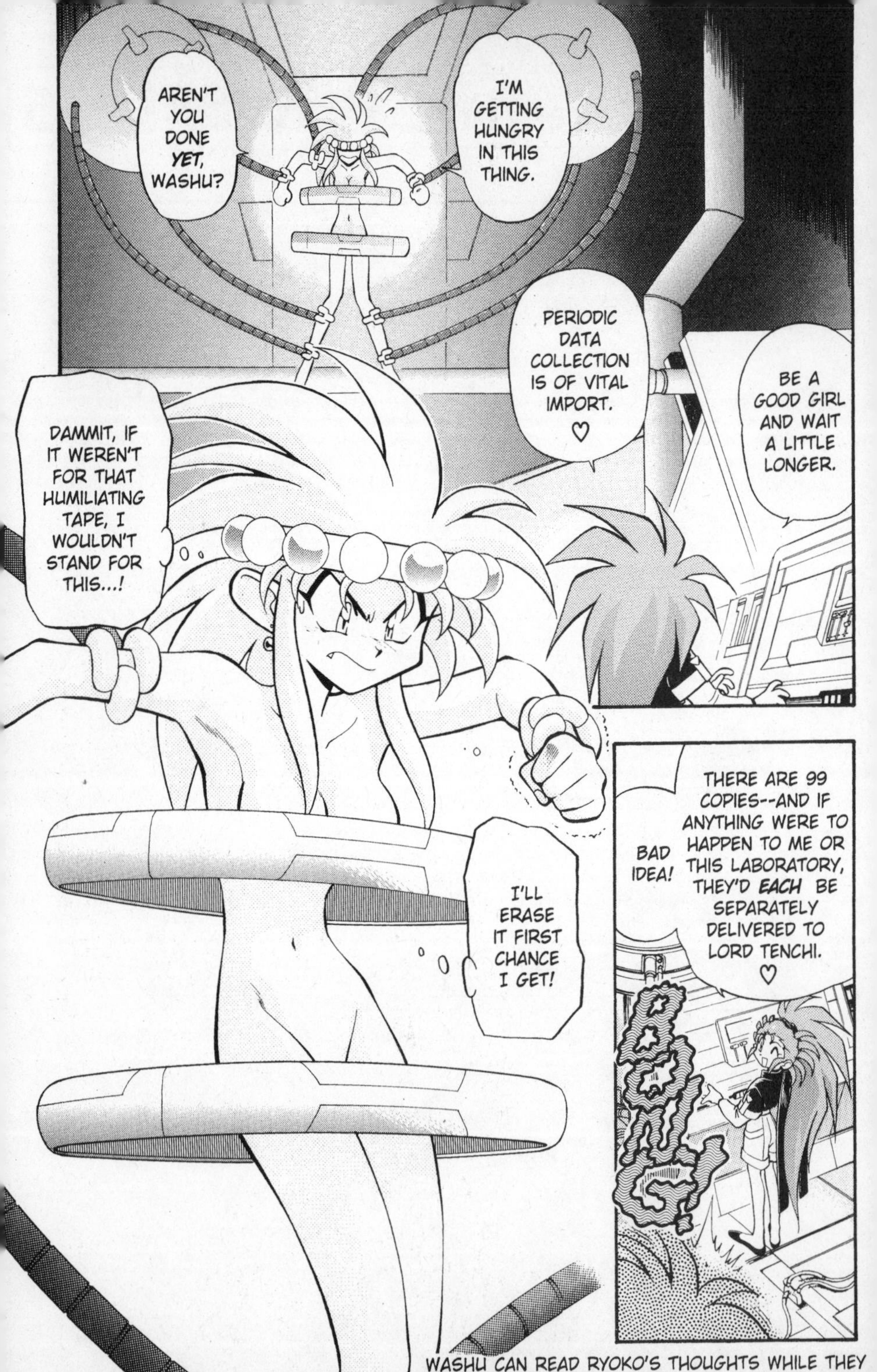
AREN'T YOU DONE *YET*, WASHU?
I'M GETTING HUNGRY IN THIS THING.
PERIODIC DATA COLLECTION IS OF VITAL IMPORT. ♡
BE A GOOD GIRL AND WAIT A LITTLE LONGER.
DAMMIT, IF IT WEREN'T FOR THAT HUMILIATING TAPE, I WOULDN'T STAND FOR THIS...!
I'LL ERASE IT FIRST CHANCE I GET!
BAD IDEA!
THERE ARE 99 COPIES--AND IF ANYTHING WERE TO HAPPEN TO ME OR THIS LABORATORY, THEY'D *EACH* BE SEPARATELY DELIVERED TO LORD TENCHI. ♡

WASHU CAN READ RYOKO'S THOUGHTS WHILE THEY ARE CONNECTED BY THE ASTRAL RING.

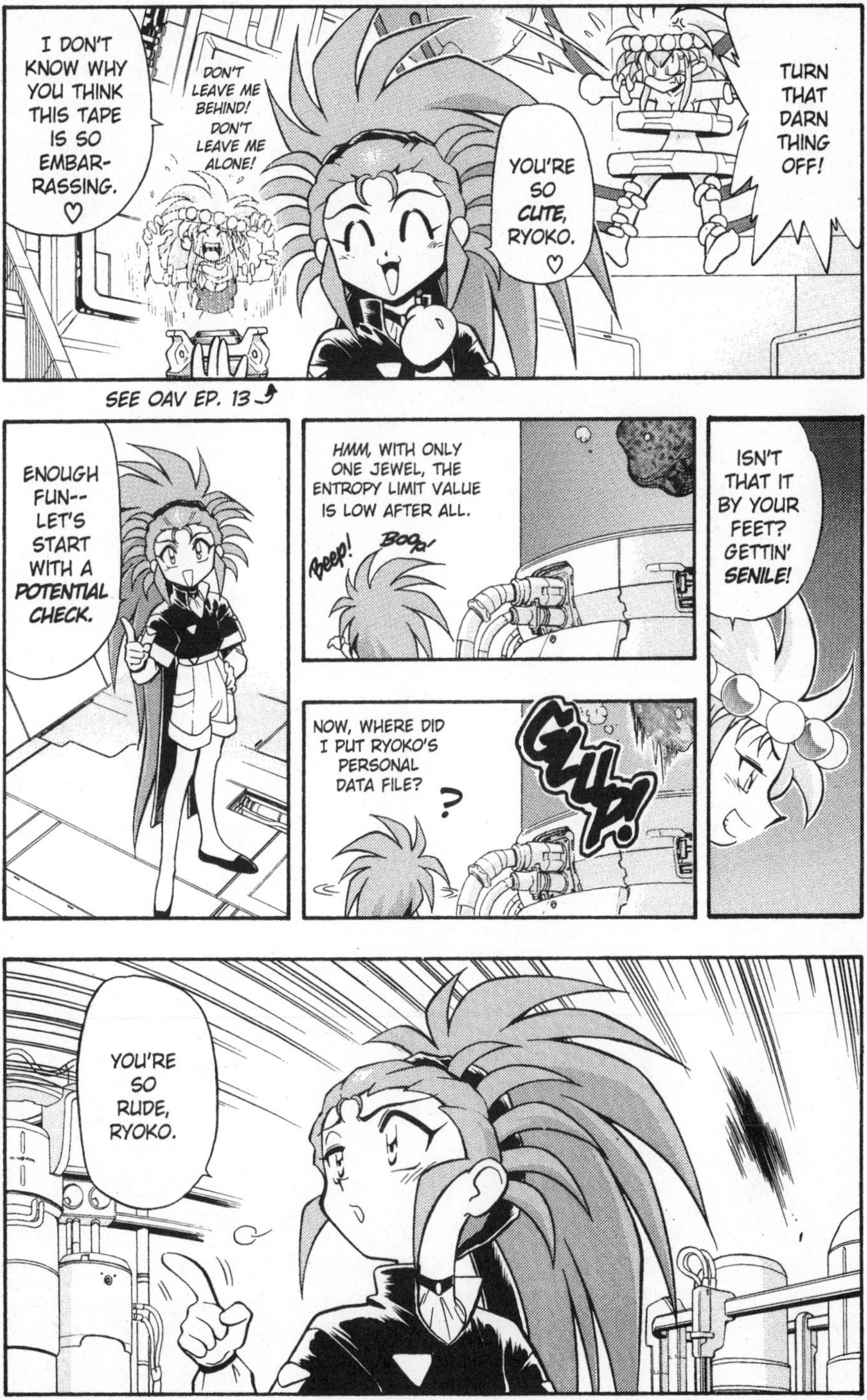
I DON'T KNOW WHY YOU THINK THIS TAPE IS SO EMBARRASSING. ♡
DON'T LEAVE ME BEHIND! DON'T LEAVE ME ALONE!
YOU'RE SO CUTE, RYOKO. ♡
TURN THAT DARN THING OFF!
SEE OAV EP. 13
ENOUGH FUN-- LET'S START WITH A POTENTIAL CHECK.
HMM, WITH ONLY ONE JEWEL, THE ENTROPY LIMIT VALUE IS LOW AFTER ALL.
Beep! Boop!
NOW, WHERE DID I PUT RYOKO'S PERSONAL DATA FILE?
?
GULP!
ISN'T THAT IT BY YOUR FEET? GETTIN' SENILE!
YOU'RE SO RUDE, RYOKO.

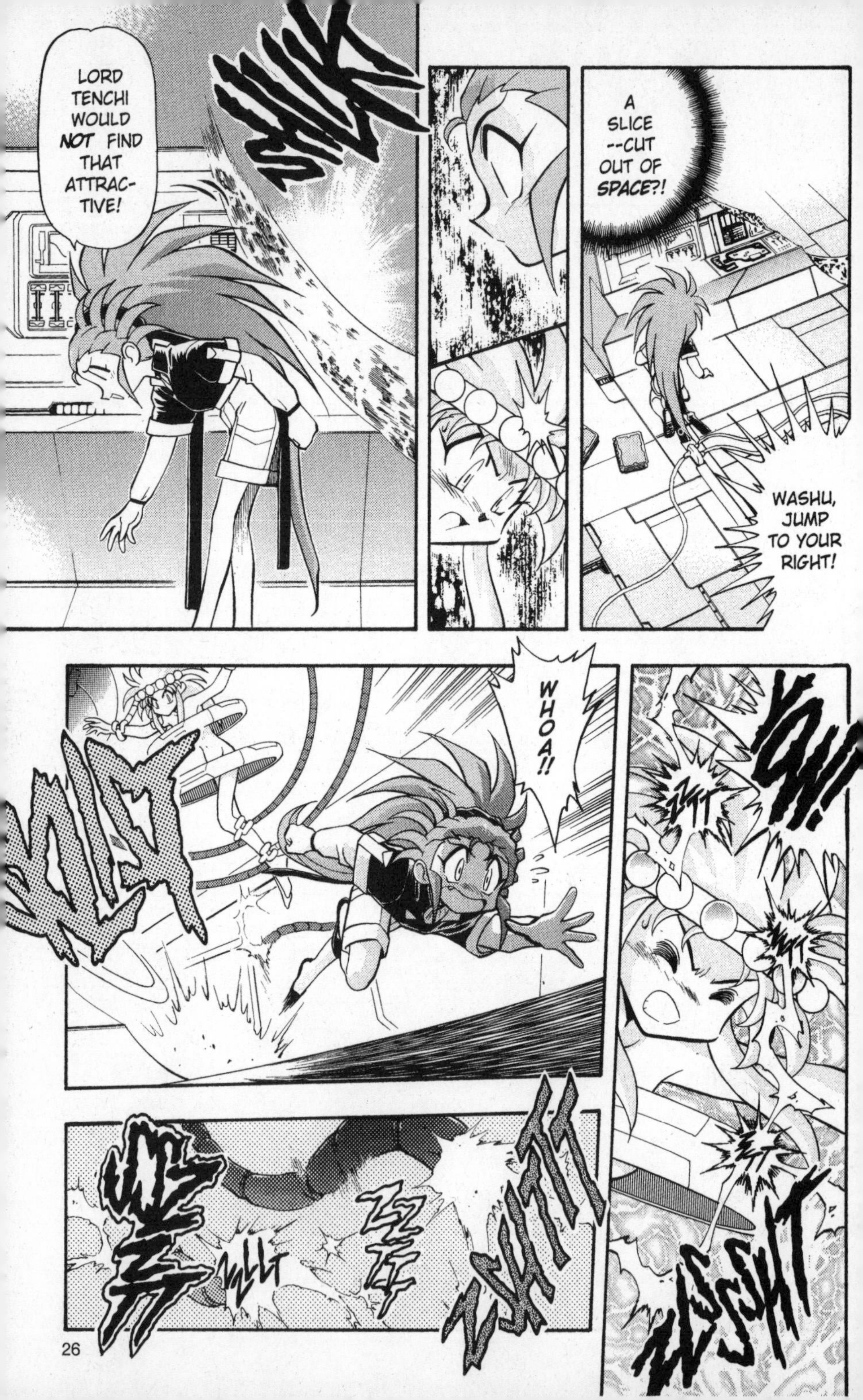
LORD TENCHI WOULD NOT FIND THAT ATTRACTIVE!
A SLICE --CUT OUT OF SPACE?!
WASHU, JUMP TO YOUR RIGHT!
WHOA!!

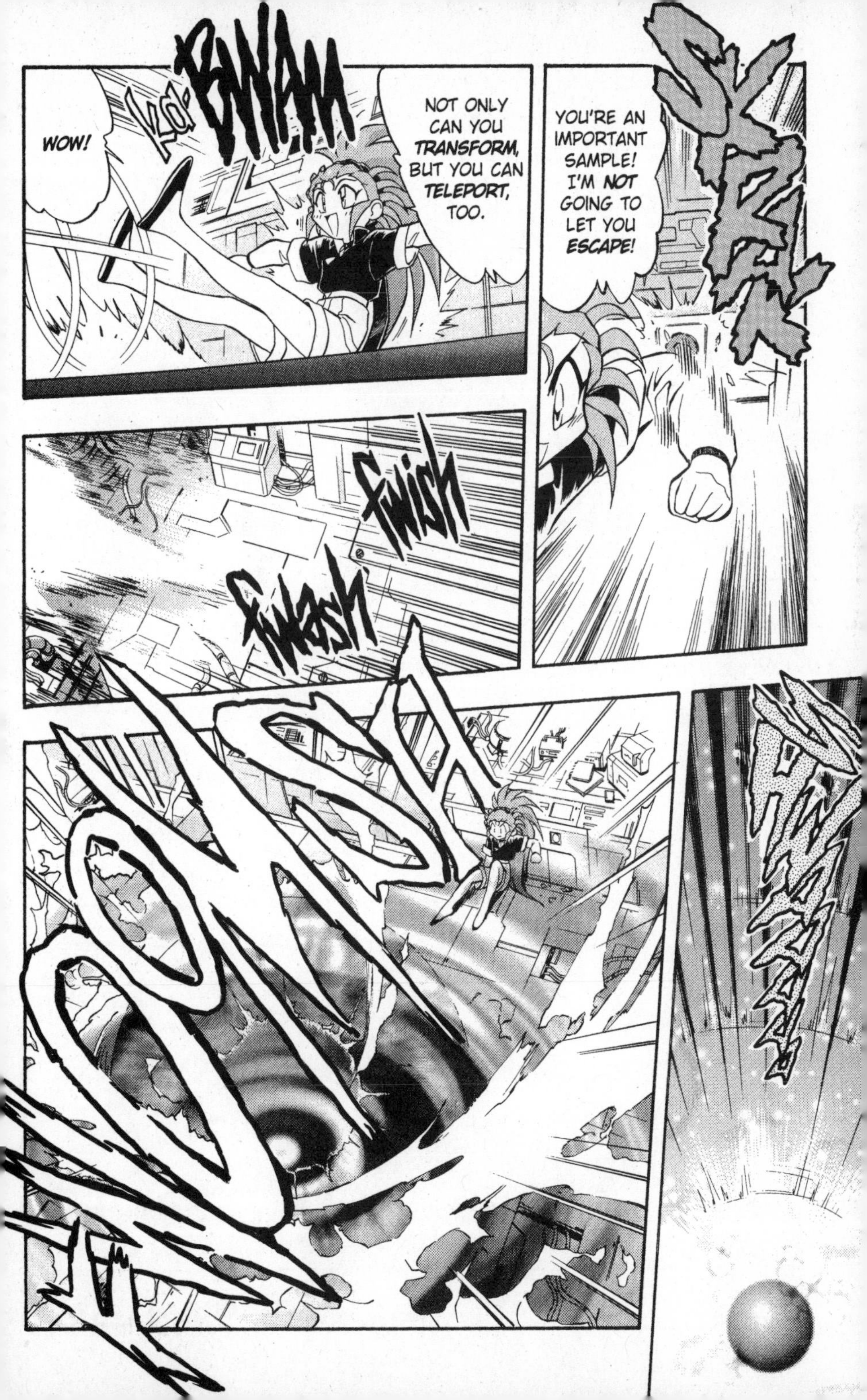
WOW!
ka-BWAM
NOT ONLY CAN YOU *TRANSFORM,* BUT YOU CAN *TELEPORT,* TOO.
YOU'RE AN IMPORTANT SAMPLE! I'M *NOT* GOING TO LET YOU *ESCAPE!*
fwish
fwash

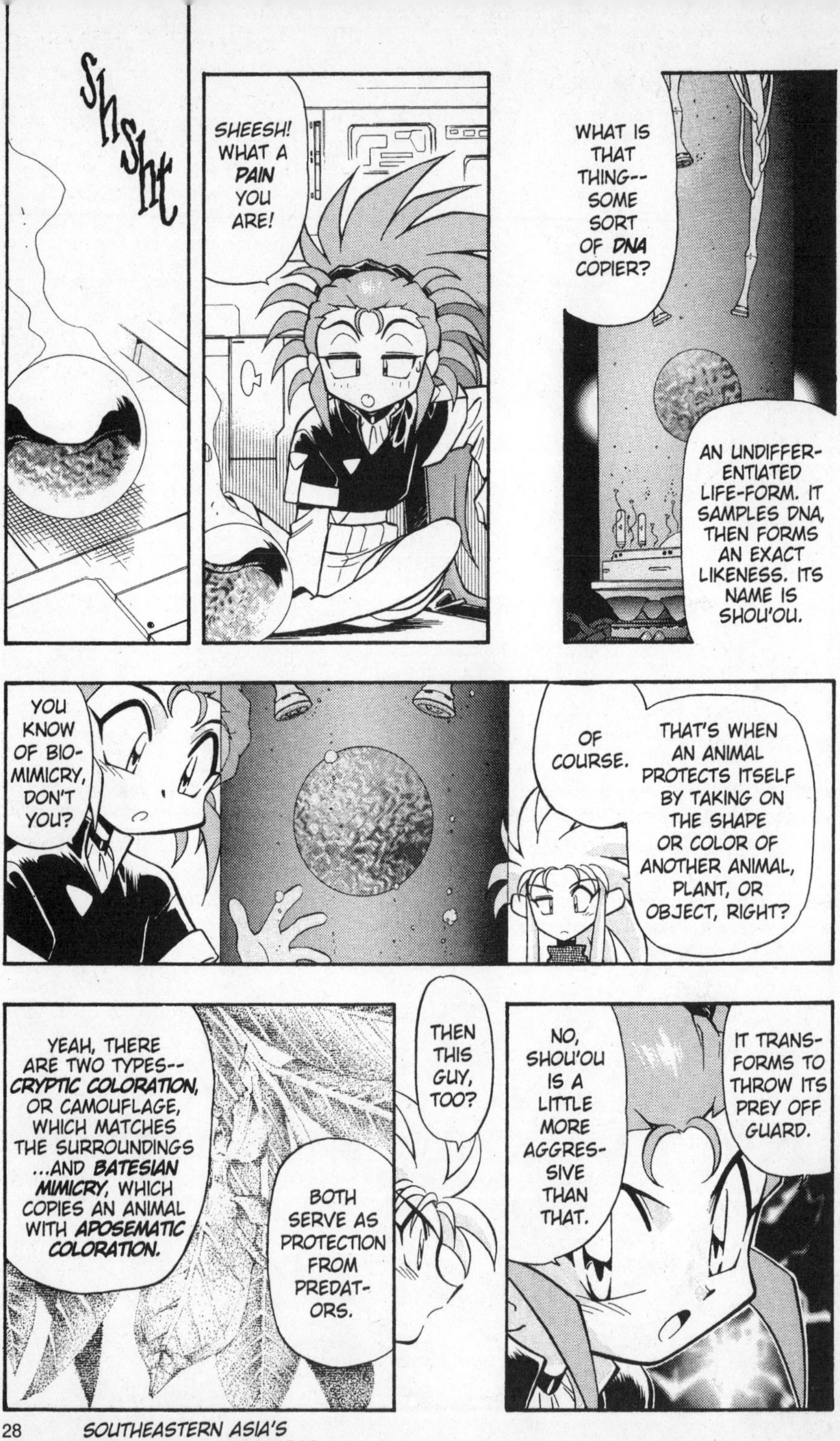
SHSHT
SHEESH! WHAT A PAIN YOU ARE!
WHAT IS THAT THING-- SOME SORT OF DNA COPIER?
AN UNDIFFERENTIATED LIFE-FORM. IT SAMPLES DNA, THEN FORMS AN EXACT LIKENESS. ITS NAME IS SHOU'OU.
YOU KNOW OF BIO-MIMICRY, DON'T YOU?
OF COURSE.
THAT'S WHEN AN ANIMAL PROTECTS ITSELF BY TAKING ON THE SHAPE OR COLOR OF ANOTHER ANIMAL, PLANT, OR OBJECT, RIGHT?
YEAH, THERE ARE TWO TYPES-- CRYPTIC COLORATION, OR CAMOUFLAGE, WHICH MATCHES THE SURROUNDINGS ...AND BATESIAN MIMICRY, WHICH COPIES AN ANIMAL WITH APOSEMATIC COLORATION.
THEN THIS GUY, TOO?
BOTH SERVE AS PROTECTION FROM PREDATORS.
NO, SHOU'OU IS A LITTLE MORE AGGRESSIVE THAN THAT.
IT TRANSFORMS TO THROW ITS PREY OFF GUARD.

SOUTHEASTERN ASIA'S CAMOUFLAGED LEAF INSECT

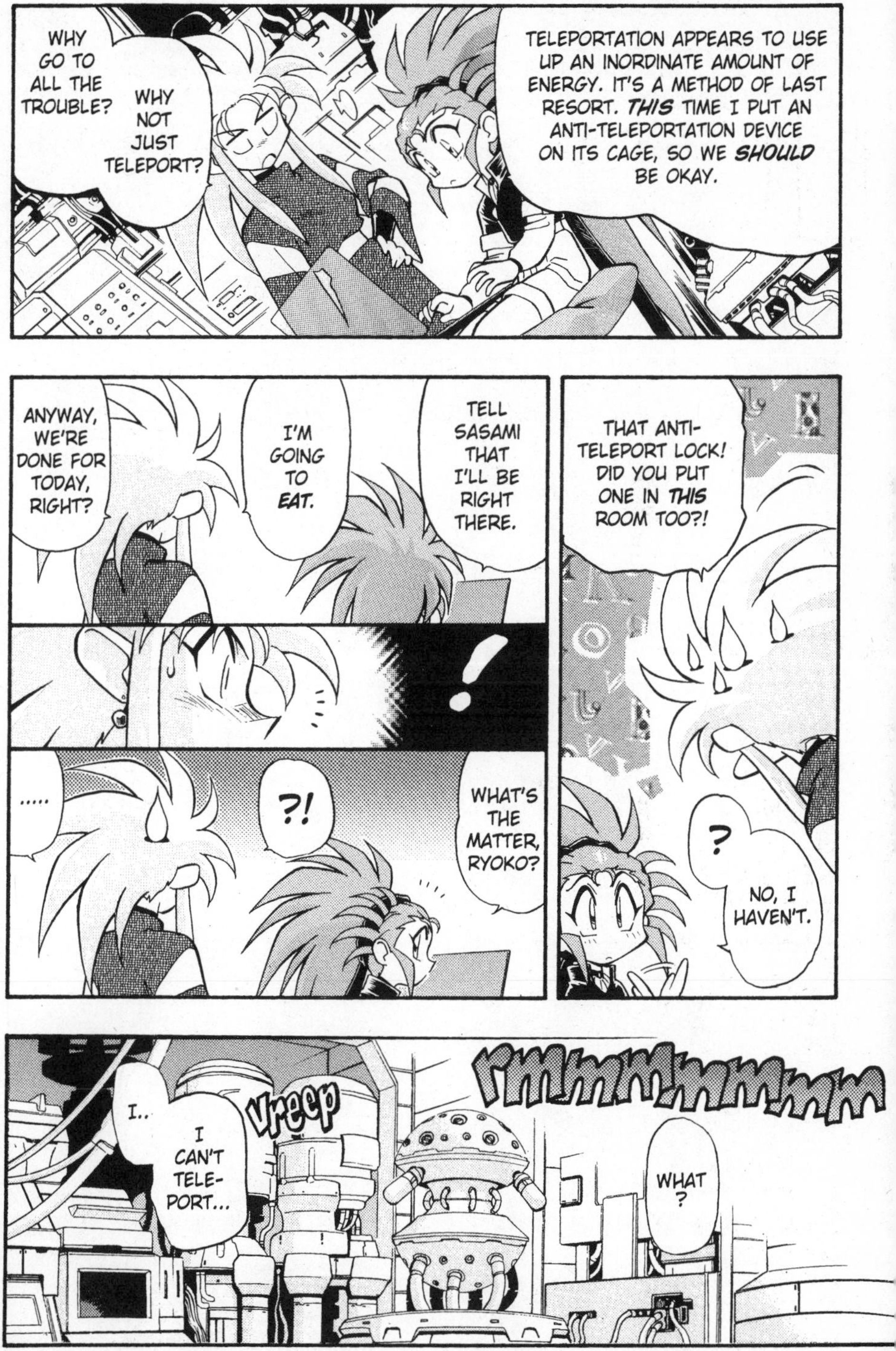
WHY GO TO ALL THE TROUBLE?
WHY NOT JUST TELEPORT?
TELEPORTATION APPEARS TO USE UP AN INORDINATE AMOUNT OF ENERGY. IT'S A METHOD OF LAST RESORT. *THIS* TIME I PUT AN ANTI-TELEPORTATION DEVICE ON ITS CAGE, SO WE *SHOULD* BE OKAY.
ANYWAY, WE'RE DONE FOR TODAY, RIGHT?
I'M GOING TO *EAT*.
TELL SASAMI THAT I'LL BE RIGHT THERE.
!
.....
?!
WHAT'S THE MATTER, RYOKO?
THAT ANTI-TELEPORT LOCK! DID YOU PUT ONE IN *THIS* ROOM TOO?!
?
NO, I HAVEN'T.
I..
I CAN'T TELE-PORT...
VREEP
RMMMMMMMMM
WHAT?

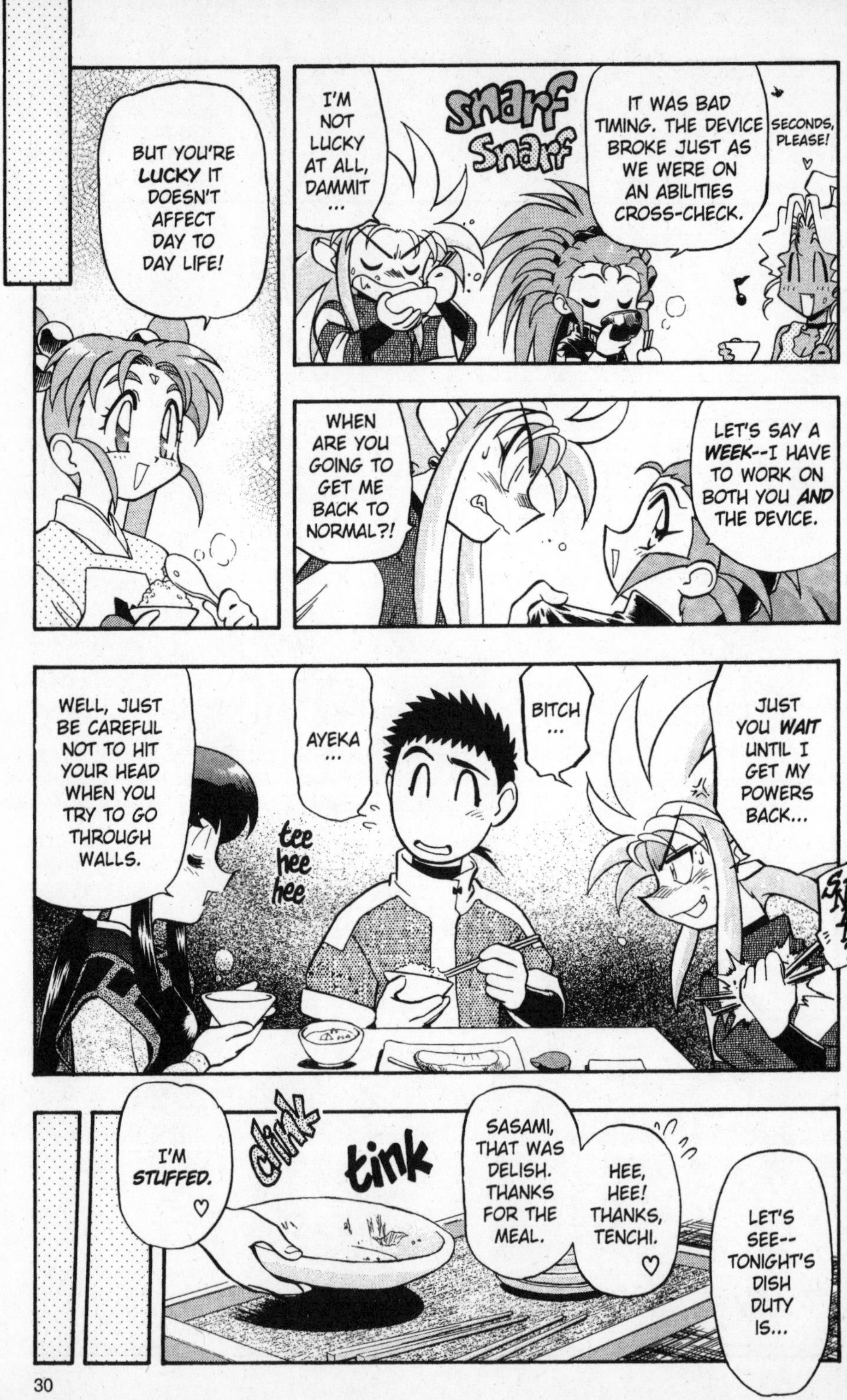

BUT YOU'RE **LUCKY** IT DOESN'T AFFECT DAY TO DAY LIFE!
I'M NOT LUCKY AT ALL, DAMMIT...
snarf snarf
IT WAS BAD TIMING. THE DEVICE BROKE JUST AS WE WERE ON AN ABILITIES CROSS-CHECK.
SECONDS, PLEASE! ♡
WHEN ARE YOU GOING TO GET ME BACK TO NORMAL?!
LET'S SAY A **WEEK**--I HAVE TO WORK ON BOTH YOU **AND** THE DEVICE.
WELL, JUST BE CAREFUL NOT TO HIT YOUR HEAD WHEN YOU TRY TO GO THROUGH WALLS.
AYEKA...
tee hee hee
BITCH...
JUST YOU **WAIT** UNTIL I GET MY POWERS BACK...
I'M **STUFFED.** ♡
clink
tink
SASAMI, THAT WAS DELISH. THANKS FOR THE MEAL.
HEE, HEE! THANKS, TENCHI. ♡
LET'S SEE-- TONIGHT'S DISH DUTY IS...

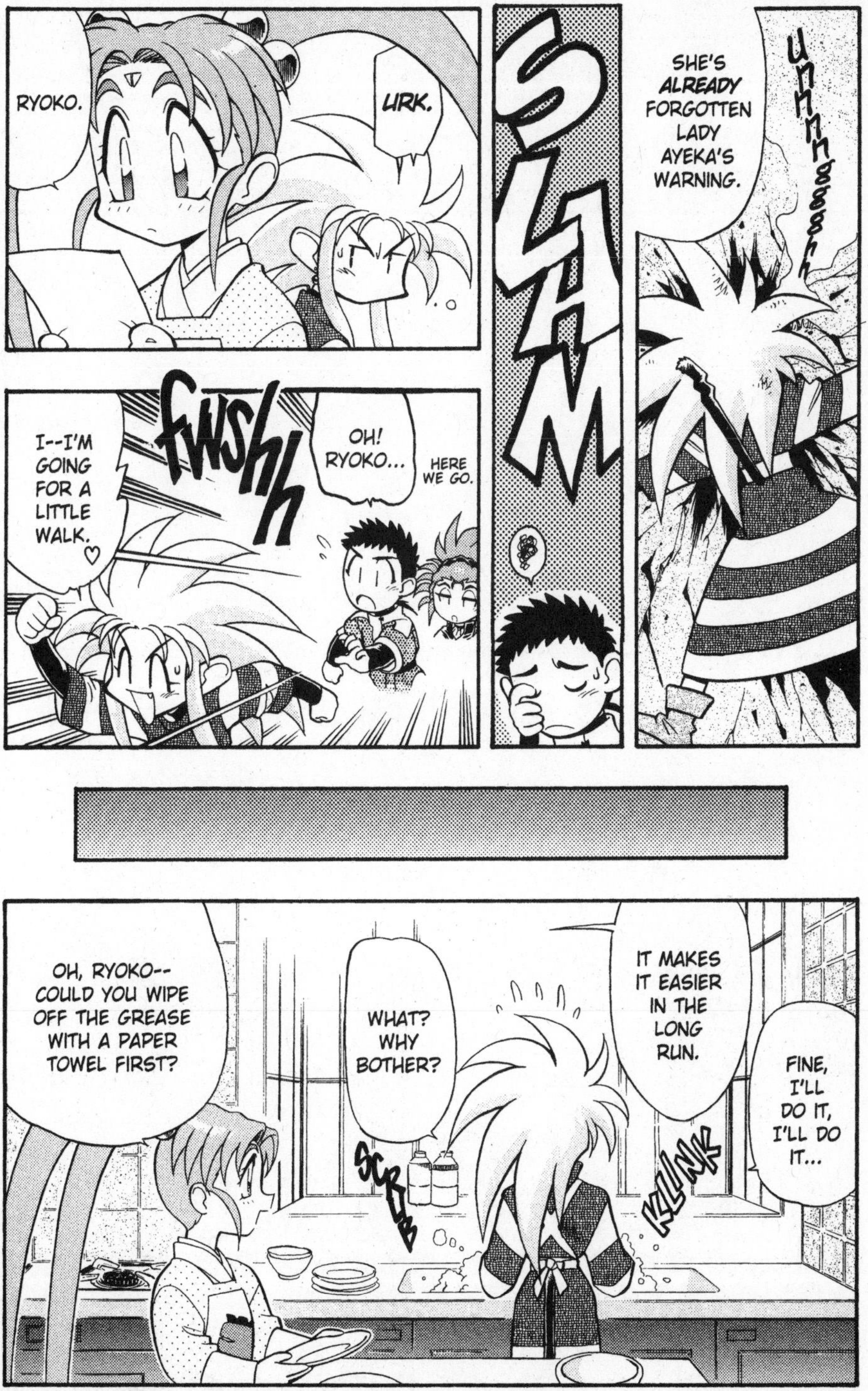
RYOKO.
URK.
I--I'M GOING FOR A LITTLE WALK. ♡
fwshh
OH! RYOKO...
HERE WE GO.
SLAM
SHE'S ALREADY FORGOTTEN LADY AYEKA'S WARNING.
unnnngggggh
OH, RYOKO-- COULD YOU WIPE OFF THE GREASE WITH A PAPER TOWEL FIRST?
WHAT? WHY BOTHER?
SCRUB
IT MAKES IT EASIER IN THE LONG RUN.
KLUNK
FINE, I'LL DO IT, I'LL DO IT...

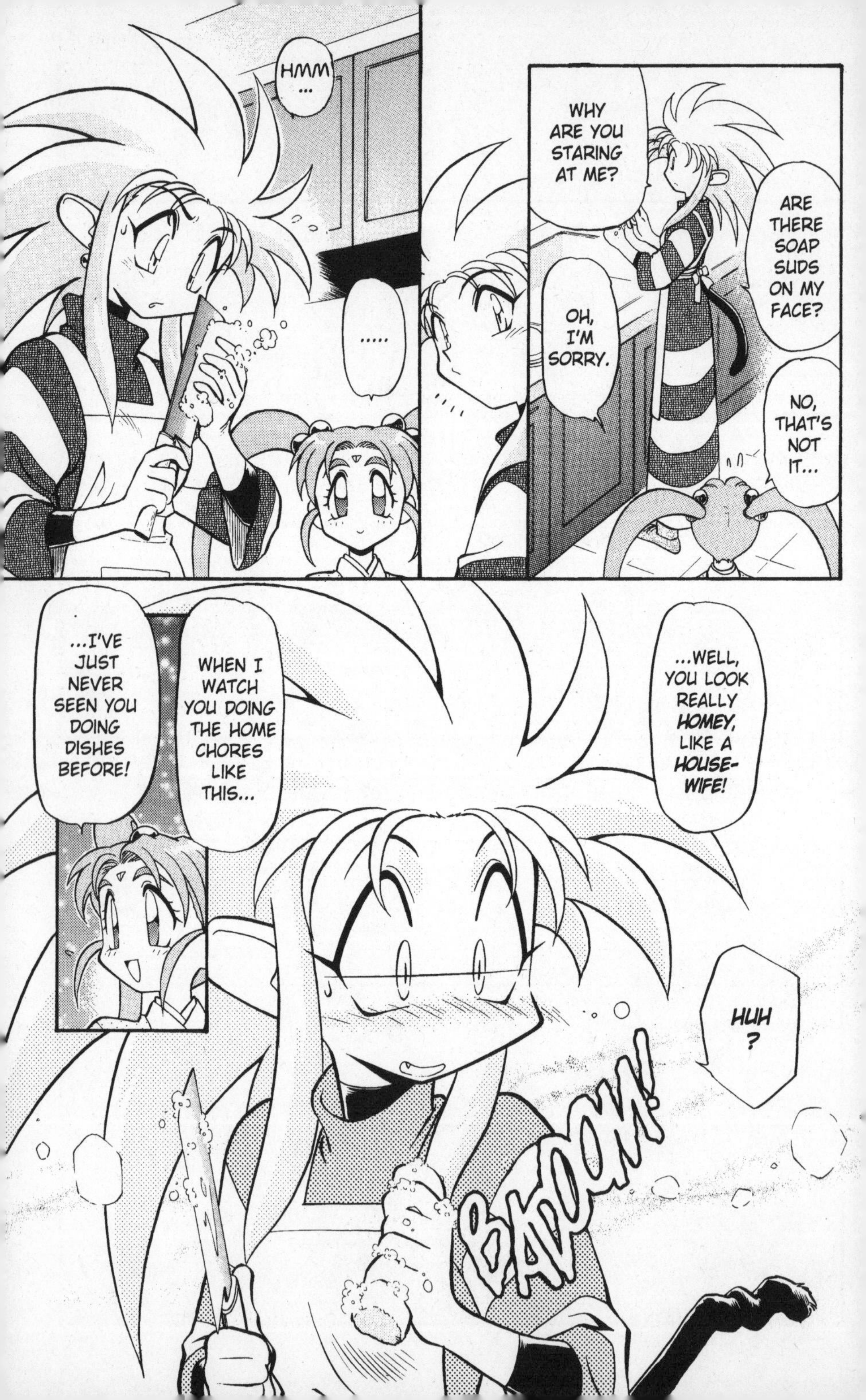

HMM ...
.....
WHY ARE YOU STARING AT ME?
OH, I'M SORRY.
ARE THERE SOAP SUDS ON MY FACE?
NO, THAT'S NOT IT...
...I'VE JUST NEVER SEEN YOU DOING DISHES BEFORE!
WHEN I WATCH YOU DOING THE HOME CHORES LIKE THIS...
...WELL, YOU LOOK REALLY HOMEY, LIKE A HOUSE-WIFE!
HUH ?
BADOOM!

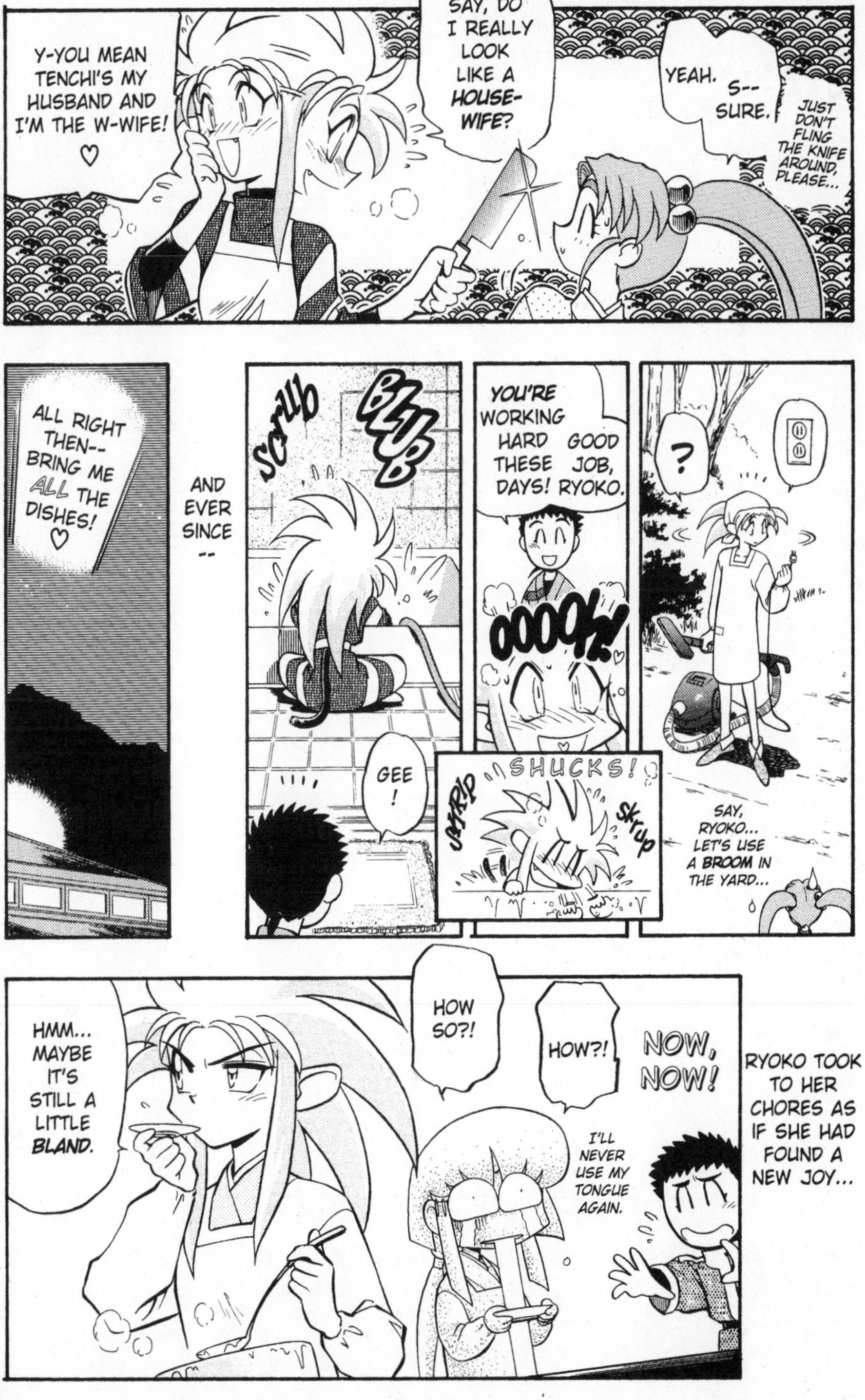
Y-YOU MEAN TENCHI'S MY HUSBAND AND I'M THE W-WIFE! ♡
SAY, DO I REALLY LOOK LIKE A **HOUSE-WIFE?**
YEAH.
S-- SURE.
JUST DON'T FLING THE KNIFE AROUND, PLEASE...
ALL RIGHT THEN-- BRING ME *ALL* THE DISHES! ♡
AND EVER SINCE --
SCRUB
BLUB
GEE!
YOU'RE WORKING HARD THESE DAYS!
GOOD JOB, RYOKO.
OOOOH!
SHUCKS!
SKRIP
SKRUP
?
SAY, RYOKO... LET'S USE A **BROOM** IN THE YARD...
HMM... MAYBE IT'S STILL A LITTLE **BLAND.**
HOW SO?!
HOW?!
NOW, NOW!
I'LL NEVER USE MY TONGUE AGAIN.
RYOKO TOOK TO HER CHORES AS IF SHE HAD FOUND A NEW JOY...

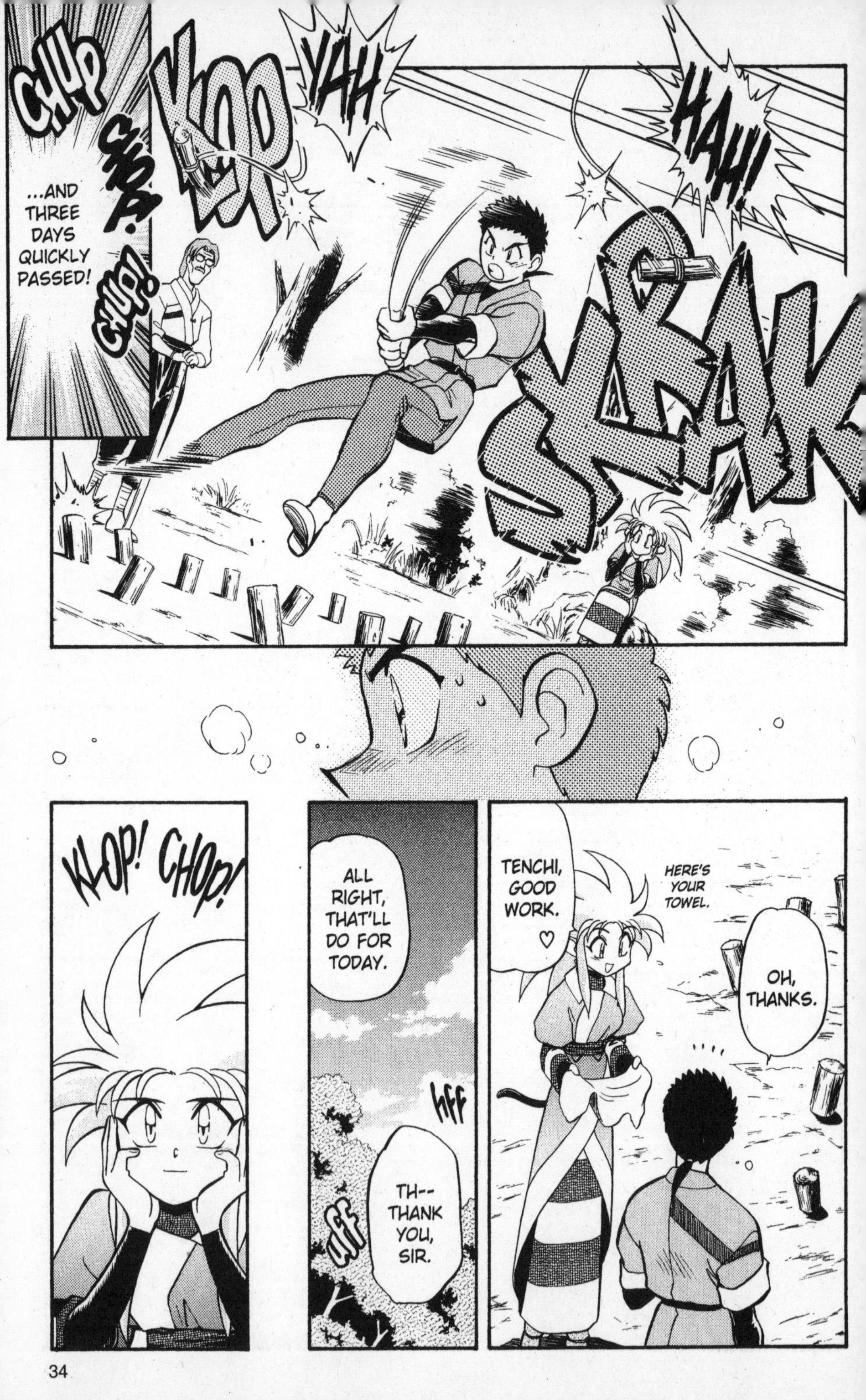
CHUP
...AND THREE DAYS QUICKLY PASSED!
CHOP!
CHUP!
KLOP
YAH
KAH!
SHAK
KLOP! CHOP!
ALL RIGHT, THAT'LL DO FOR TODAY.
hff
uff
TH-- THANK YOU, SIR.
TENCHI, GOOD WORK. ♡
HERE'S YOUR TOWEL.
OH, THANKS.
...

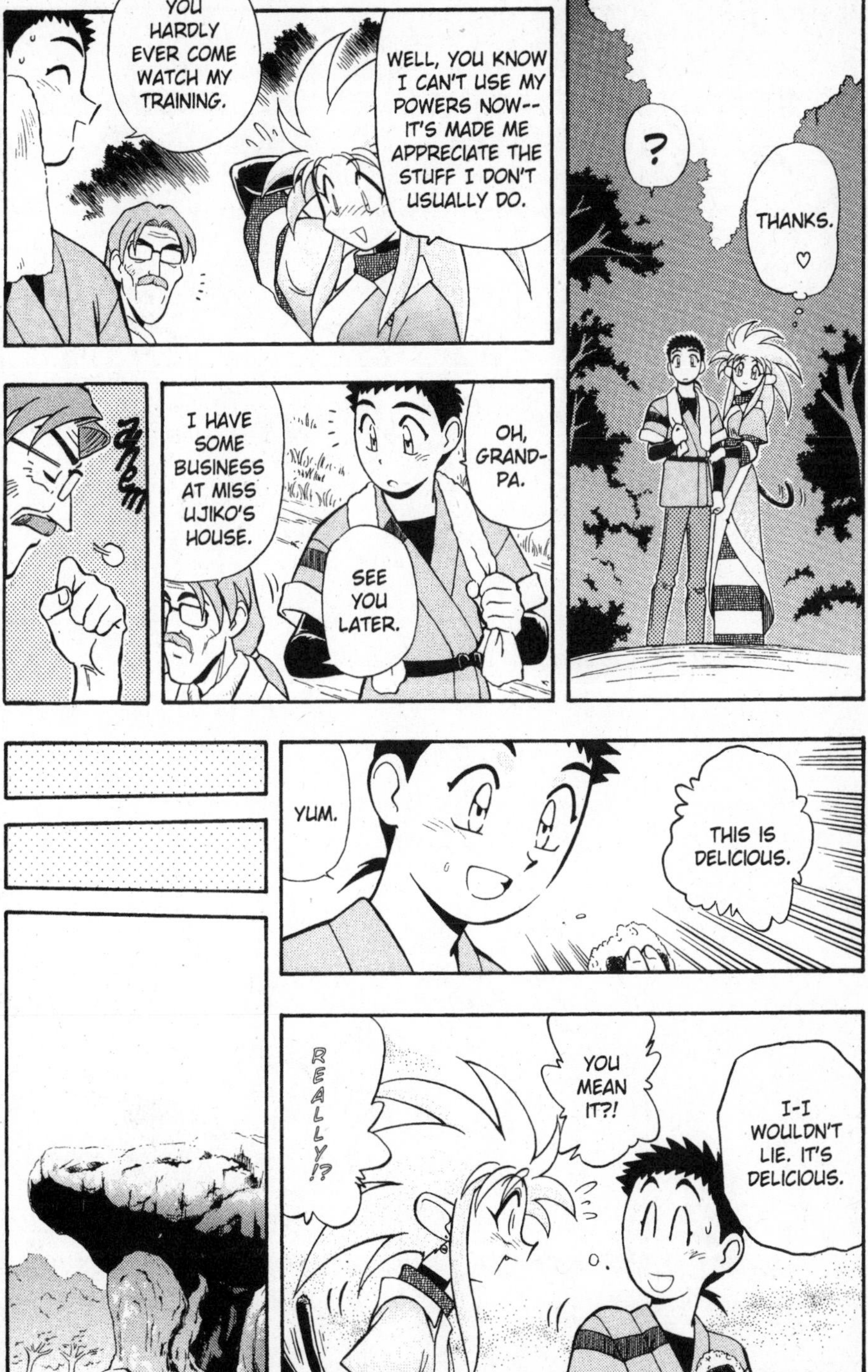
YOU HARDLY EVER COME WATCH MY TRAINING.
WELL, YOU KNOW I CAN'T USE MY POWERS NOW-- IT'S MADE ME APPRECIATE THE STUFF I DON'T USUALLY DO.
I HAVE SOME BUSINESS AT MISS UJIKO'S HOUSE.
OH, GRAND-PA.
SEE YOU LATER.
?
THANKS. ♡
YUM.
THIS IS DELICIOUS.
REALLY!?
YOU MEAN IT?!
I-I WOULDN'T LIE. IT'S DELICIOUS.

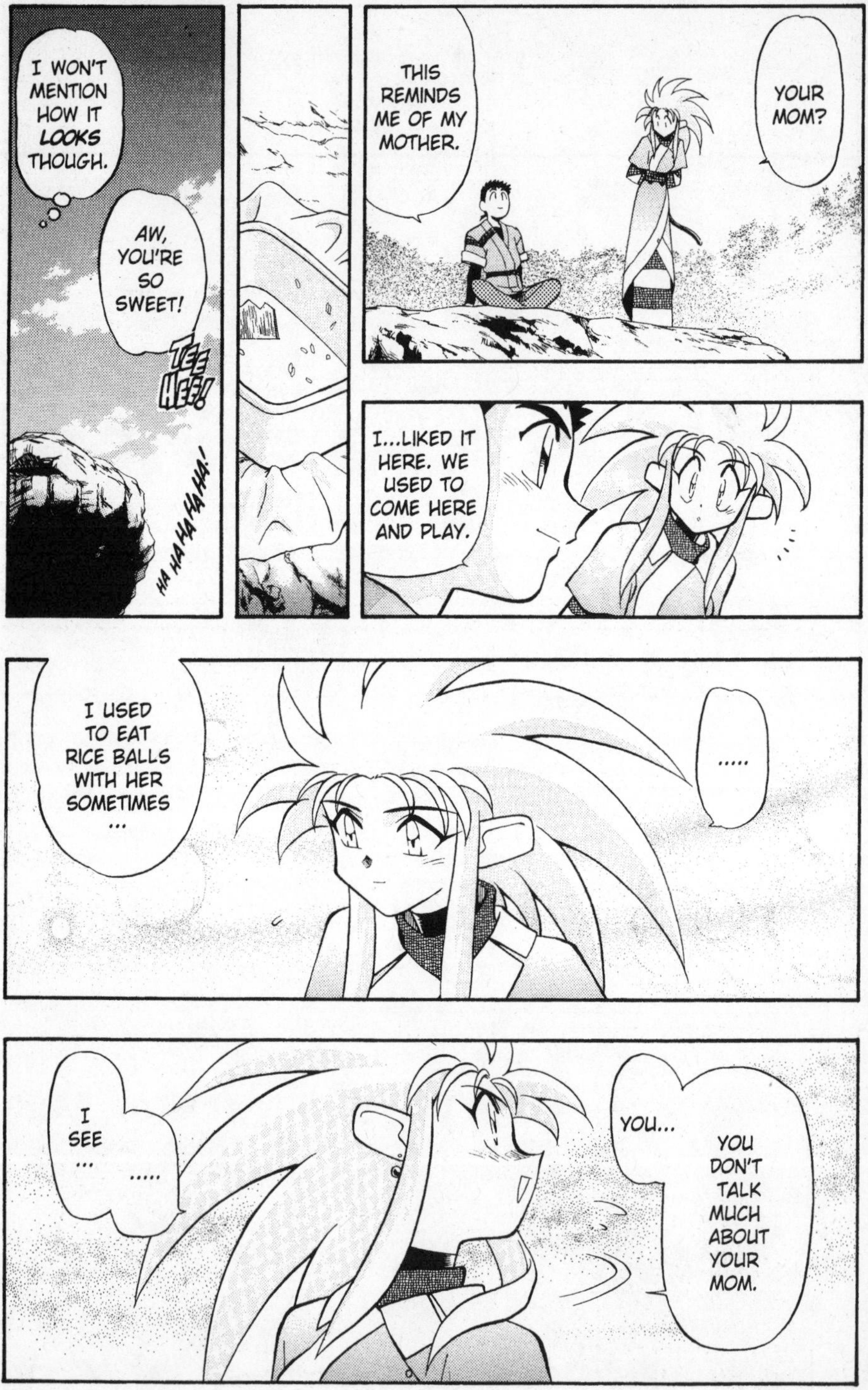

I WON'T MENTION HOW IT LOOKS THOUGH.
AW, YOU'RE SO SWEET!
TEE HEE!
HA HA HA HA HA!
THIS REMINDS ME OF MY MOTHER.
YOUR MOM?
I...LIKED IT HERE. WE USED TO COME HERE AND PLAY.
I USED TO EAT RICE BALLS WITH HER SOMETIMES ...
.....
I SEE ...
.....
YOU...
YOU DON'T TALK MUCH ABOUT YOUR MOM.

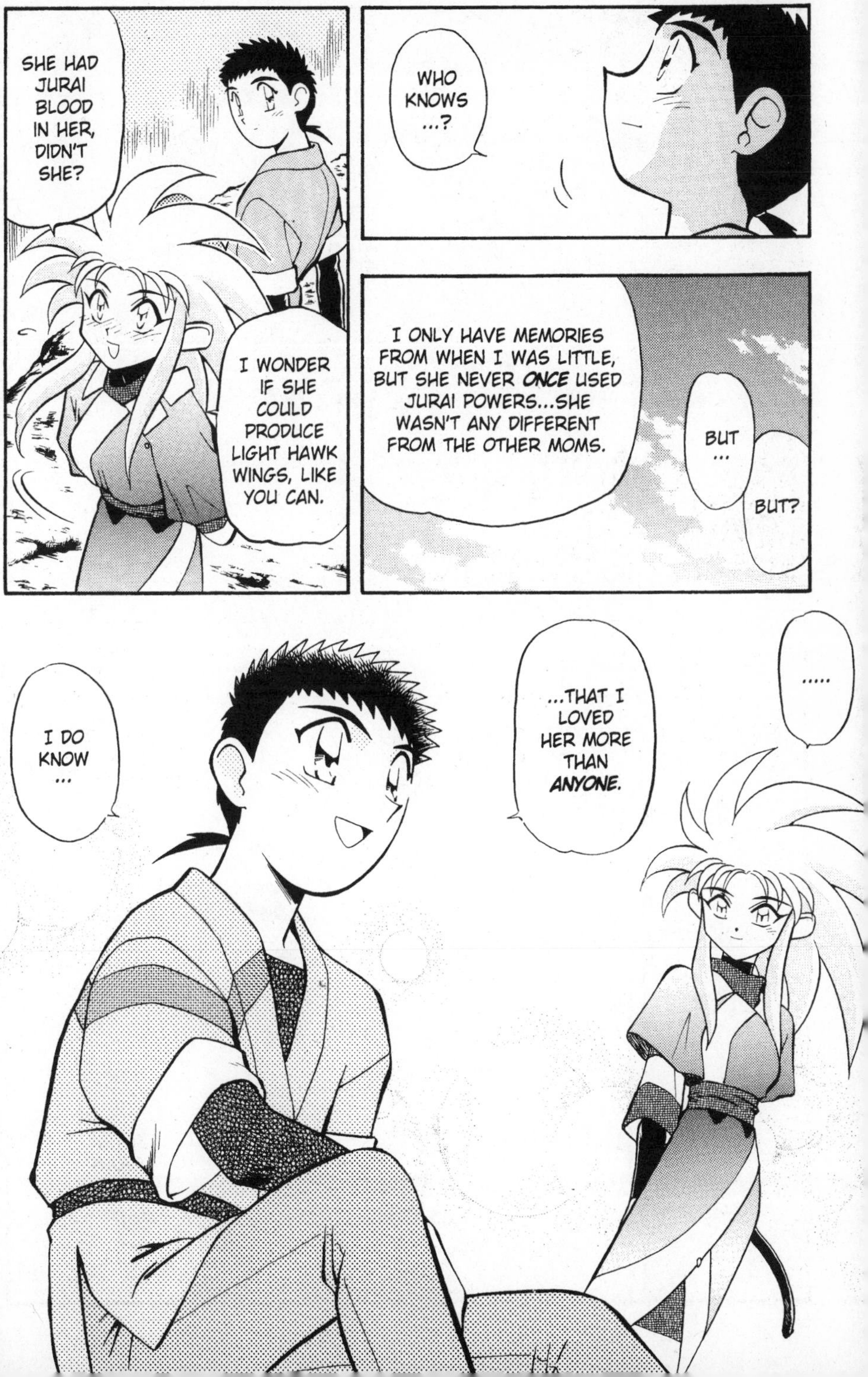
SHE HAD JURAI BLOOD IN HER, DIDN'T SHE?
I WONDER IF SHE COULD PRODUCE LIGHT HAWK WINGS, LIKE YOU CAN.
WHO KNOWS ...?
I ONLY HAVE MEMORIES FROM WHEN I WAS LITTLE, BUT SHE NEVER *ONCE* USED JURAI POWERS...SHE WASN'T ANY DIFFERENT FROM THE OTHER MOMS.
BUT ...
BUT?
I DO KNOW ...
...THAT I LOVED HER MORE THAN *ANYONE*.
.....

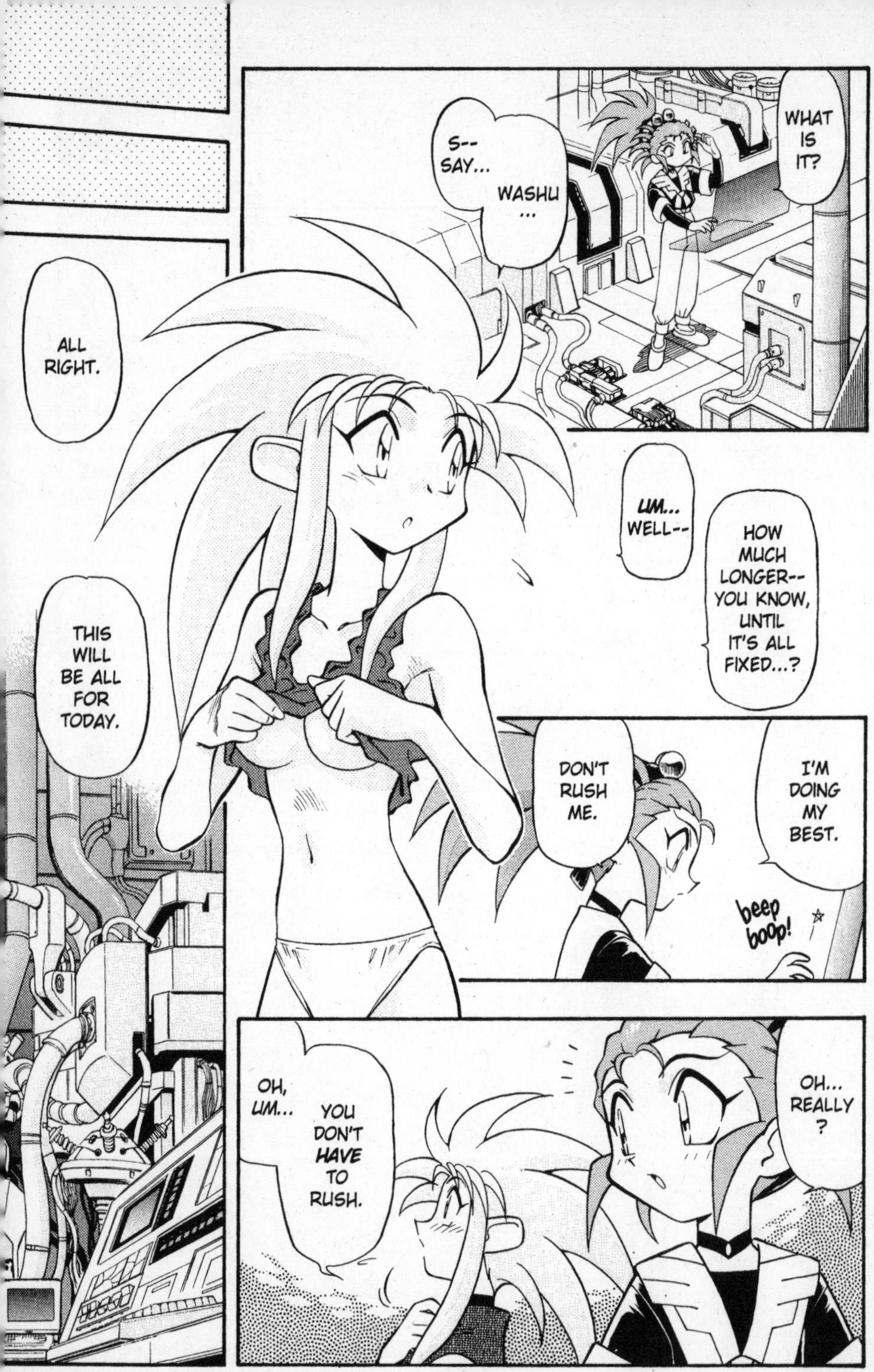

S-- SAY...
WASHU ...
WHAT IS IT?
ALL RIGHT.
THIS WILL BE ALL FOR TODAY.
UM... WELL--
HOW MUCH LONGER-- YOU KNOW, UNTIL IT'S ALL FIXED...?
DON'T RUSH ME.
I'M DOING MY BEST.
beep boop!
OH, UM...
YOU DON'T *HAVE* TO RUSH.
OH... REALLY ?

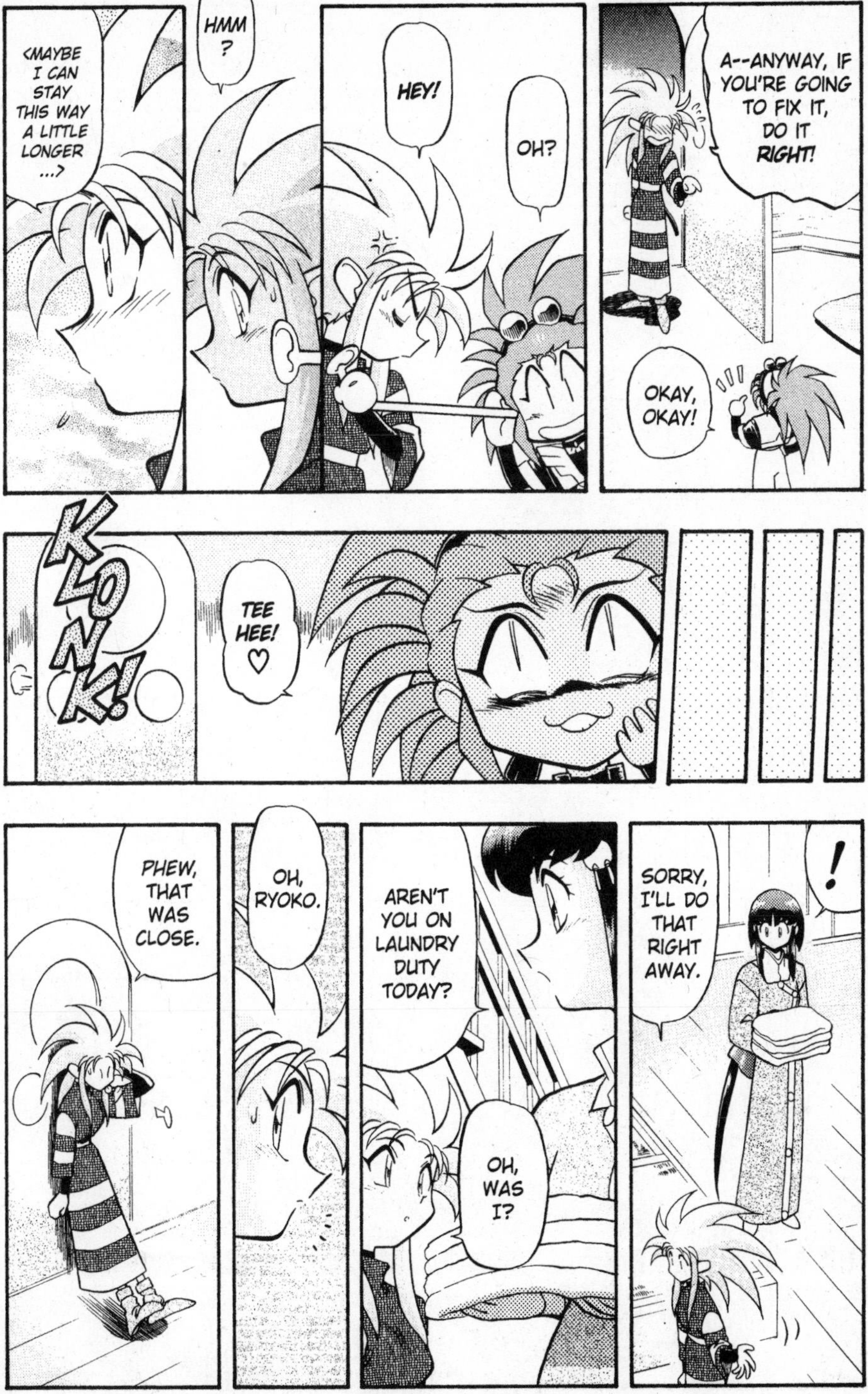
<MAYBE I CAN STAY THIS WAY A LITTLE LONGER ...>
HMM ?
HEY!
OH?
A--ANYWAY, IF YOU'RE GOING TO FIX IT, DO IT RIGHT!
OKAY, OKAY!
KLONK!
TEE HEE! ♡
PHEW, THAT WAS CLOSE.
OH, RYOKO.
AREN'T YOU ON LAUNDRY DUTY TODAY?
OH, WAS I?
SORRY, I'LL DO THAT RIGHT AWAY.
!

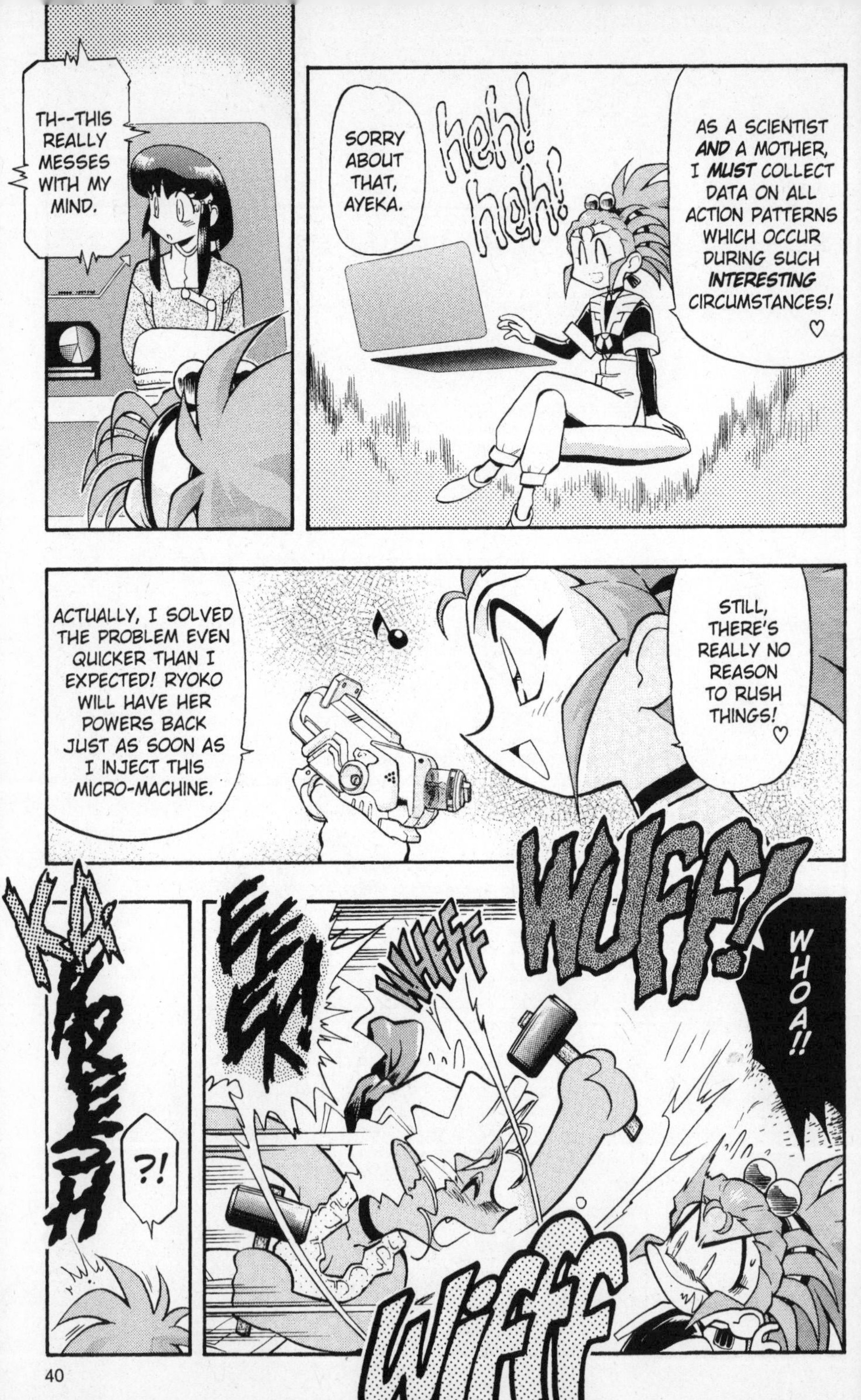
TH--THIS REALLY MESSES WITH MY MIND.
SORRY ABOUT THAT, AYEKA.
heh! heh!
AS A SCIENTIST **AND** A MOTHER, I **MUST** COLLECT DATA ON ALL ACTION PATTERNS WHICH OCCUR DURING SUCH **INTERESTING** CIRCUMSTANCES! ♡
ACTUALLY, I SOLVED THE PROBLEM EVEN QUICKER THAN I EXPECTED! RYOKO WILL HAVE HER POWERS BACK JUST AS SOON AS I INJECT THIS MICRO-MACHINE.
STILL, THERE'S REALLY NO REASON TO RUSH THINGS! ♡
?!
WHIFF
WUFF!
WHOA!!
Wiff

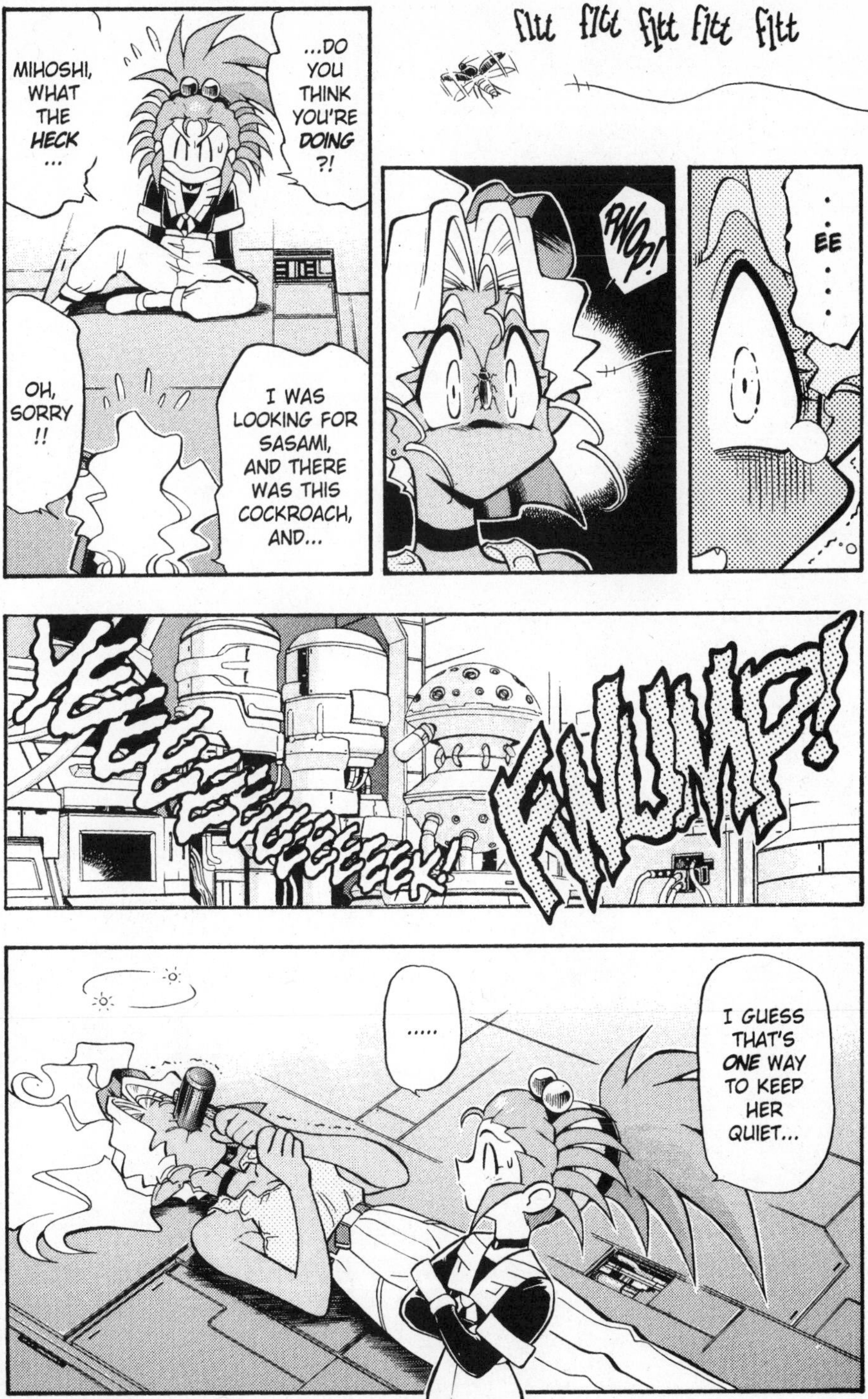
MIHOSHI, WHAT THE HECK...
...DO YOU THINK YOU'RE DOING?!
OH, SORRY!!
I WAS LOOKING FOR SASAMI, AND THERE WAS THIS COCKROACH, AND...
fltt fltt fltt fltt fltt
RWOP!
...EE....
YEEEEEEEEEEEEEEK!
FWUMP!
.....
I GUESS THAT'S ONE WAY TO KEEP HER QUIET...

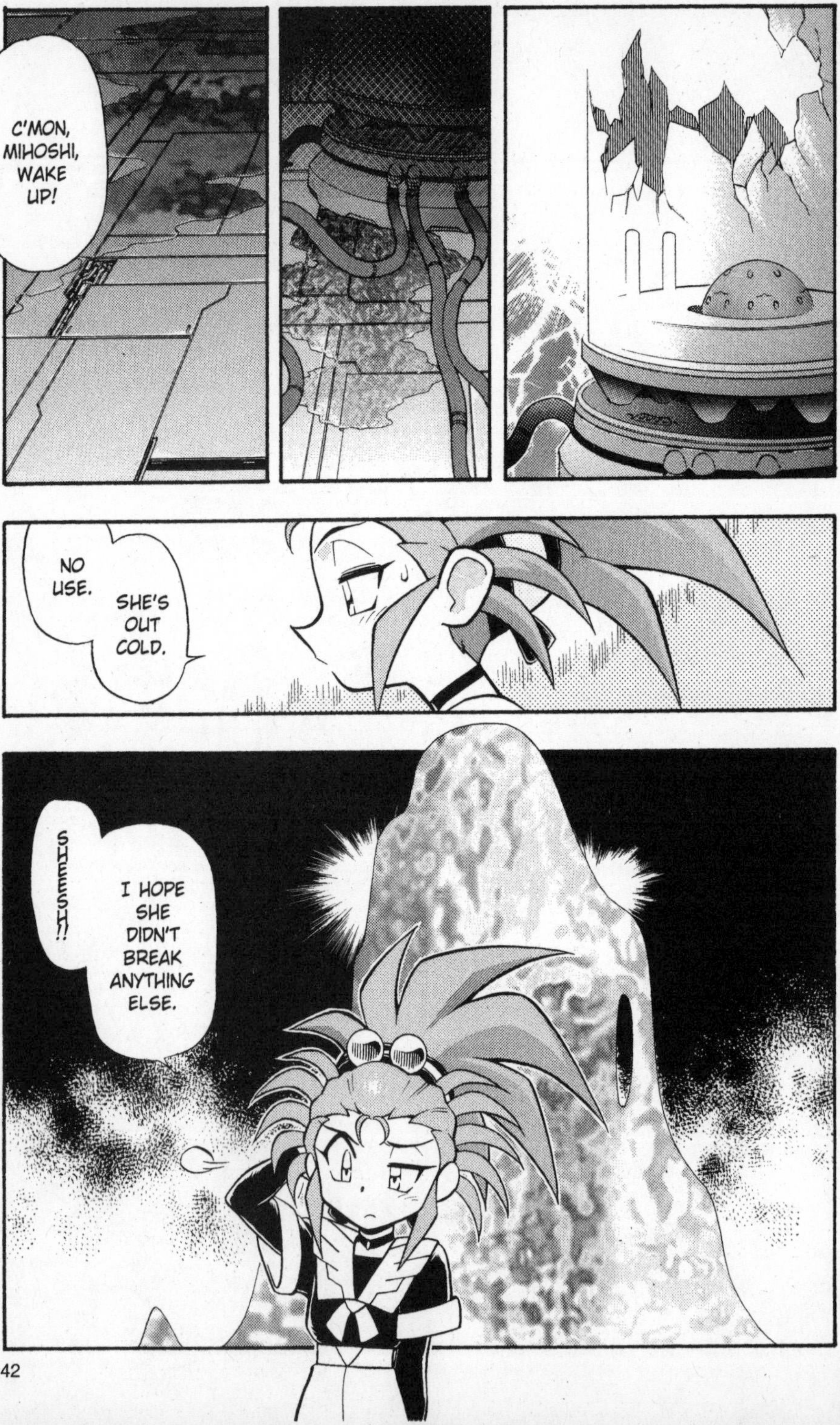
C'MON, MIHOSHI, WAKE UP!
NO USE.
SHE'S OUT COLD.
SHEESH!!
I HOPE SHE DIDN'T BREAK ANYTHING ELSE.

Tales of Tenchi #3:
A SHOU'OU THING

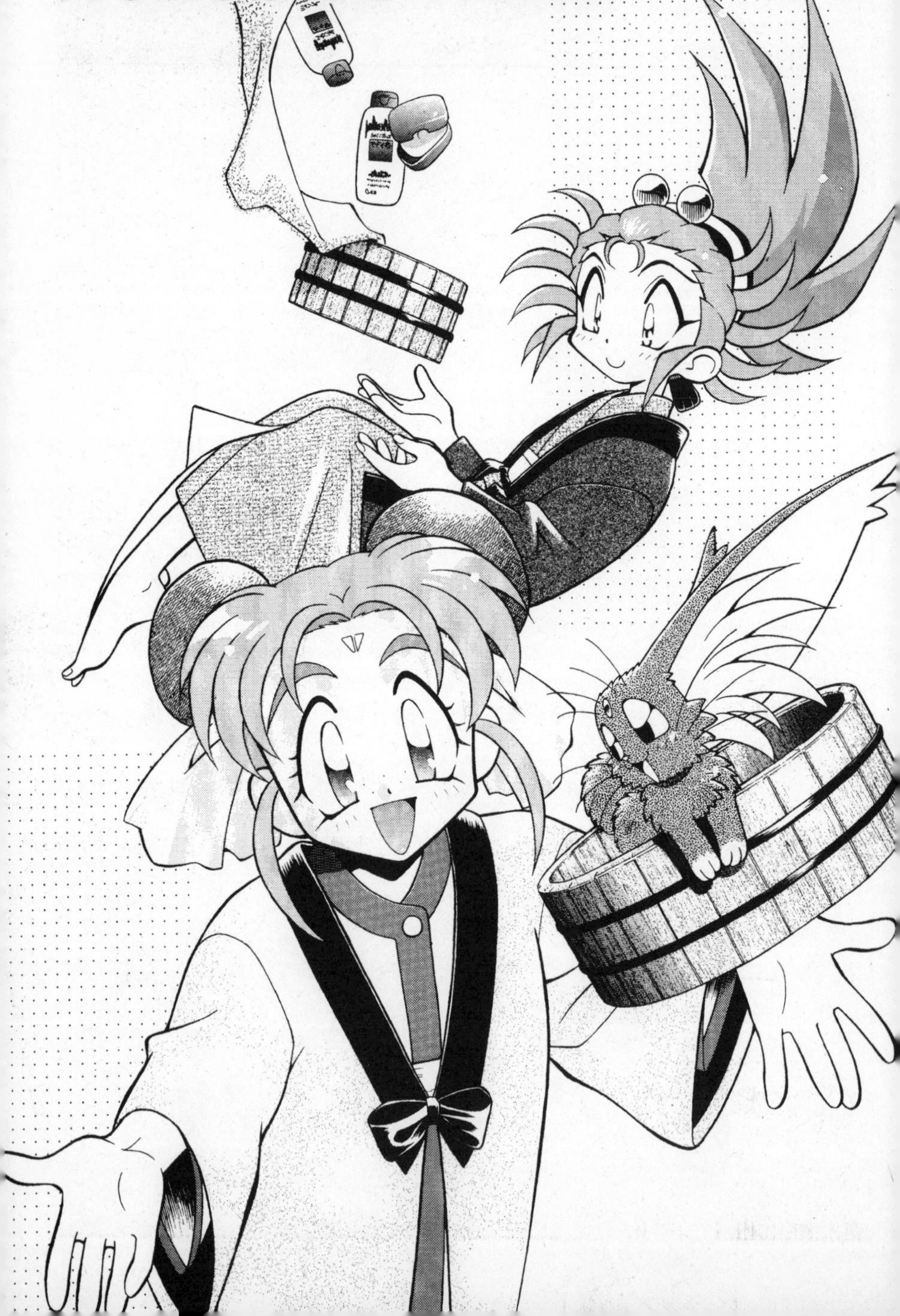

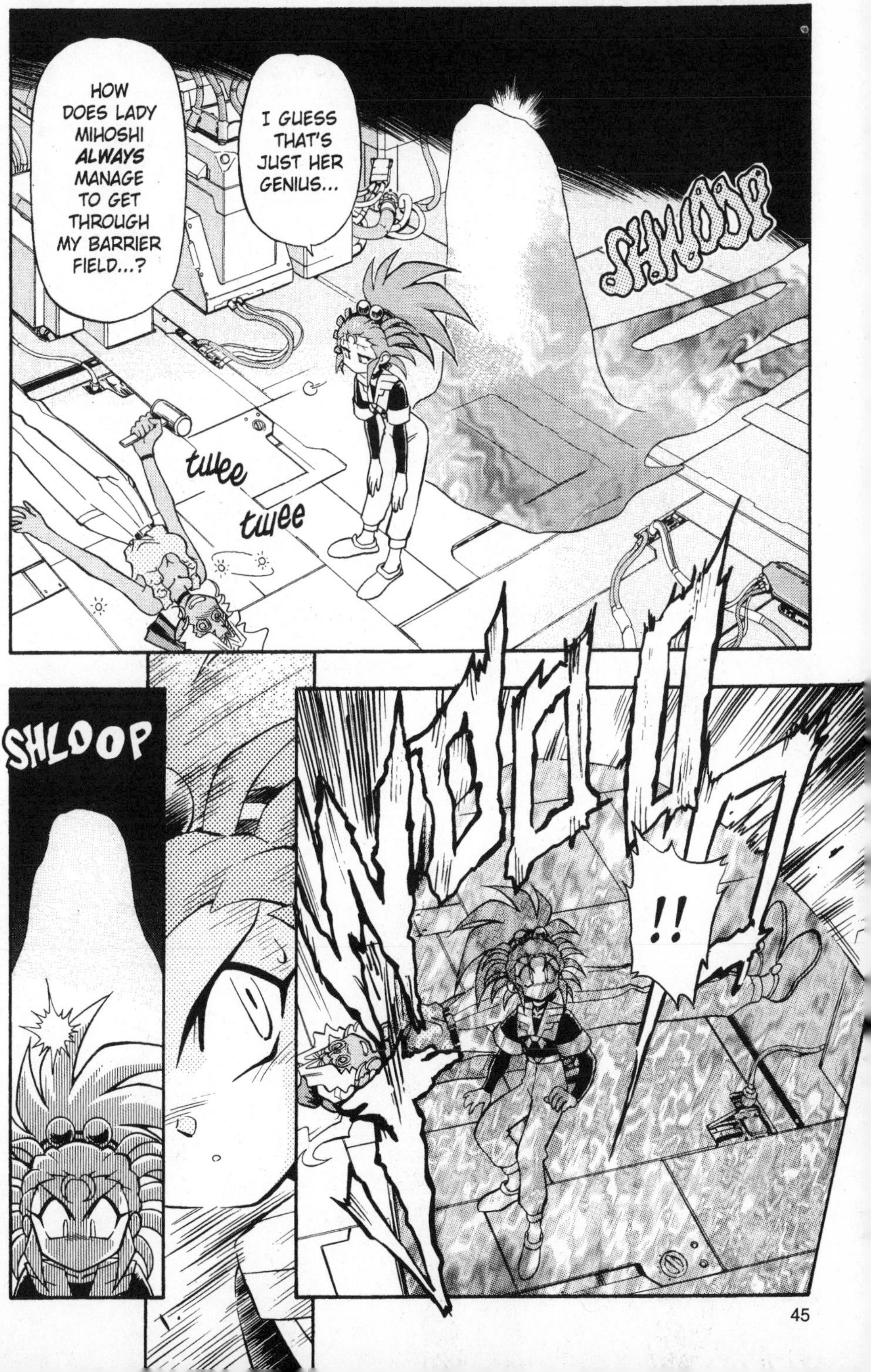
HOW DOES LADY MIHOSHI **ALWAYS** MANAGE TO GET THROUGH MY BARRIER FIELD...?
I GUESS THAT'S JUST HER GENIUS...
twee
twee
SHLOOP
!!

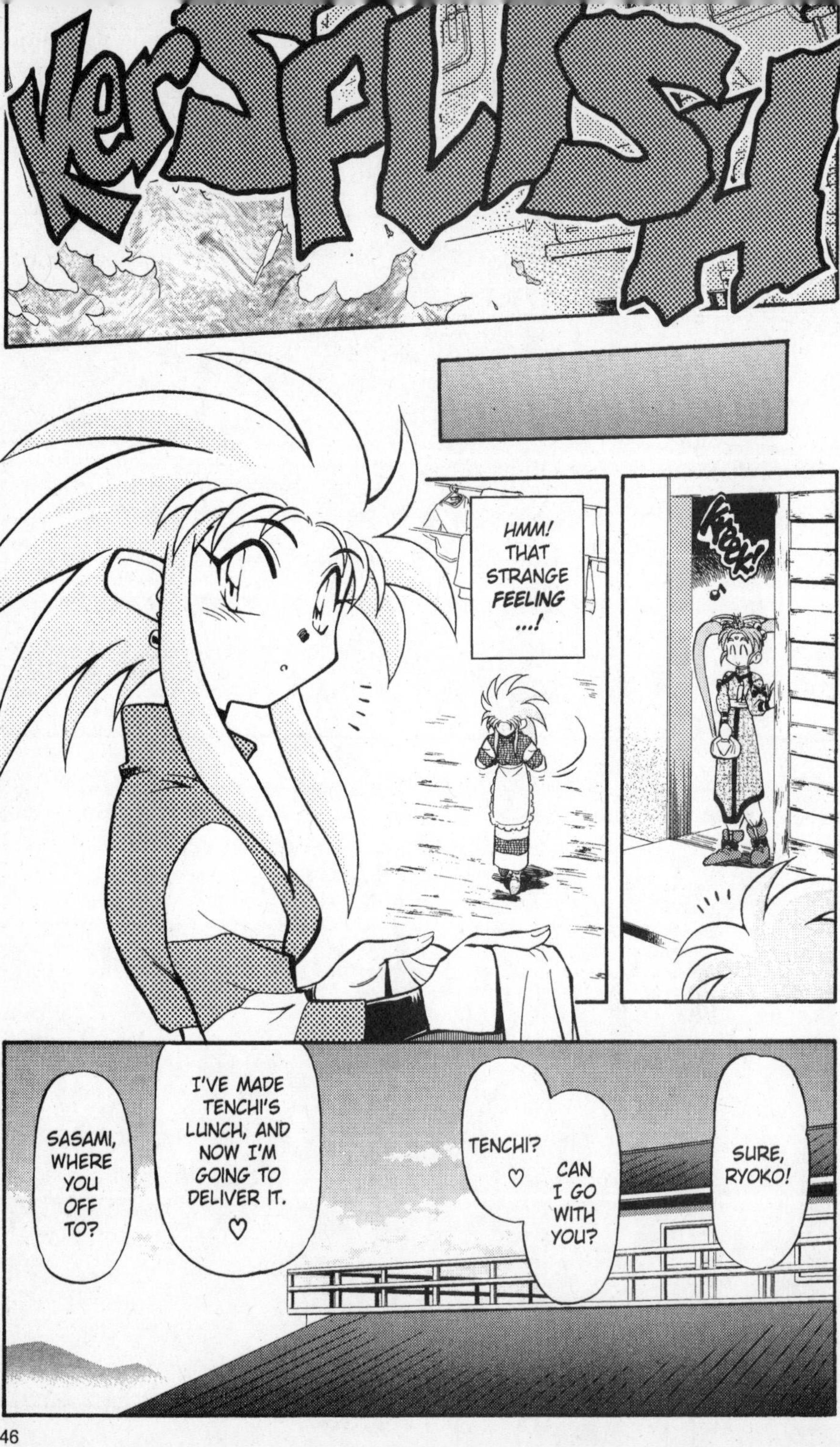
HMM! THAT STRANGE FEELING ...!
SASAMI, WHERE YOU OFF TO?
I'VE MADE TENCHI'S LUNCH, AND NOW I'M GOING TO DELIVER IT. ♡
TENCHI? ♡
CAN I GO WITH YOU?
SURE, RYOKO!

SPLIP

SPLOOP

THE FEEDING PATTERNS OF WASHU'S NEW LIFE FORM WERE *VERY* PECULIAR.

UNGH...

BLUP!

ME, THE *GENIUS*...

...MY ENERGY DRAINING AWAY. AWFUL!

THE *SHOU'OU* NEITHER KILLS ITS PREY NOR LETS THEM LIVE, BUT GRADUALLY ABSORBS THEIR ENERGY...

BLOOP!

?! IT'S SENSING A LARGE ENERGY SOURCE...

WHAT! I WASN'T ENOUGH!?

COULD IT BE...?!

FWD

SHU

47

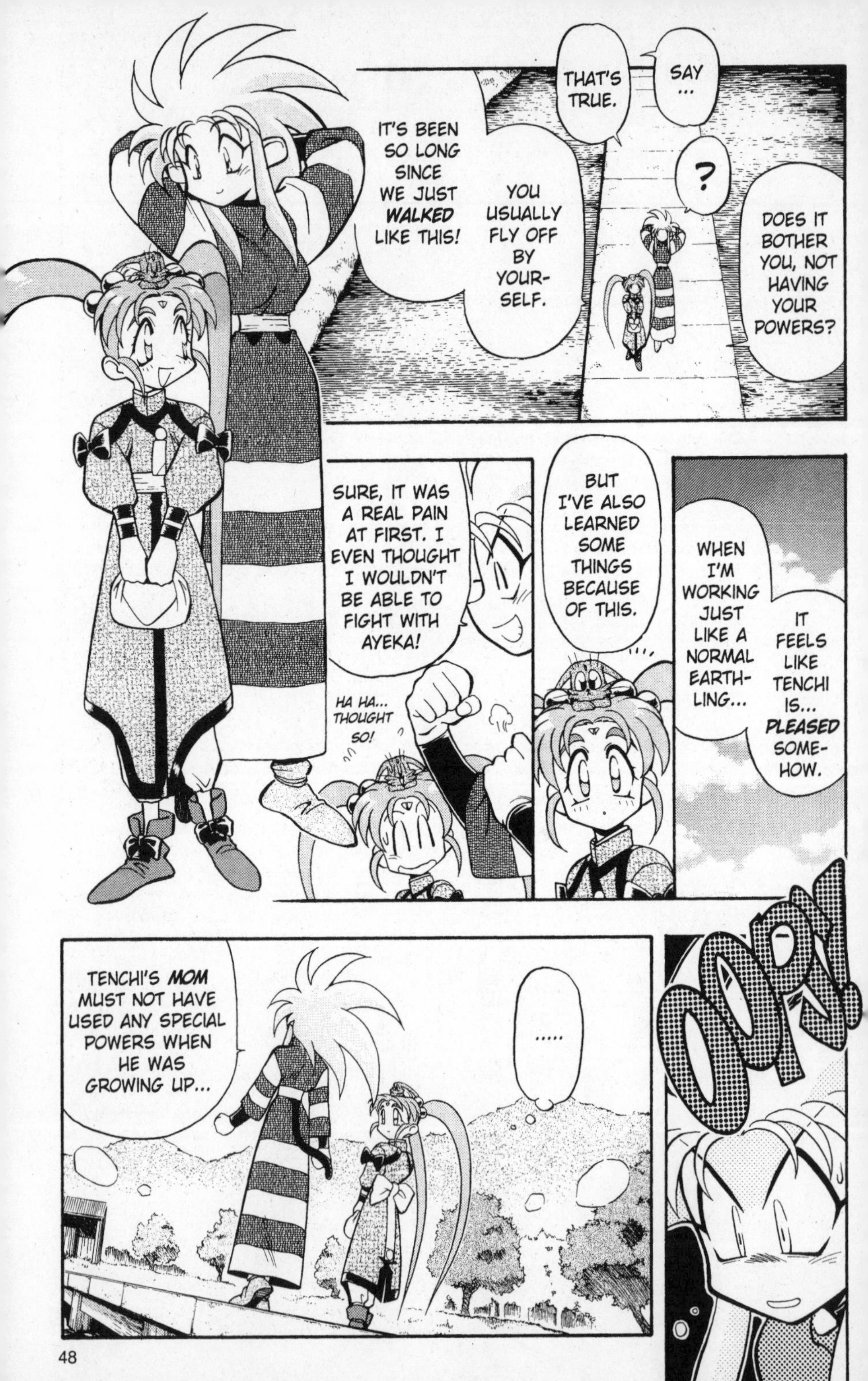
IT'S BEEN SO LONG SINCE WE JUST **WALKED** LIKE THIS!
YOU USUALLY FLY OFF BY YOURSELF.
THAT'S TRUE.
SAY ...
?
DOES IT BOTHER YOU, NOT HAVING YOUR POWERS?
SURE, IT WAS A REAL PAIN AT FIRST. I EVEN THOUGHT I WOULDN'T BE ABLE TO FIGHT WITH AYEKA!
HA HA... THOUGHT SO!
BUT I'VE ALSO LEARNED SOME THINGS BECAUSE OF THIS.
WHEN I'M WORKING JUST LIKE A NORMAL EARTHLING...
IT FEELS LIKE TENCHI IS... **PLEASED** SOMEHOW.
TENCHI'S **MOM** MUST NOT HAVE USED ANY SPECIAL POWERS WHEN HE WAS GROWING UP...
.....
OOPS!

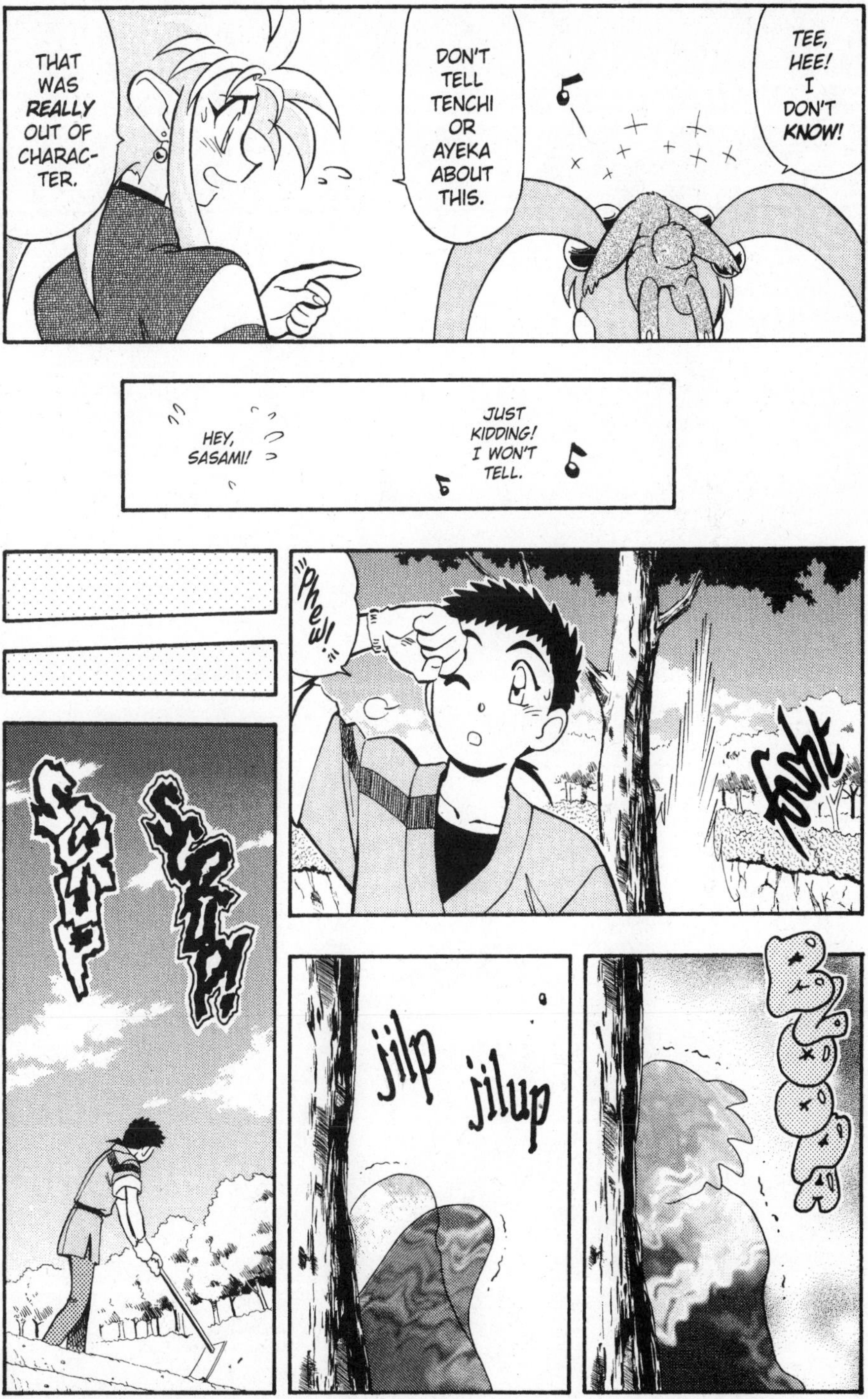
THAT WAS REALLY OUT OF CHARACTER.
DON'T TELL TENCHI OR AYEKA ABOUT THIS.
TEE, HEE! I DON'T KNOW!
HEY, SASAMI!
JUST KIDDING! I WON'T TELL.
Phew!
jilp
jilup

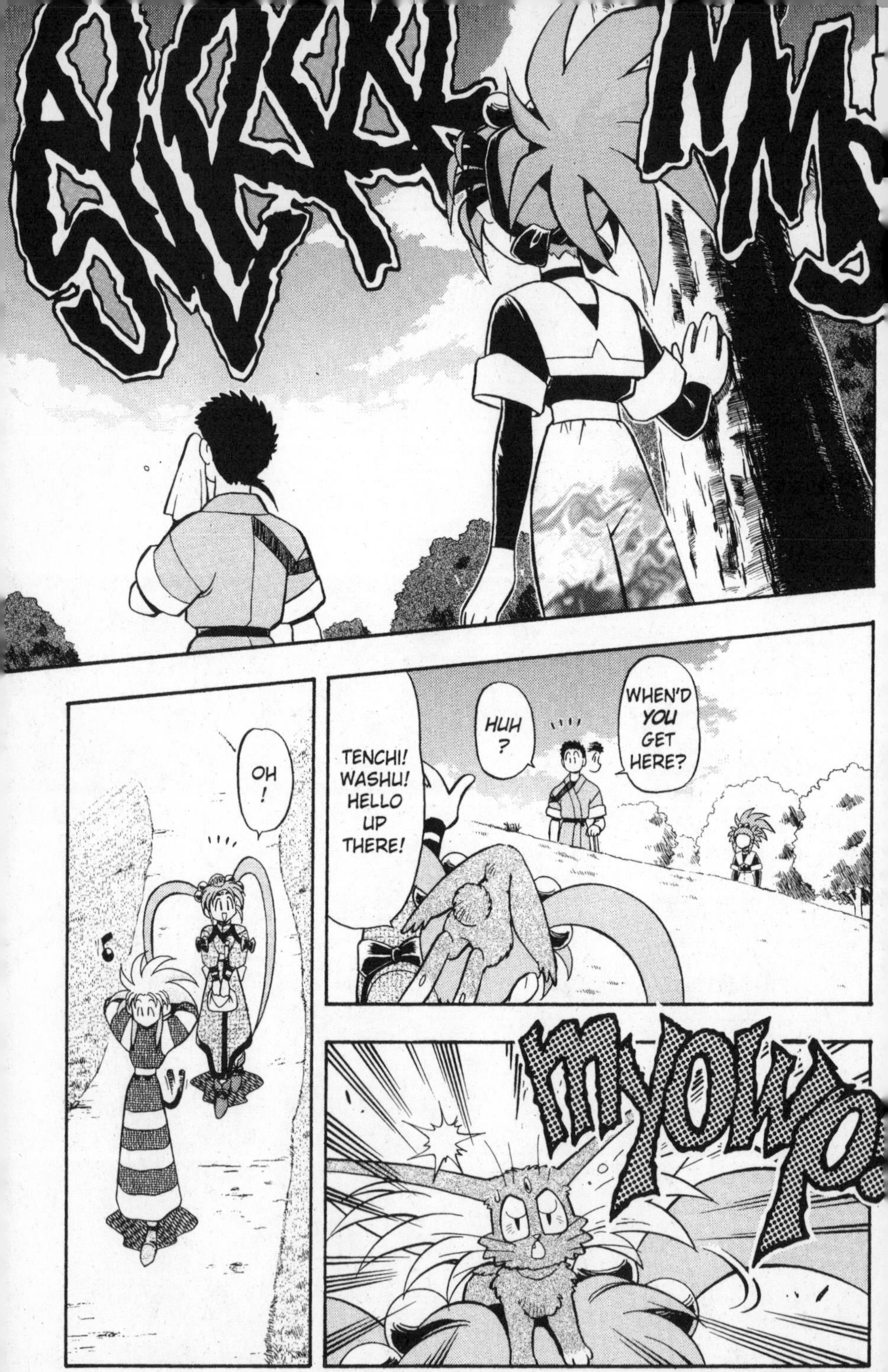
OH!
TENCHI! WASHU! HELLO UP THERE!
HUH?
WHEN'D YOU GET HERE?
myowa.

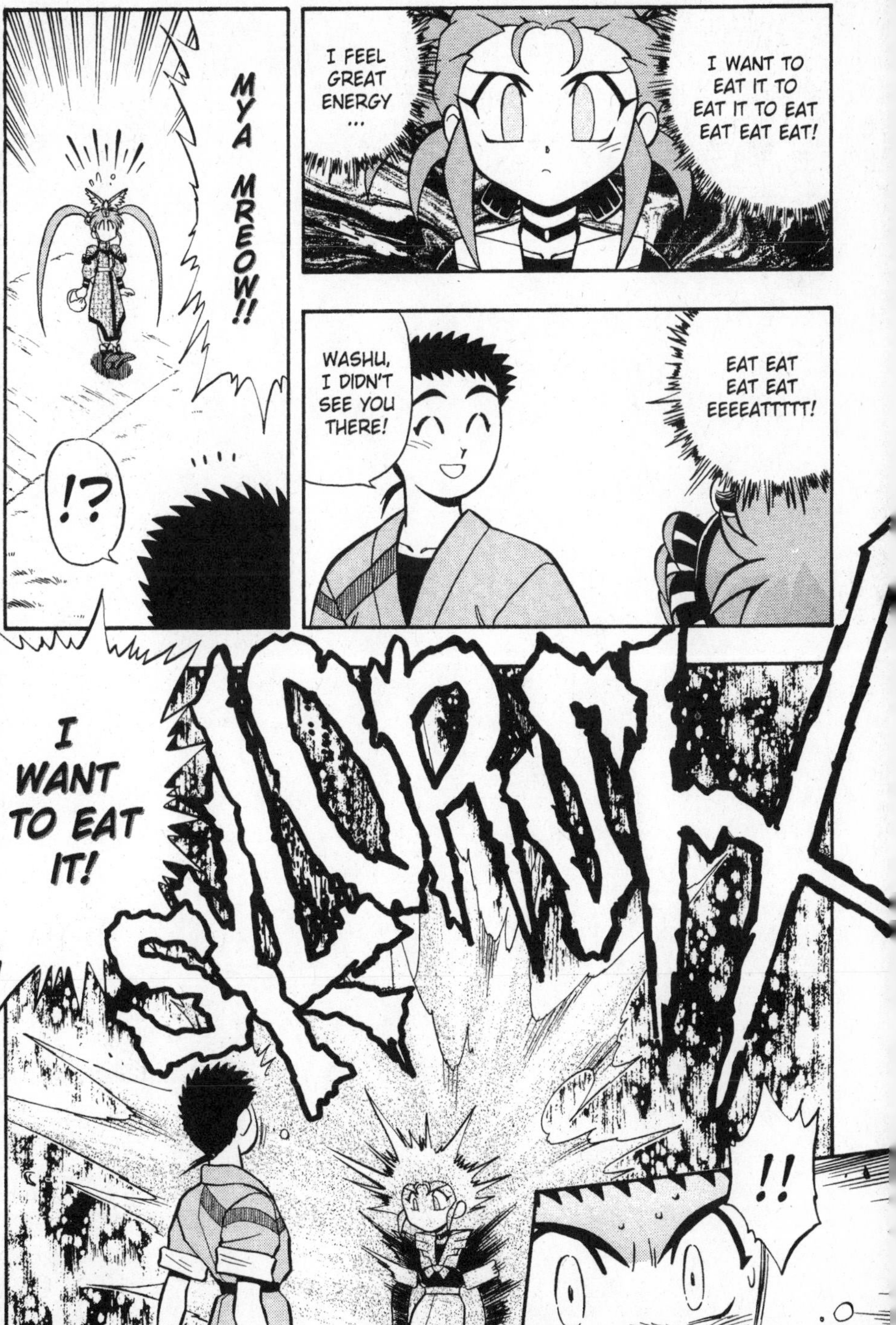
MYA MREOW!!
!?
...
I FEEL GREAT ENERGY ...
I WANT TO EAT IT TO EAT IT TO EAT EAT EAT EAT!
WASHU, I DIDN'T SEE YOU THERE!
EAT EAT EAT EAT EEEEATTTTT!
I WANT TO EAT IT!
!!

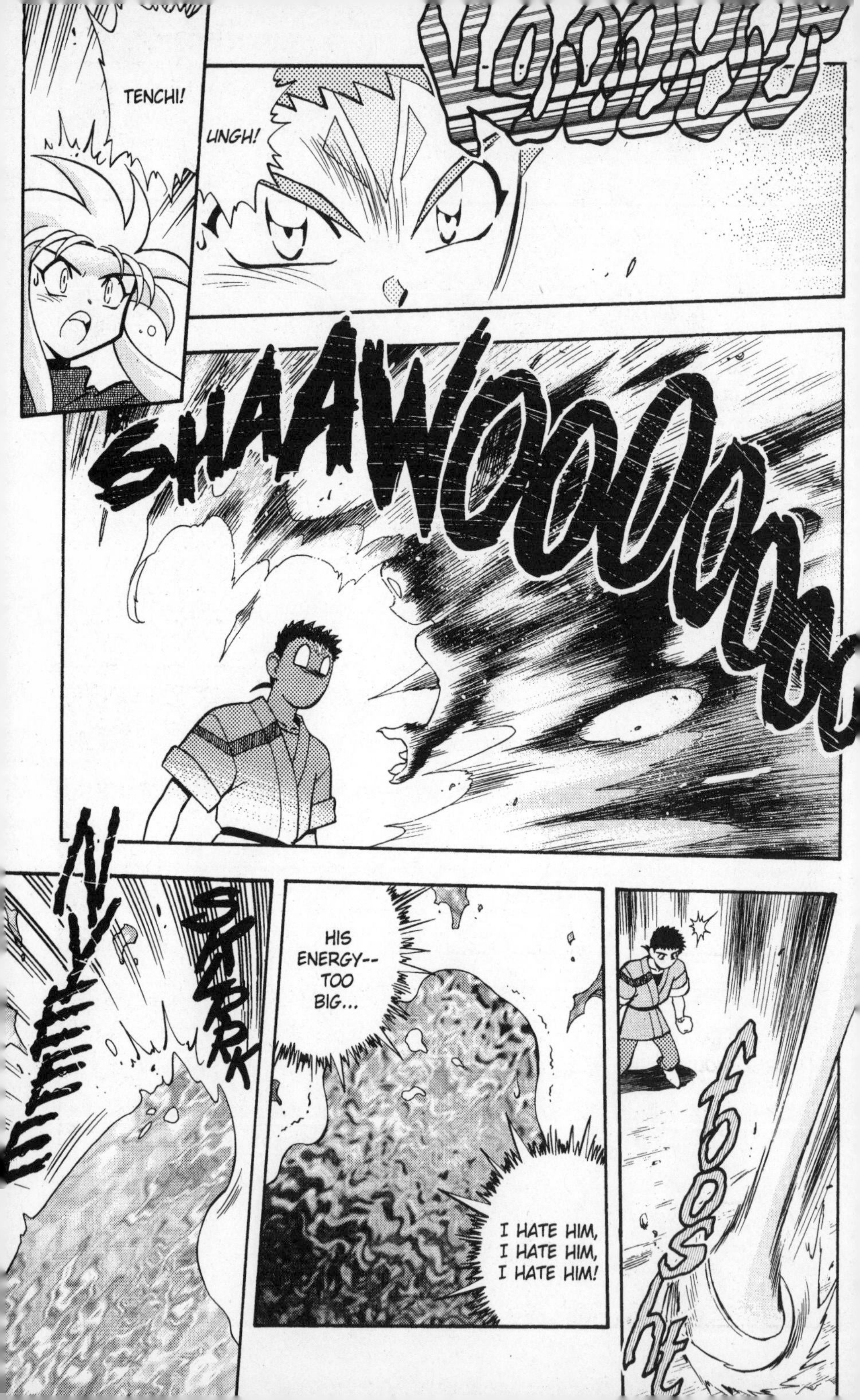
TENCHI!
UNGH!
HIS ENERGY-- TOO BIG...
I HATE HIM, I HATE HIM, I HATE HIM!

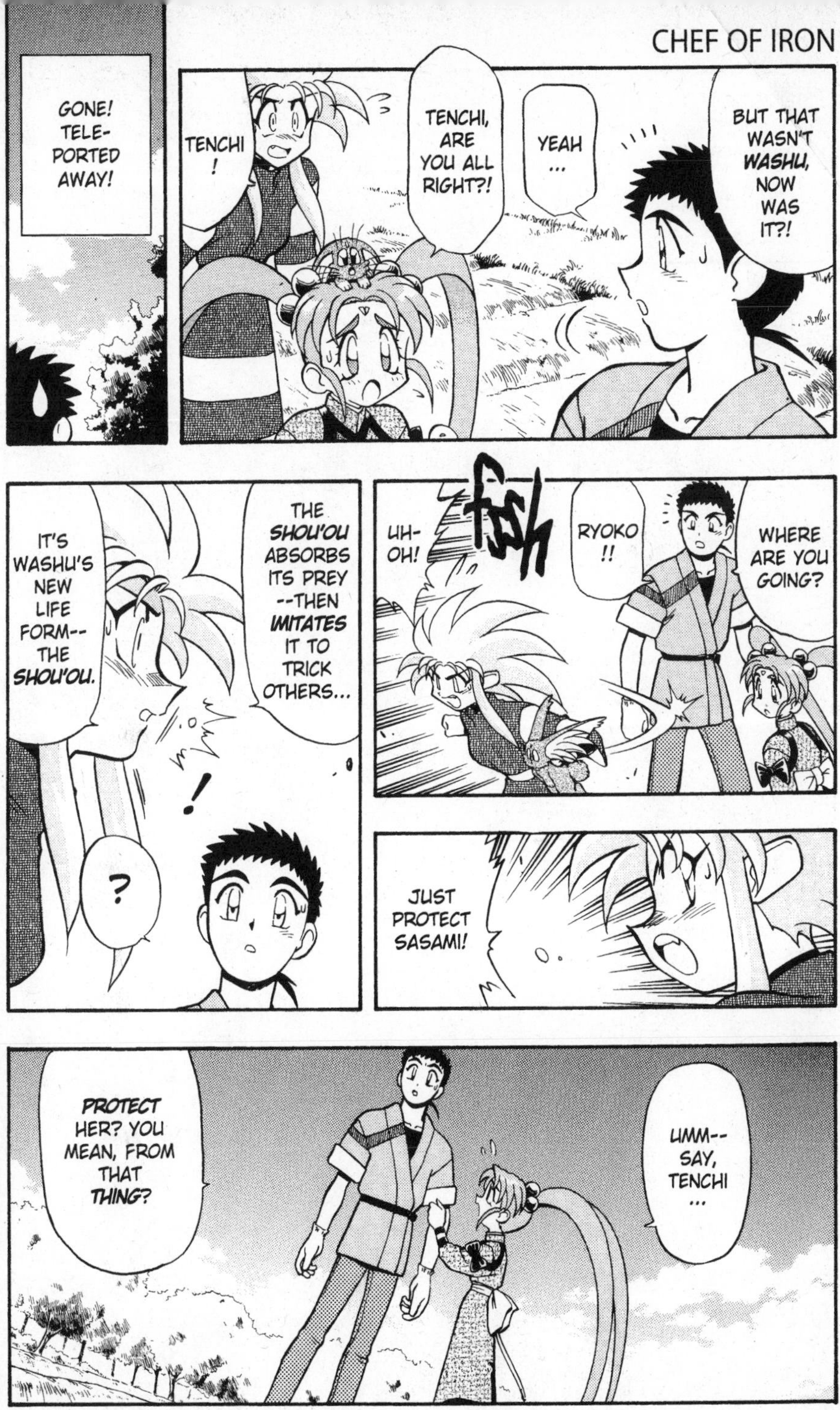
GONE! TELE-PORTED AWAY!
TENCHI!
TENCHI, ARE YOU ALL RIGHT?!
YEAH...
BUT THAT WASN'T *WASHU*, NOW WAS IT?!
IT'S WASHU'S NEW LIFE FORM--THE *SHOU'OU*.
THE *SHOU'OU* ABSORBS ITS PREY--THEN *IMITATES* IT TO TRICK OTHERS...
?
UH-OH!
fsh
RYOKO!!
WHERE ARE YOU GOING?
JUST PROTECT SASAMI!
PROTECT HER? YOU MEAN, FROM THAT *THING*?
UMM--SAY, TENCHI...

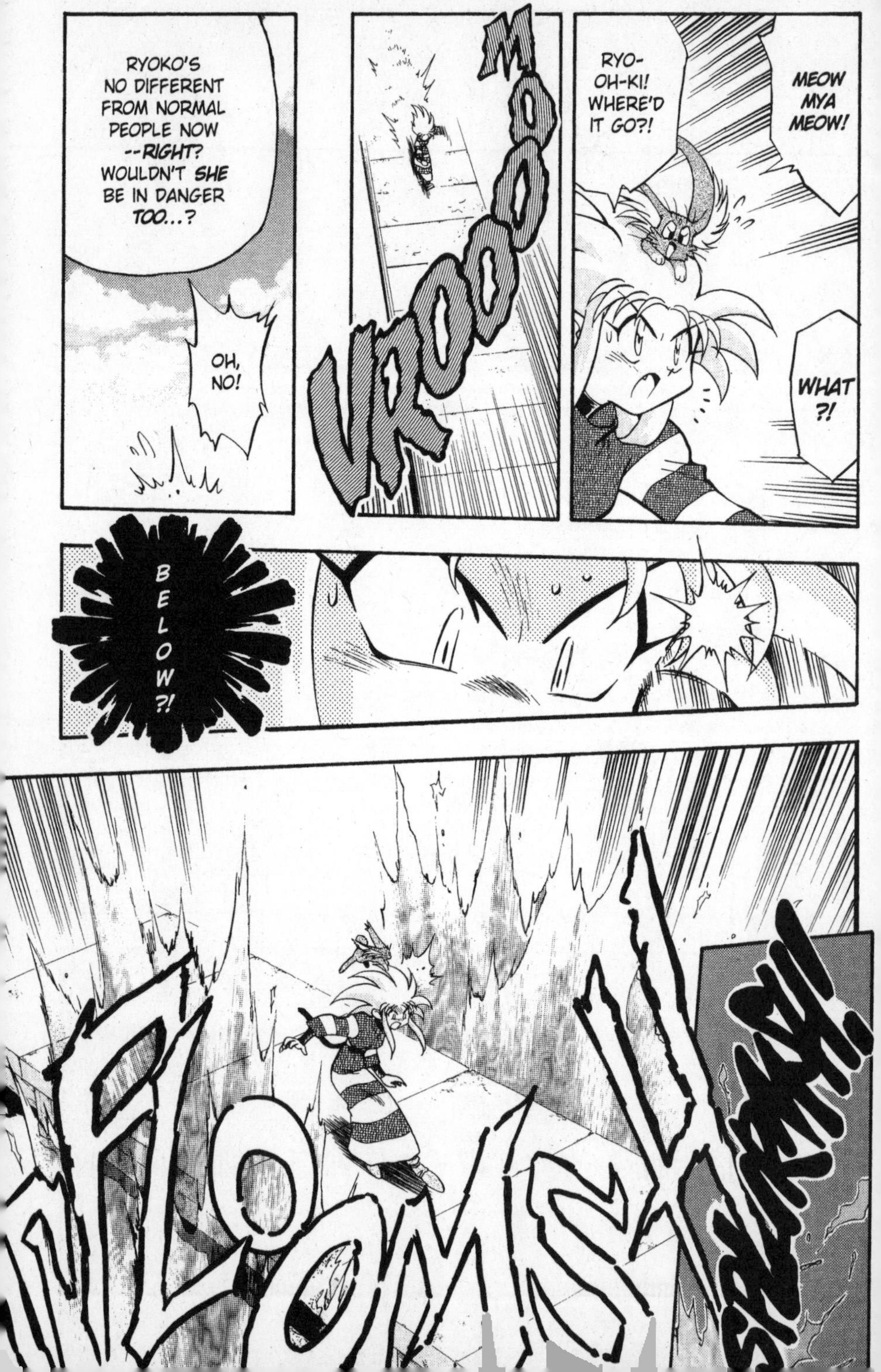
RYOKO'S NO DIFFERENT FROM NORMAL PEOPLE NOW --RIGHT? WOULDN'T SHE BE IN DANGER TOO...?
OH, NO!
VROOOOOM
RYO-OH-KI! WHERE'D IT GO?!
MEOW MYA MEOW!
WHAT?!
BELOW?!

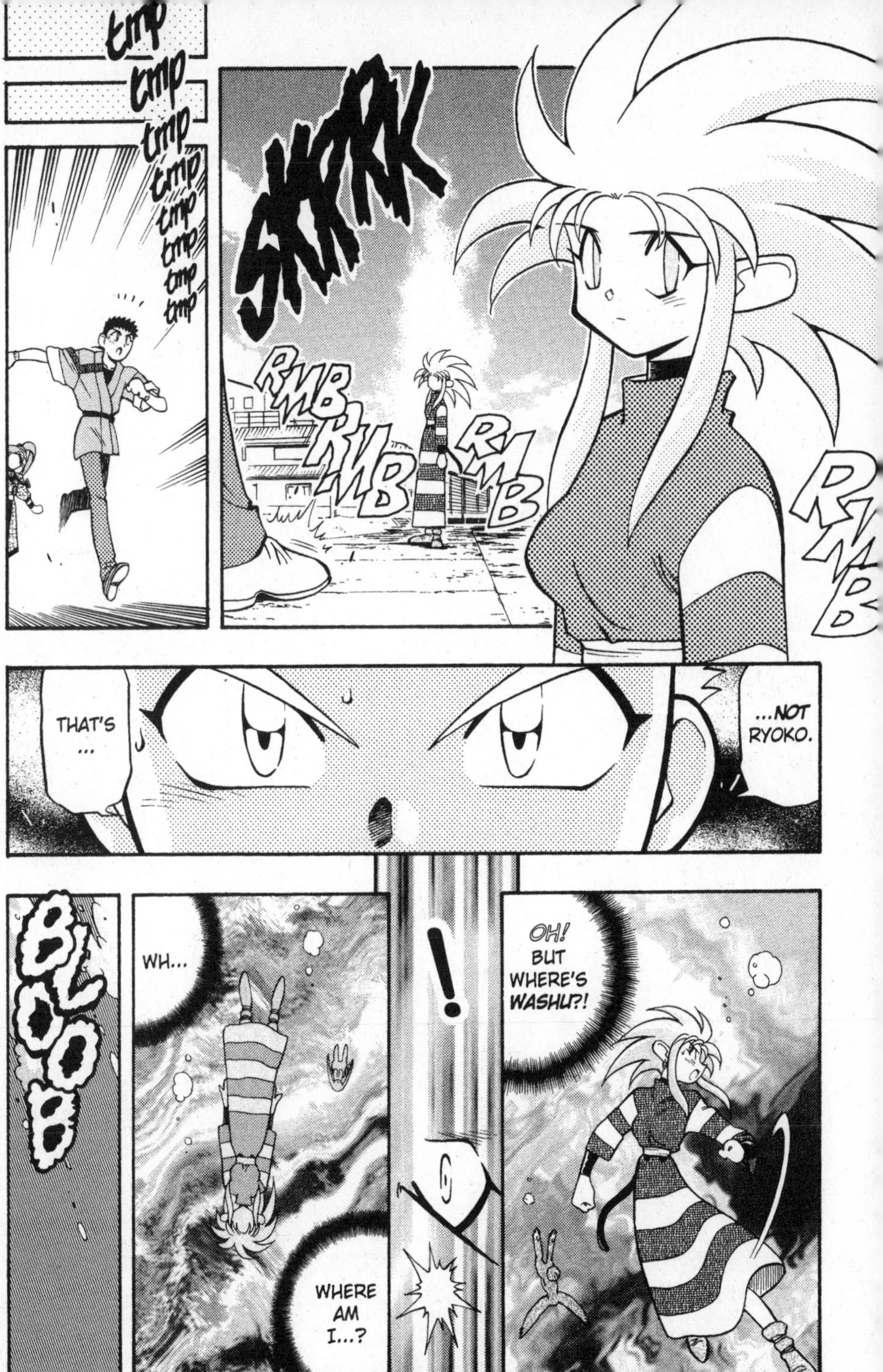
tmp tmp tmp tmp tmp tmp tmp tmp
SKRRK
RMB RMB RMB
RMB
THAT'S ...
...NOT RYOKO.
BLOOOB
WH...
WHERE AM I...?
!
OH! BUT WHERE'S WASHU?!

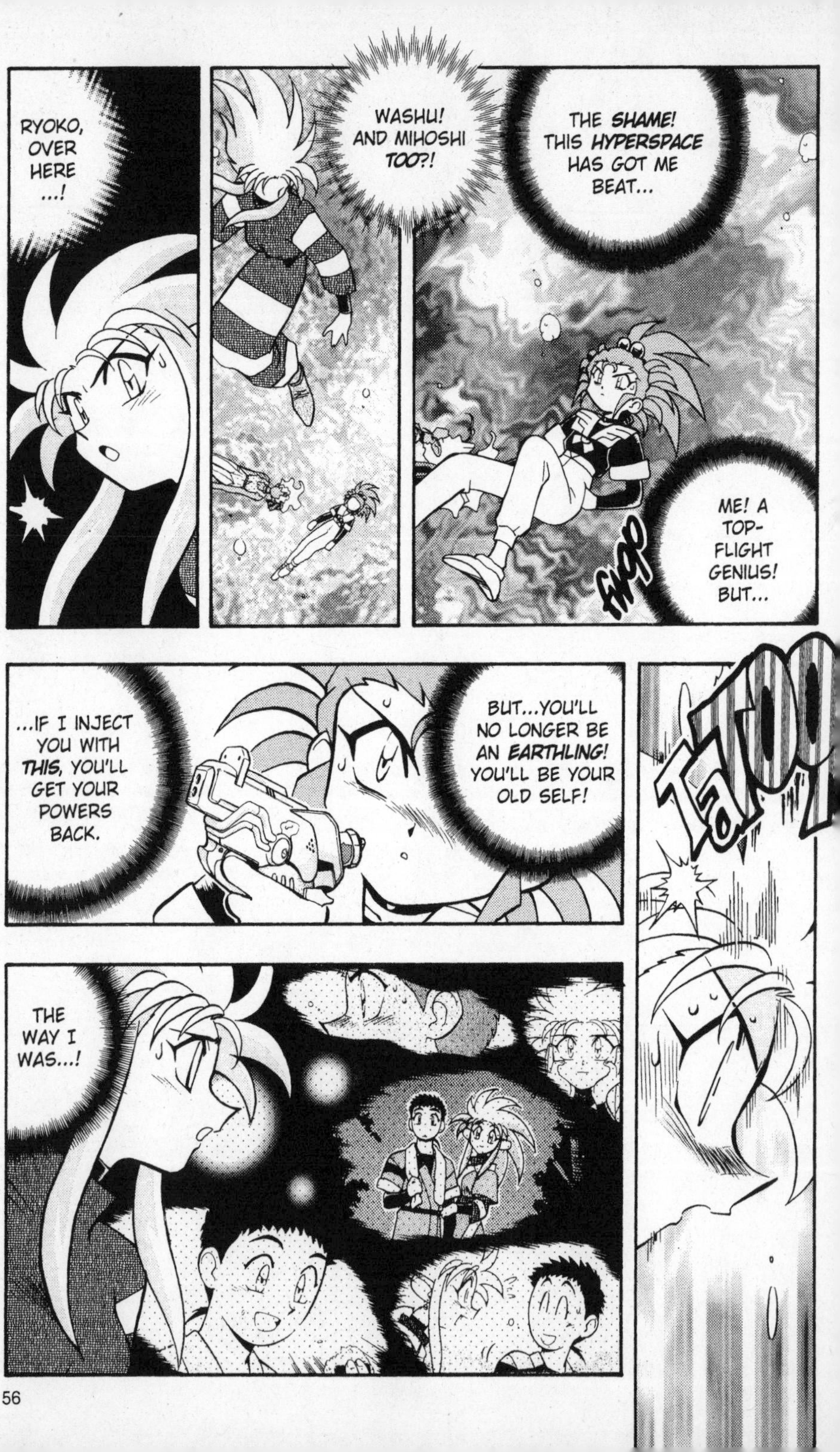
RYOKO, OVER HERE ...!
WASHU! AND MIHOSHI TOO?!
THE SHAME! THIS HYPERSPACE HAS GOT ME BEAT...
ME! A TOP-FLIGHT GENIUS! BUT...
...IF I INJECT YOU WITH THIS, YOU'LL GET YOUR POWERS BACK.
BUT...YOU'LL NO LONGER BE AN EARTHLING! YOU'LL BE YOUR OLD SELF!
THE WAY I WAS...!

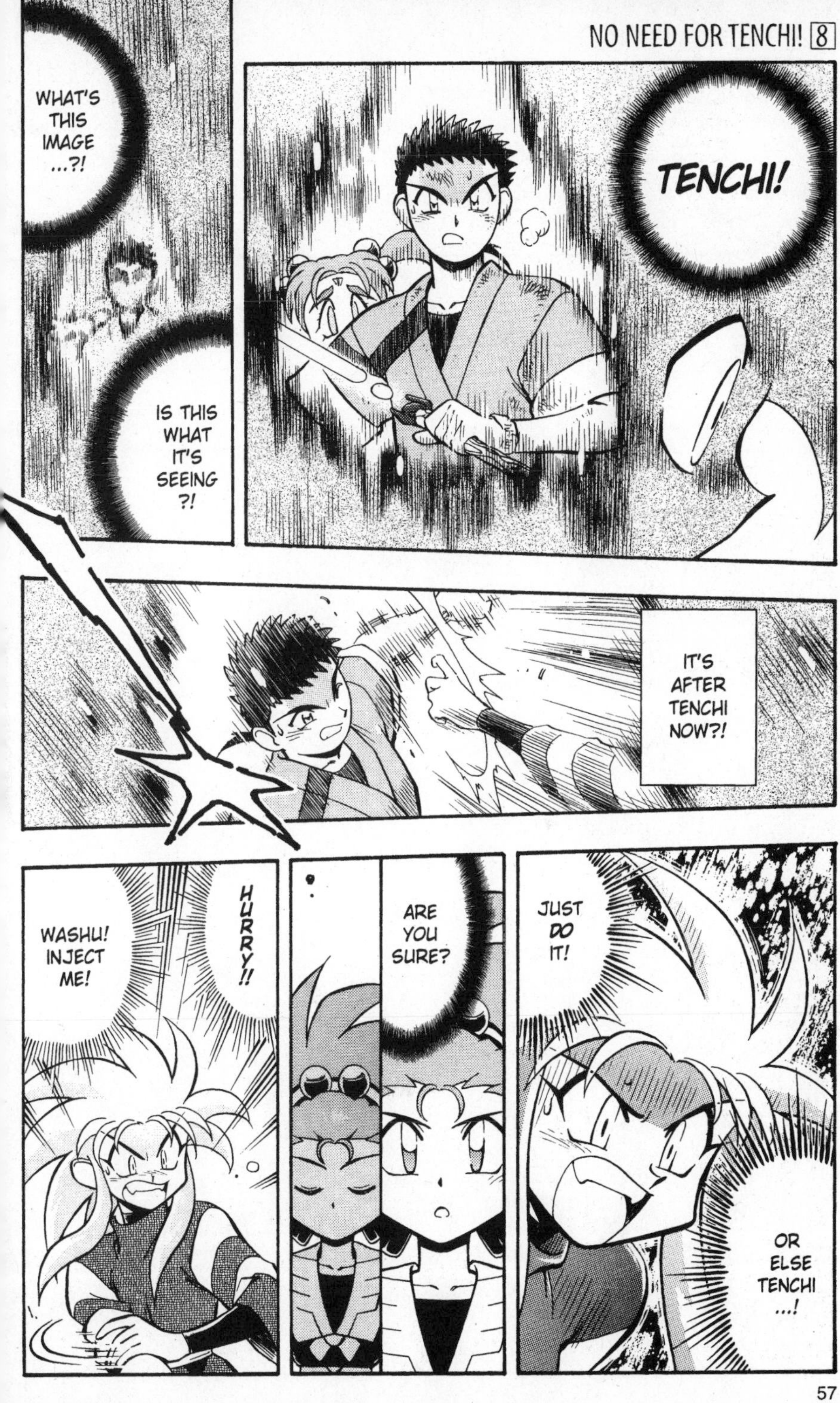
WHAT'S THIS IMAGE ...?!
IS THIS WHAT IT'S SEEING ?!
TENCHI!
IT'S AFTER TENCHI NOW?!
WASHU! INJECT ME!
HURRY!!
ARE YOU SURE?
JUST DO IT!
OR ELSE TENCHI ...!

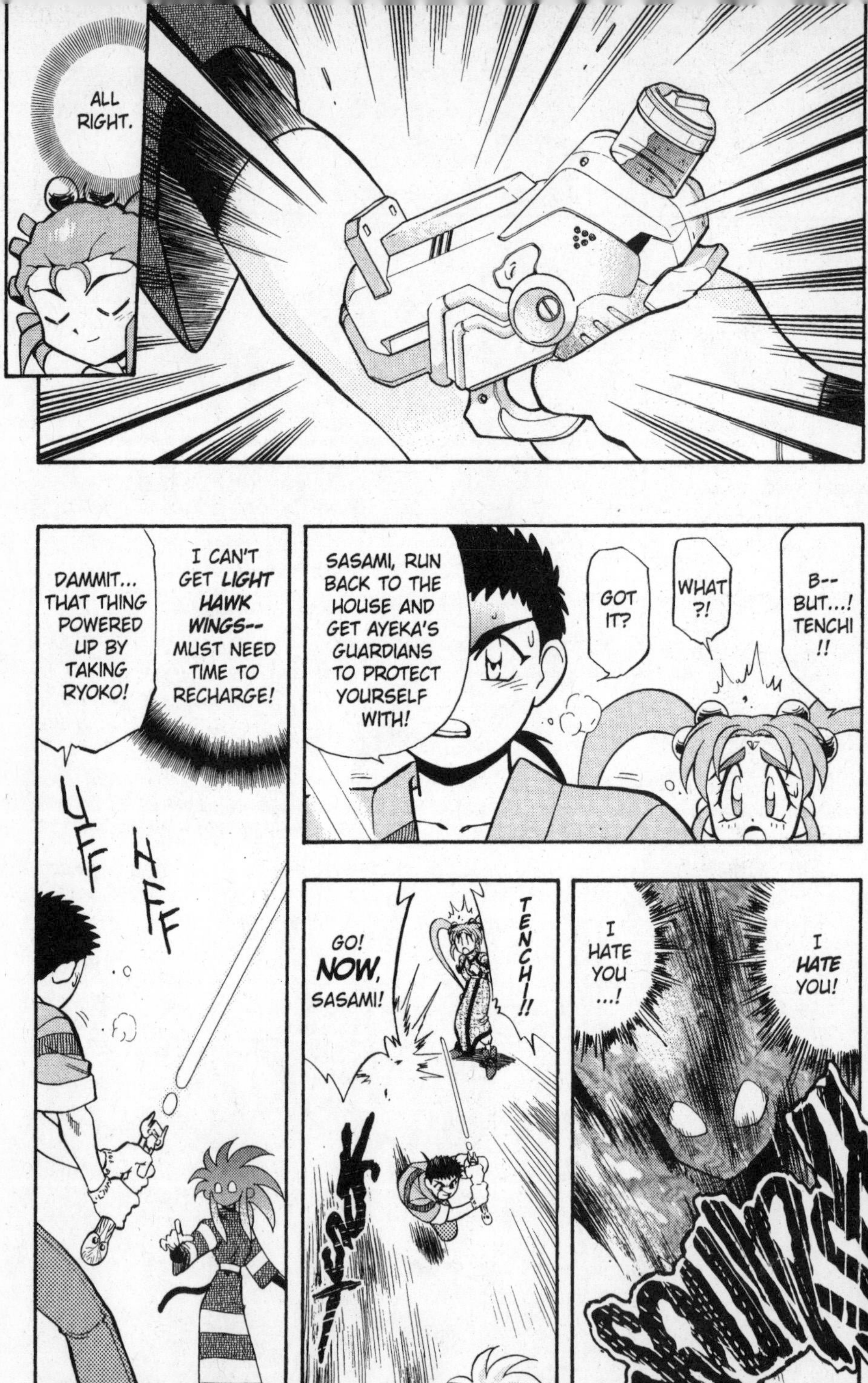

ALL RIGHT.
DAMMIT... THAT THING POWERED UP BY TAKING RYOKO!
I CAN'T GET LIGHT HAWK WINGS-- MUST NEED TIME TO RECHARGE!
UFF
HFF
SASAMI, RUN BACK TO THE HOUSE AND GET AYEKA'S GUARDIANS TO PROTECT YOURSELF WITH!
GOT IT?
WHAT?!
B-- BUT...! TENCHI!!
GO! NOW, SASAMI!
TENCHI!!
I HATE YOU...!
I HATE YOU!

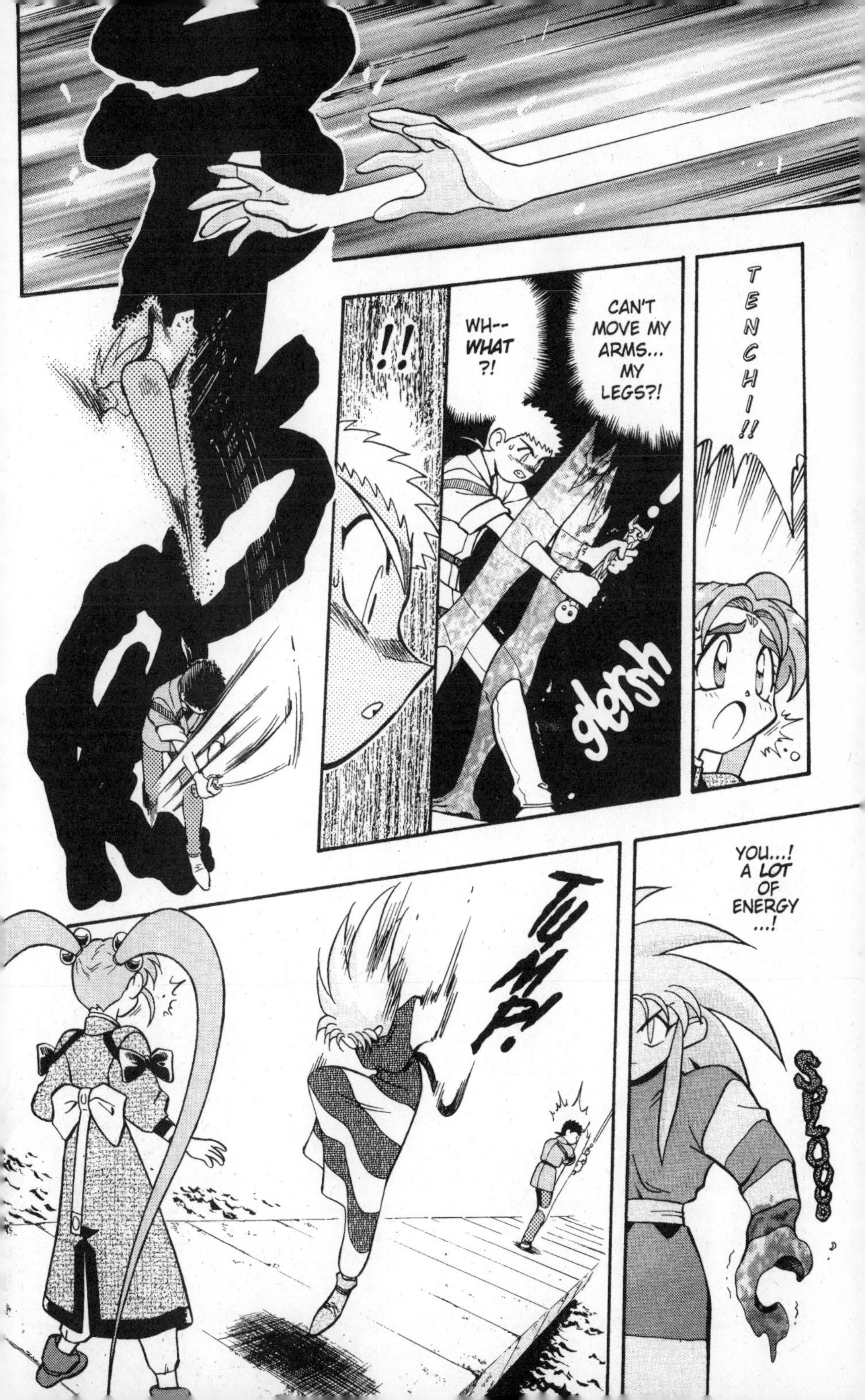
!!
WH-- WHAT?!
CAN'T MOVE MY ARMS... MY LEGS?!
glrsh
TENCHI!!
THUMP!
YOU...! A LOT OF ENERGY...!
SPLOOOO

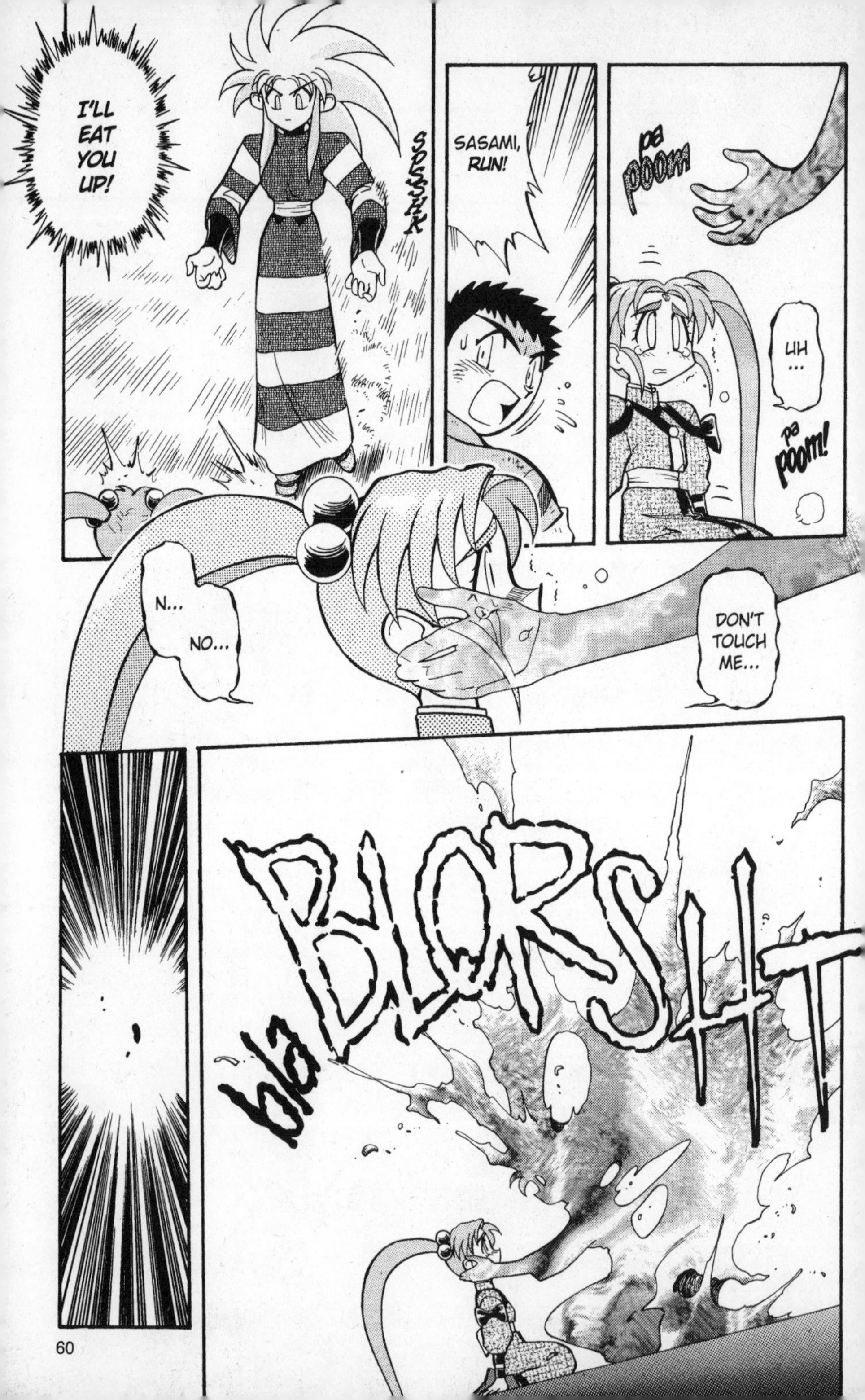
I'LL EAT YOU UP!
SOSSHK
SASAMI, RUN!
pa poom
UH ...
pa poom!
N... NO...
DON'T TOUCH ME...
bla BLORSHHT!

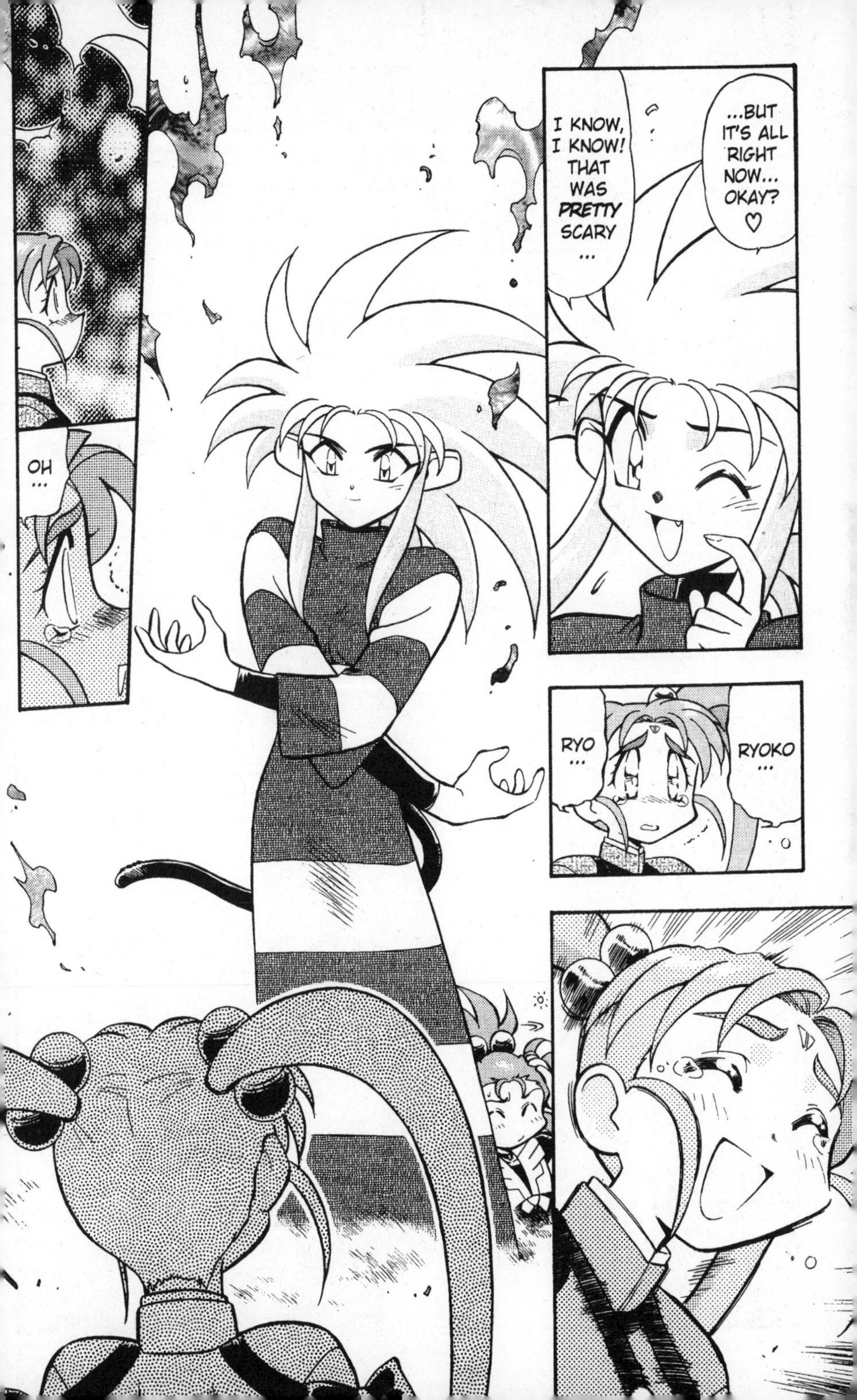
OH ...
I KNOW, I KNOW! THAT WAS **PRETTY** SCARY ...
...BUT IT'S ALL RIGHT NOW... OKAY? ♡
RYO ...
RYOKO ...

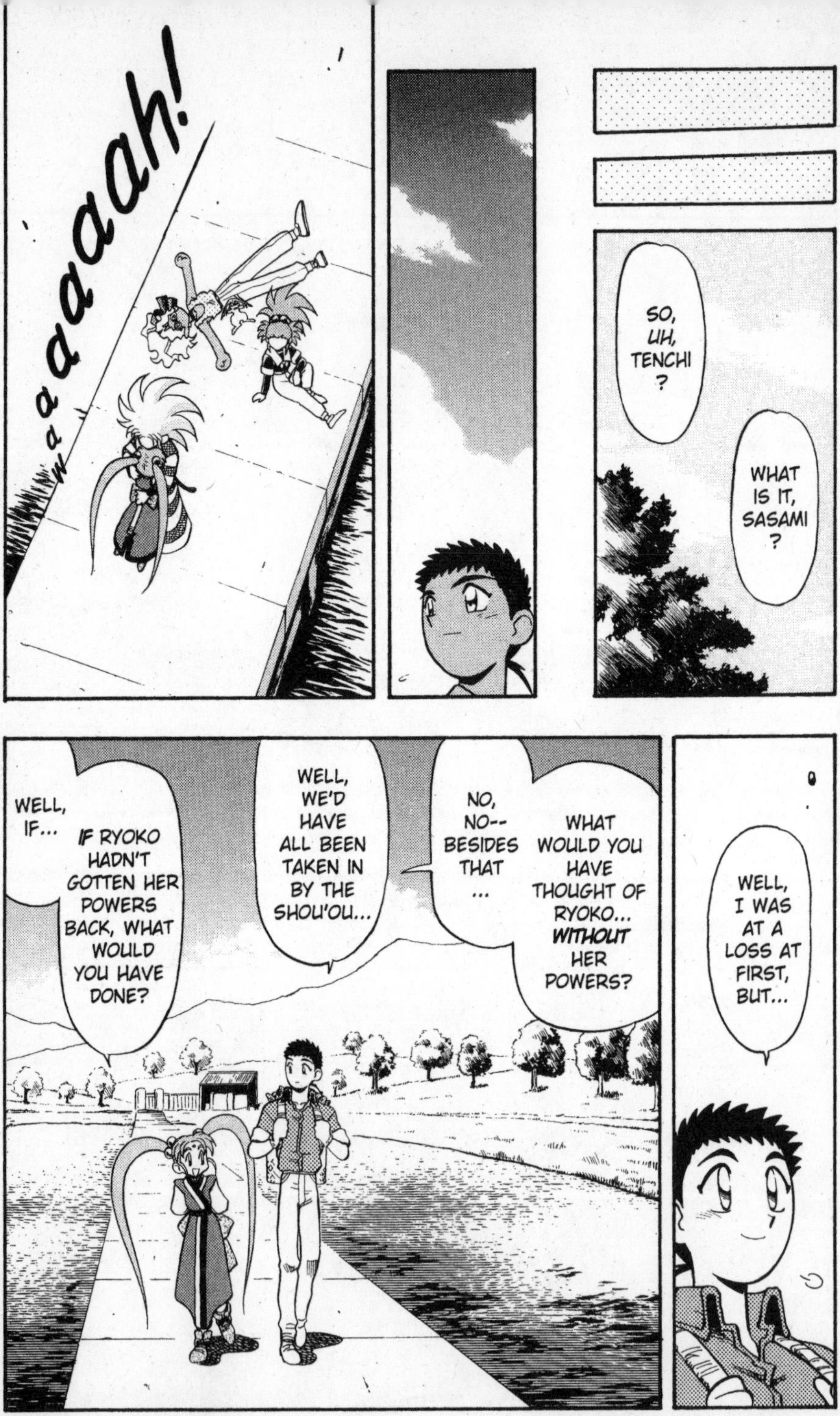

waaaaah!
SO, UH, TENCHI?
WHAT IS IT, SASAMI?
WELL, IF... IF RYOKO HADN'T GOTTEN HER POWERS BACK, WHAT WOULD YOU HAVE DONE?
WELL, WE'D HAVE ALL BEEN TAKEN IN BY THE SHOU'OU...
NO, NO-- BESIDES THAT...
WHAT WOULD YOU HAVE THOUGHT OF RYOKO... WITHOUT HER POWERS?
WELL, I WAS AT A LOSS AT FIRST, BUT...

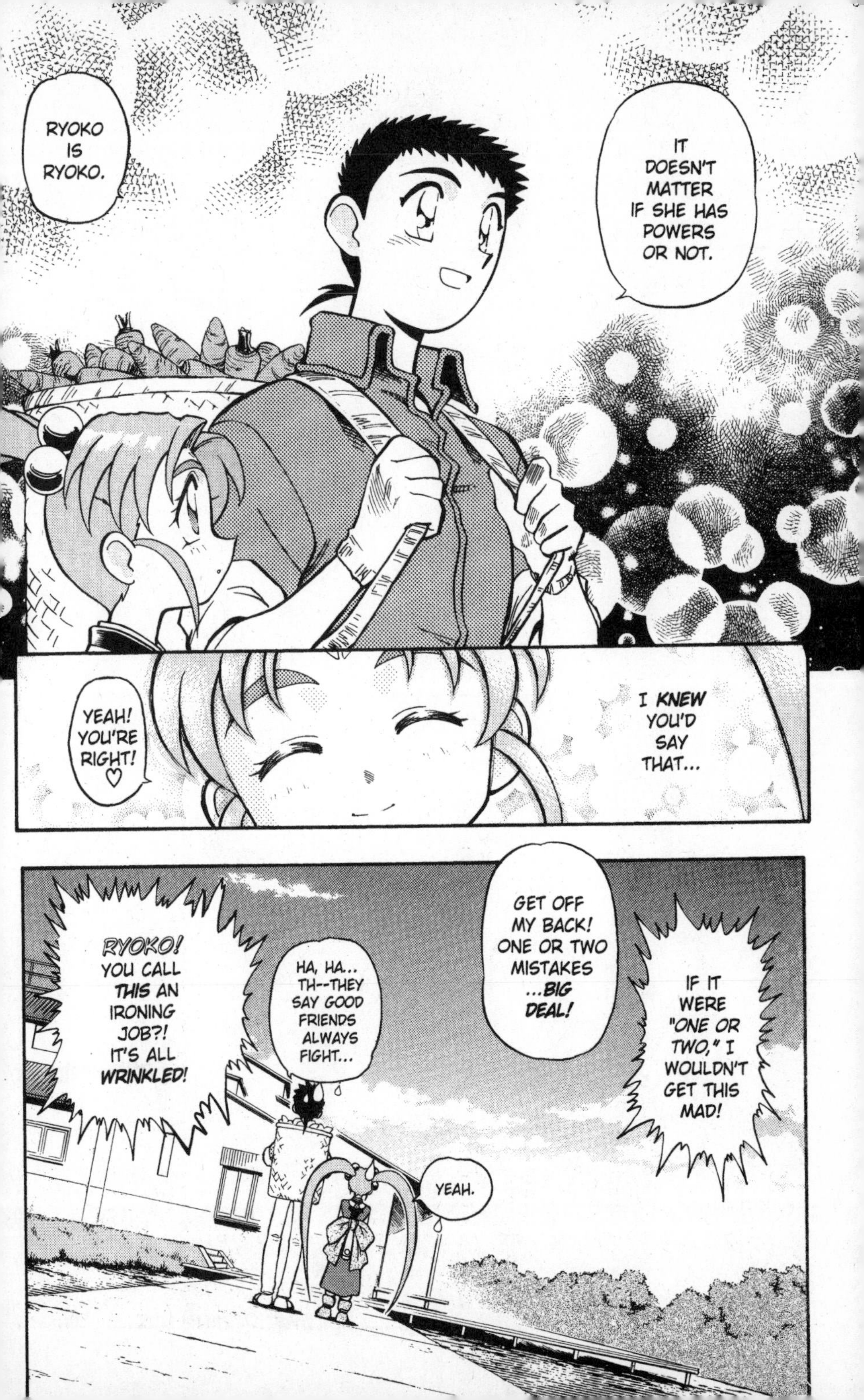
RYOKO IS RYOKO.
IT DOESN'T MATTER IF SHE HAS POWERS OR NOT.
YEAH! YOU'RE RIGHT! ♡
I *KNEW* YOU'D SAY THAT...
RYOKO! YOU CALL *THIS* AN IRONING JOB?! IT'S ALL *WRINKLED!*
HA, HA... TH--THEY SAY GOOD FRIENDS ALWAYS FIGHT...
GET OFF MY BACK! ONE OR TWO MISTAKES ...*BIG DEAL!*
IF IT WERE *"ONE OR TWO,"* I WOULDN'T GET THIS MAD!
YEAH.

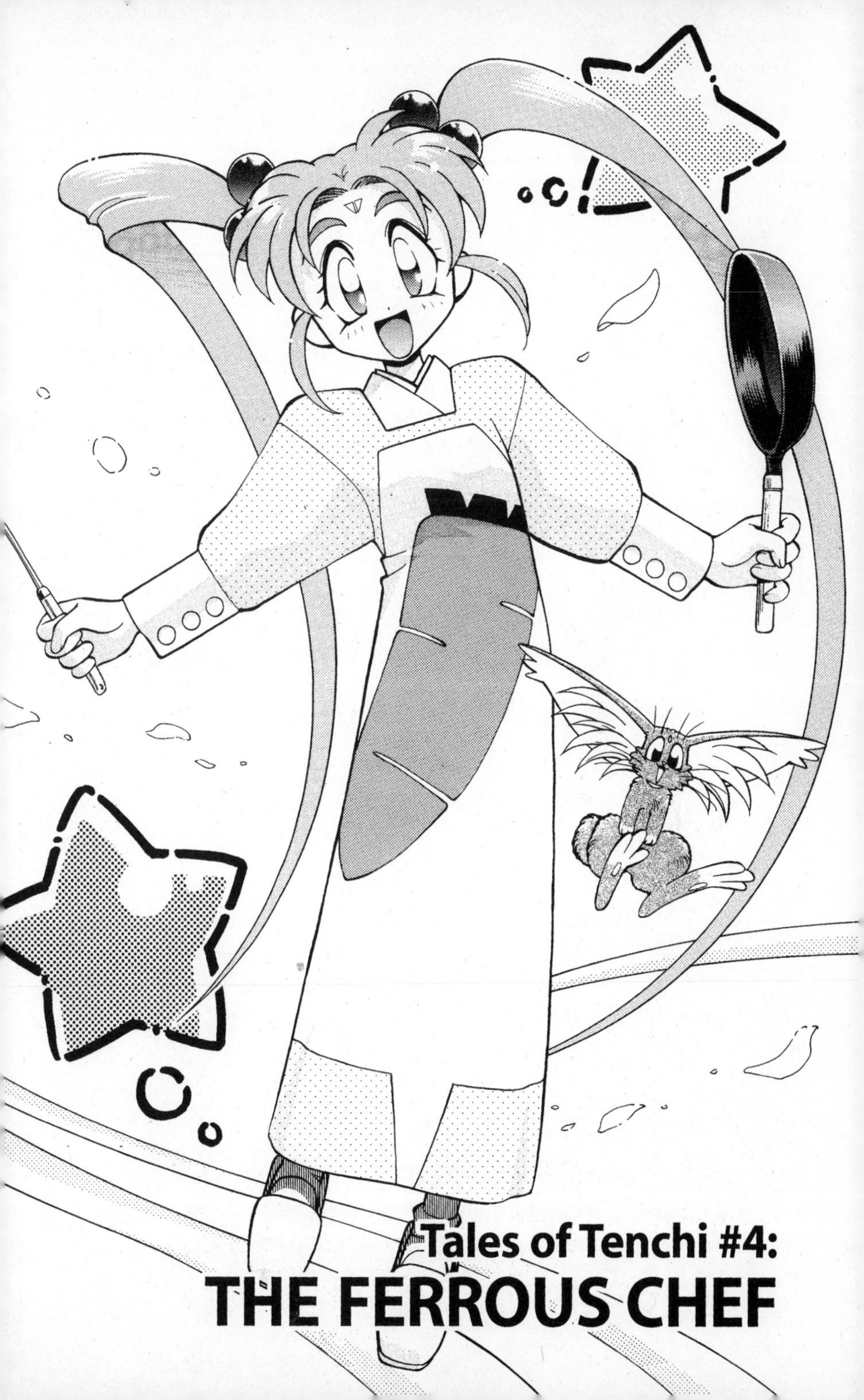

Tales of Tenchi #4:
THE FERROUS CHEF

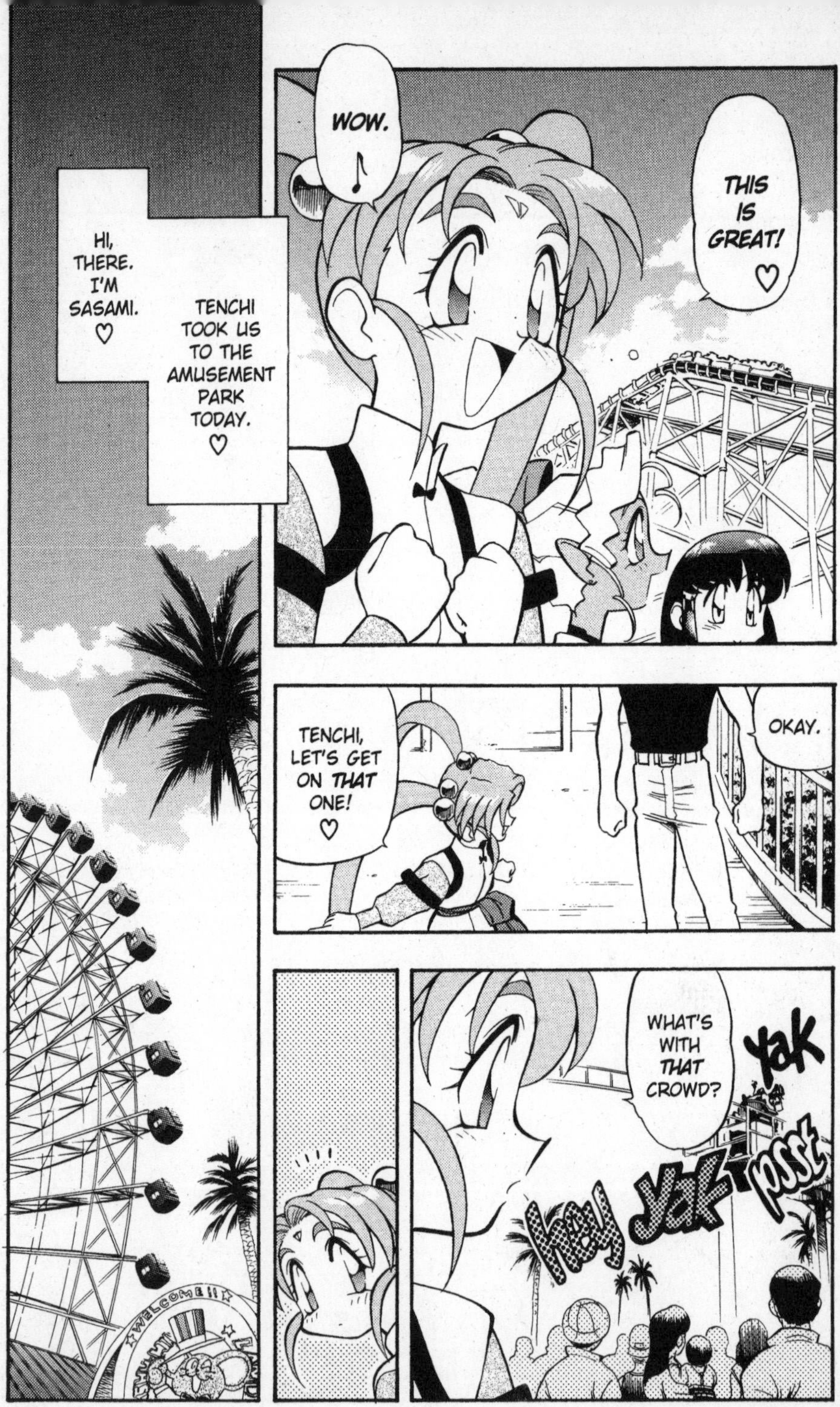
HI, THERE. I'M SASAMI. ♡
TENCHI TOOK US TO THE AMUSEMENT PARK TODAY. ♡
WELCOME!!
WOW. ♪
THIS IS GREAT! ♡
TENCHI, LET'S GET ON *THAT* ONE! ♡
OKAY.
WHAT'S WITH *THAT* CROWD?
YAK
HEY
YAK
PSST

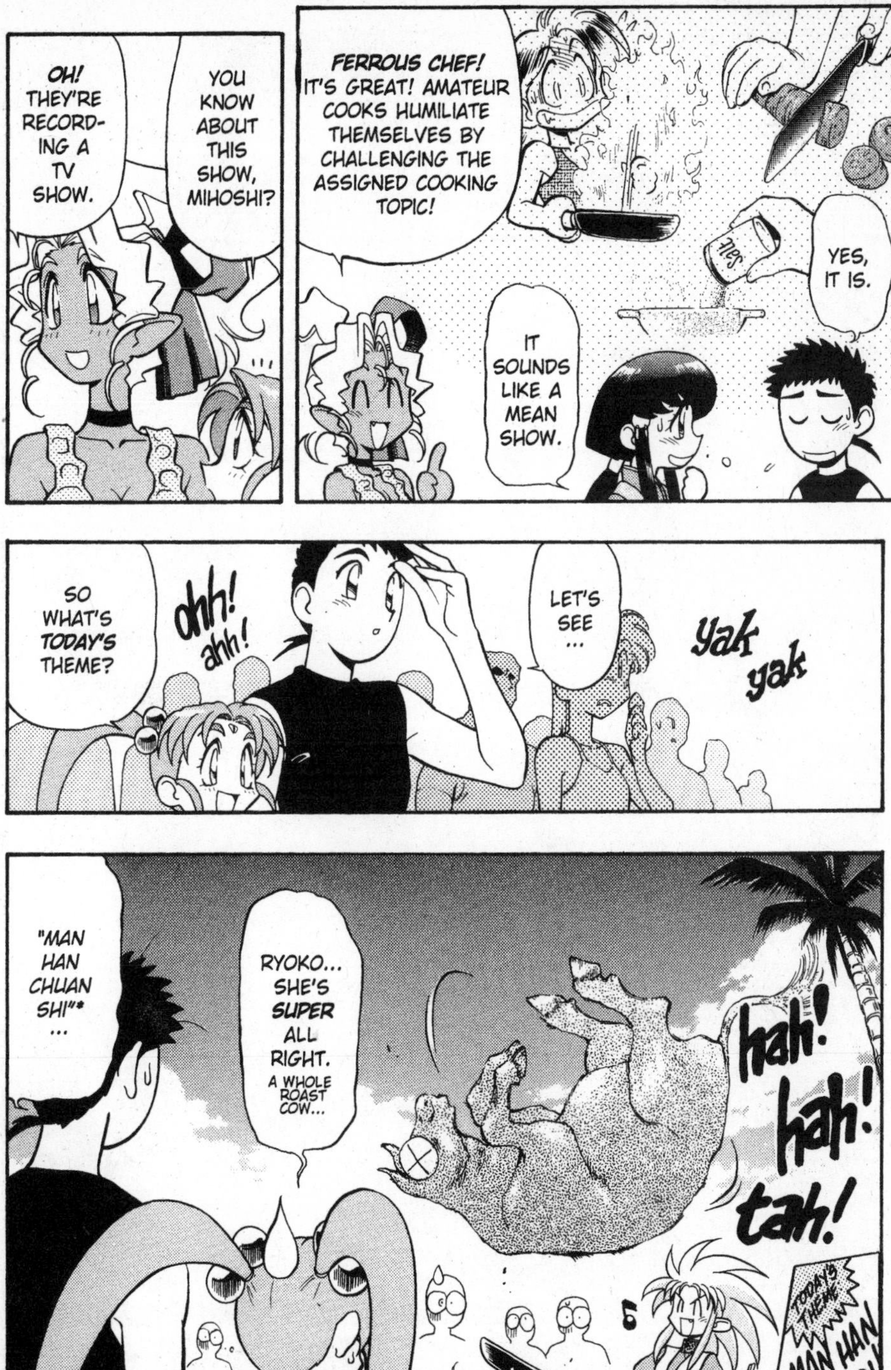
OH! THEY'RE RECORDING A TV SHOW.
YOU KNOW ABOUT THIS SHOW, MIHOSHI?
FERROUS CHEF! IT'S GREAT! AMATEUR COOKS HUMILIATE THEMSELVES BY CHALLENGING THE ASSIGNED COOKING TOPIC!
YES, IT IS.
IT SOUNDS LIKE A MEAN SHOW.
SO WHAT'S TODAY'S THEME?
ohh! ahh!
LET'S SEE ...
yak yak
"MAN HAN CHUAN SHI"* ...
RYOKO... SHE'S SUPER ALL RIGHT.
A WHOLE ROAST COW...
hah! hah! tah!
TODAY'S THEME
MAN HAN CHUAN SH

*COOKING FOR THE CHINESE IMPERIAL COURT.
SUPER DELUXE, SUPER LUXURY, SUPER VOLUME.

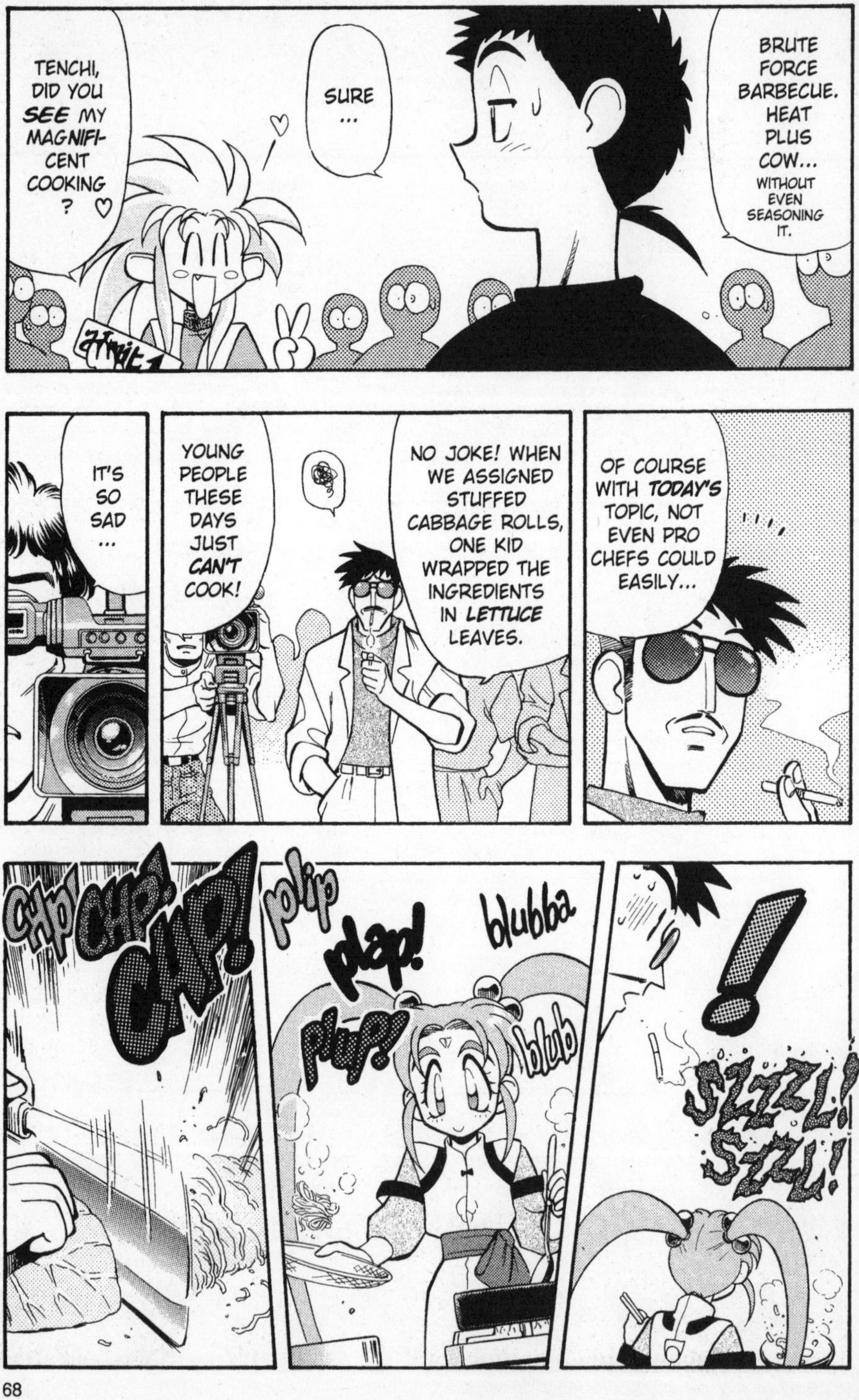

TENCHI, DID YOU SEE MY MAGNIFICENT COOKING? ♡
SURE ...
BRUTE FORCE BARBECUE. HEAT PLUS COW... WITHOUT EVEN SEASONING IT.
IT'S SO SAD ...
YOUNG PEOPLE THESE DAYS JUST CAN'T COOK!
NO JOKE! WHEN WE ASSIGNED STUFFED CABBAGE ROLLS, ONE KID WRAPPED THE INGREDIENTS IN LETTUCE LEAVES.
OF COURSE WITH TODAY'S TOPIC, NOT EVEN PRO CHEFS COULD EASILY...
CHOP! CHOP! CHOP!
plip
plap!
plop!
blubba
blub
!
SIZZL! SIZZL!

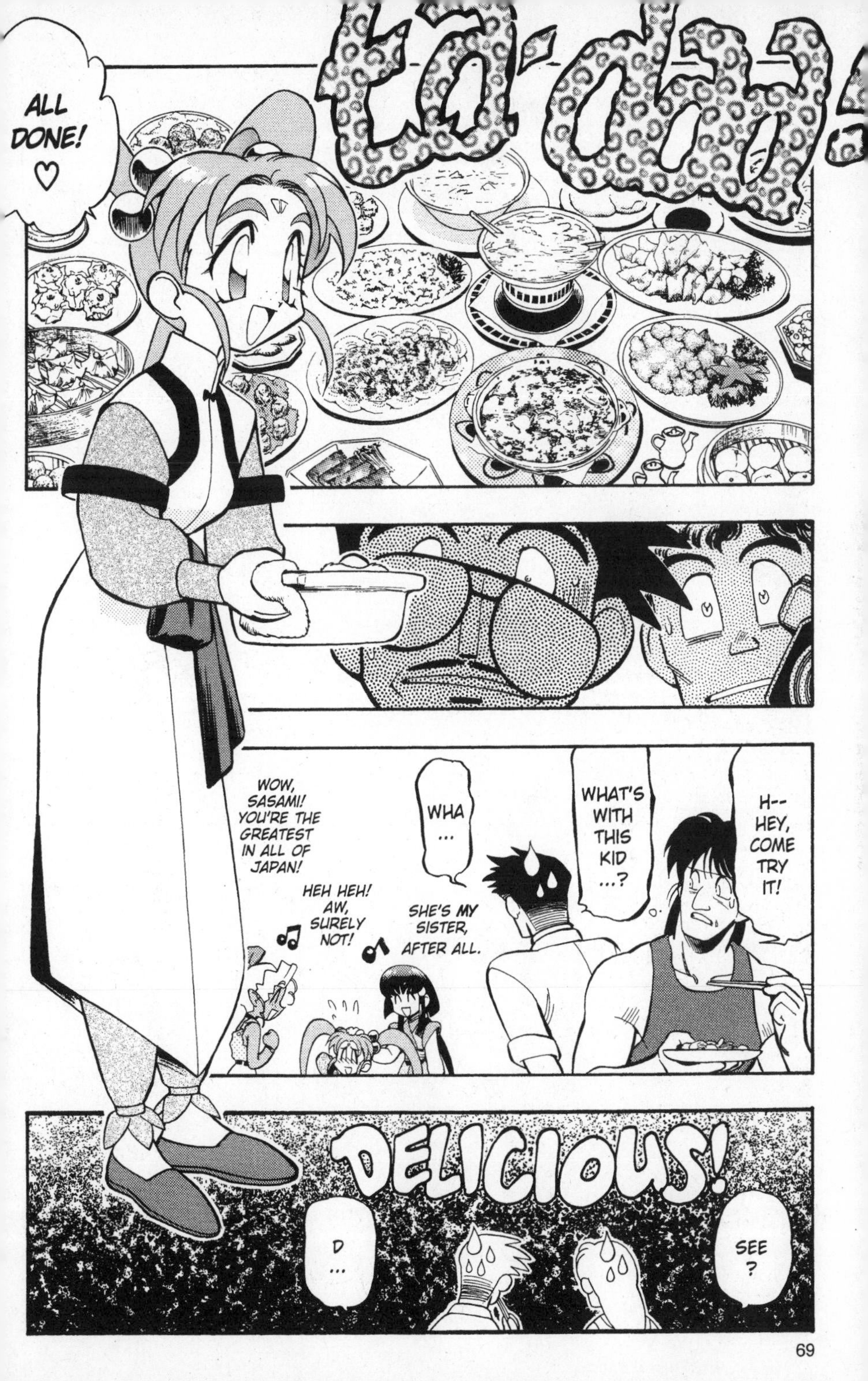
ALL DONE! ♡
WOW, SASAMI! YOU'RE THE GREATEST IN ALL OF JAPAN!
HEH HEH! AW, SURELY NOT!
WHA ...
SHE'S MY SISTER, AFTER ALL.
WHAT'S WITH THIS KID ...?
H-- HEY, COME TRY IT!
DELICIOUS!
D ...
SEE ?

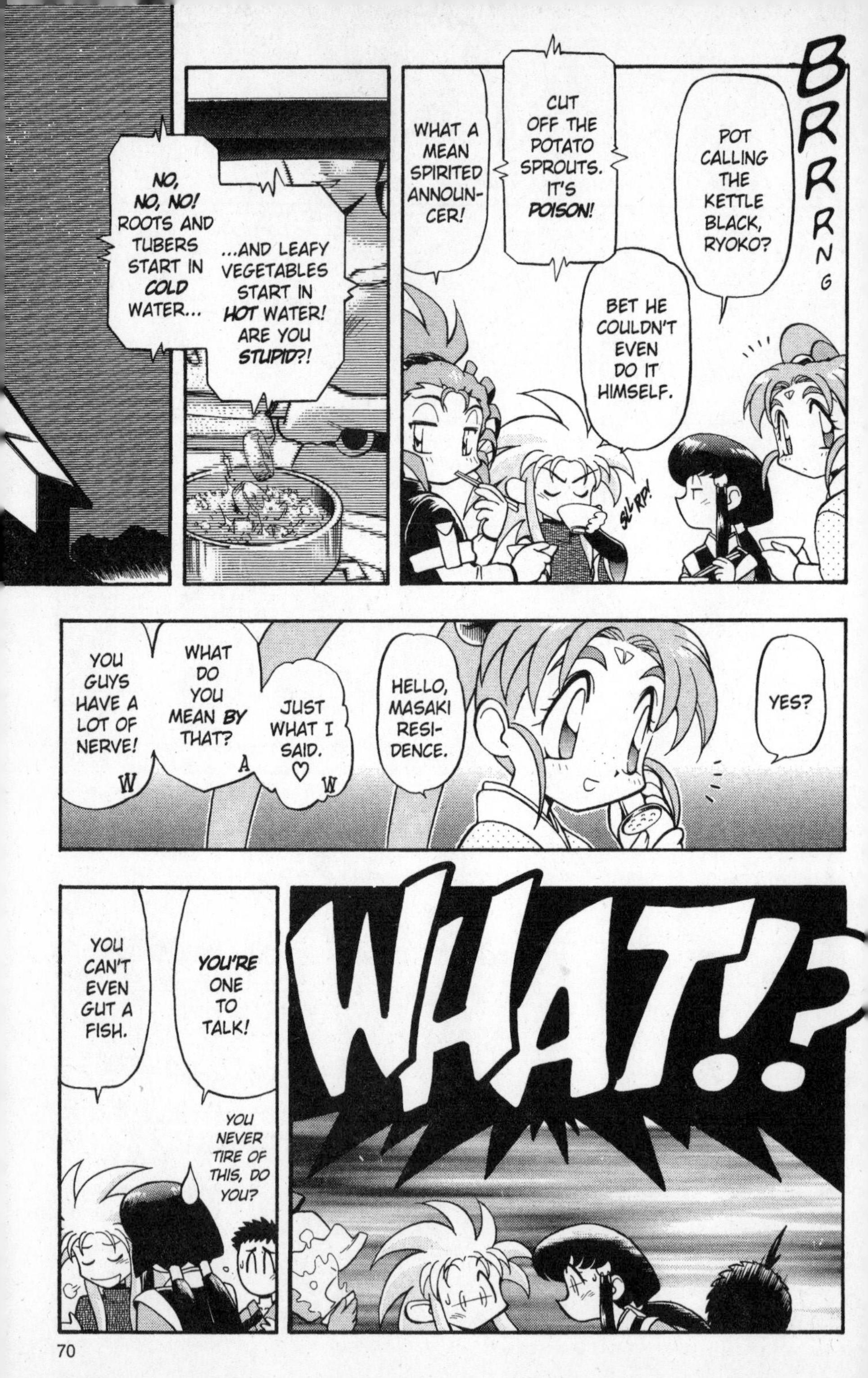
NO, NO, NO! ROOTS AND TUBERS START IN COLD WATER...
...AND LEAFY VEGETABLES START IN HOT WATER! ARE YOU STUPID?!
WHAT A MEAN SPIRITED ANNOUNCER!
CUT OFF THE POTATO SPROUTS. IT'S POISON!
BET HE COULDN'T EVEN DO IT HIMSELF.
POT CALLING THE KETTLE BLACK, RYOKO?
BRRRRNG
SLURP!
YOU GUYS HAVE A LOT OF NERVE!
W
WHAT DO YOU MEAN BY THAT?
A
JUST WHAT I SAID. ♡
W
HELLO, MASAKI RESIDENCE.
YES?
YOU CAN'T EVEN GUT A FISH.
YOU'RE ONE TO TALK!
WHAT!?
YOU NEVER TIRE OF THIS, DO YOU?

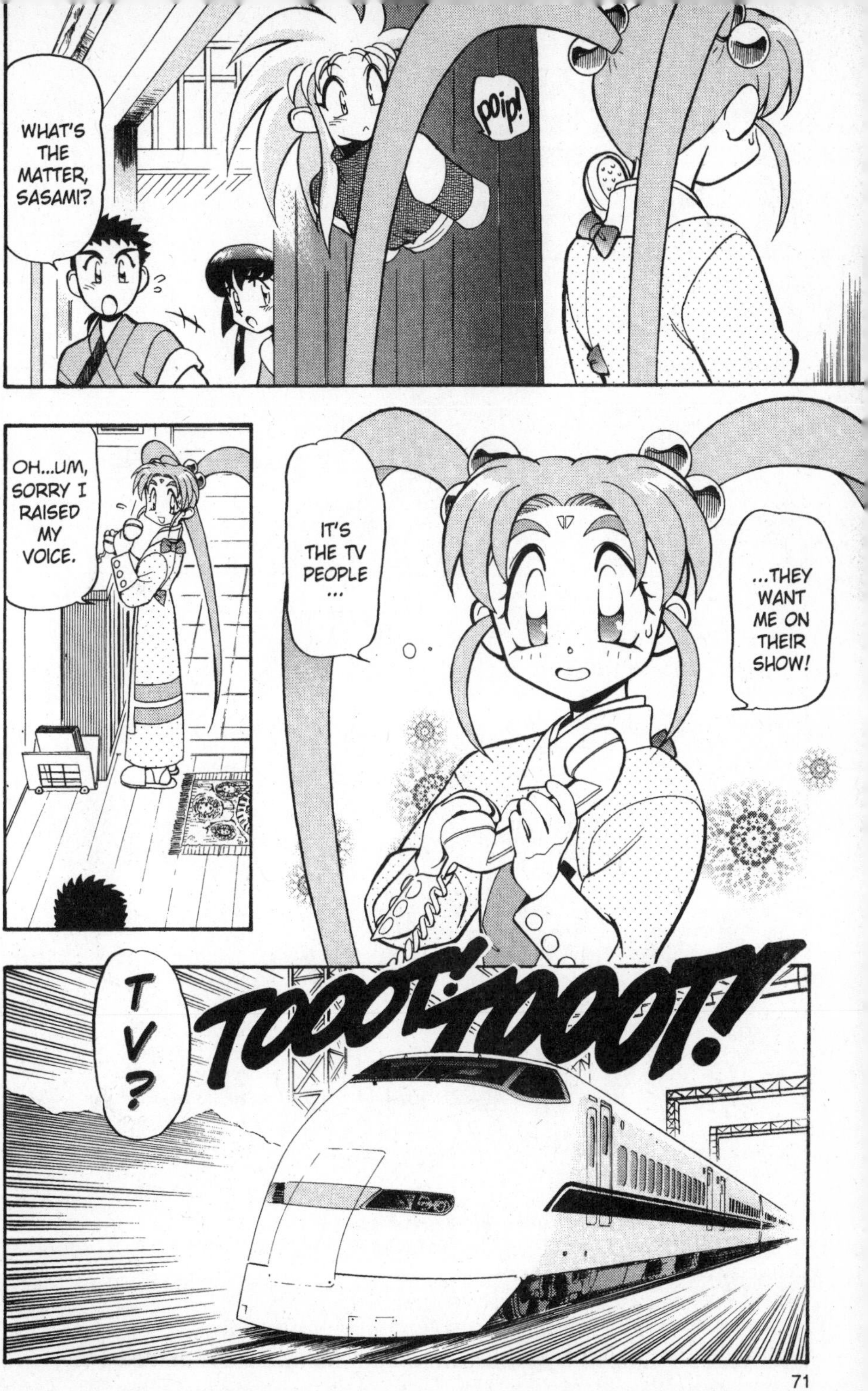

WHAT'S THE MATTER, SASAMI?
poip!
OH...UM, SORRY I RAISED MY VOICE.
IT'S THE TV PEOPLE ...
...THEY WANT ME ON THEIR SHOW!
TV?
TOOOT! TOOOT!

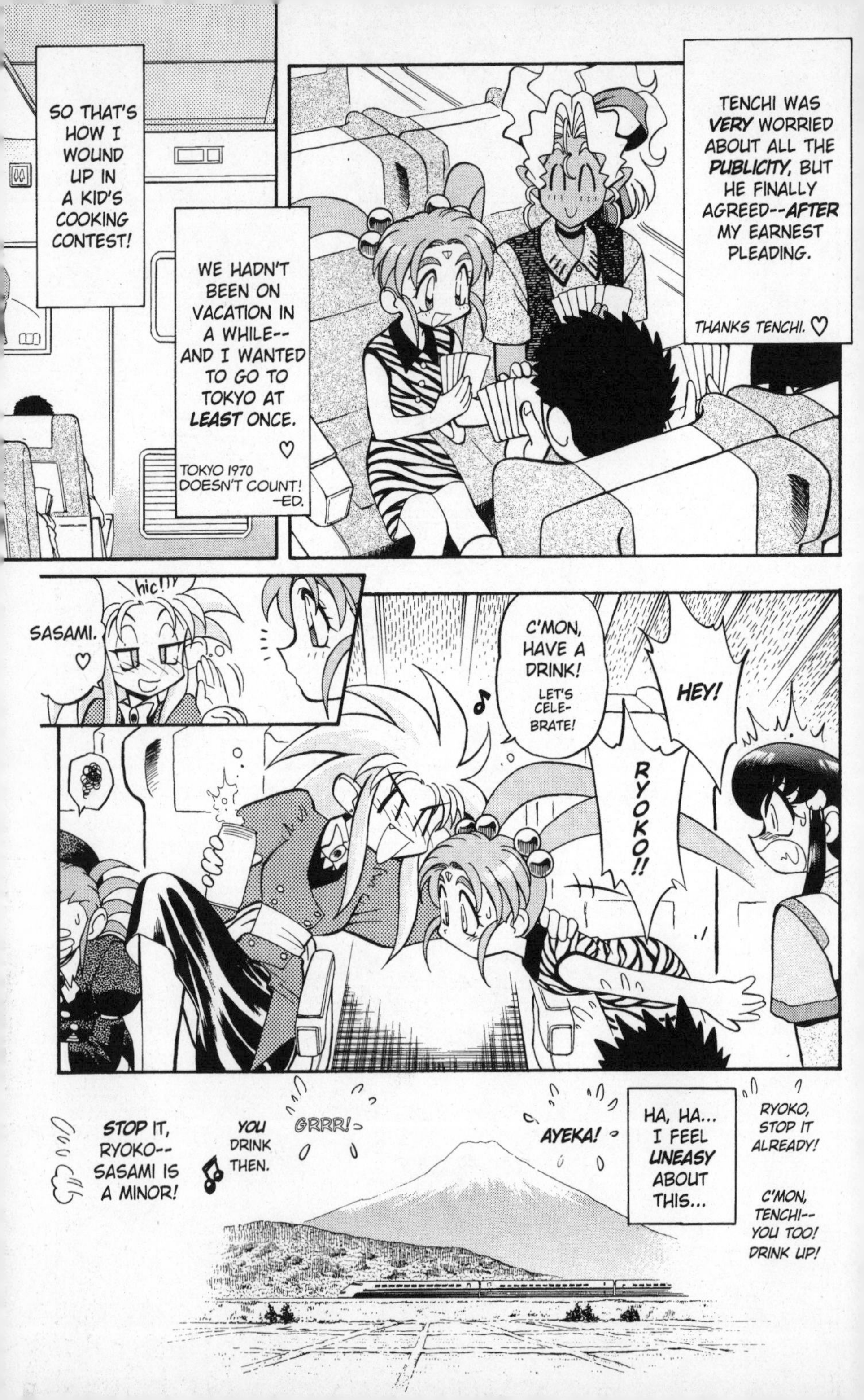
SO THAT'S HOW I WOUND UP IN A KID'S COOKING CONTEST!
WE HADN'T BEEN ON VACATION IN A WHILE-- AND I WANTED TO GO TO TOKYO AT LEAST ONCE. ♡
TOKYO 1970 DOESN'T COUNT! —ED.
TENCHI WAS VERY WORRIED ABOUT ALL THE PUBLICITY, BUT HE FINALLY AGREED--AFTER MY EARNEST PLEADING.
THANKS TENCHI. ♡
hic!!
SASAMI. ♡
C'MON, HAVE A DRINK!
LET'S CELEBRATE!
HEY!
RYOKO!!
STOP IT, RYOKO-- SASAMI IS A MINOR!
YOU DRINK THEN.
GRRR!
AYEKA!
HA, HA... I FEEL UNEASY ABOUT THIS...
RYOKO, STOP IT ALREADY!
C'MON, TENCHI-- YOU TOO! DRINK UP!

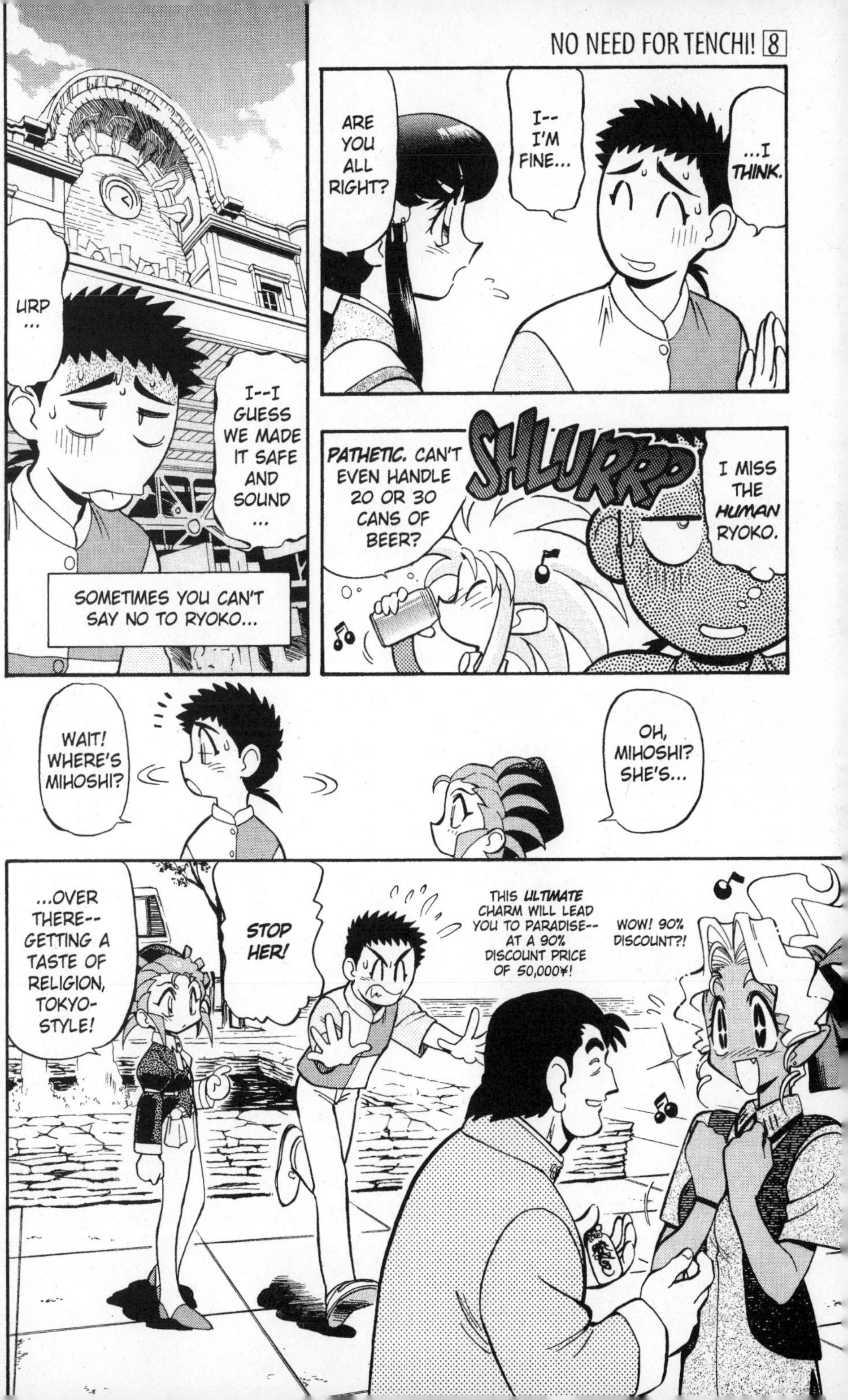
URP ...
I--I GUESS WE MADE IT SAFE AND SOUND ...
SOMETIMES YOU CAN'T SAY NO TO RYOKO...
ARE YOU ALL RIGHT?
I-- I'M FINE...
...I THINK.
PATHETIC. CAN'T EVEN HANDLE 20 OR 30 CANS OF BEER?
SHLURRP
I MISS THE HUMAN RYOKO.
WAIT! WHERE'S MIHOSHI?
OH, MIHOSHI? SHE'S...
...OVER THERE-- GETTING A TASTE OF RELIGION, TOKYO-STYLE!
STOP HER!
THIS ULTIMATE CHARM WILL LEAD YOU TO PARADISE-- AT A 90% DISCOUNT PRICE OF 50,000¥!
WOW! 90% DISCOUNT?!

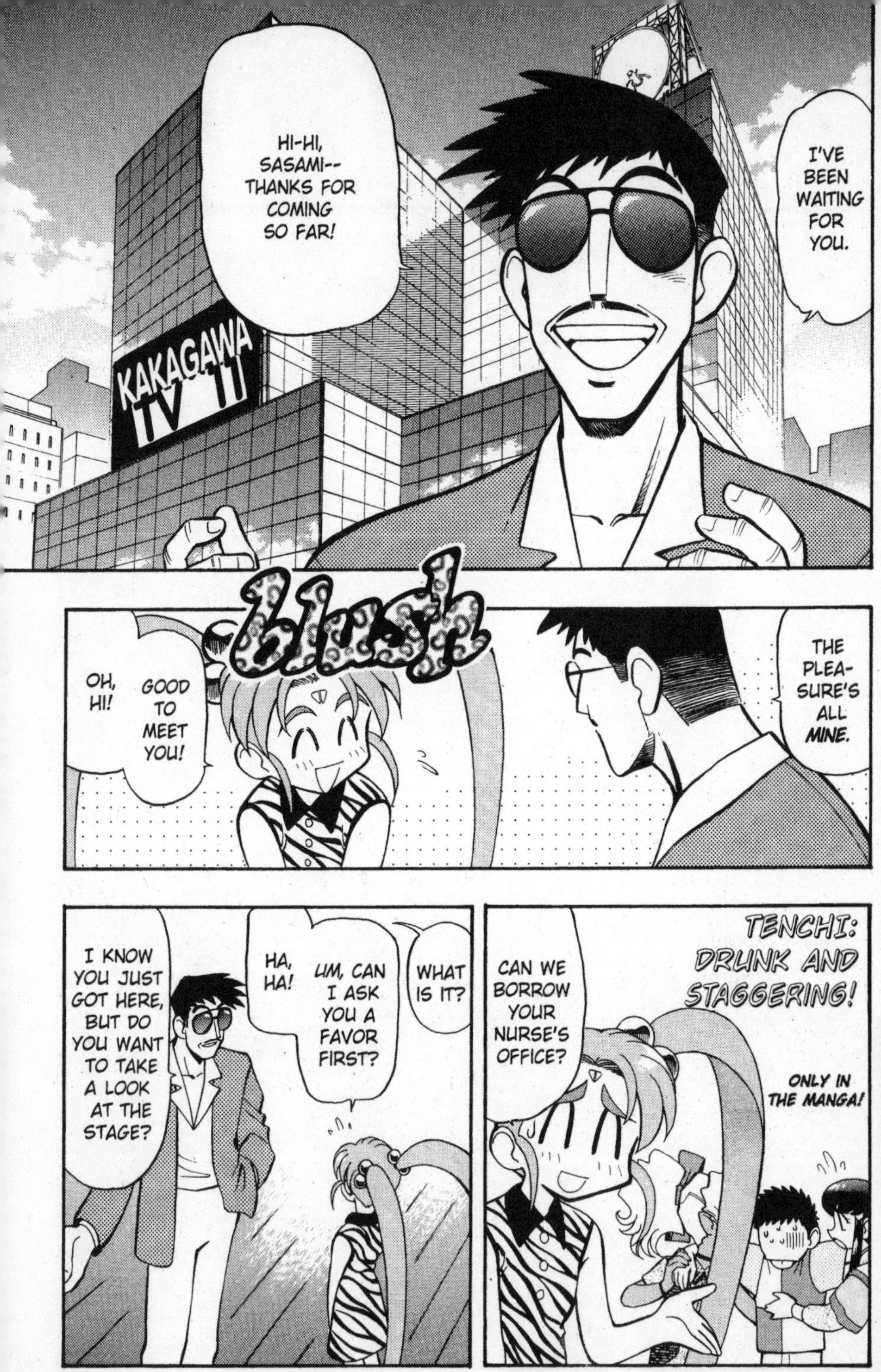

KAKAGAWA TV 11
HI-HI, SASAMI-- THANKS FOR COMING SO FAR!
I'VE BEEN WAITING FOR YOU.
blush
OH, HI!
GOOD TO MEET YOU!
THE PLEA-SURE'S ALL MINE.
I KNOW YOU JUST GOT HERE, BUT DO YOU WANT TO TAKE A LOOK AT THE STAGE?
HA, HA!
UM, CAN I ASK YOU A FAVOR FIRST?
WHAT IS IT?
CAN WE BORROW YOUR NURSE'S OFFICE?
TENCHI: DRUNK AND STAGGERING!
ONLY IN THE MANGA!

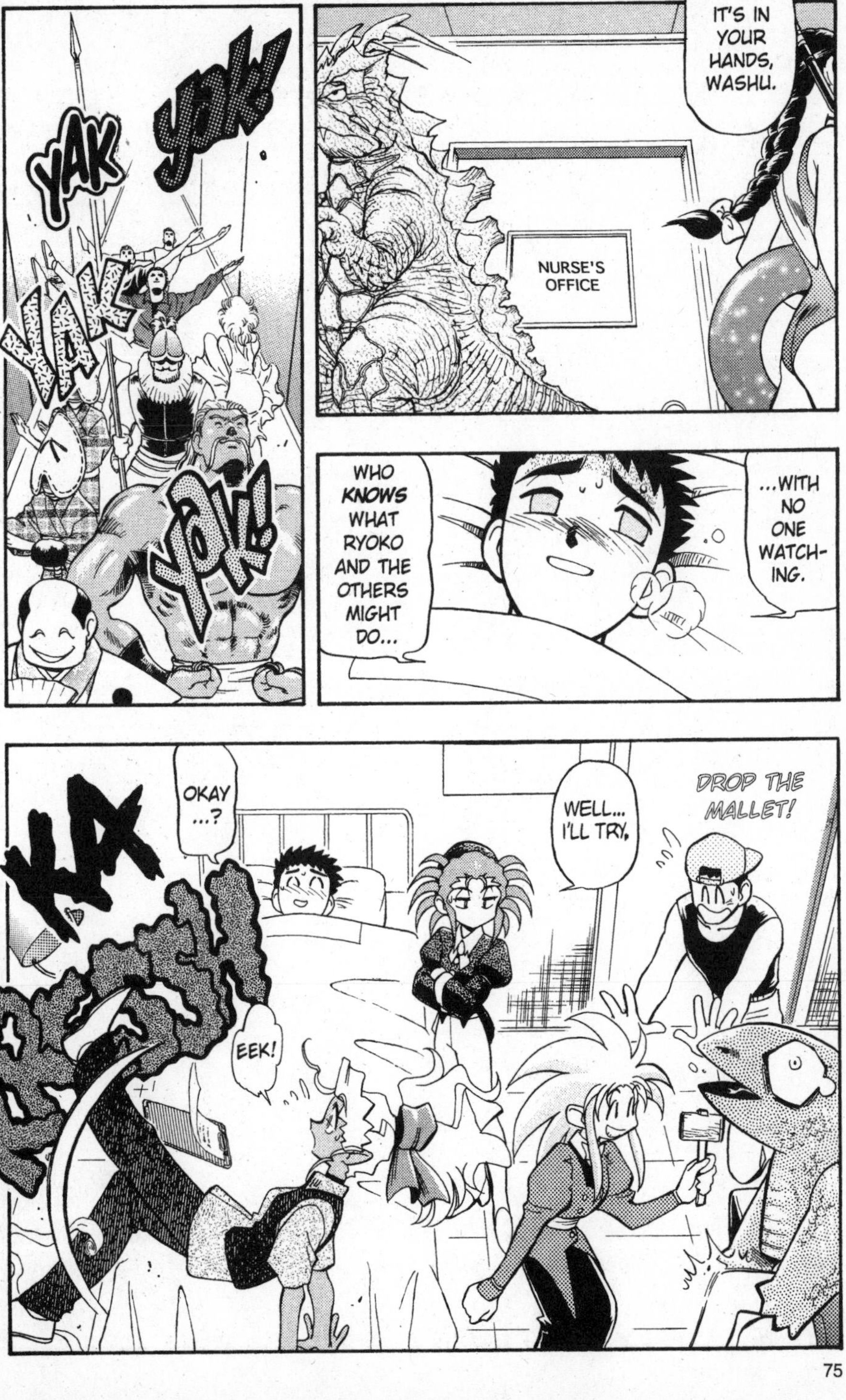

YAK
yak!
YAK
yak!
NURSE'S OFFICE
IT'S IN YOUR HANDS, WASHU.
WHO KNOWS WHAT RYOKO AND THE OTHERS MIGHT DO...
...WITH NO ONE WATCHING.
KA
OKAY ...?
WELL... I'LL TRY.
DROP THE MALLET!
EEK!

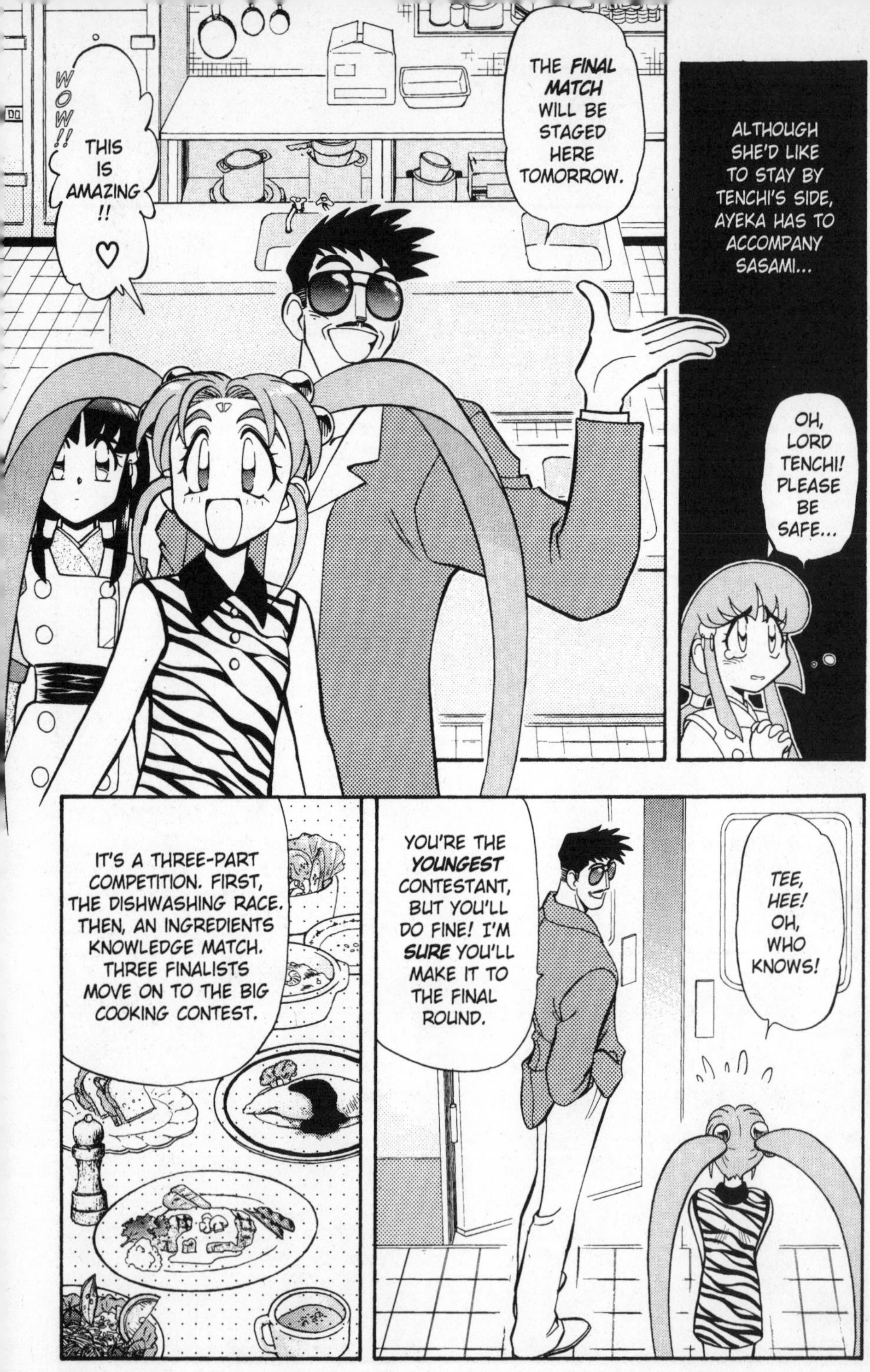
WOW!!
THIS IS AMAZING!! ♡
THE FINAL MATCH WILL BE STAGED HERE TOMORROW.
ALTHOUGH SHE'D LIKE TO STAY BY TENCHI'S SIDE, AYEKA HAS TO ACCOMPANY SASAMI...
OH, LORD TENCHI! PLEASE BE SAFE...
IT'S A THREE-PART COMPETITION. FIRST, THE DISHWASHING RACE. THEN, AN INGREDIENTS KNOWLEDGE MATCH. THREE FINALISTS MOVE ON TO THE BIG COOKING CONTEST.
YOU'RE THE YOUNGEST CONTESTANT, BUT YOU'LL DO FINE! I'M SURE YOU'LL MAKE IT TO THE FINAL ROUND.
TEE, HEE! OH, WHO KNOWS!

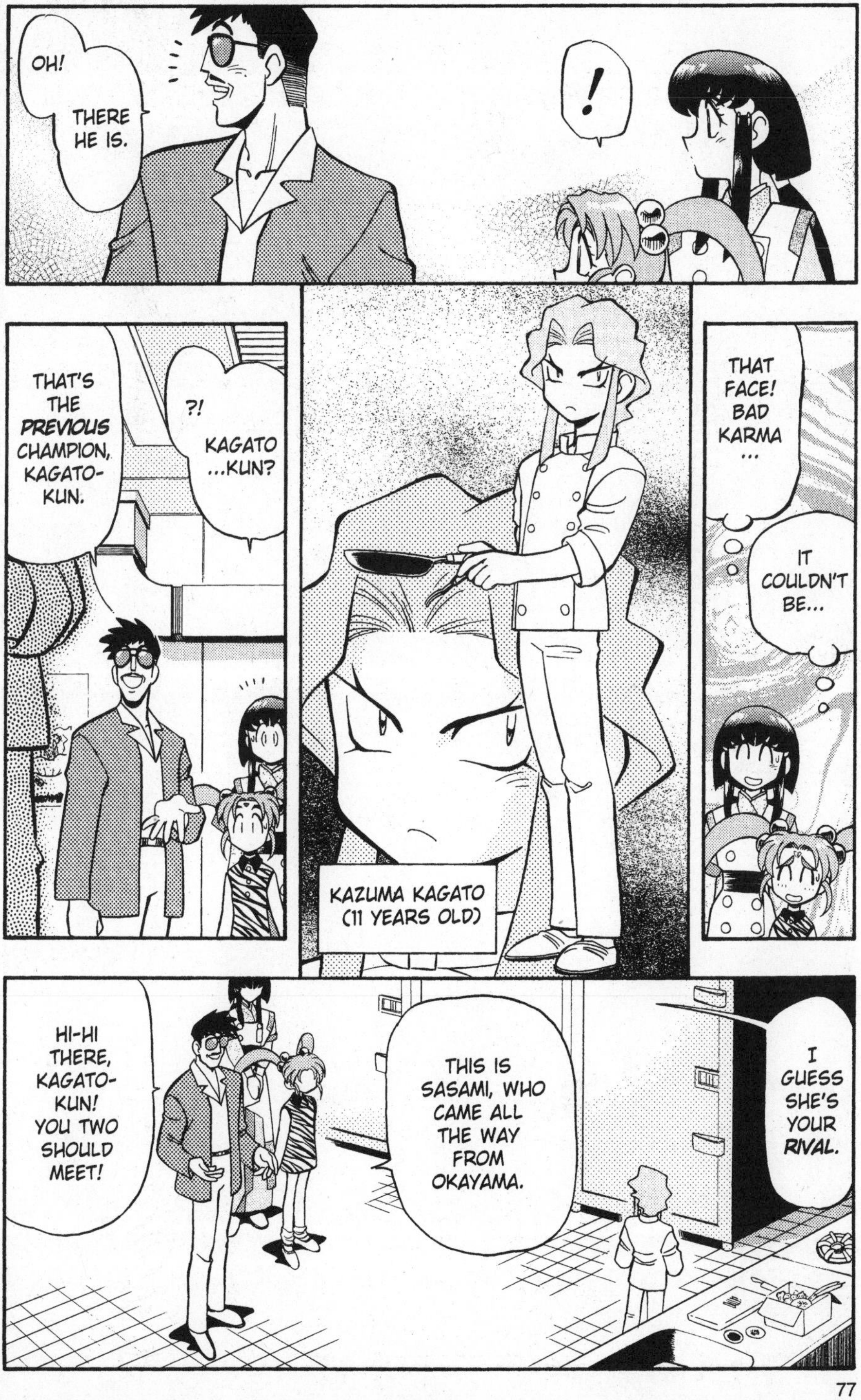
OH!
THERE HE IS.
!
THAT'S THE PREVIOUS CHAMPION, KAGATO-KUN.
?!
KAGATO ...KUN?
KAZUMA KAGATO (11 YEARS OLD)
THAT FACE! BAD KARMA ...
IT COULDN'T BE...
HI-HI THERE, KAGATO-KUN! YOU TWO SHOULD MEET!
THIS IS SASAMI, WHO CAME ALL THE WAY FROM OKAYAMA.
I GUESS SHE'S YOUR RIVAL.

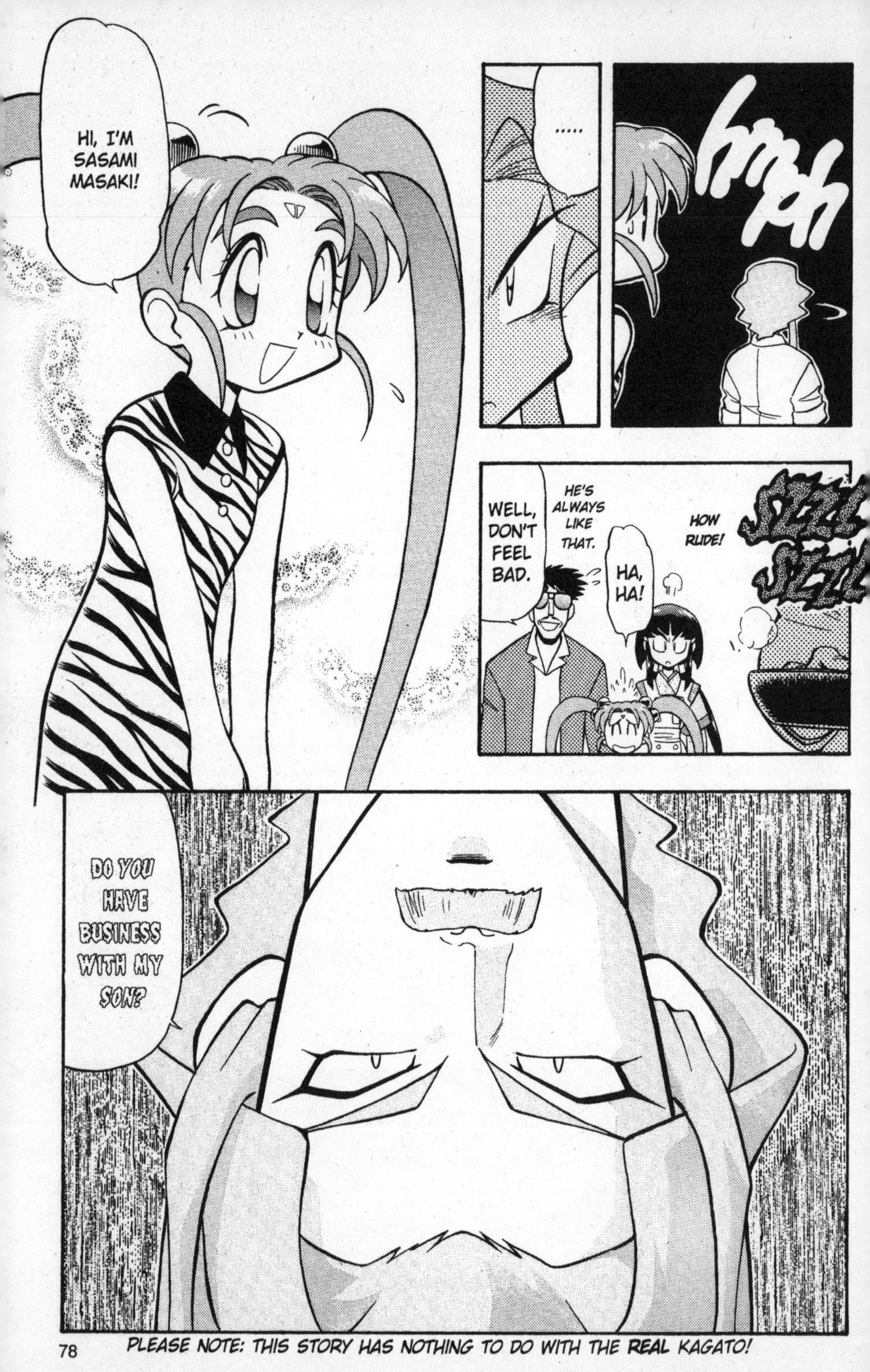
HI, I'M SASAMI MASAKI!
.....
hmph
WELL, DON'T FEEL BAD.
HE'S ALWAYS LIKE THAT.
HA, HA!
HOW RUDE!
DO YOU HAVE BUSINESS WITH MY SON?

PLEASE NOTE: THIS STORY HAS NOTHING TO DO WITH THE **REAL** KAGATO!

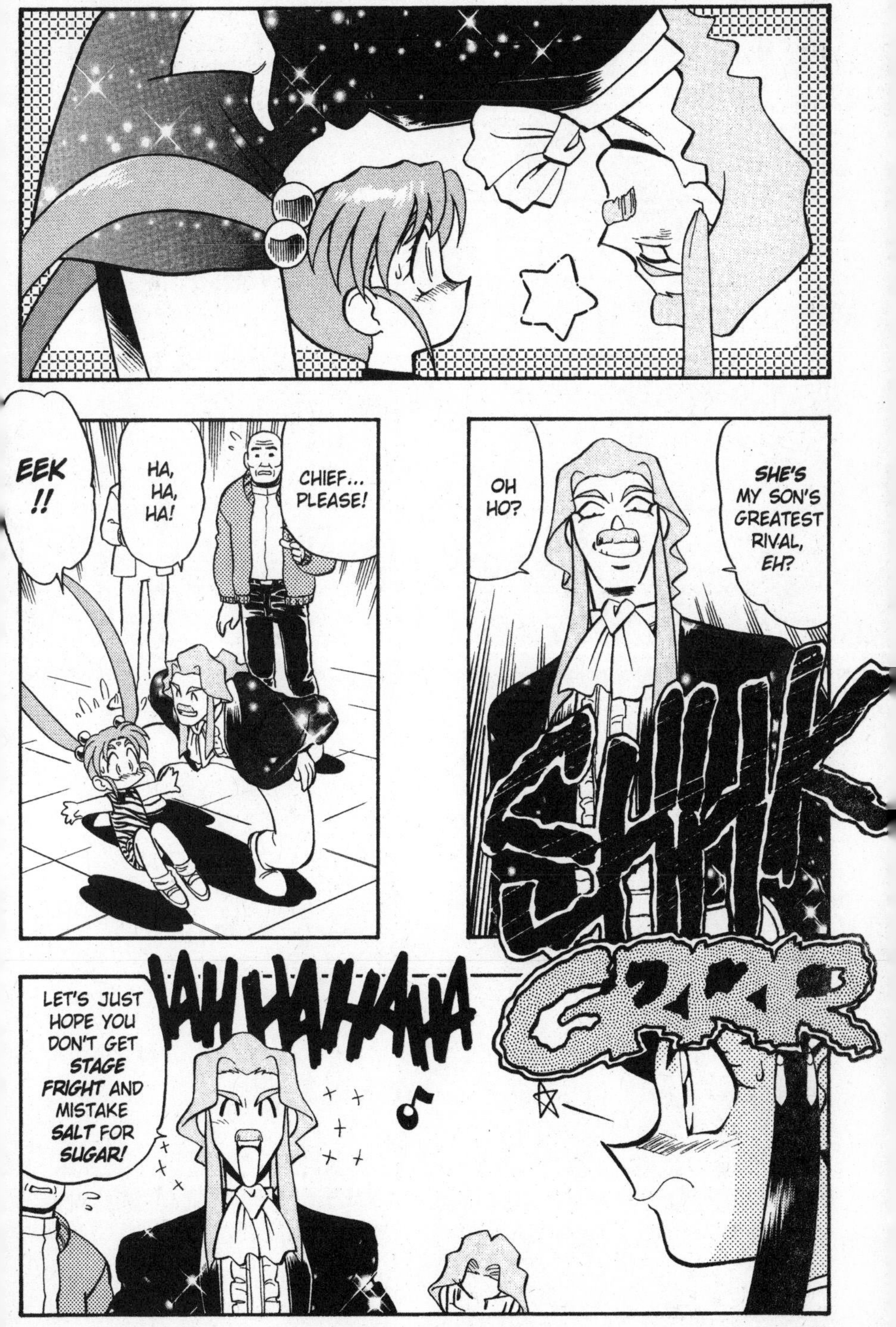
EEK!!
HA, HA, HA!
CHIEF... PLEASE!
OH HO?
SHE'S MY SON'S GREATEST RIVAL, EH?
LET'S JUST HOPE YOU DON'T GET STAGE FRIGHT AND MISTAKE SALT FOR SUGAR!

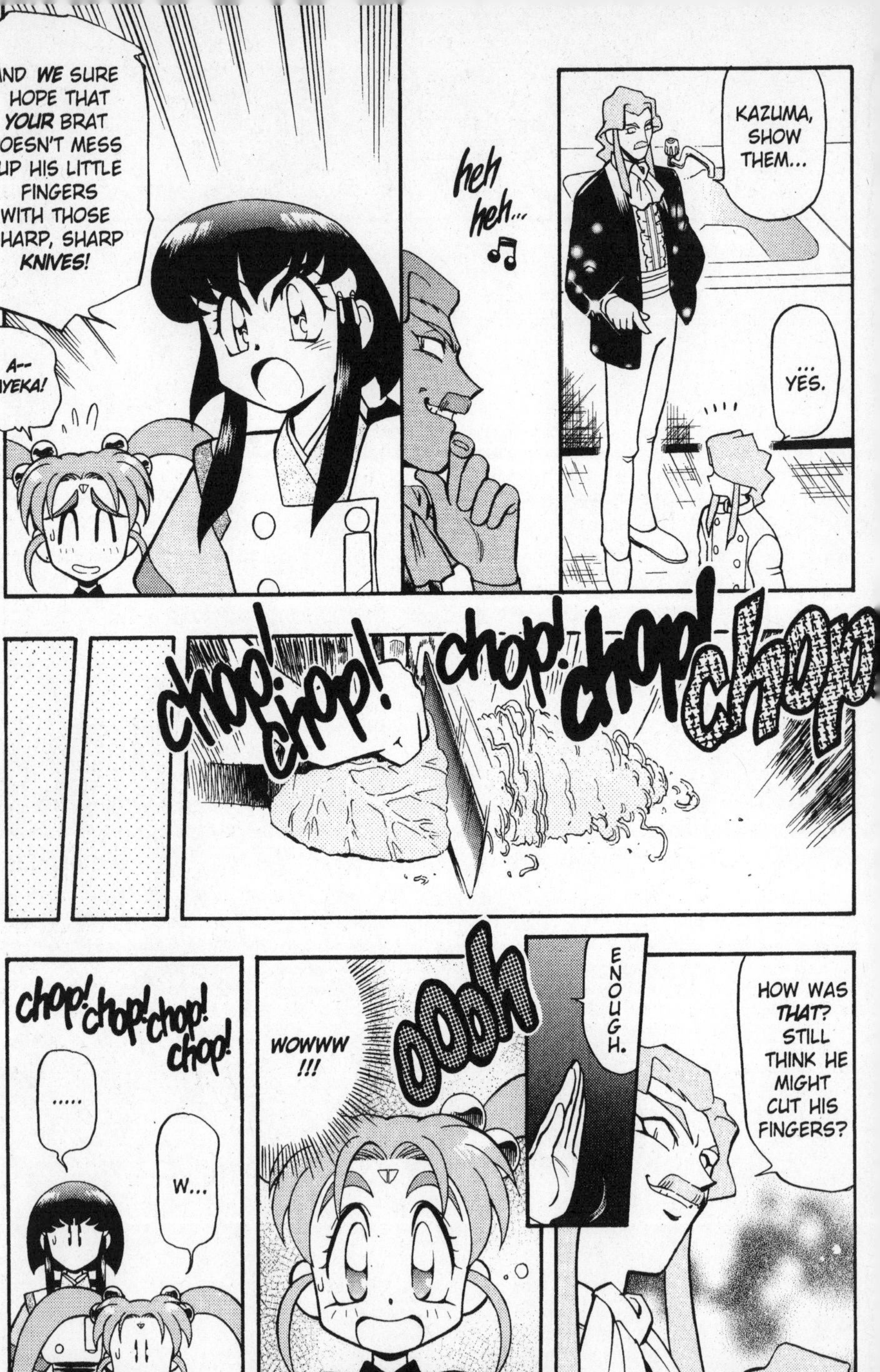

AND WE SURE HOPE THAT YOUR BRAT DOESN'T MESS UP HIS LITTLE FINGERS WITH THOSE SHARP, SHARP KNIVES!
A-- AYEKA!
heh heh...
KAZUMA, SHOW THEM...
... YES.
chop! chop! chop! chop! chop
chop! chop! chop! chop!
.....
W...
WOWWW !!!
oooh
ENOUGH.
HOW WAS THAT? STILL THINK HE MIGHT CUT HIS FINGERS?

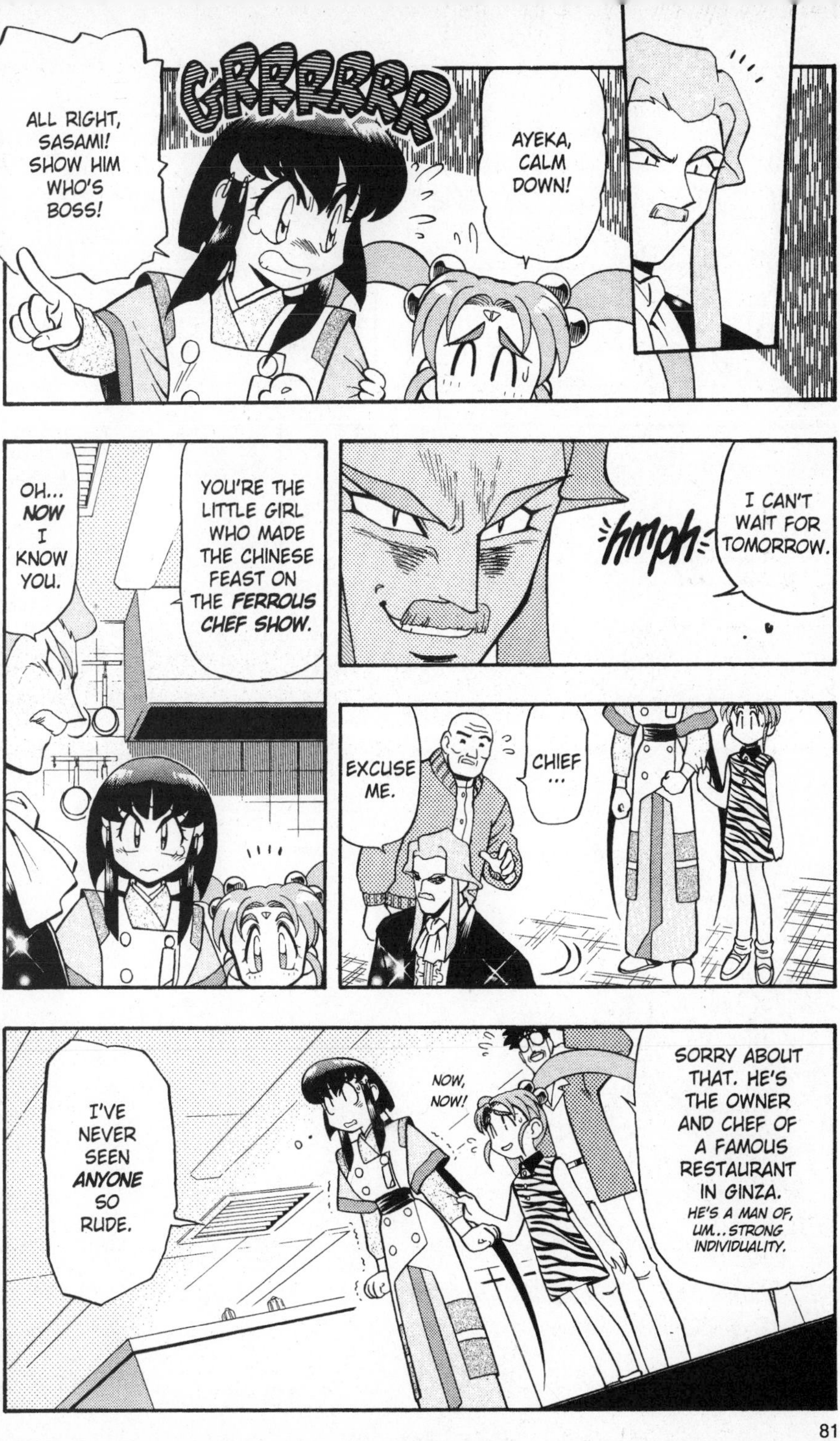

ALL RIGHT, SASAMI! SHOW HIM WHO'S BOSS!
GRRRRRRR
AYEKA, CALM DOWN!
OH... NOW I KNOW YOU.
YOU'RE THE LITTLE GIRL WHO MADE THE CHINESE FEAST ON THE FERROUS CHEF SHOW.
hmph
I CAN'T WAIT FOR TOMORROW.
EXCUSE ME.
CHIEF ...
I'VE NEVER SEEN ANYONE SO RUDE.
NOW, NOW!
SORRY ABOUT THAT. HE'S THE OWNER AND CHEF OF A FAMOUS RESTAURANT IN GINZA.
HE'S A MAN OF, UM...STRONG INDIVIDUALITY.

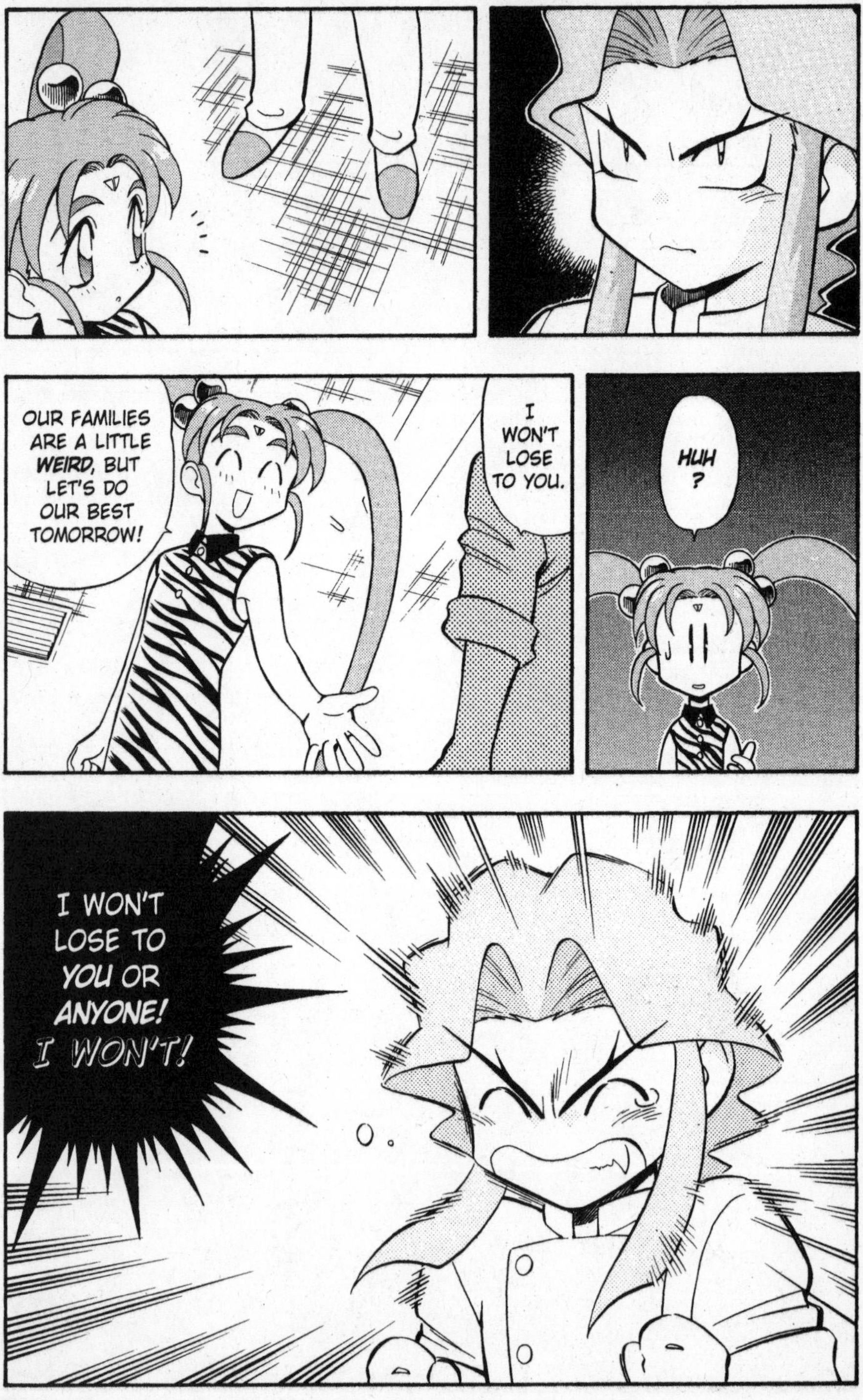
OUR FAMILIES ARE A LITTLE WEIRD, BUT LET'S DO OUR BEST TOMORROW!
I WON'T LOSE TO YOU.
HUH ?
I WON'T LOSE TO YOU OR ANYONE! I WON'T!

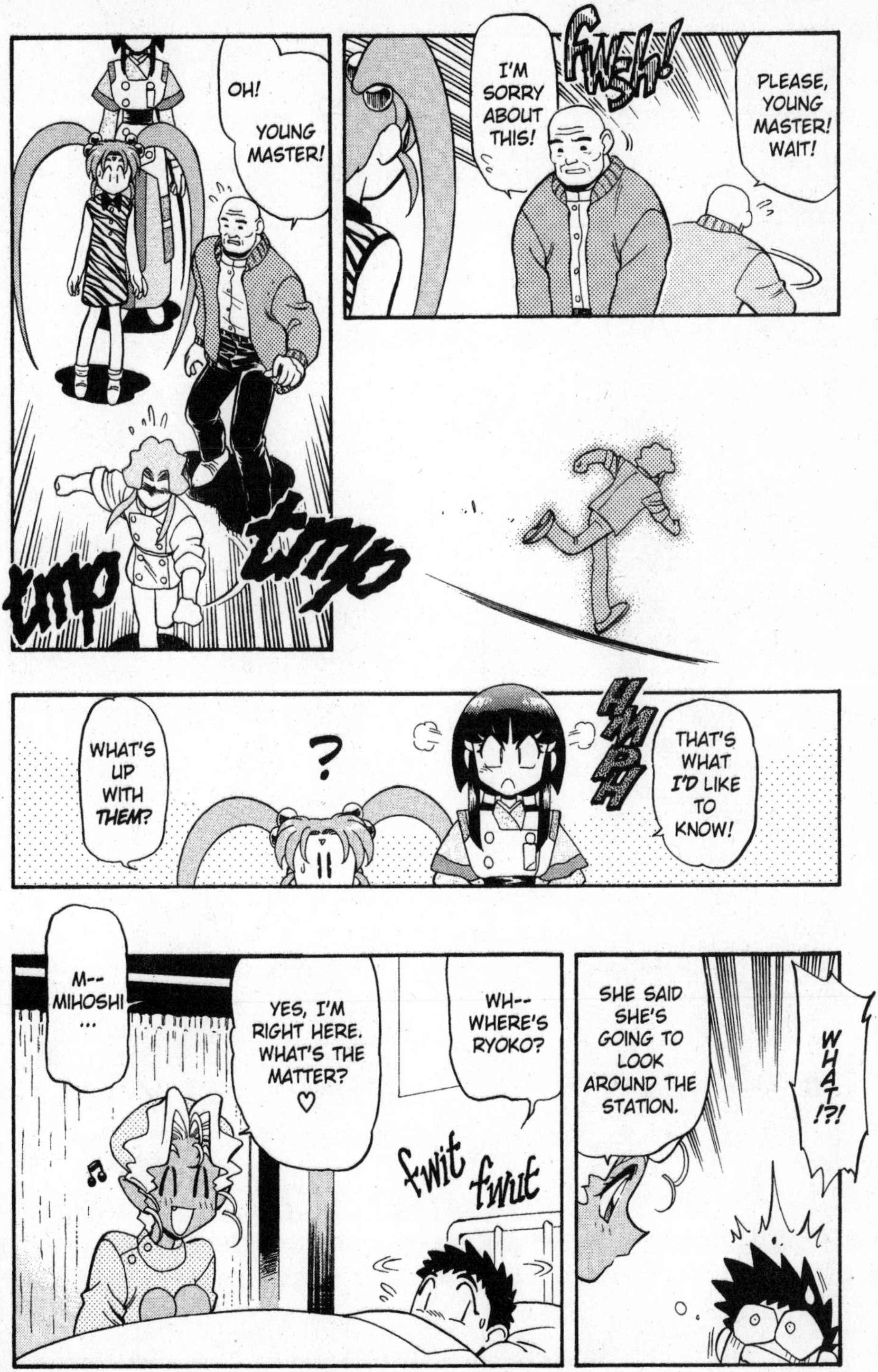
OH!
YOUNG MASTER!
tmp
tmp
I'M SORRY ABOUT THIS!
FWSH!
PLEASE, YOUNG MASTER! WAIT!
WHAT'S UP WITH *THEM*?
?
HMPH
THAT'S WHAT *I'D* LIKE TO KNOW!
M-- MIHOSHI ...
YES, I'M RIGHT HERE. WHAT'S THE MATTER? ♡
WH-- WHERE'S RYOKO?
fwit
fwut
SHE SAID SHE'S GOING TO LOOK AROUND THE STATION.
WHAT!?!

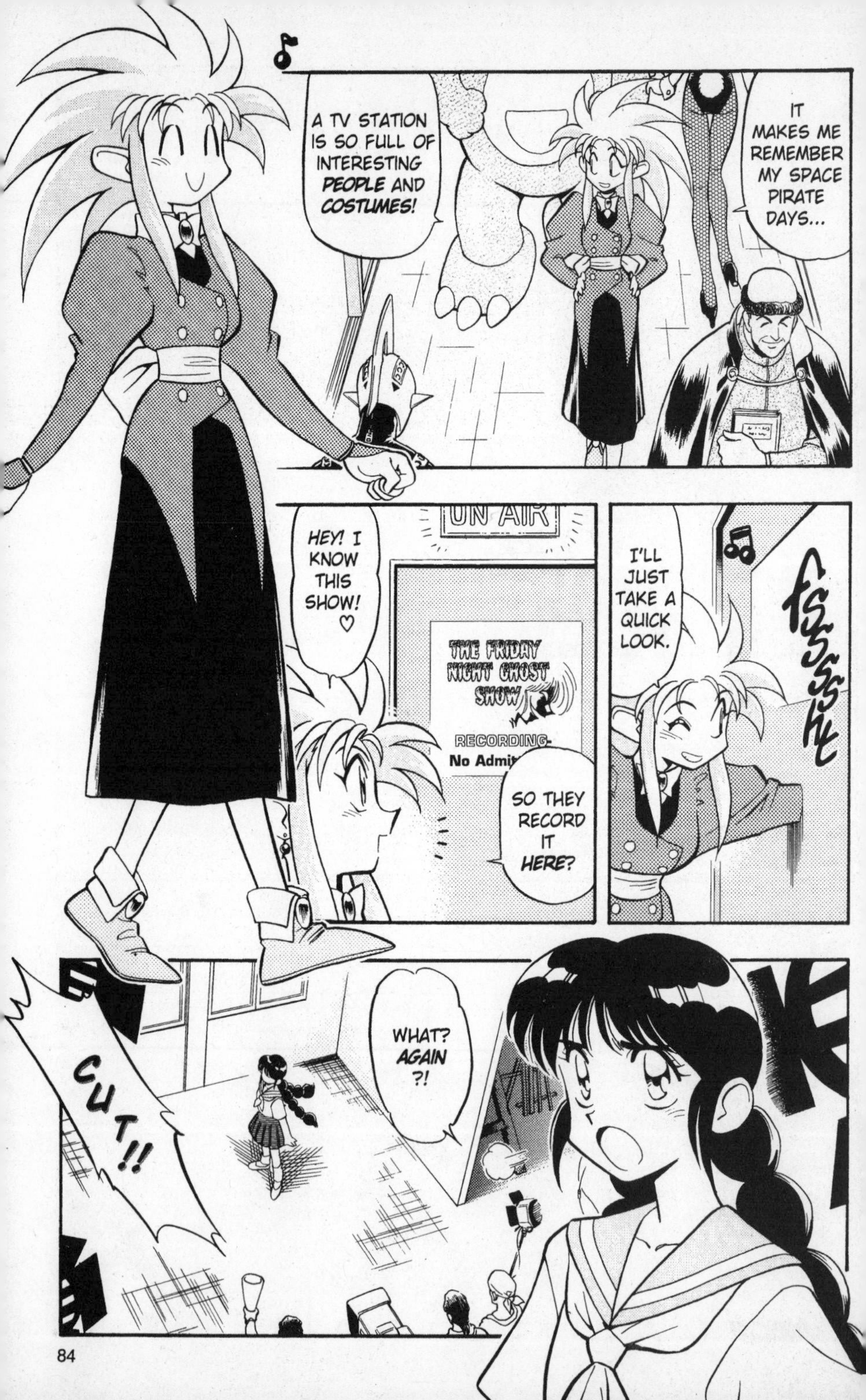
A TV STATION IS SO FULL OF INTERESTING PEOPLE AND COSTUMES!
IT MAKES ME REMEMBER MY SPACE PIRATE DAYS...
ON AIR
HEY! I KNOW THIS SHOW! ♡
THE FRIDAY NIGHT GHOST SHOW
RECORDING-
No Admit
SO THEY RECORD IT HERE?
I'LL JUST TAKE A QUICK LOOK.
FSSSSHK
CUT!!
WHAT? AGAIN ?!

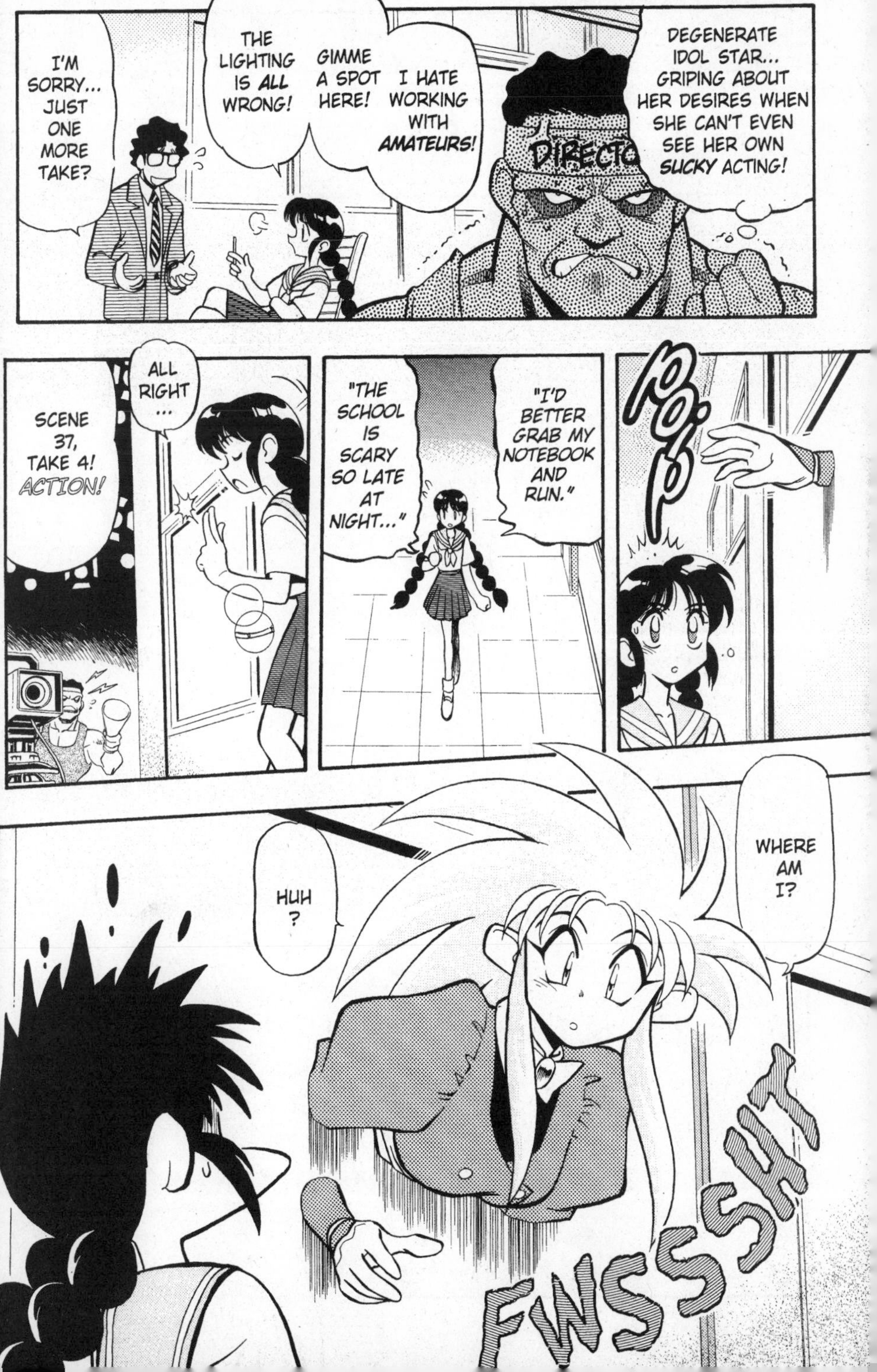
I'M SORRY... JUST ONE MORE TAKE?
THE LIGHTING IS **ALL** WRONG!
GIMME A SPOT HERE!
I HATE WORKING WITH ***AMATEURS!***
DIRECTO
DEGENERATE IDOL STAR... GRIPING ABOUT HER DESIRES WHEN SHE CAN'T EVEN SEE HER OWN ***SUCKY*** ACTING!
SCENE 37, TAKE 4! *ACTION!*
ALL RIGHT ...
"THE SCHOOL IS SCARY SO LATE AT NIGHT..."
"I'D BETTER GRAB MY NOTEBOOK AND RUN."
POP
HUH ?
WHERE AM I?
FWSSSHT

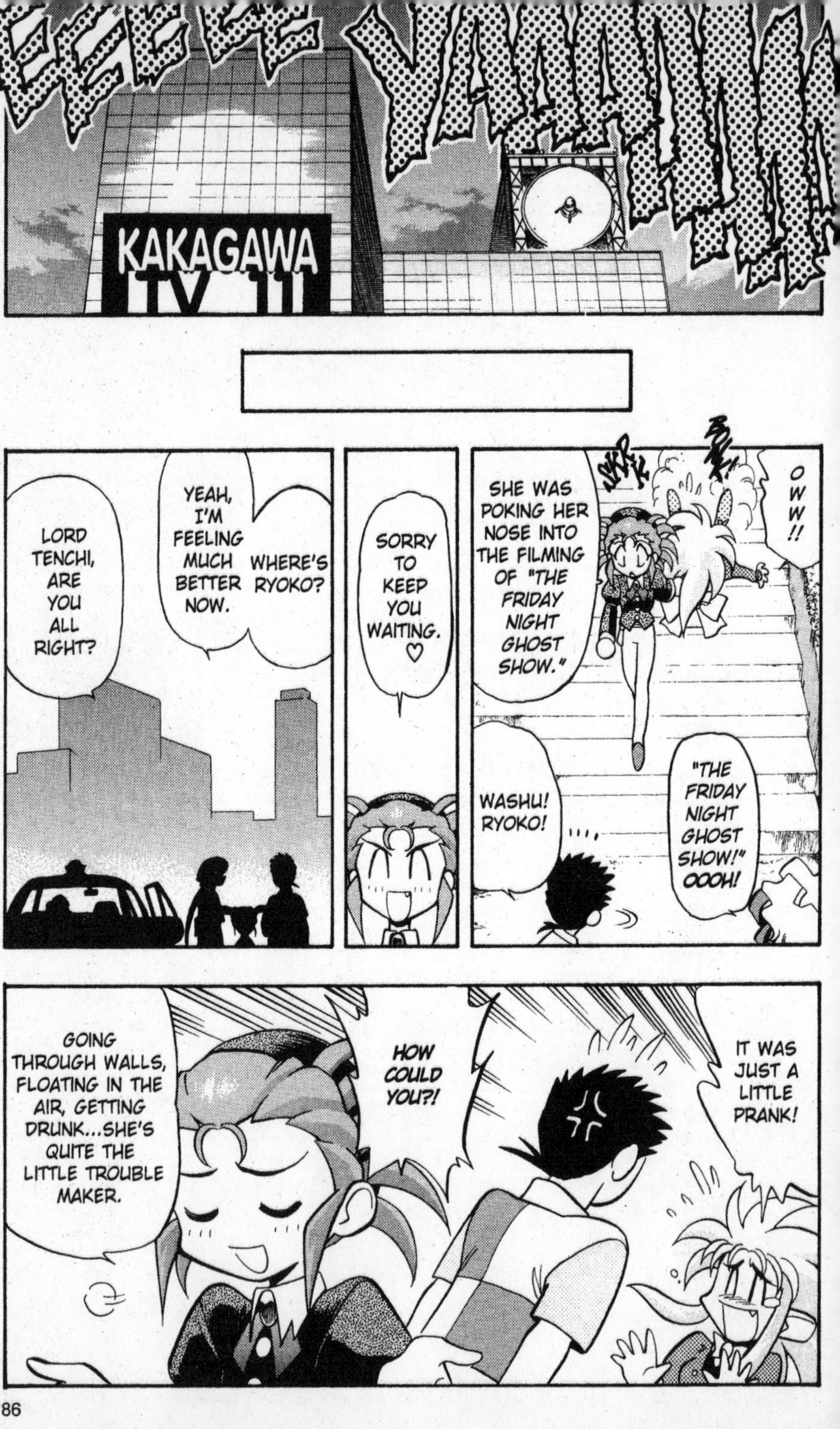
KAKAGAWA
TV 11
LORD TENCHI, ARE YOU ALL RIGHT?
YEAH, I'M FEELING MUCH BETTER NOW. WHERE'S RYOKO?
SORRY TO KEEP YOU WAITING. ♡
SHE WAS POKING HER NOSE INTO THE FILMING OF "THE FRIDAY NIGHT GHOST SHOW."
OWW!!
WASHU! RYOKO!
...
"THE FRIDAY NIGHT GHOST SHOW!" OOOH!
GOING THROUGH WALLS, FLOATING IN THE AIR, GETTING DRUNK...SHE'S QUITE THE LITTLE TROUBLE MAKER.
HOW COULD YOU?!
IT WAS JUST A LITTLE PRANK!

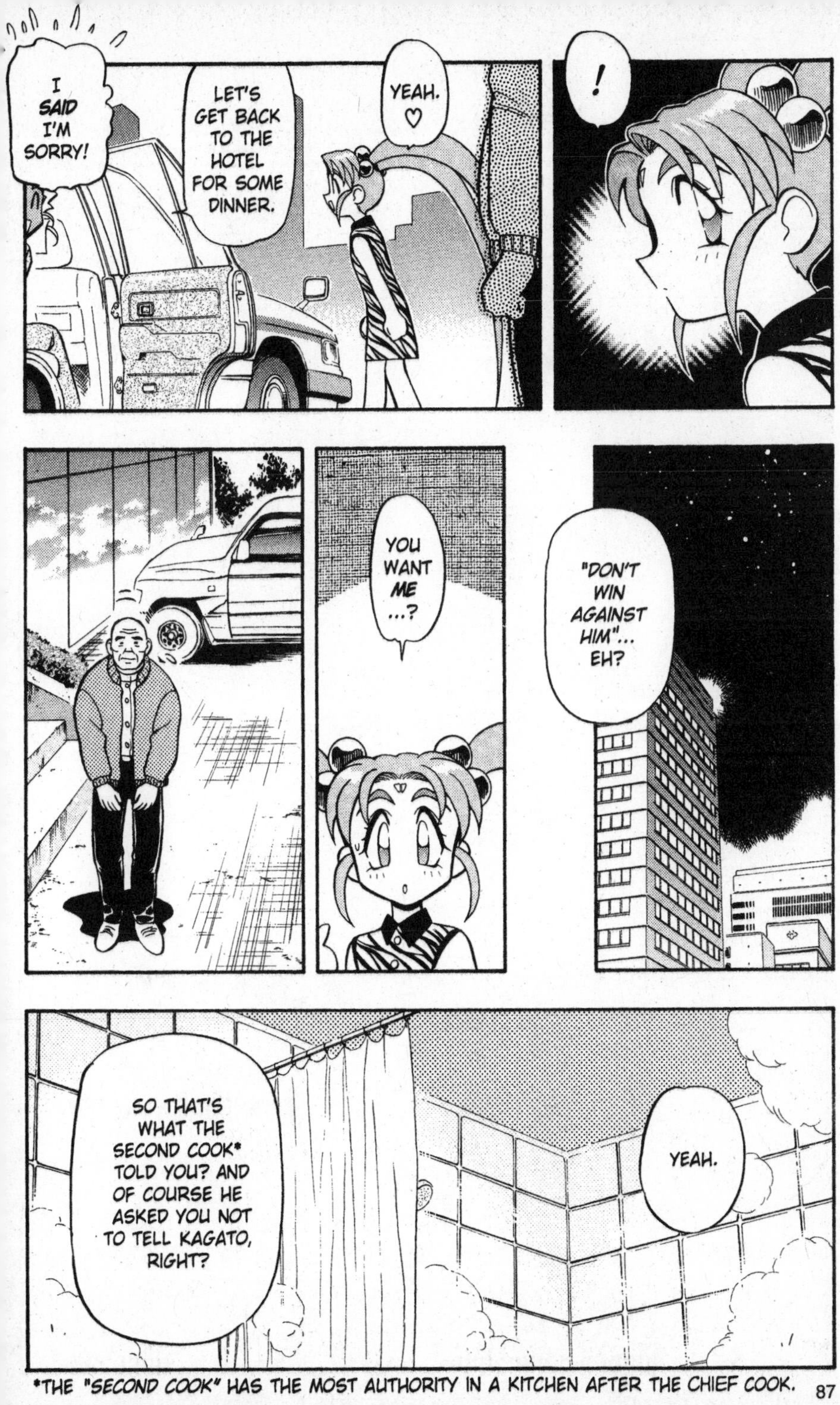
I SAID I'M SORRY!
LET'S GET BACK TO THE HOTEL FOR SOME DINNER.
YEAH. ♡
!
YOU WANT ME ...?
"DON'T WIN AGAINST HIM"... EH?
SO THAT'S WHAT THE SECOND COOK* TOLD YOU? AND OF COURSE HE ASKED YOU NOT TO TELL KAGATO, RIGHT?
YEAH.

*THE "SECOND COOK" HAS THE MOST AUTHORITY IN A KITCHEN AFTER THE CHIEF COOK.

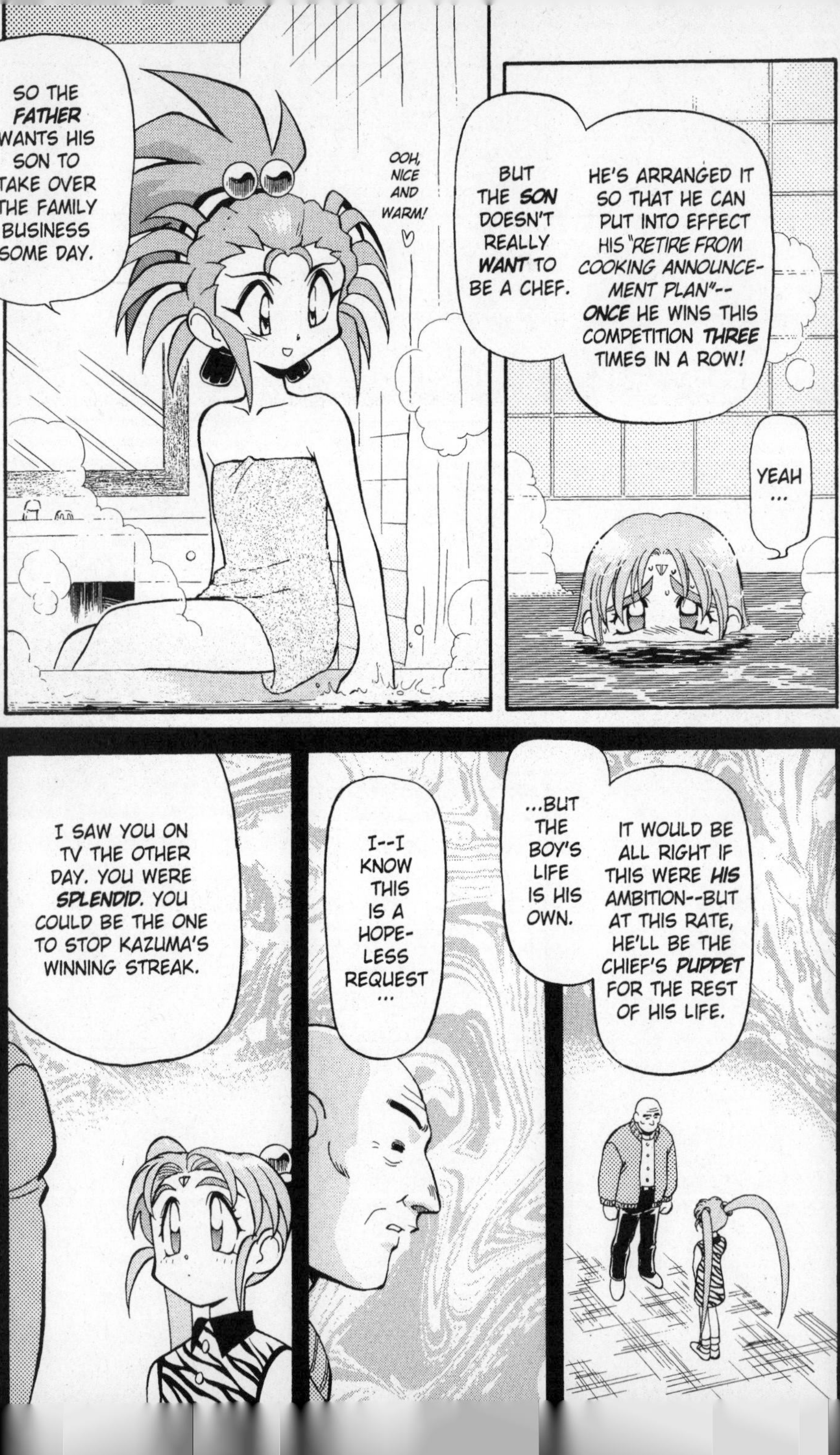
SO THE FATHER WANTS HIS SON TO TAKE OVER THE FAMILY BUSINESS SOME DAY.
OOH, NICE AND WARM! ♡
BUT THE SON DOESN'T REALLY WANT TO BE A CHEF.
HE'S ARRANGED IT SO THAT HE CAN PUT INTO EFFECT HIS "RETIRE FROM COOKING ANNOUNCE-MENT PLAN"-- ONCE HE WINS THIS COMPETITION THREE TIMES IN A ROW!
YEAH ...
I SAW YOU ON TV THE OTHER DAY. YOU WERE SPLENDID. YOU COULD BE THE ONE TO STOP KAZUMA'S WINNING STREAK.
I--I KNOW THIS IS A HOPE-LESS REQUEST ...
...BUT THE BOY'S LIFE IS HIS OWN.
IT WOULD BE ALL RIGHT IF THIS WERE HIS AMBITION--BUT AT THIS RATE, HE'LL BE THE CHIEF'S PUPPET FOR THE REST OF HIS LIFE.

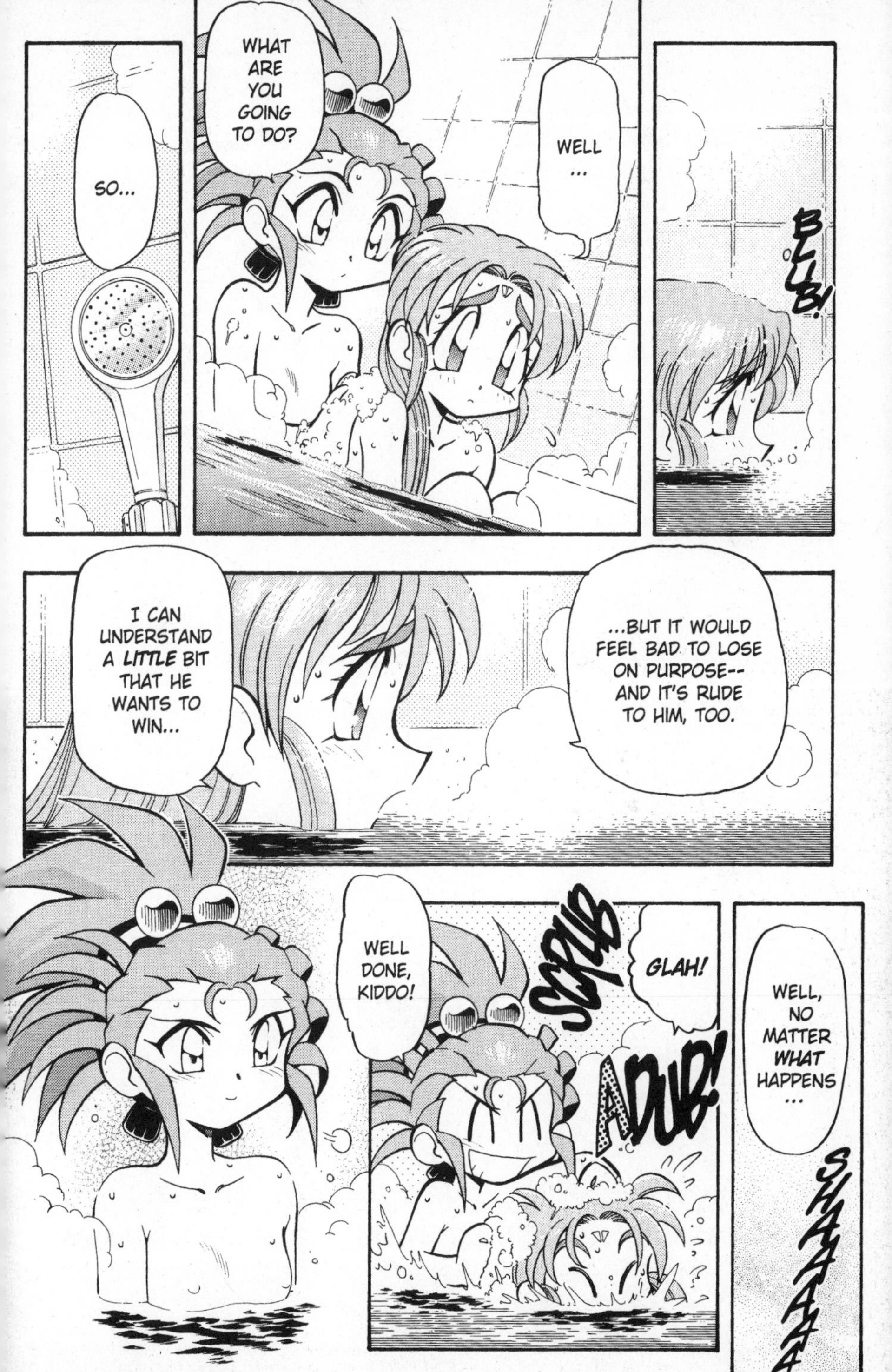

SO...
WHAT ARE YOU GOING TO DO?
WELL ...
BLUB!
I CAN UNDERSTAND A *LITTLE* BIT THAT HE WANTS TO WIN...
...BUT IT WOULD FEEL BAD TO LOSE ON PURPOSE-- AND IT'S RUDE TO HIM, TOO.
WELL DONE, KIDDO!
SCRUB
GLAH!
ADUB!
WELL, NO MATTER *WHAT* HAPPENS ...
SHAAAAAA

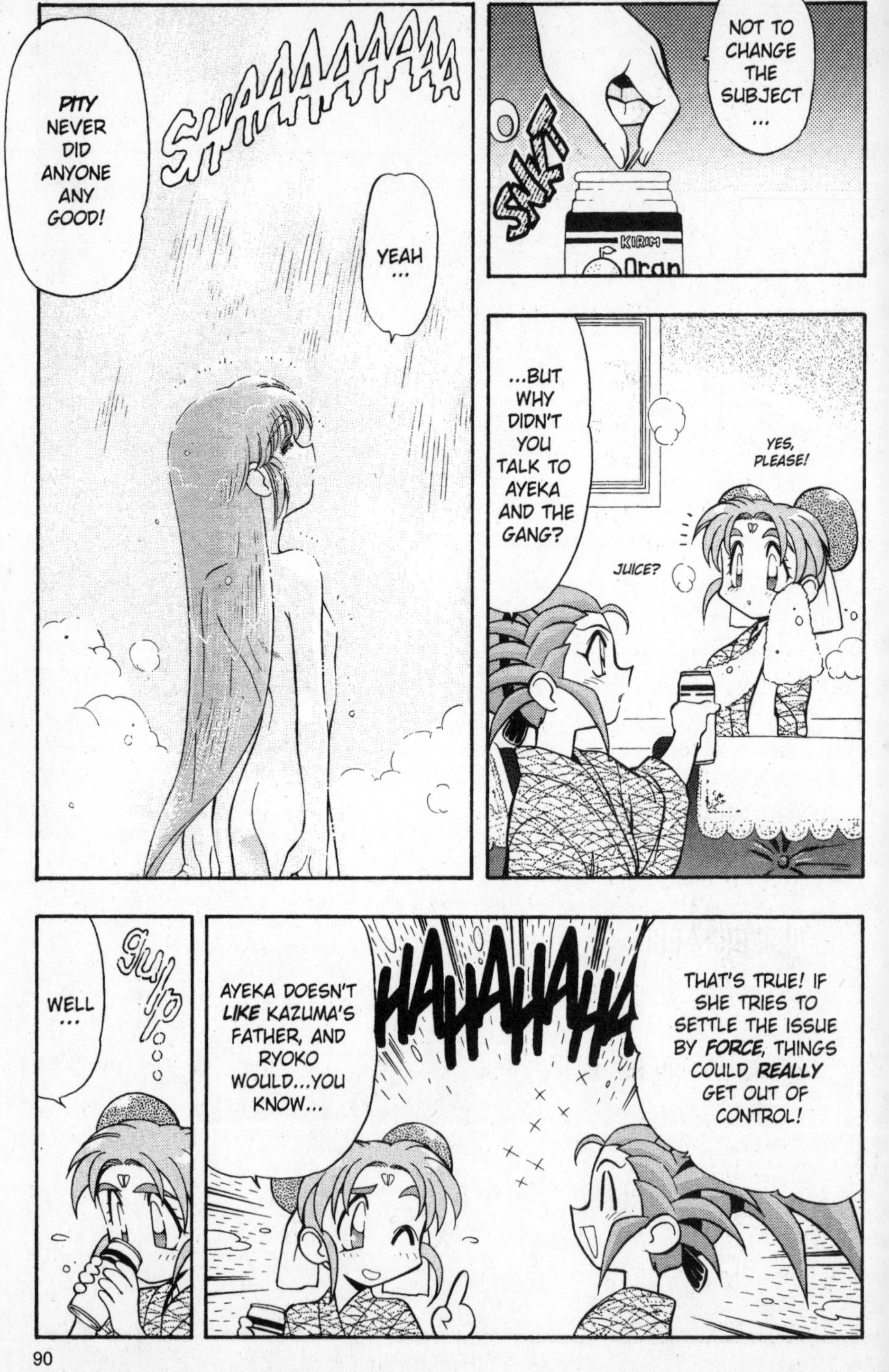
PITY NEVER DID ANYONE ANY GOOD!
SHAAAAAAAA
YEAH ...
NOT TO CHANGE THE SUBJECT ...
SNKT
KIRIM
Oran
...BUT WHY DIDN'T YOU TALK TO AYEKA AND THE GANG?
JUICE?
YES, PLEASE!
WELL ...
gulp
AYEKA DOESN'T LIKE KAZUMA'S FATHER, AND RYOKO WOULD...YOU KNOW...
HAHAHAHA
THAT'S TRUE! IF SHE TRIES TO SETTLE THE ISSUE BY FORCE, THINGS COULD REALLY GET OUT OF CONTROL!

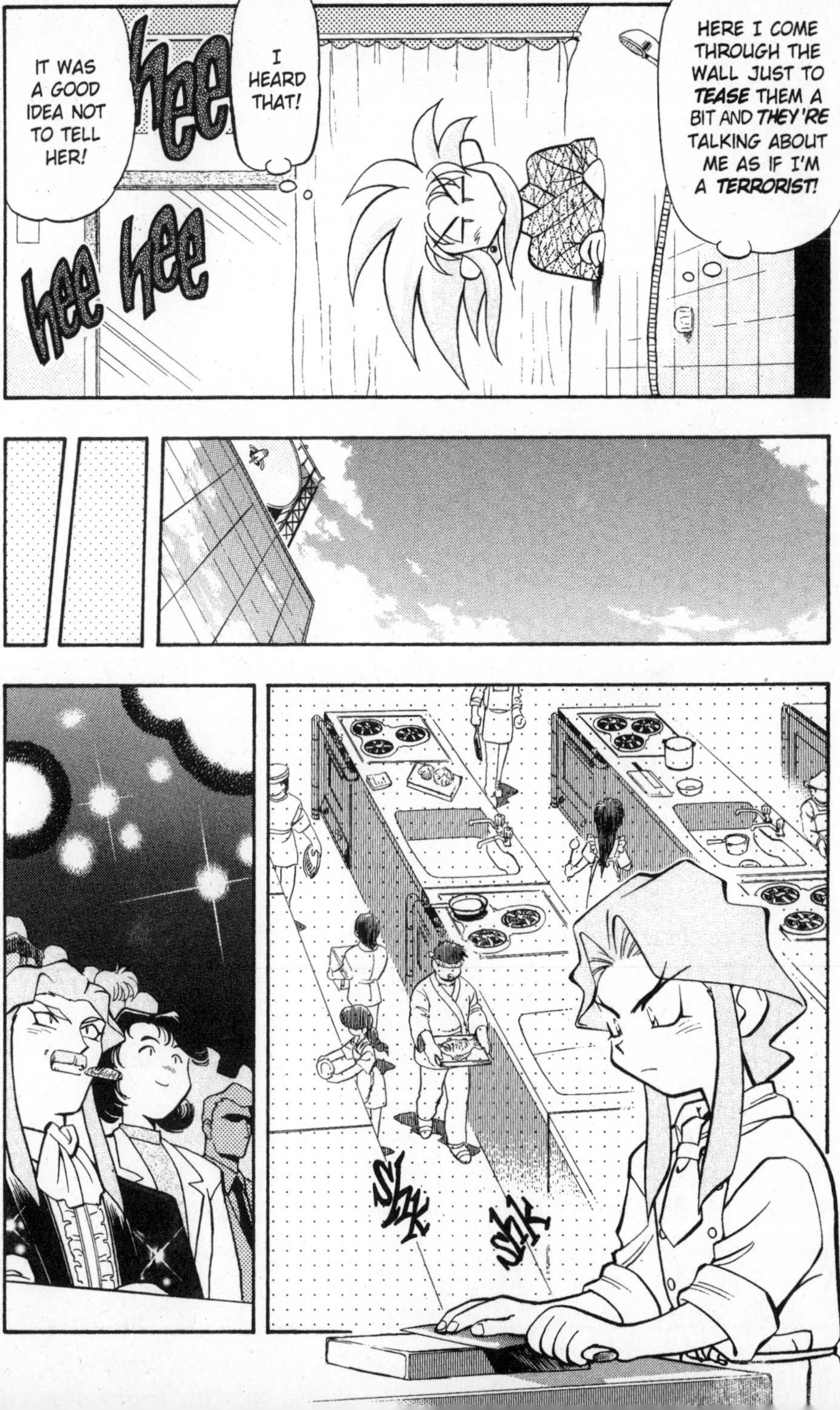
hee
hee hee
IT WAS A GOOD IDEA NOT TO TELL HER!
I HEARD THAT!
HERE I COME THROUGH THE WALL JUST TO TEASE THEM A BIT AND THEY'RE TALKING ABOUT ME AS IF I'M A TERRORIST!
shk
shk

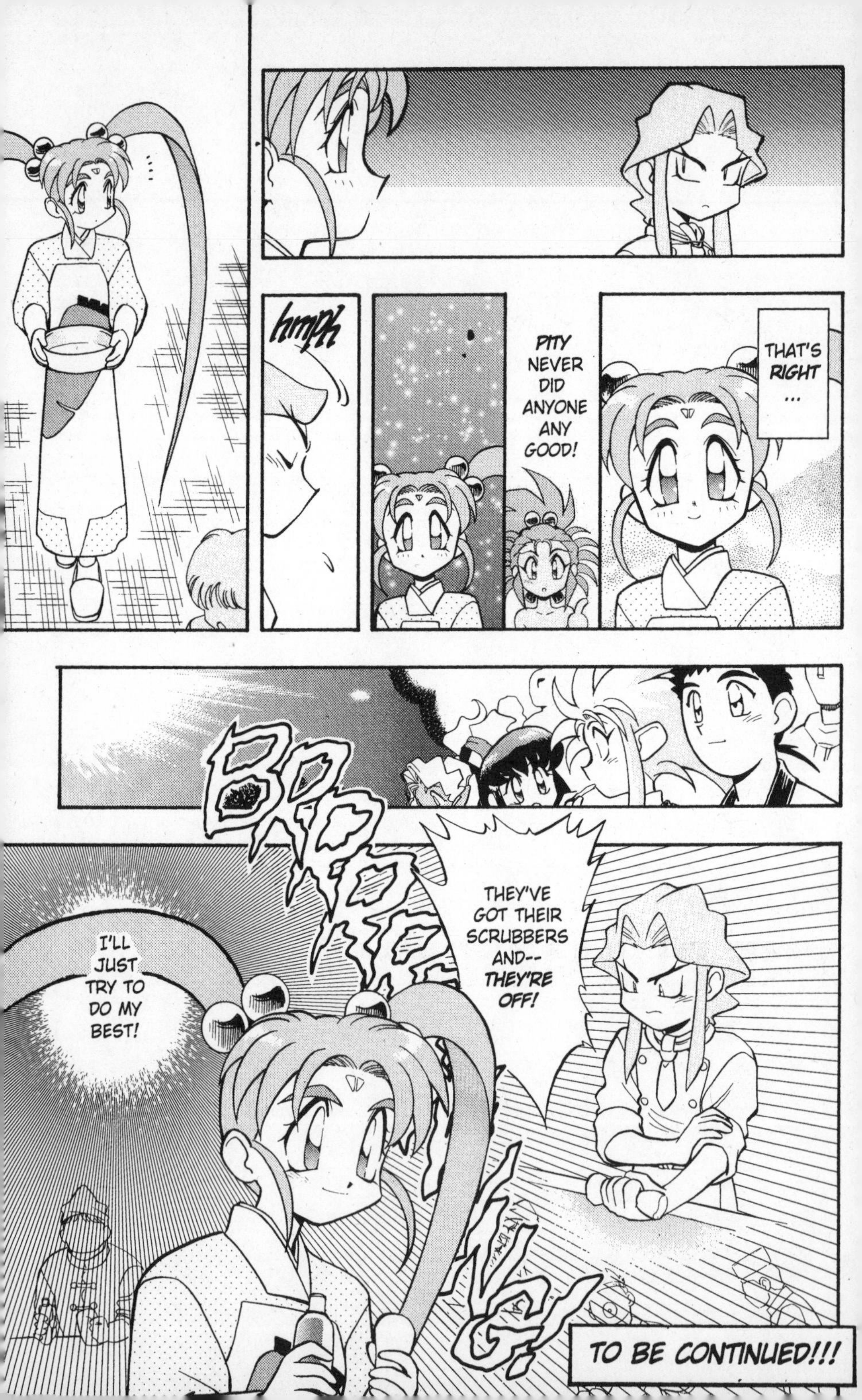
...
hmph
PITY NEVER DID ANYONE ANY GOOD!
THAT'S RIGHT ...
BOOM
THEY'VE GOT THEIR SCRUBBERS AND-- THEY'RE OFF!
I'LL JUST TRY TO DO MY BEST!
TO BE CONTINUED!!!

Tales of Tenchi #5:
THE BLAME GAME

AND THE GRADE SCHOOL COOKING CHAMPIONSHIP HAS STARTED! FIRST UP IS THE "DISHWASHING RACE"--A BRAND NEW EVENT FOR US!

BRRRING

OUR COMMENTARY, AS YOU KNOW, IS BY MASTER CHEF HATTARI. SO, WHAT DO YOU THINK OF THIS MATCH?

THE ONE TO WATCH IS DEFINITELY THE CURRENT CHAMPION FOR TWO YEARS RUNNING, KAGATO KAZUMA.

WILL HE PULL OFF A *THIRD* WIN IN A ROW-- A FEAT *UNEQUALED*? I THINK IT COULD HAPPEN!

OH, SASAMI ...GOOD LUCK!

HMPH. WASHING DISHES-- SO... BASIC.

WE DIDN'T TRAIN HIM AS A *DISH BOY*!

GOOD LUCK, YOUNG MASTER!

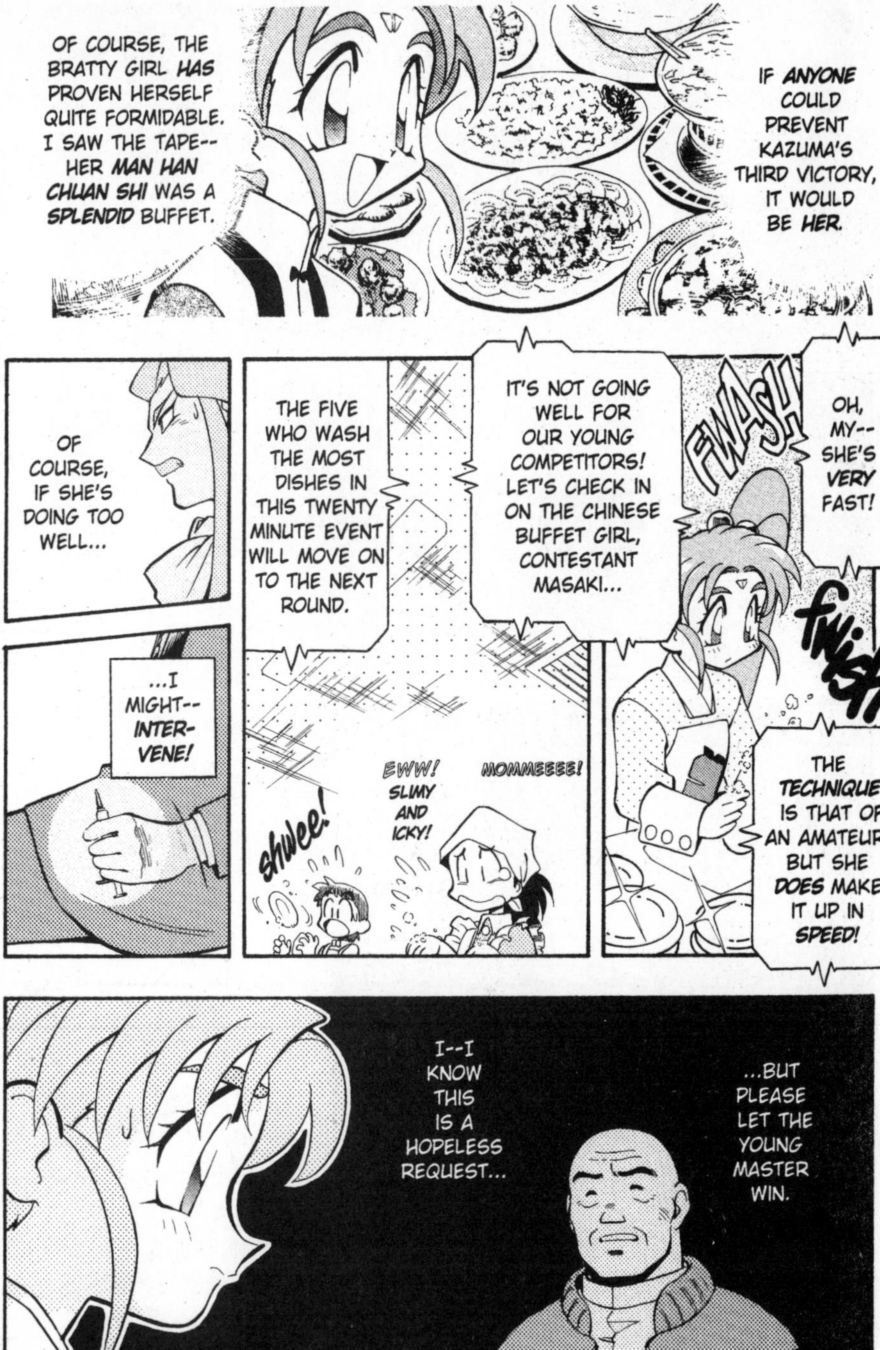

OF COURSE, THE BRATTY GIRL HAS PROVEN HERSELF QUITE FORMIDABLE. I SAW THE TAPE-- HER MAN HAN CHUAN SHI WAS A SPLENDID BUFFET.
IF ANYONE COULD PREVENT KAZUMA'S THIRD VICTORY, IT WOULD BE HER.
OF COURSE, IF SHE'S DOING TOO WELL...
...I MIGHT-- INTERVENE!
THE FIVE WHO WASH THE MOST DISHES IN THIS TWENTY MINUTE EVENT WILL MOVE ON TO THE NEXT ROUND.
IT'S NOT GOING WELL FOR OUR YOUNG COMPETITORS! LET'S CHECK IN ON THE CHINESE BUFFET GIRL, CONTESTANT MASAKI...
EWW! SLIMY AND ICKY!
MOMMEEEE!
shwee!
FWASH
OH, MY-- SHE'S VERY FAST!
fwish
THE TECHNIQUE IS THAT OF AN AMATEUR, BUT SHE DOES MAKE IT UP IN SPEED!
I--I KNOW THIS IS A HOPELESS REQUEST...
...BUT PLEASE LET THE YOUNG MASTER WIN.

SKURRK

......

WH-- WHAT'S WRONG ...? IS SHE OKAY?

......

SASAMI...

NO MATTER **WHAT** HAPPENS, I'M GOING TO TO DO MY BEST.

THAT'S WHAT I DECIDED...

...NO.

I **CAN'T** SLACK OFF HERE.

!!

WHA ...!

WHAT **SPEED!**

I CAN EVEN SEE THE **SOUND EFFECT** ...!

fwish

fwash

fwish

fwash

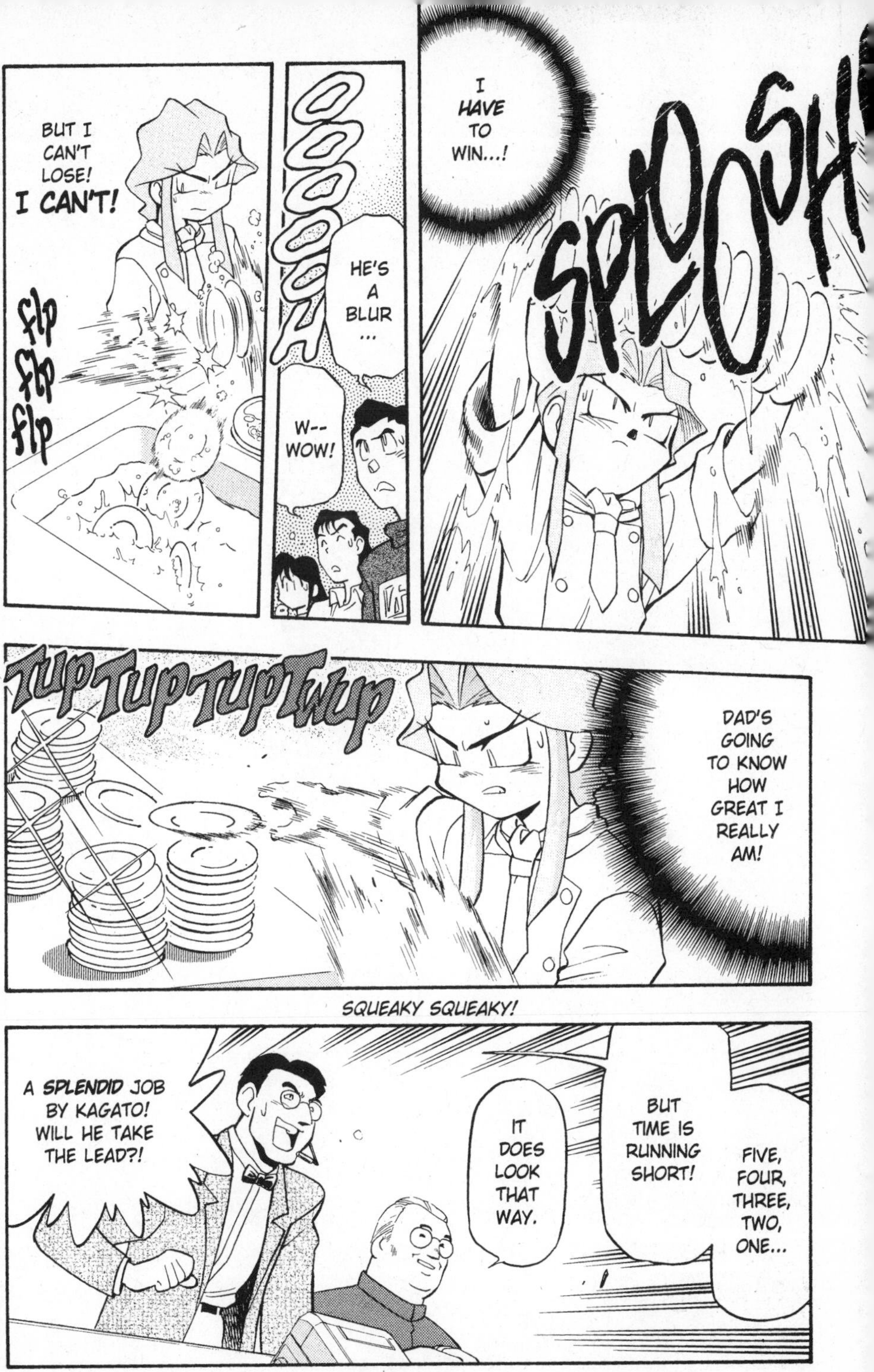
BUT I CAN'T LOSE! I CAN'T!
flp flp flp
HE'S A BLUR...
W-- WOW!
I HAVE TO WIN...!
SPLOOSH
TUP TUP TUP TWUP
DAD'S GOING TO KNOW HOW GREAT I REALLY AM!
SQUEAKY SQUEAKY!
A SPLENDID JOB BY KAGATO! WILL HE TAKE THE LEAD?!
IT DOES LOOK THAT WAY.
BUT TIME IS RUNNING SHORT!
FIVE, FOUR, THREE, TWO, ONE...

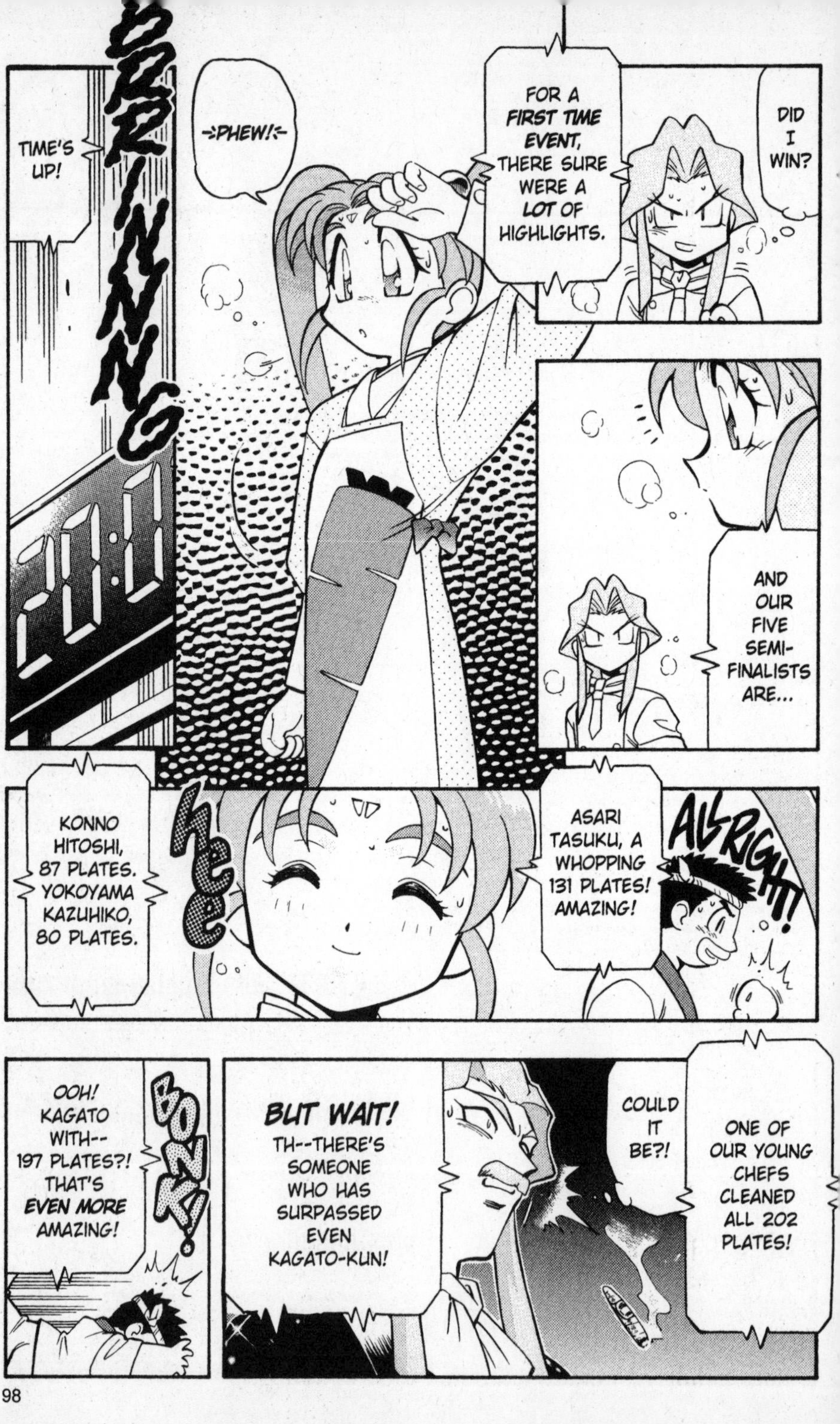

TIME'S UP!
BZZINNNG
-PHEW!-
FOR A FIRST TIME EVENT, THERE SURE WERE A LOT OF HIGHLIGHTS.
DID I WIN?
AND OUR FIVE SEMI-FINALISTS ARE...
KONNO HITOSHI, 87 PLATES. YOKOYAMA KAZUHIKO, 80 PLATES.
hee
ASARI TASUKU, A WHOPPING 131 PLATES! AMAZING!
ALRIGHT!
OOH! KAGATO WITH-- 197 PLATES?! THAT'S EVEN MORE AMAZING!
BONK!
BUT WAIT! TH--THERE'S SOMEONE WHO HAS SURPASSED EVEN KAGATO-KUN!
COULD IT BE?!
ONE OF OUR YOUNG CHEFS CLEANED ALL 202 PLATES!

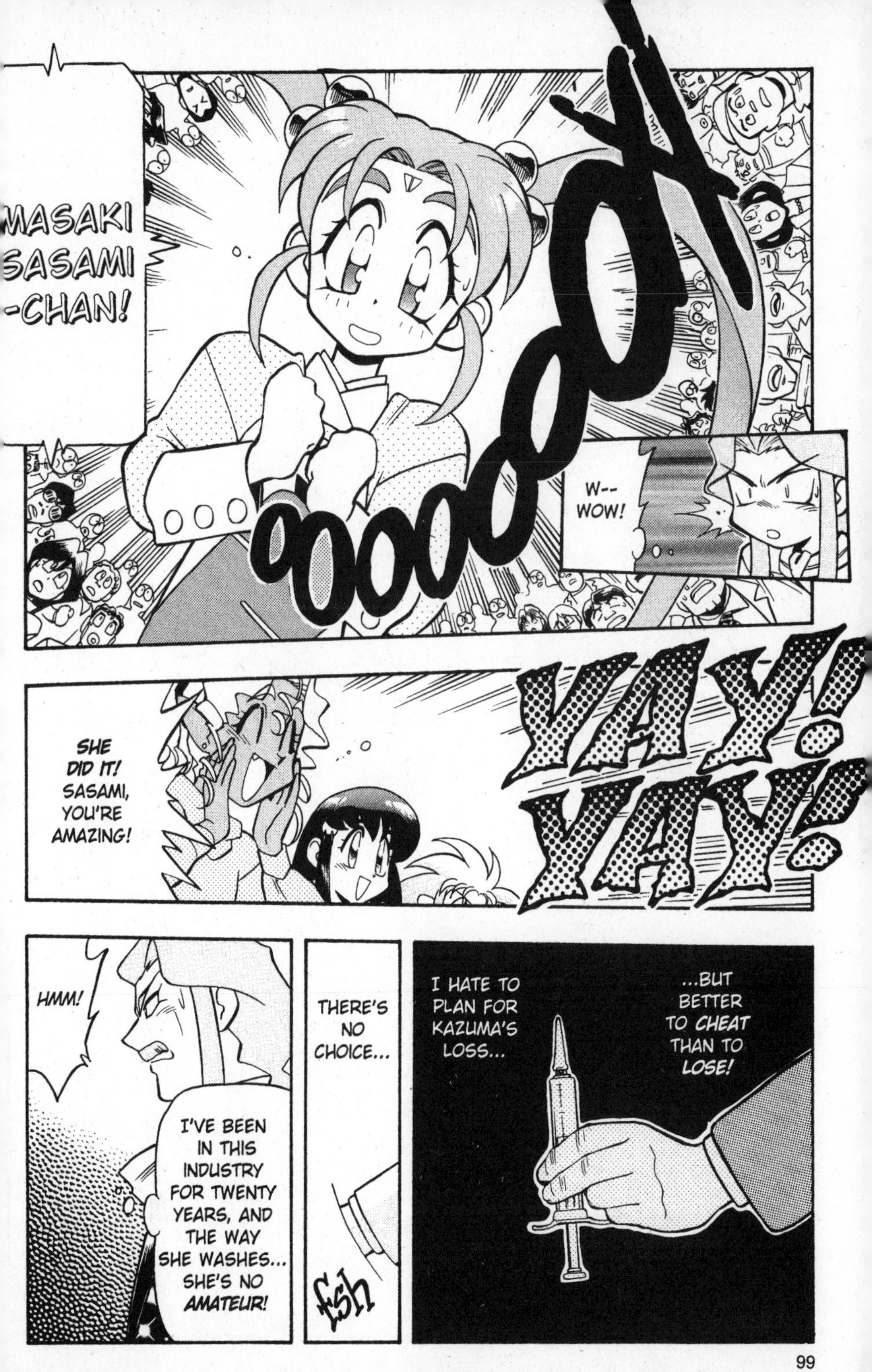
MASAKI SASAMI -CHAN!
OOOOOOOH!
W-- WOW!
SHE DID IT! SASAMI, YOU'RE AMAZING!
YAY! YAY!
HMM!
I'VE BEEN IN THIS INDUSTRY FOR TWENTY YEARS, AND THE WAY SHE WASHES... SHE'S NO AMATEUR!
THERE'S NO CHOICE...
fsh
I HATE TO PLAN FOR KAZUMA'S LOSS...
...BUT BETTER TO CHEAT THAN TO LOSE!

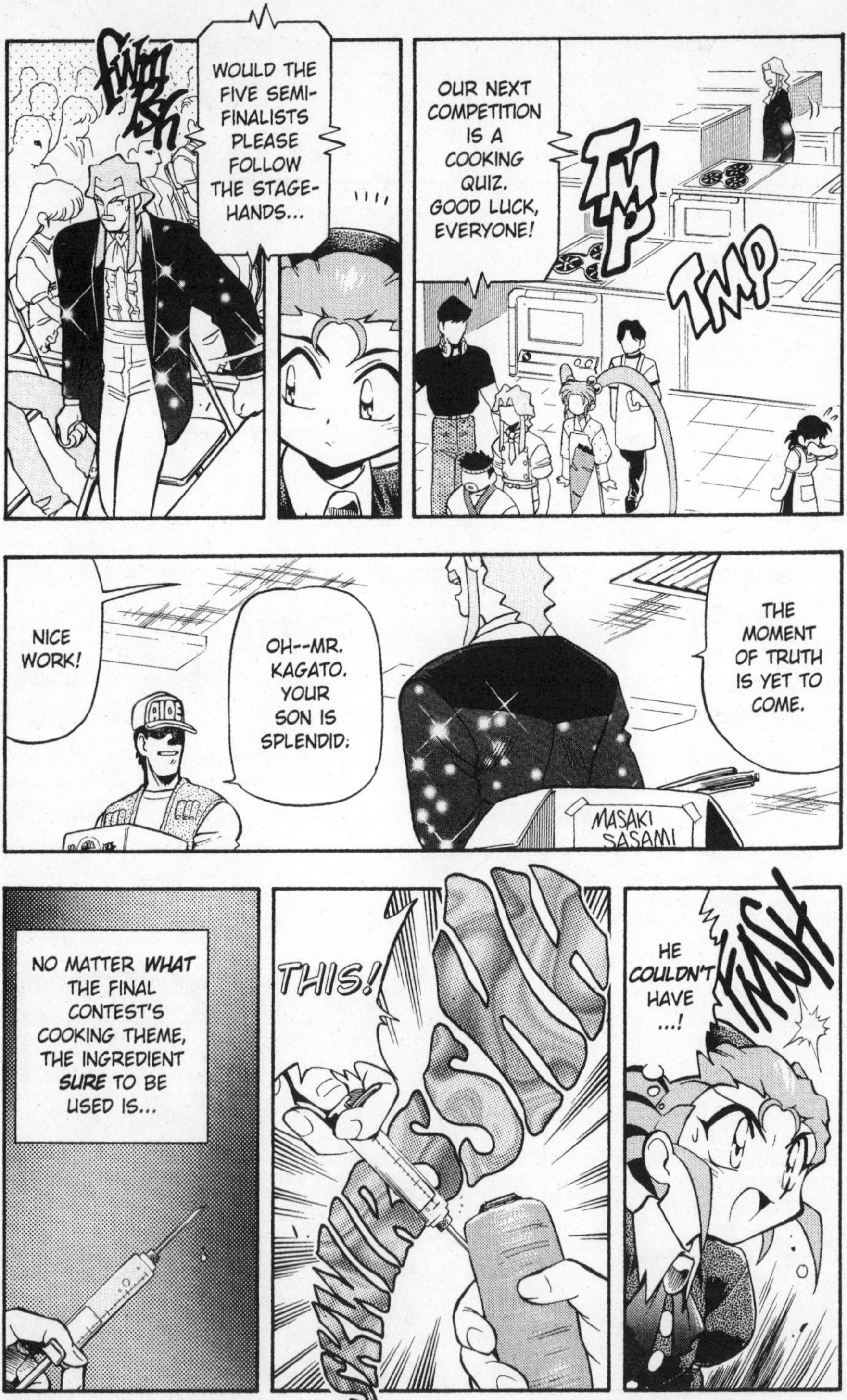
FWMISH
WOULD THE FIVE SEMI-FINALISTS PLEASE FOLLOW THE STAGE-HANDS...
OUR NEXT COMPETITION IS A COOKING QUIZ. GOOD LUCK, EVERYONE!
TMP
TMP
NICE WORK!
OH--MR. KAGATO. YOUR SON IS SPLENDID.
THE MOMENT OF TRUTH IS YET TO COME.
MASAKI SASAMI
NO MATTER WHAT THE FINAL CONTEST'S COOKING THEME, THE INGREDIENT SURE TO BE USED IS...
THIS!
HE COULDN'T HAVE ...!
TWISH

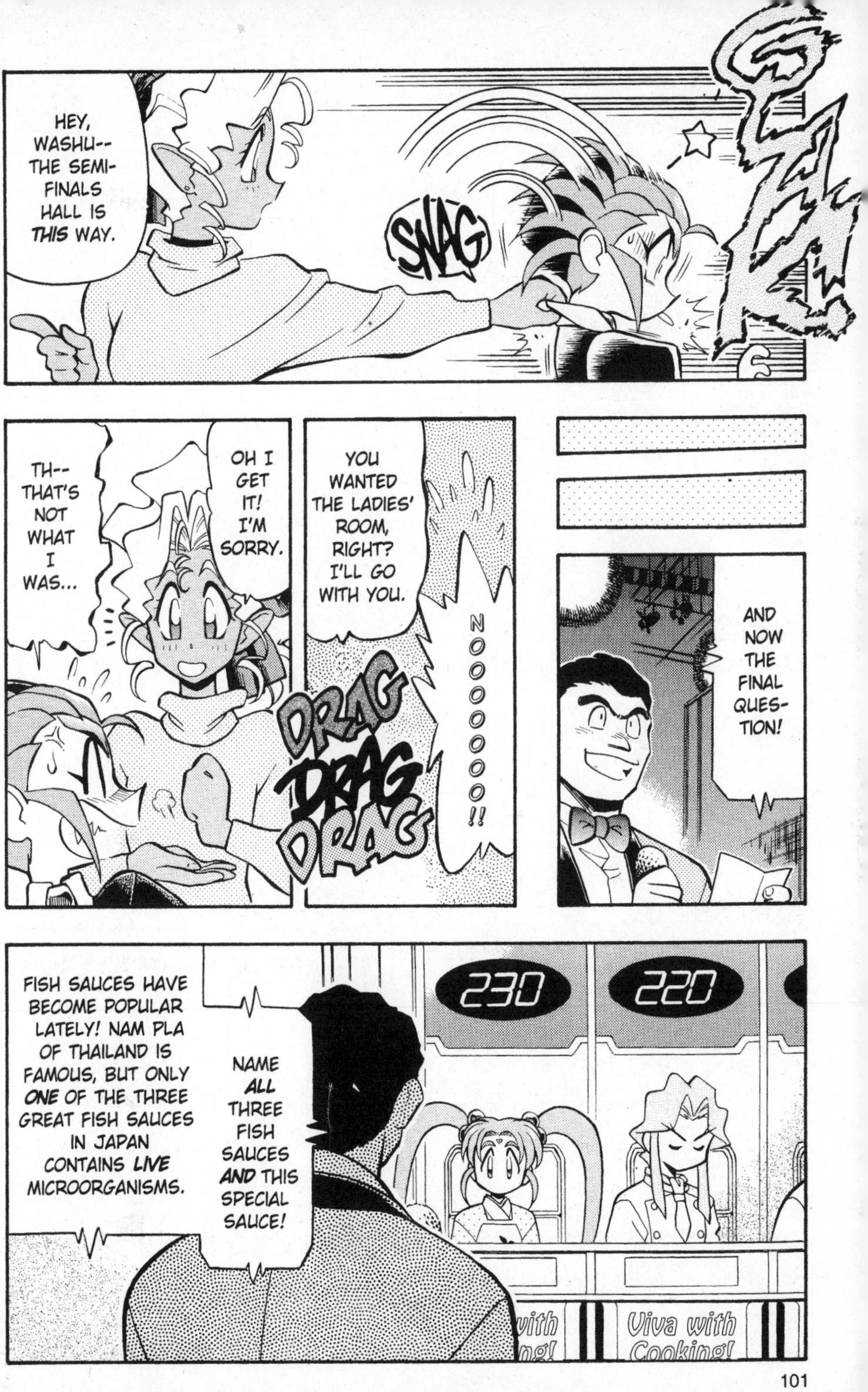

HEY, WASHU-- THE SEMI-FINALS HALL IS THIS WAY.
SNAG
TH-- THAT'S NOT WHAT I WAS...
OH I GET IT! I'M SORRY.
YOU WANTED THE LADIES' ROOM, RIGHT? I'LL GO WITH YOU.
DRAG DRAG DRAG
NOOOOOOOOO!!
AND NOW THE FINAL QUES-TION!
FISH SAUCES HAVE BECOME POPULAR LATELY! NAM PLA OF THAILAND IS FAMOUS, BUT ONLY ONE OF THE THREE GREAT FISH SAUCES IN JAPAN CONTAINS LIVE MICROORGANISMS.
NAME ALL THREE FISH SAUCES AND THIS SPECIAL SAUCE!
230
220
Viva with Cooking!

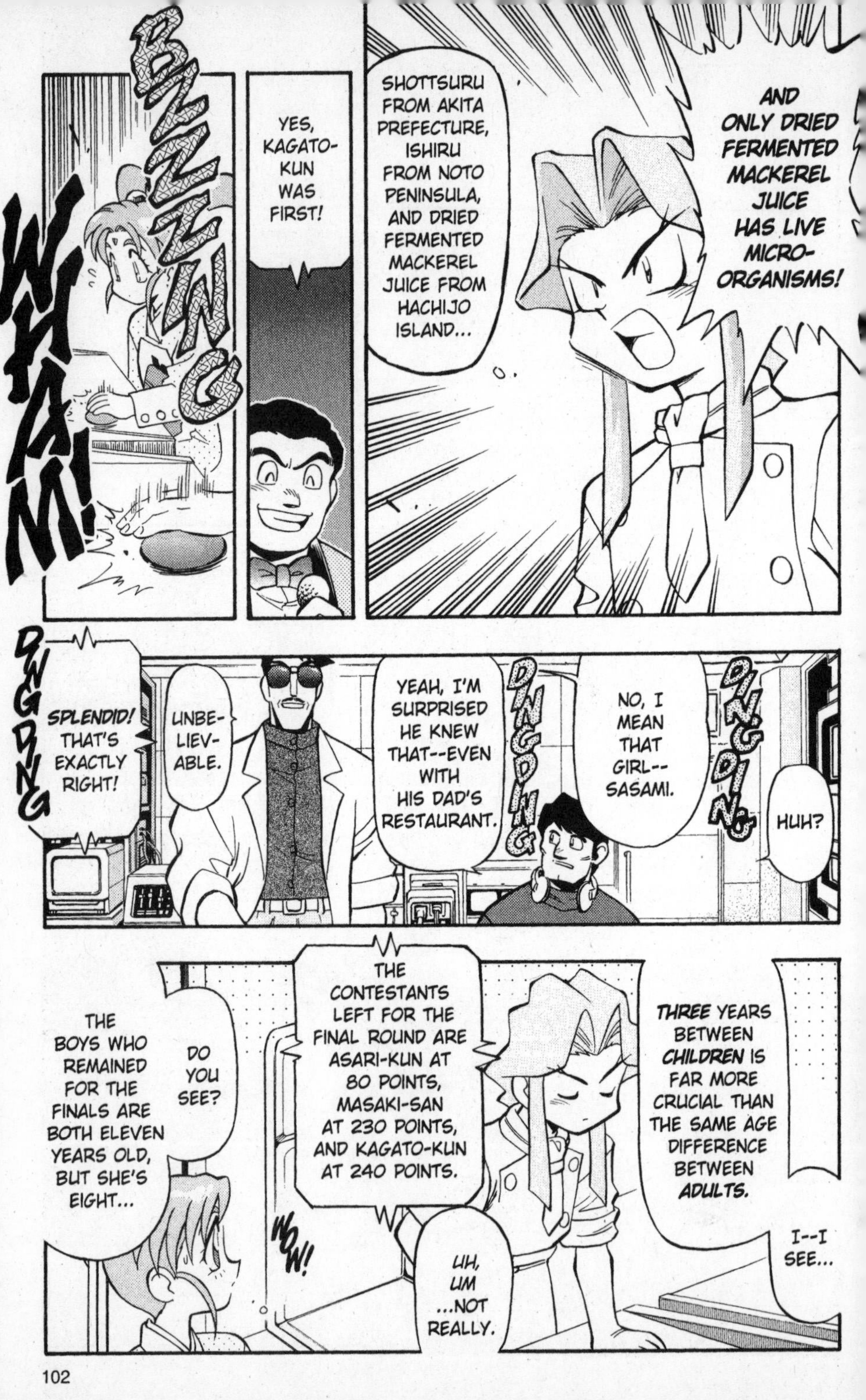
BONNNG
WHAM!
YES, KAGATO-KUN WAS FIRST!
SHOTTSURU FROM AKITA PREFECTURE, ISHIRU FROM NOTO PENINSULA, AND DRIED FERMENTED MACKEREL JUICE FROM HACHIJO ISLAND...
AND ONLY DRIED FERMENTED MACKEREL JUICE HAS LIVE MICRO-ORGANISMS!
DING DING
SPLENDID! THAT'S EXACTLY RIGHT!
UNBE-LIEV-ABLE.
YEAH, I'M SURPRISED HE KNEW THAT--EVEN WITH HIS DAD'S RESTAURANT.
DING DING
NO, I MEAN THAT GIRL--SASAMI.
DING DING
HUH?
THE BOYS WHO REMAINED FOR THE FINALS ARE BOTH ELEVEN YEARS OLD, BUT SHE'S EIGHT...
DO YOU SEE?
THE CONTESTANTS LEFT FOR THE FINAL ROUND ARE ASARI-KUN AT 80 POINTS, MASAKI-SAN AT 230 POINTS, AND KAGATO-KUN AT 240 POINTS.
WOW!
UH, UM ...NOT REALLY.
THREE YEARS BETWEEN CHILDREN IS FAR MORE CRUCIAL THAN THE SAME AGE DIFFERENCE BETWEEN ADULTS.
I--I SEE...

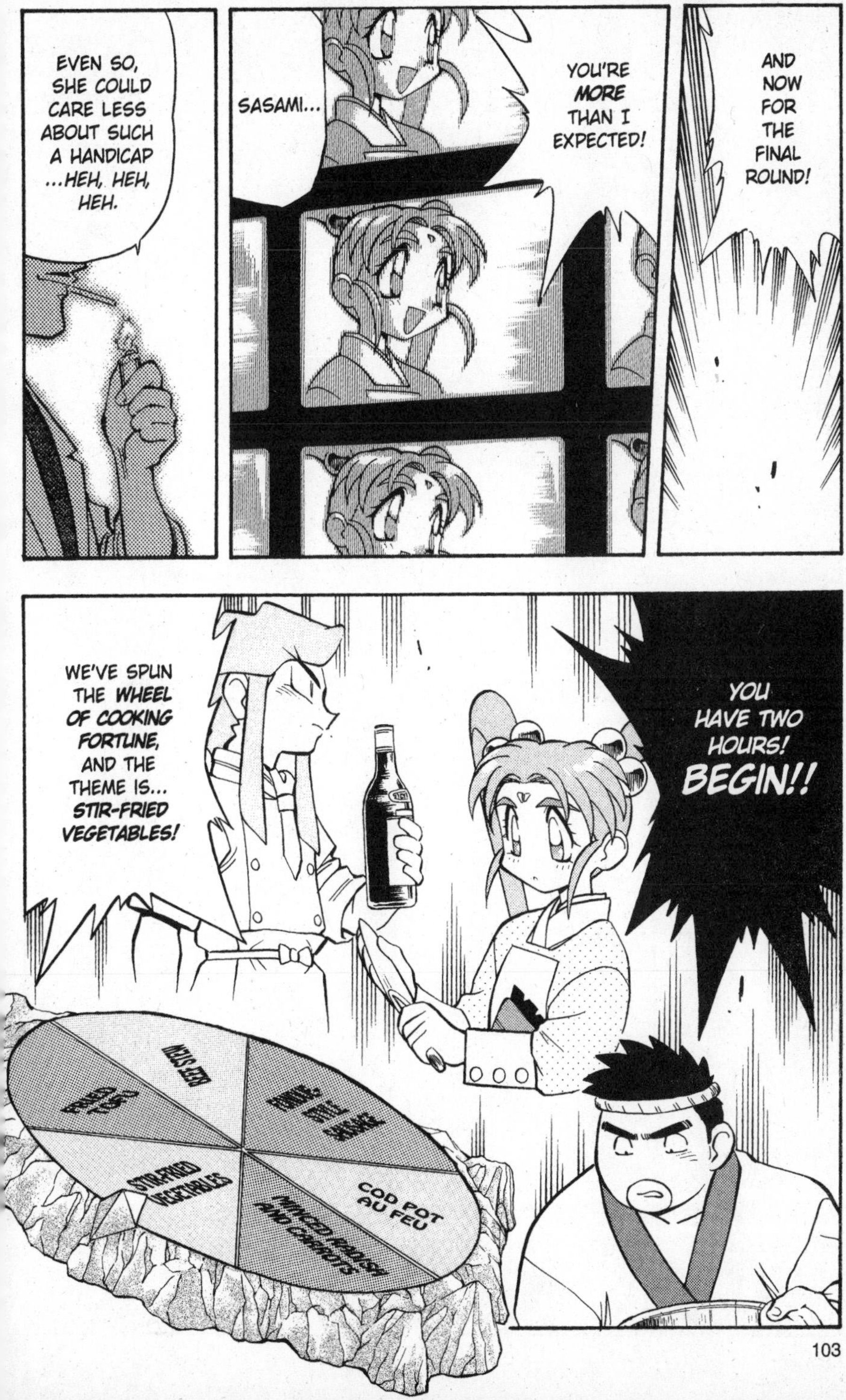
EVEN SO, SHE COULD CARE LESS ABOUT SUCH A HANDICAP ...HEH, HEH, HEH.
SASAMI...
YOU'RE MORE THAN I EXPECTED!
AND NOW FOR THE FINAL ROUND!
WE'VE SPUN THE WHEEL OF COOKING FORTUNE, AND THE THEME IS... STIR-FRIED VEGETABLES!
YOU HAVE TWO HOURS! BEGIN!!
BEEF STEW
FRIED TOFU
STIR-FRIED VEGETABLES
MINCED RADISH AND CARROTS
COD POT AU FEU

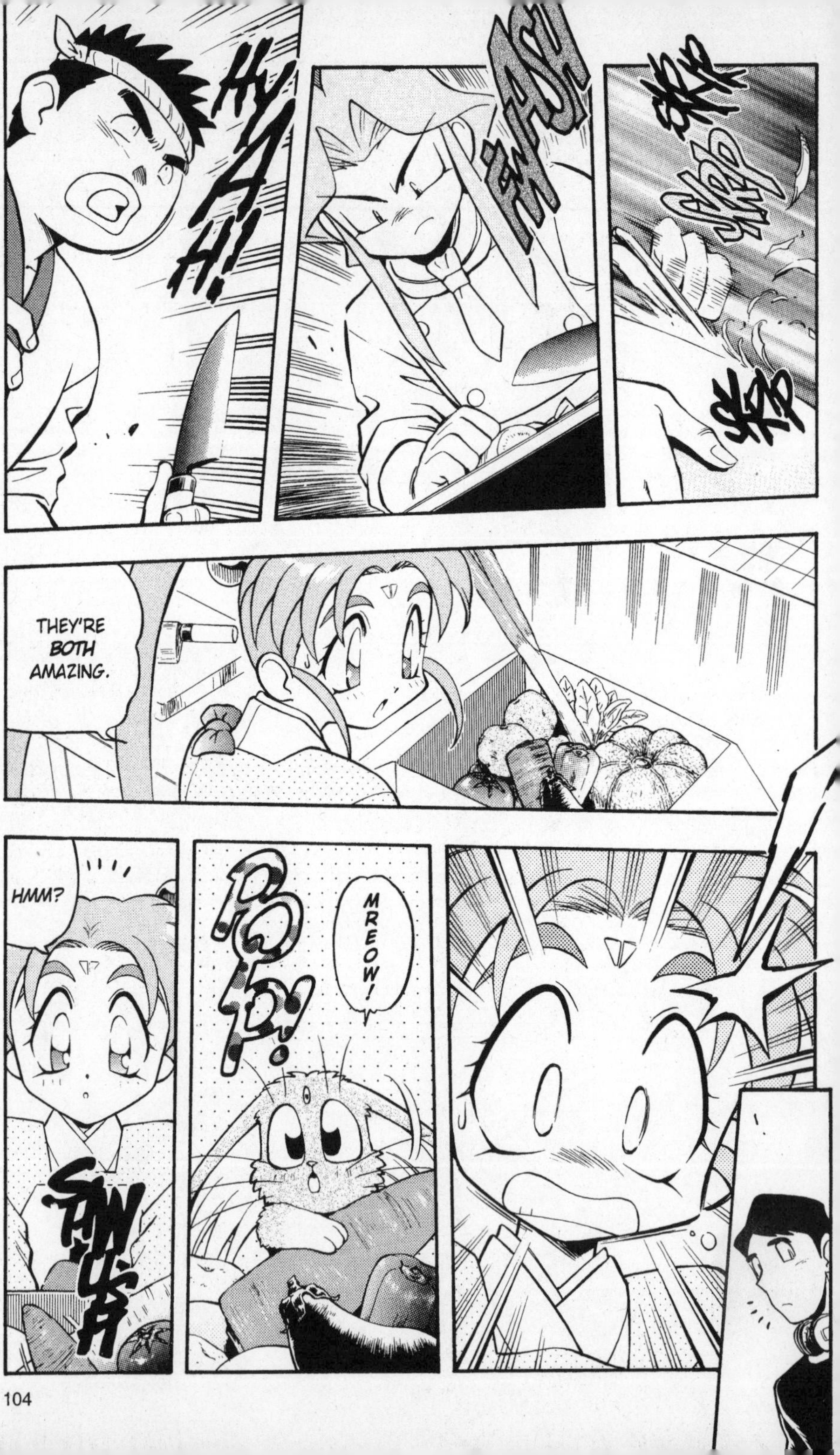
HYAAH!!
SKRP
SKRP
THEY'RE BOTH AMAZING.
HMM?
MREOW!

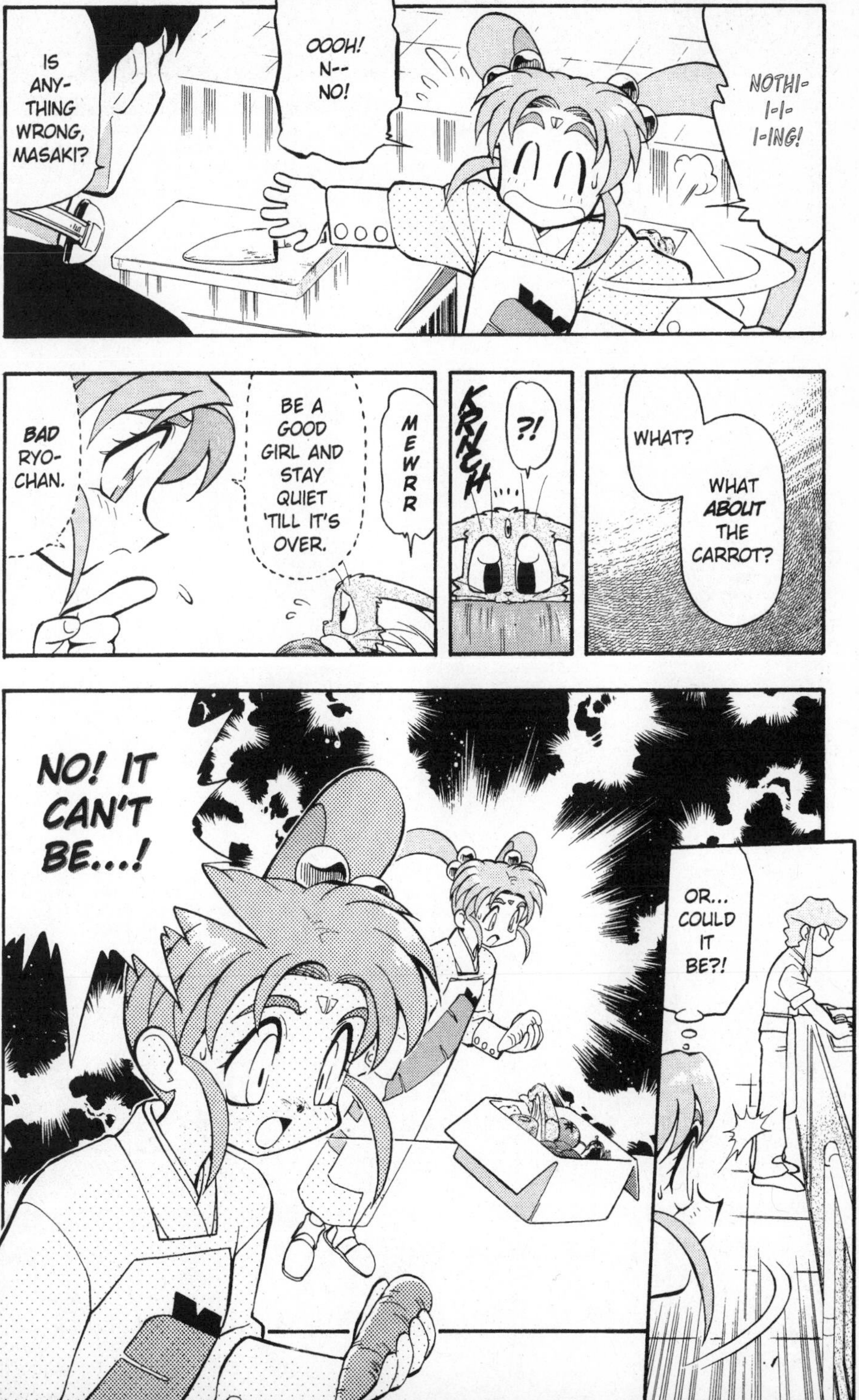
IS ANY-THING WRONG, MASAKI?
OOOH! N-- NO!
NOTHI-I-I-I-ING!
BAD RYO-CHAN.
BE A GOOD GIRL AND STAY QUIET 'TILL IT'S OVER.
MEWRR
KRNCH
?!
WHAT?
WHAT ABOUT THE CARROT?
NO! IT CAN'T BE...!
OR... COULD IT BE?!

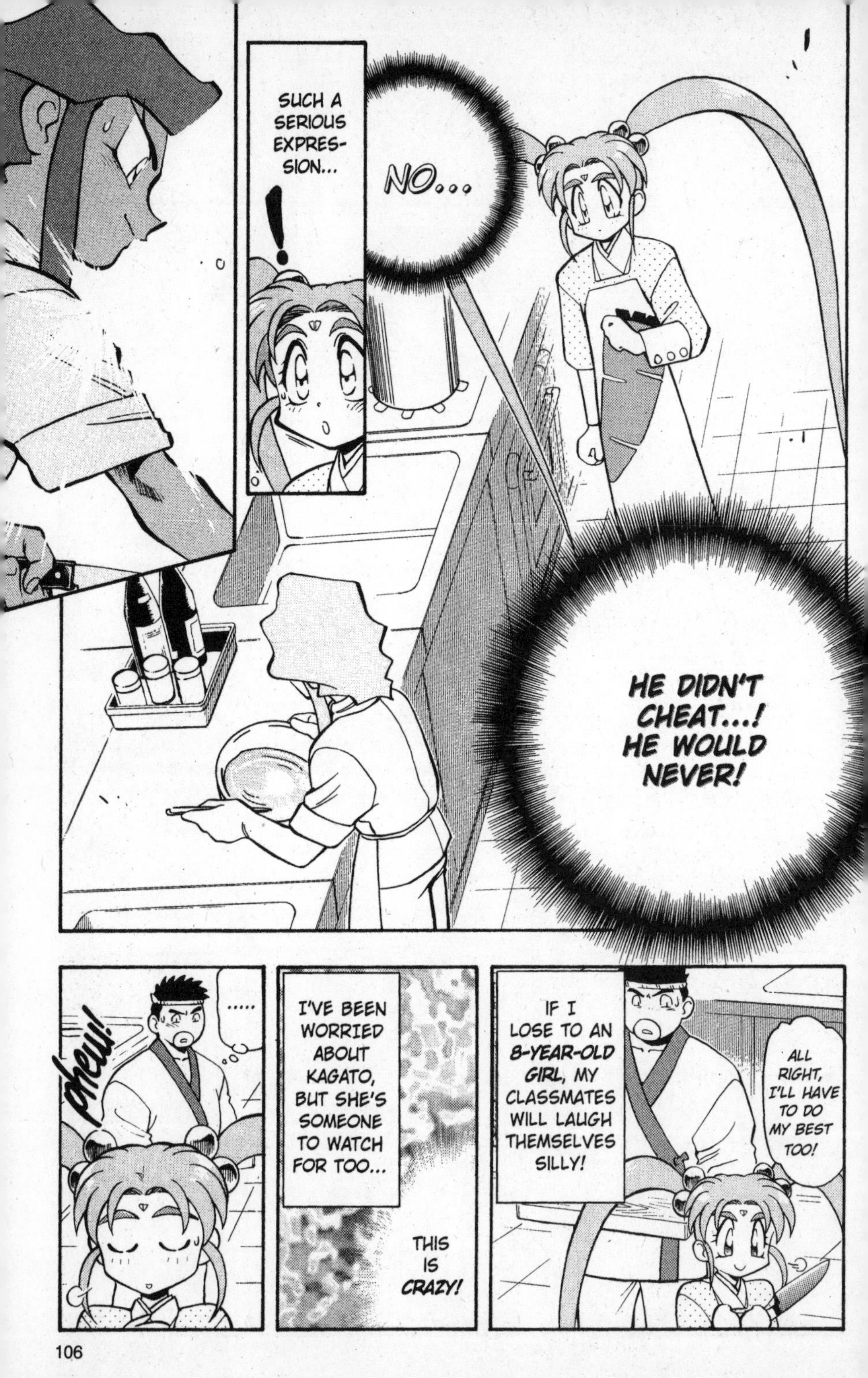

SUCH A SERIOUS EXPRES-SION...
!
NO...
HE DIDN'T CHEAT...! HE WOULD NEVER!
.....
phew!
I'VE BEEN WORRIED ABOUT KAGATO, BUT SHE'S SOMEONE TO WATCH FOR TOO...
THIS IS CRAZY!
IF I LOSE TO AN 8-YEAR-OLD GIRL, MY CLASSMATES WILL LAUGH THEMSELVES SILLY!
ALL RIGHT, I'LL HAVE TO DO MY BEST TOO!

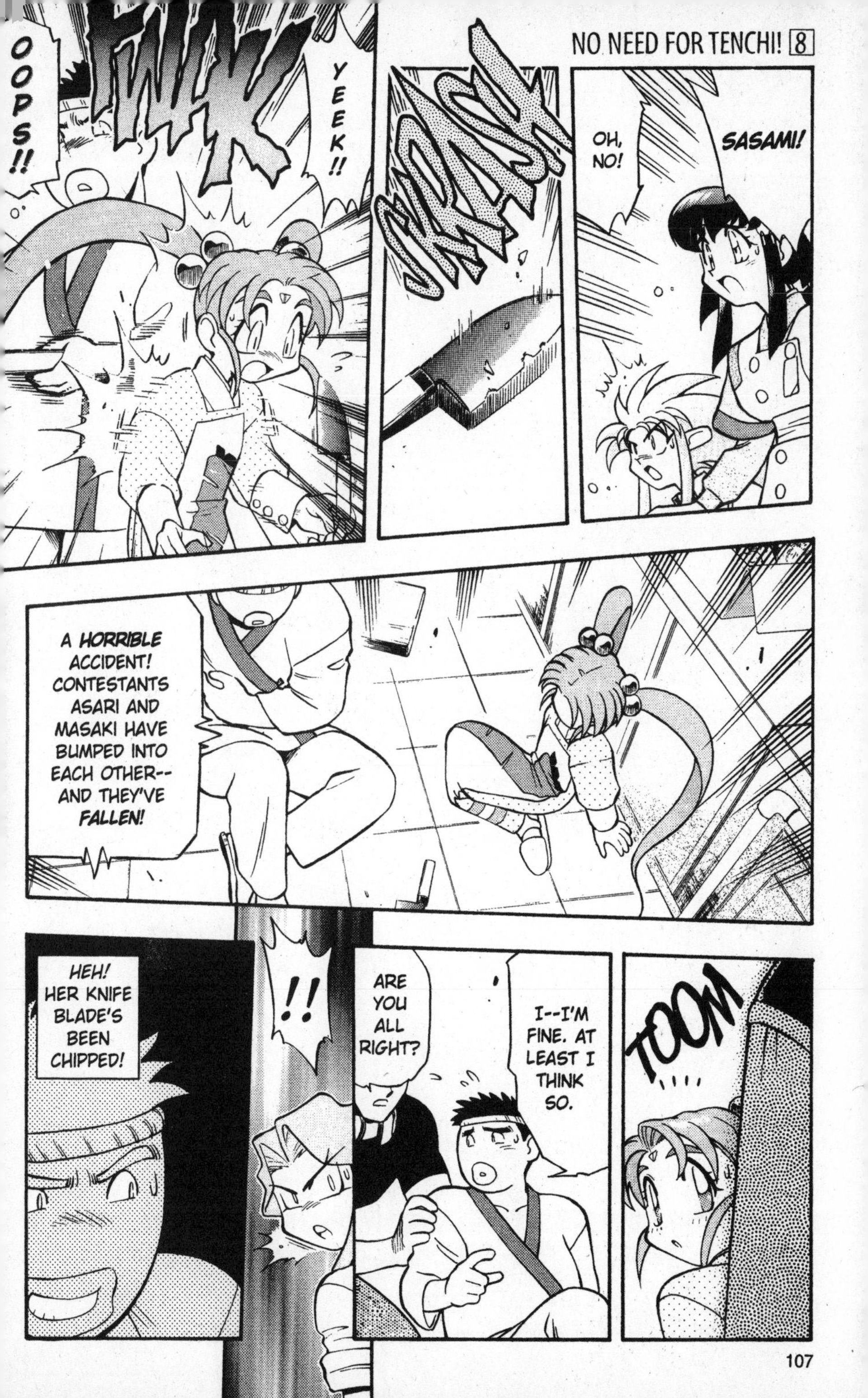
OOPS!!
THWK
YEEK!!
SKRASH
OH, NO!
SASAMI!
A HORRIBLE ACCIDENT! CONTESTANTS ASARI AND MASAKI HAVE BUMPED INTO EACH OTHER--AND THEY'VE FALLEN!
HEH! HER KNIFE BLADE'S BEEN CHIPPED!
!!
ARE YOU ALL RIGHT?
I--I'M FINE. AT LEAST I THINK SO.
TOOM

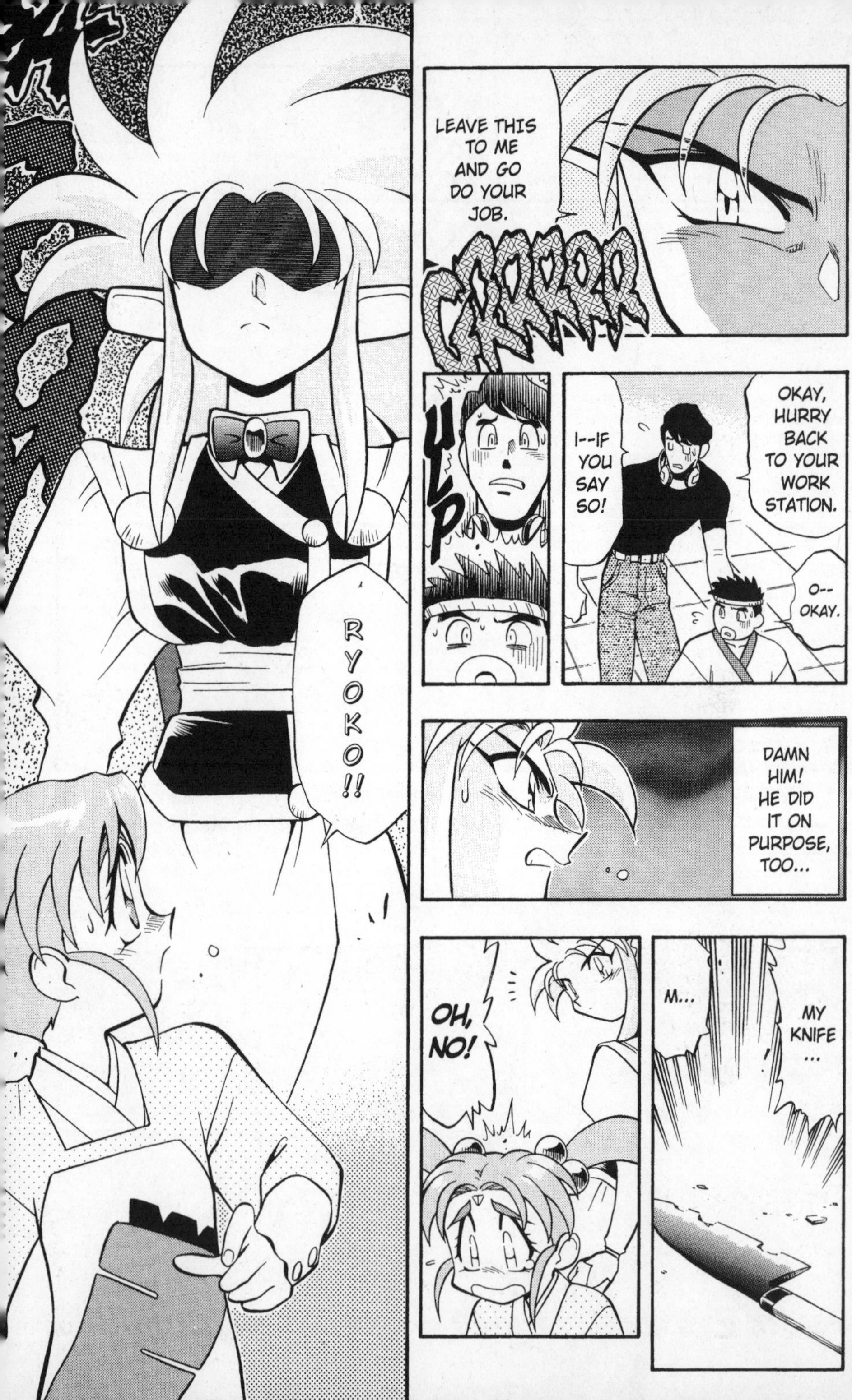
RYOKO!!
LEAVE THIS TO ME AND GO DO YOUR JOB.
GRRRRR
ULP
I--IF YOU SAY SO!
OKAY, HURRY BACK TO YOUR WORK STATION.
O--OKAY.
DAMN HIM! HE DID IT ON PURPOSE, TOO...
OH, NO!
M...
MY KNIFE ...

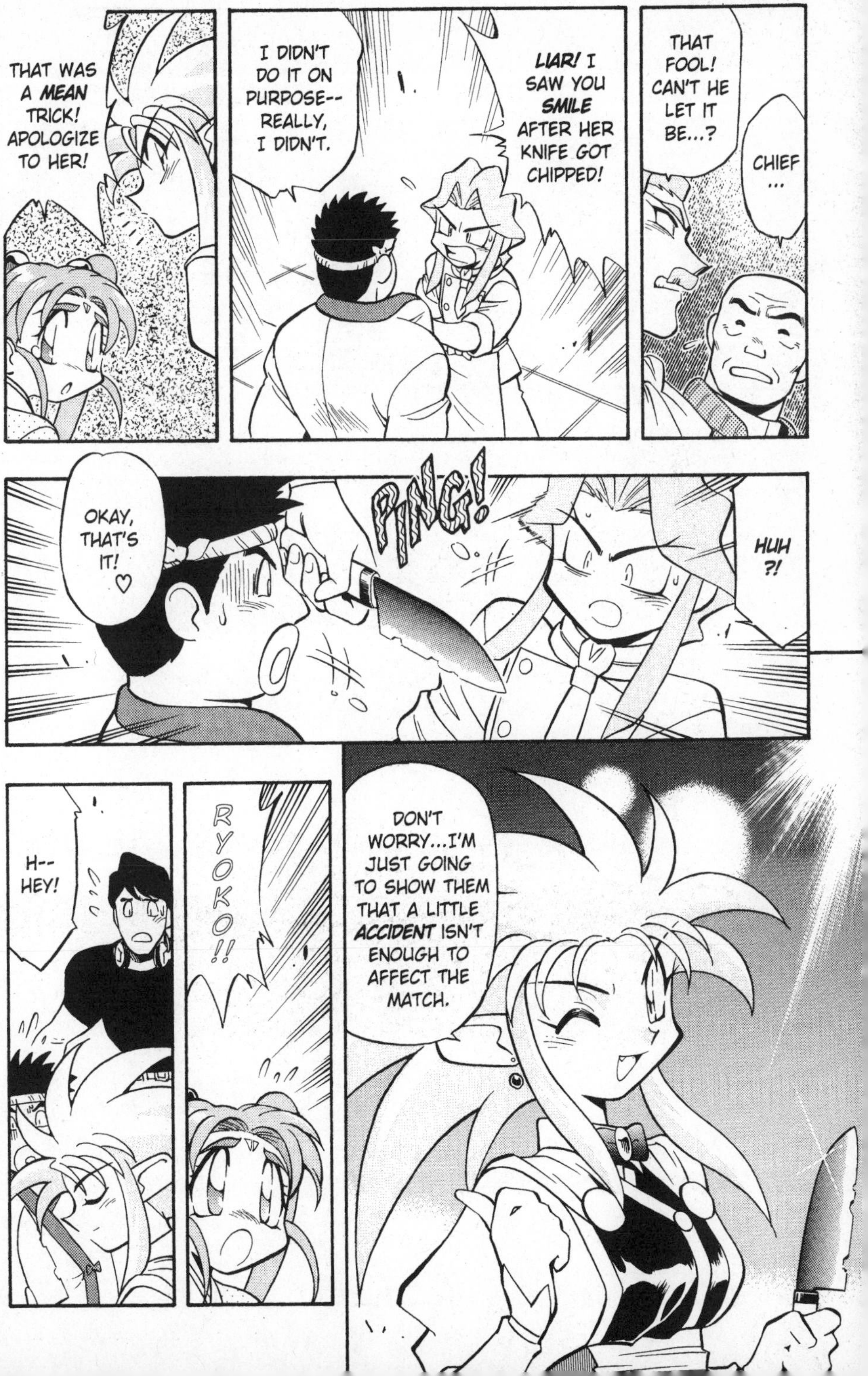
THAT WAS A MEAN TRICK! APOLOGIZE TO HER!
I DIDN'T DO IT ON PURPOSE-- REALLY, I DIDN'T.
LIAR! I SAW YOU SMILE AFTER HER KNIFE GOT CHIPPED!
THAT FOOL! CAN'T HE LET IT BE...?
CHIEF ...
OKAY, THAT'S IT! ♡
PING!
HUH ?!
H-- HEY!
RYOKO!!
DON'T WORRY...I'M JUST GOING TO SHOW THEM THAT A LITTLE ACCIDENT ISN'T ENOUGH TO AFFECT THE MATCH.

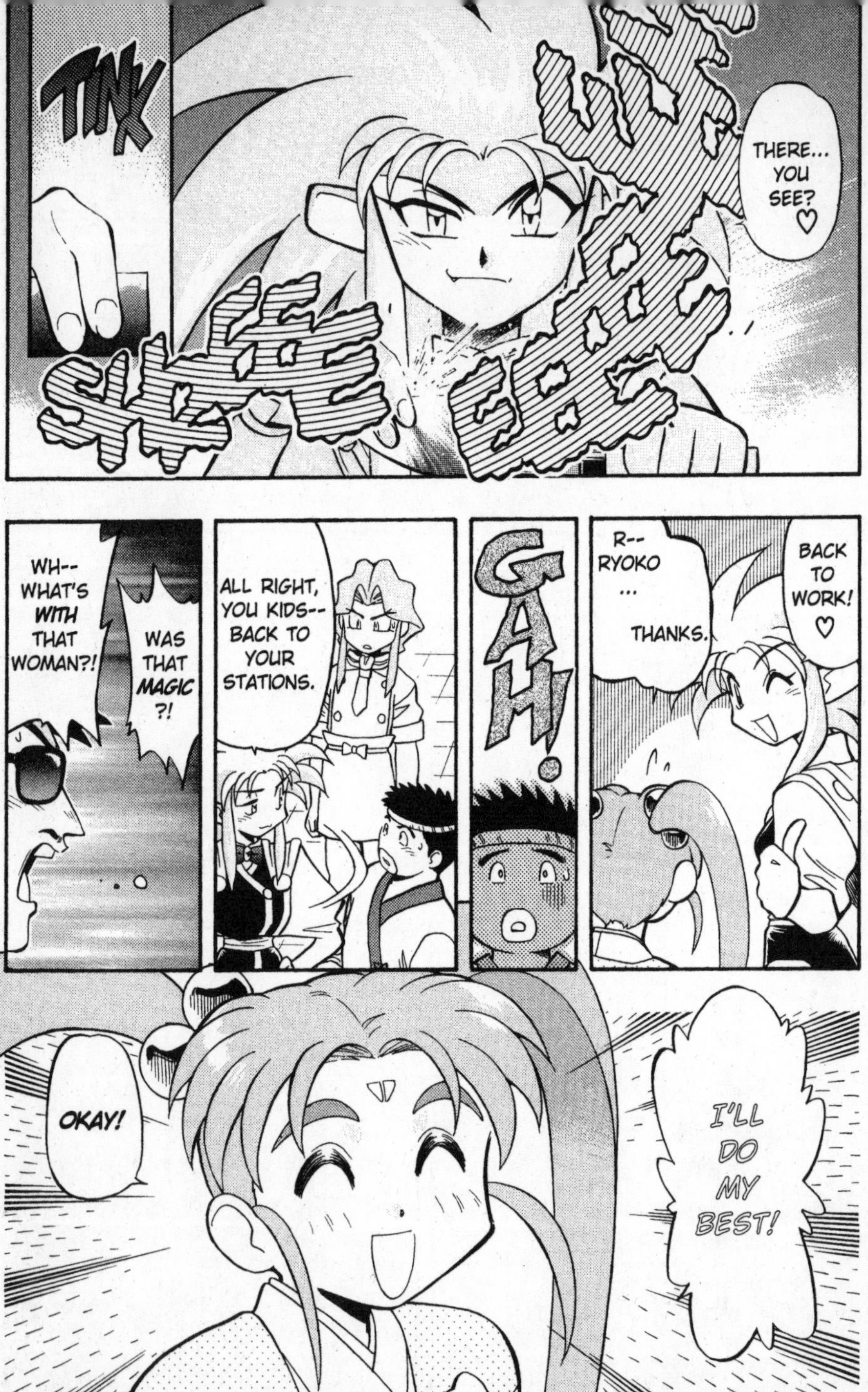
TINK
THERE... YOU SEE? ♡
SHA-SHE
CHA-CHA
WH-- WHAT'S WITH THAT WOMAN?!
WAS THAT MAGIC?!
ALL RIGHT, YOU KIDS-- BACK TO YOUR STATIONS.
GAH!
R-- RYOKO ... THANKS.
BACK TO WORK! ♡
OKAY!
I'LL DO MY BEST!

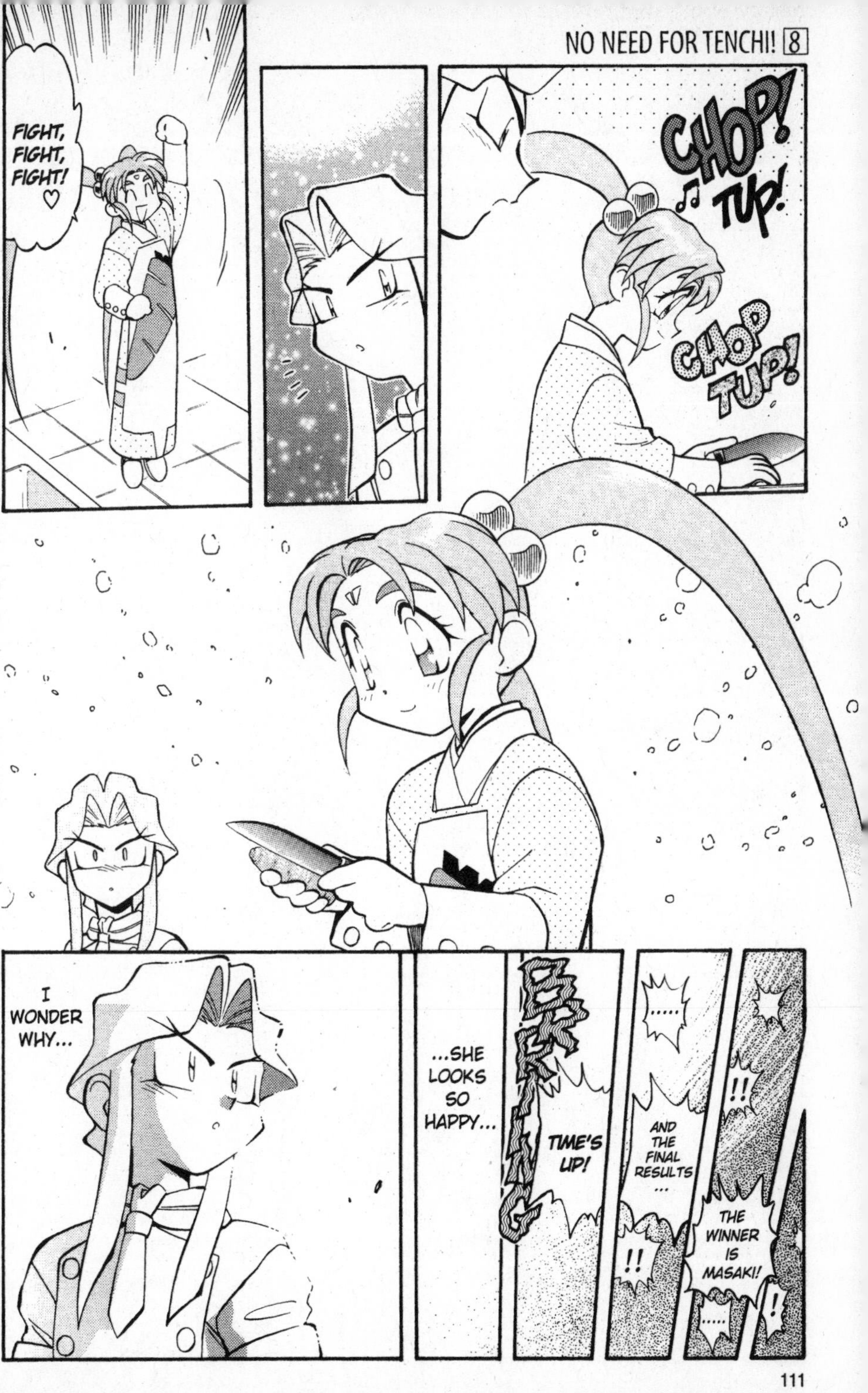
FIGHT, FIGHT, FIGHT! ♡
CHOP! ♫ TUP!
CHOP TUP!
I WONDER WHY...
...SHE LOOKS SO HAPPY...
TIME'S UP!
.....
!!
AND THE FINAL RESULTS ...
!!
THE WINNER IS MASAKI!
.....
!

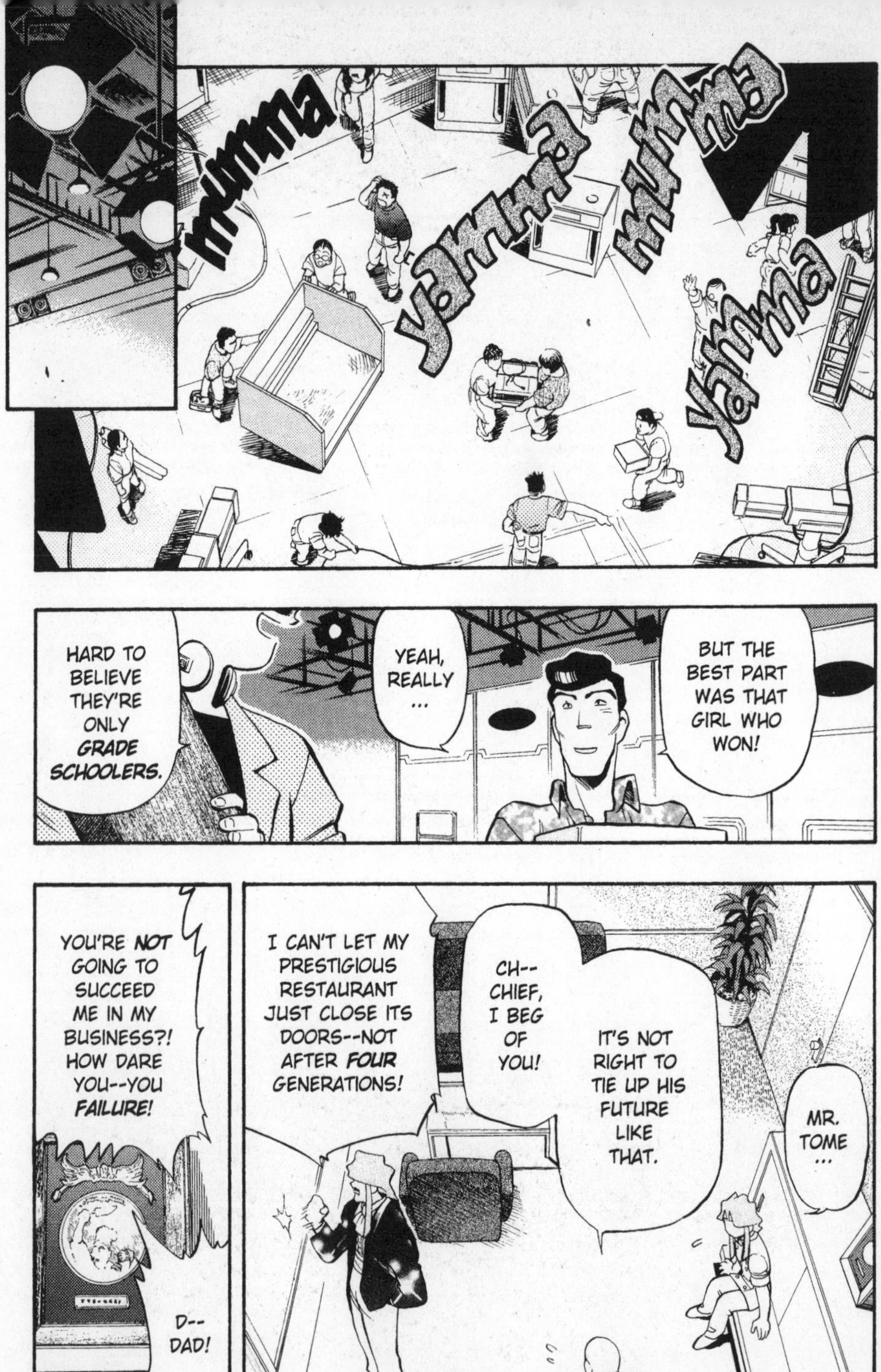
mumma
yamma
mumma
yamma
HARD TO BELIEVE THEY'RE ONLY *GRADE SCHOOLERS.*
YEAH, REALLY ...
BUT THE BEST PART WAS THAT GIRL WHO WON!
YOU'RE **NOT** GOING TO SUCCEED ME IN MY BUSINESS?! HOW DARE YOU--YOU **FAILURE!**
D-- DAD!
I CAN'T LET MY PRESTIGIOUS RESTAURANT JUST CLOSE ITS DOORS--NOT AFTER ***FOUR*** GENERATIONS!
CH-- CHIEF, I BEG OF YOU!
IT'S NOT RIGHT TO TIE UP HIS FUTURE LIKE THAT.
MR. TOME ...

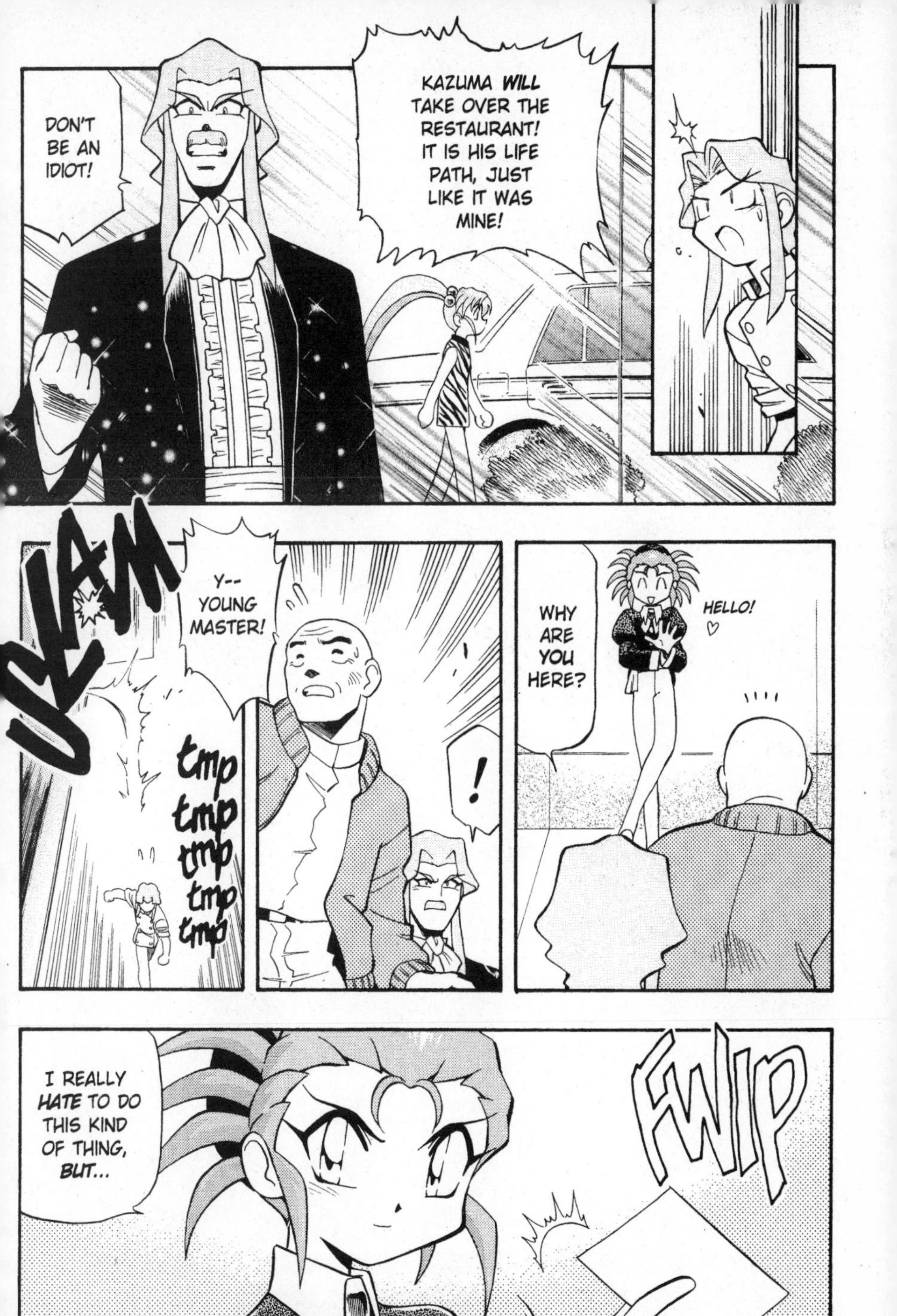
DON'T BE AN IDIOT!
KAZUMA WILL TAKE OVER THE RESTAURANT! IT IS HIS LIFE PATH, JUST LIKE IT WAS MINE!
WHAM
tmp tmp tmp tmp tmp
Y-- YOUNG MASTER!
!
WHY ARE YOU HERE?
HELLO! ♡
I REALLY HATE TO DO THIS KIND OF THING, BUT...
FWIP

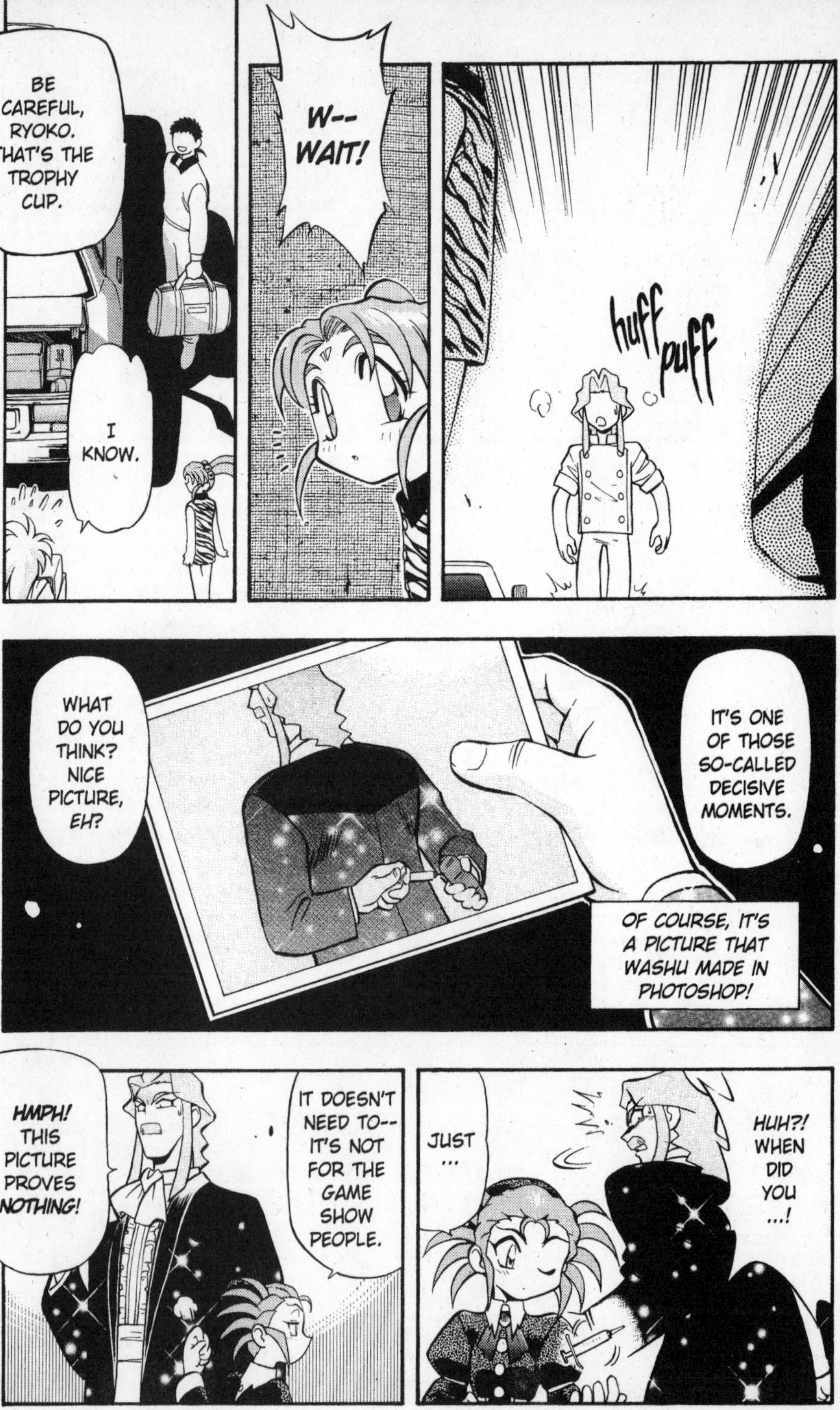
BE CAREFUL, RYOKO. THAT'S THE TROPHY CUP.
I KNOW.
W-- WAIT!
huff puff
WHAT DO YOU THINK? NICE PICTURE, EH?
IT'S ONE OF THOSE SO-CALLED DECISIVE MOMENTS.
OF COURSE, IT'S A PICTURE THAT WASHU MADE IN PHOTOSHOP!
HMPH! THIS PICTURE PROVES NOTHING!
IT DOESN'T NEED TO-- IT'S NOT FOR THE GAME SHOW PEOPLE.
JUST ...
HUH?! WHEN DID YOU ...!

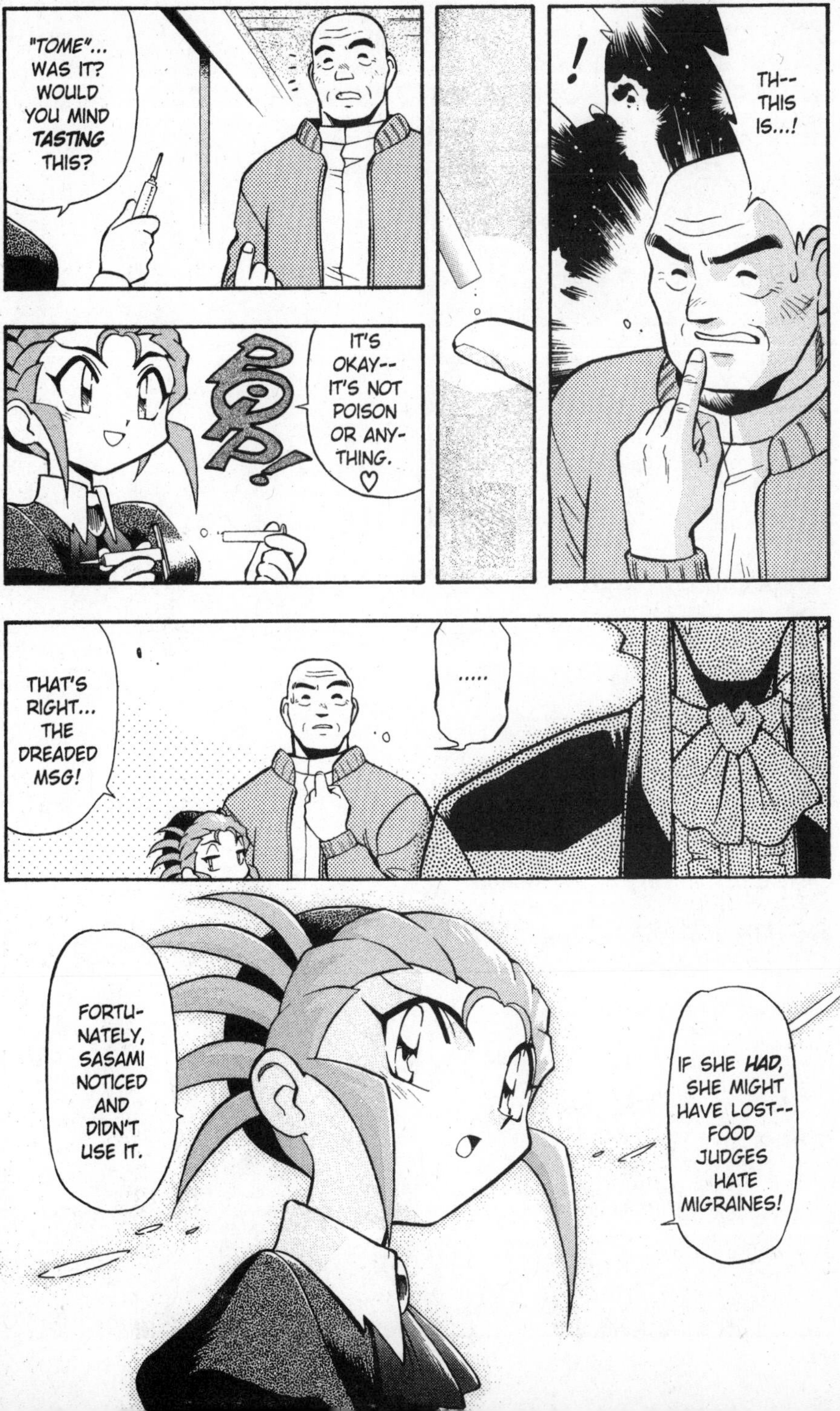
"TOME"... WAS IT? WOULD YOU MIND TASTING THIS?
IT'S OKAY-- IT'S NOT POISON OR ANY- THING. ♡
!
TH-- THIS IS...!
THAT'S RIGHT... THE DREADED MSG!
.....
FORTU- NATELY, SASAMI NOTICED AND DIDN'T USE IT.
IF SHE HAD, SHE MIGHT HAVE LOST-- FOOD JUDGES HATE MIGRAINES!

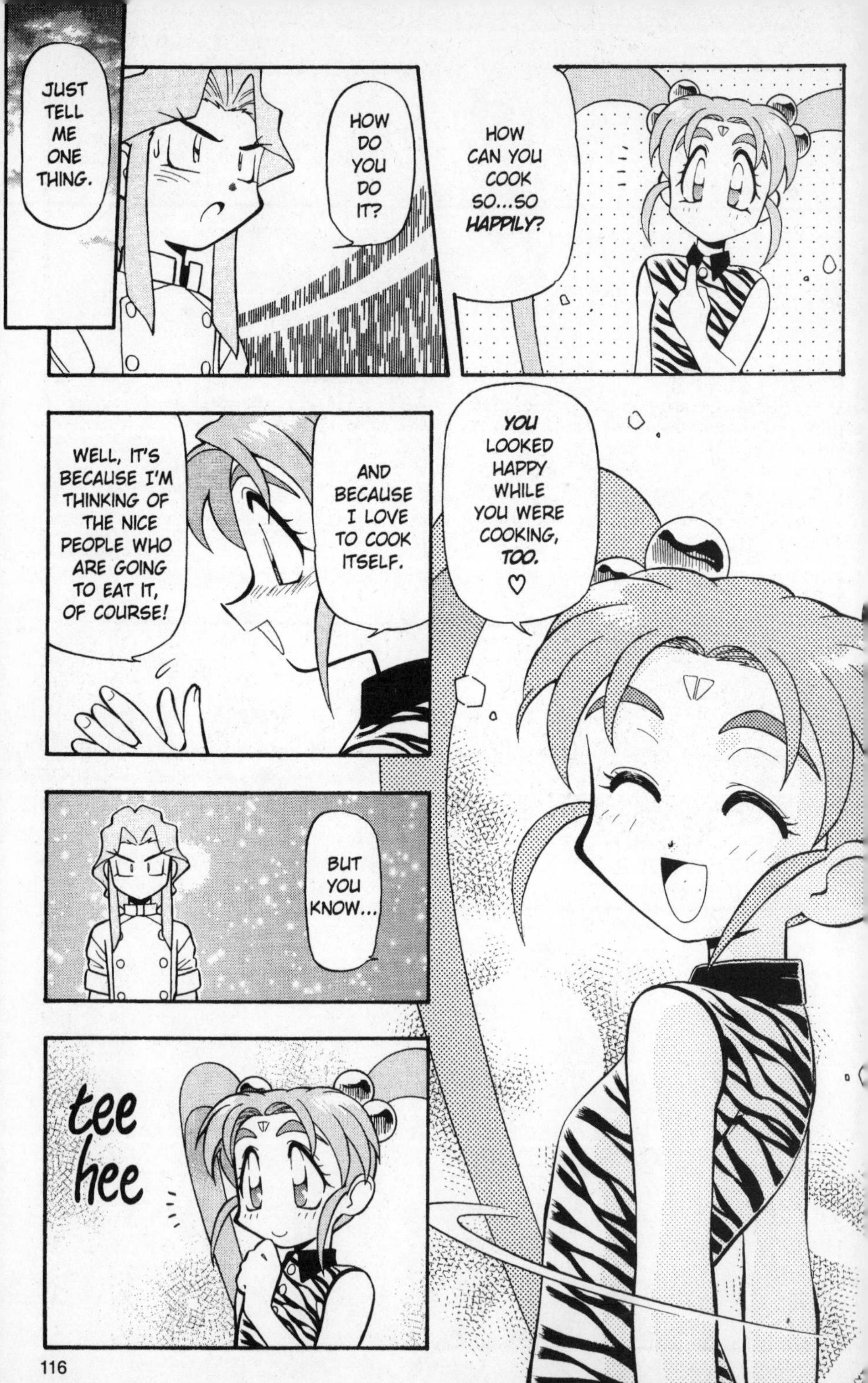
JUST TELL ME ONE THING.
HOW DO YOU DO IT?
HOW CAN YOU COOK SO...SO *HAPPILY?*
WELL, IT'S BECAUSE I'M THINKING OF THE NICE PEOPLE WHO ARE GOING TO EAT IT, OF COURSE!
AND BECAUSE I LOVE TO COOK ITSELF.
BUT YOU KNOW...
tee hee
YOU LOOKED HAPPY WHILE YOU WERE COOKING, *TOO.* ♡

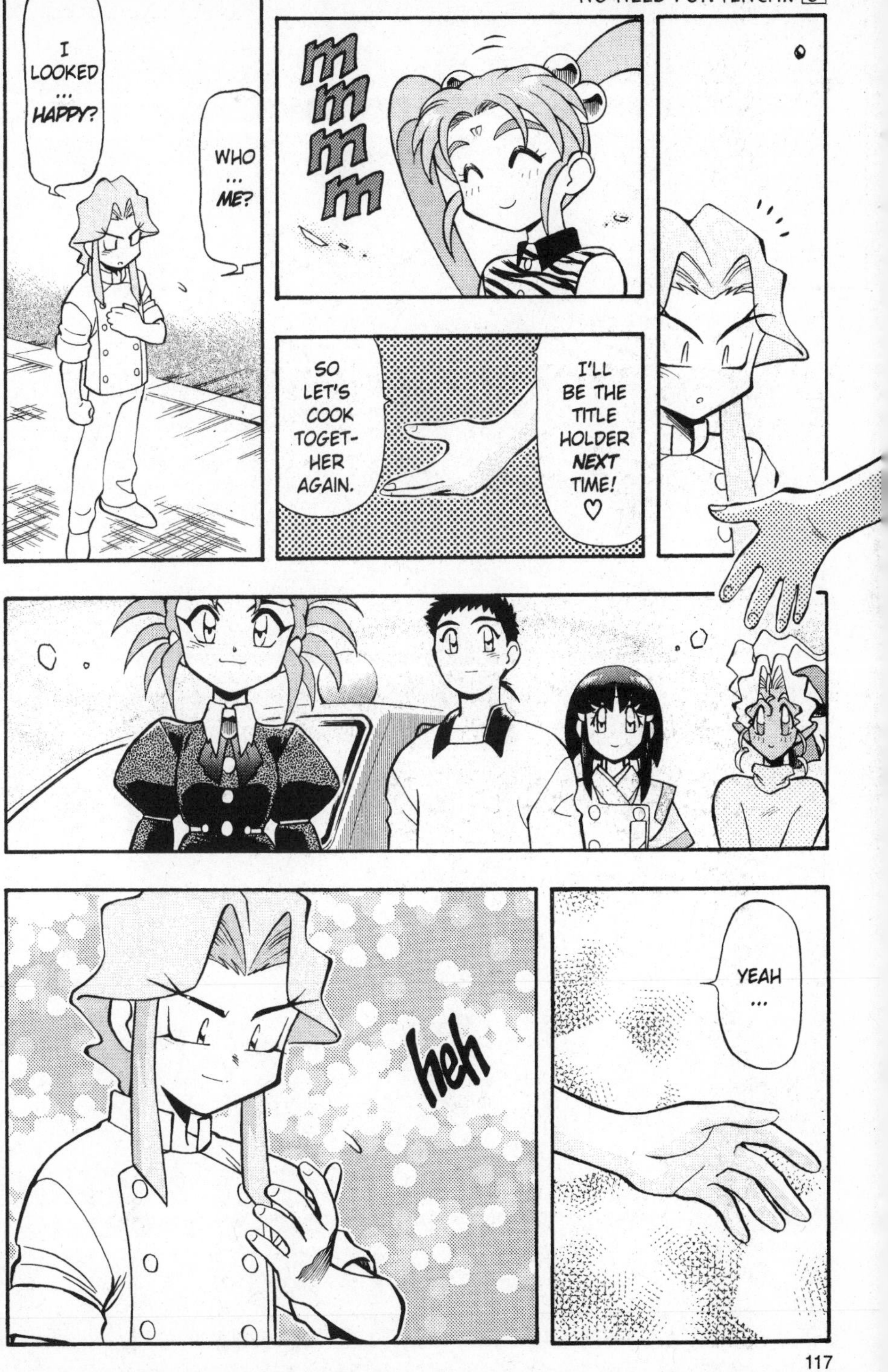
I LOOKED ... HAPPY?
WHO ... ME?
mmmm
SO LET'S COOK TOGET-HER AGAIN.
I'LL BE THE TITLE HOLDER NEXT TIME! ♡
heh
YEAH ...

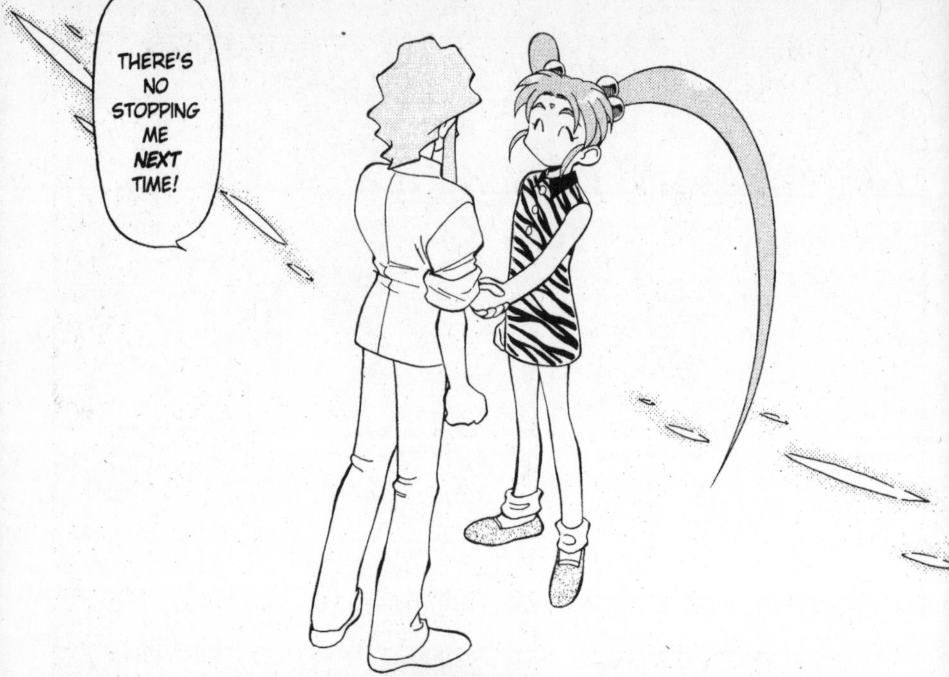
THERE'S NO STOPPING ME NEXT TIME!

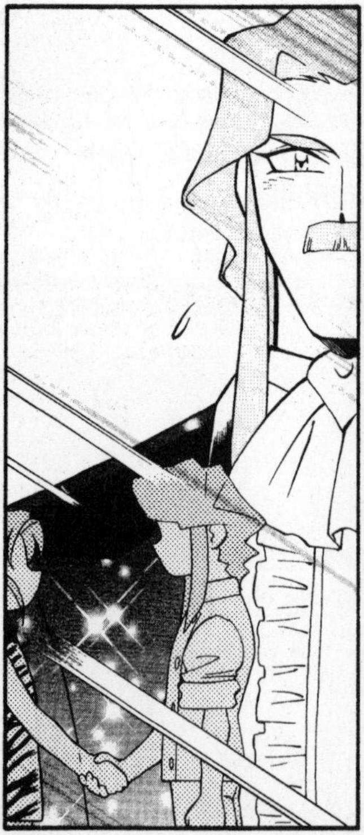

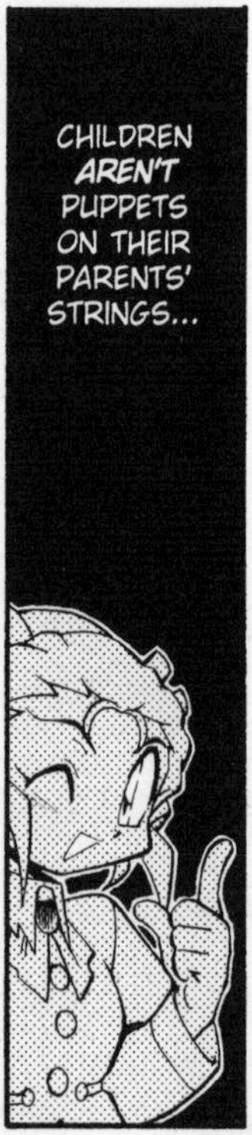
CHILDREN AREN'T PUPPETS ON THEIR PARENTS' STRINGS...

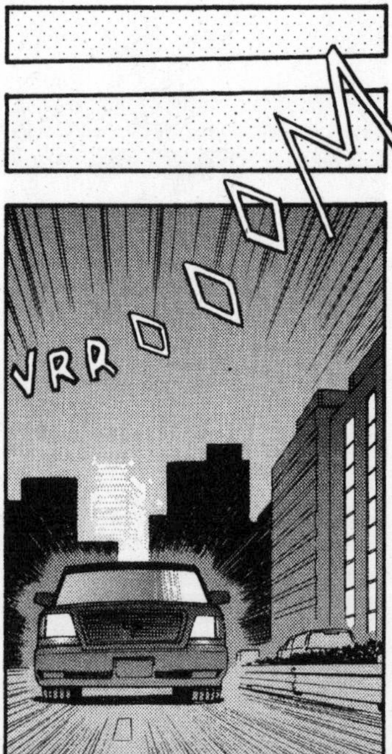
VRROOOM

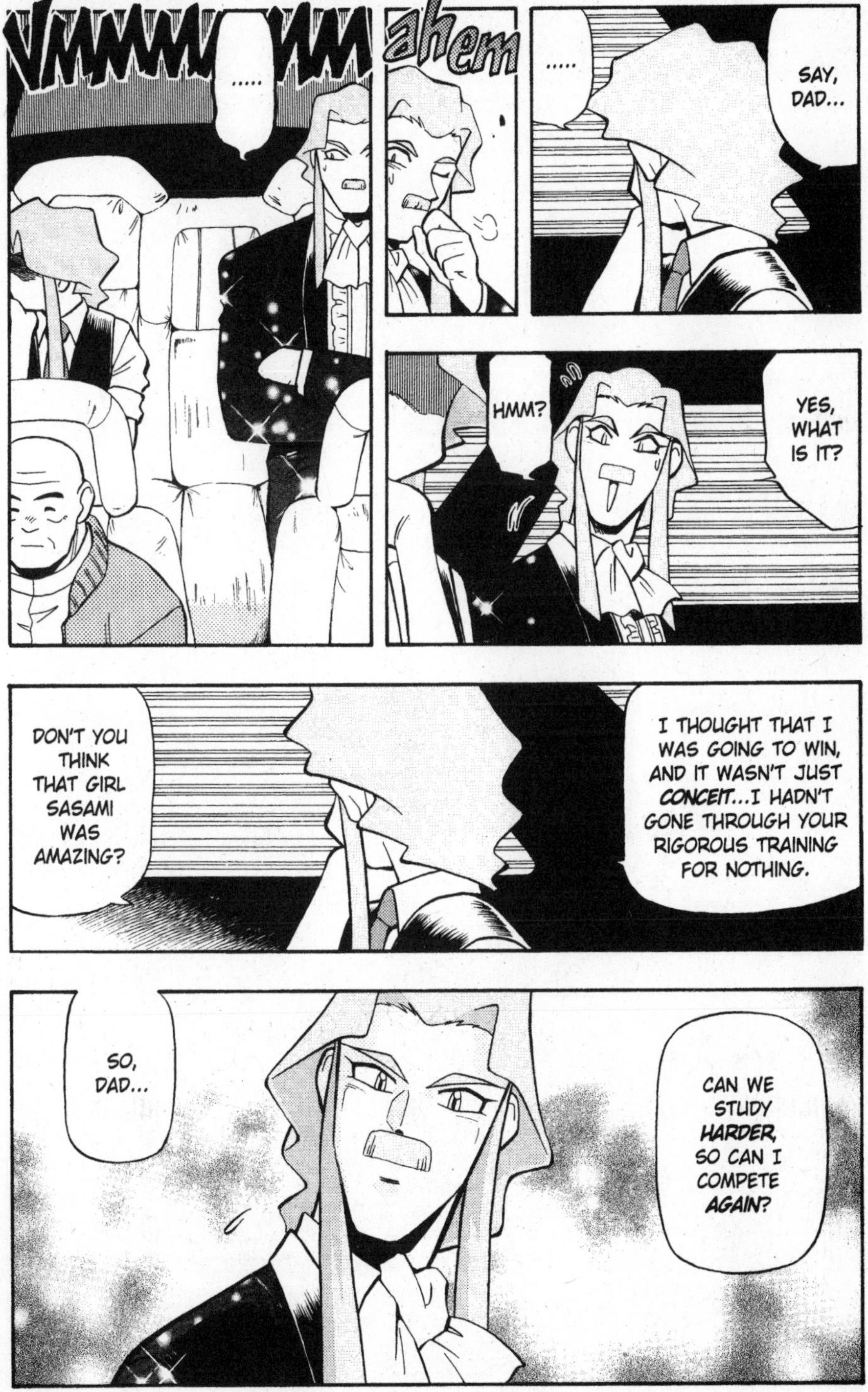
.....
ahem
.....
SAY, DAD...
HMM?
YES, WHAT IS IT?
DON'T YOU THINK THAT GIRL SASAMI WAS AMAZING?
I THOUGHT THAT I WAS GOING TO WIN, AND IT WASN'T JUST CONCEIT...I HADN'T GONE THROUGH YOUR RIGOROUS TRAINING FOR NOTHING.
SO, DAD...
CAN WE STUDY HARDER, SO CAN I COMPETE AGAIN?

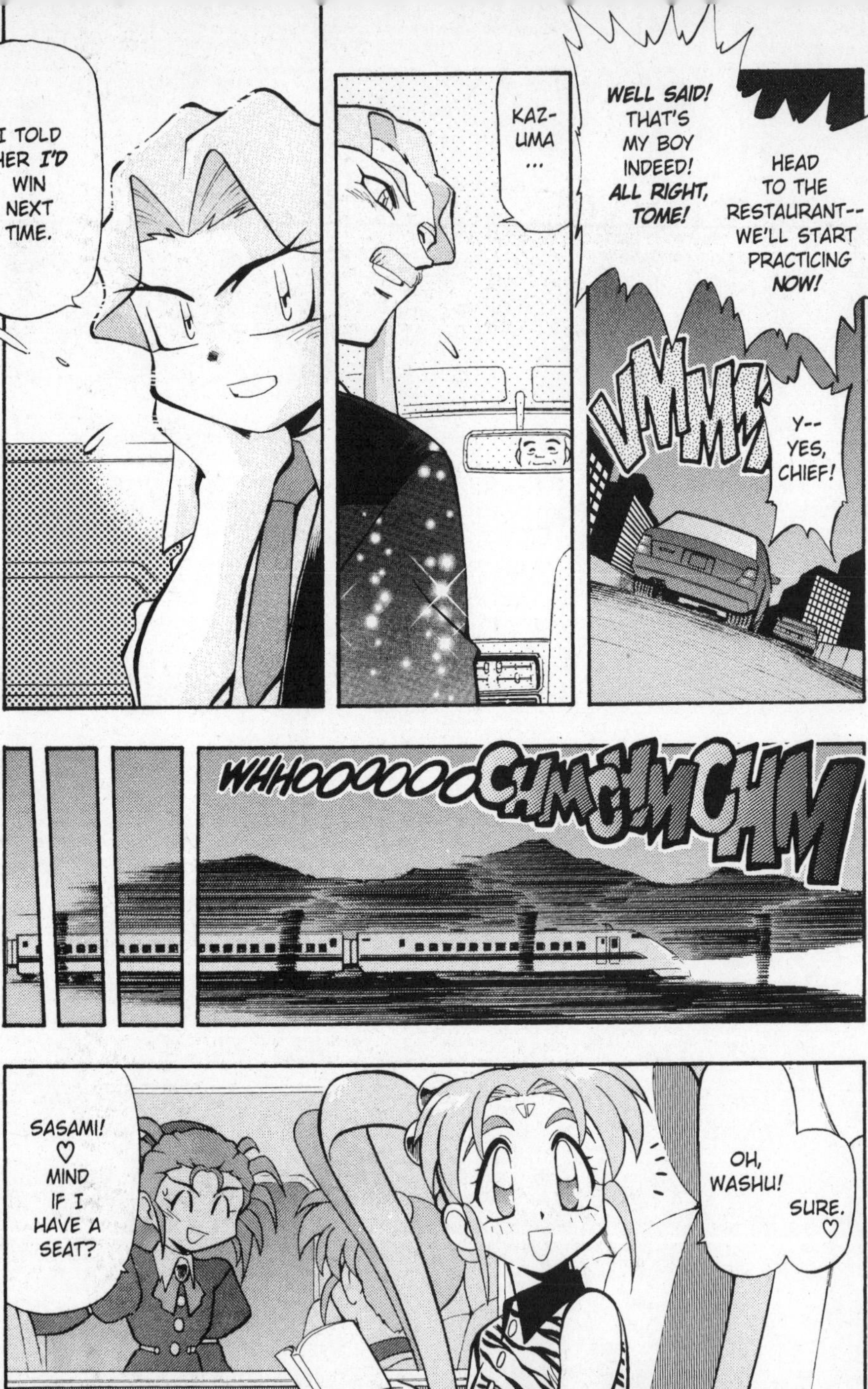
I TOLD HER I'D WIN NEXT TIME.
KAZ-UMA...
WELL SAID! THAT'S MY BOY INDEED! ALL RIGHT, TOME!
HEAD TO THE RESTAURANT-- WE'LL START PRACTICING NOW!
VMMM
Y-- YES, CHIEF!
WHHOOOOOOO
CHMCHMCHM
SASAMI! ♡ MIND IF I HAVE A SEAT?
OH, WASHU!
SURE. ♡

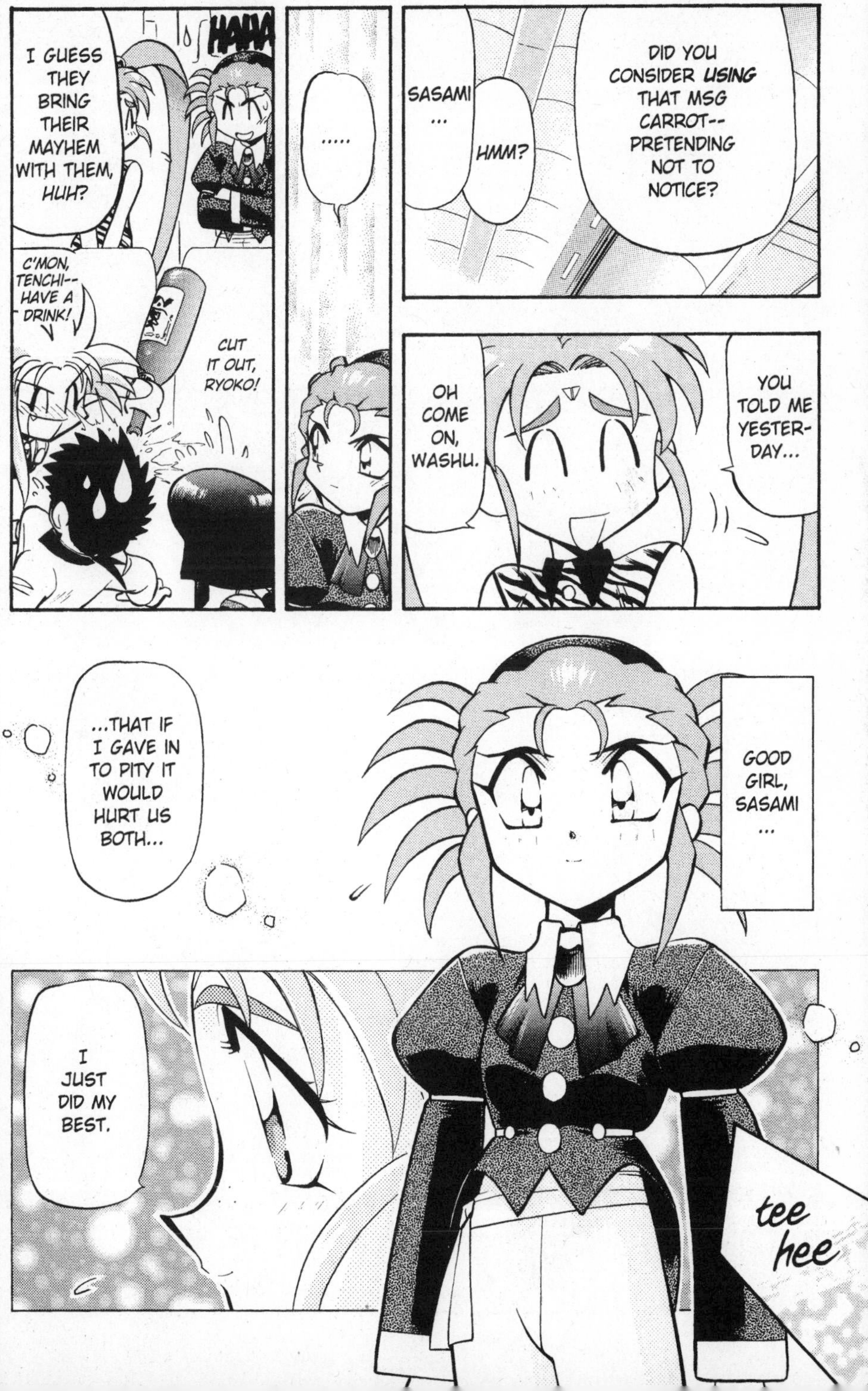
I GUESS THEY BRING THEIR MAYHEM WITH THEM, HUH?
HAHA
C'MON, TENCHI-- HAVE A DRINK!
CUT IT OUT, RYOKO!
.....
SASAMI ...
HMM?
DID YOU CONSIDER USING THAT MSG CARROT-- PRETENDING NOT TO NOTICE?
OH COME ON, WASHU.
YOU TOLD ME YESTER-DAY...
...THAT IF I GAVE IN TO PITY IT WOULD HURT US BOTH...
GOOD GIRL, SASAMI ...
I JUST DID MY BEST.
tee hee

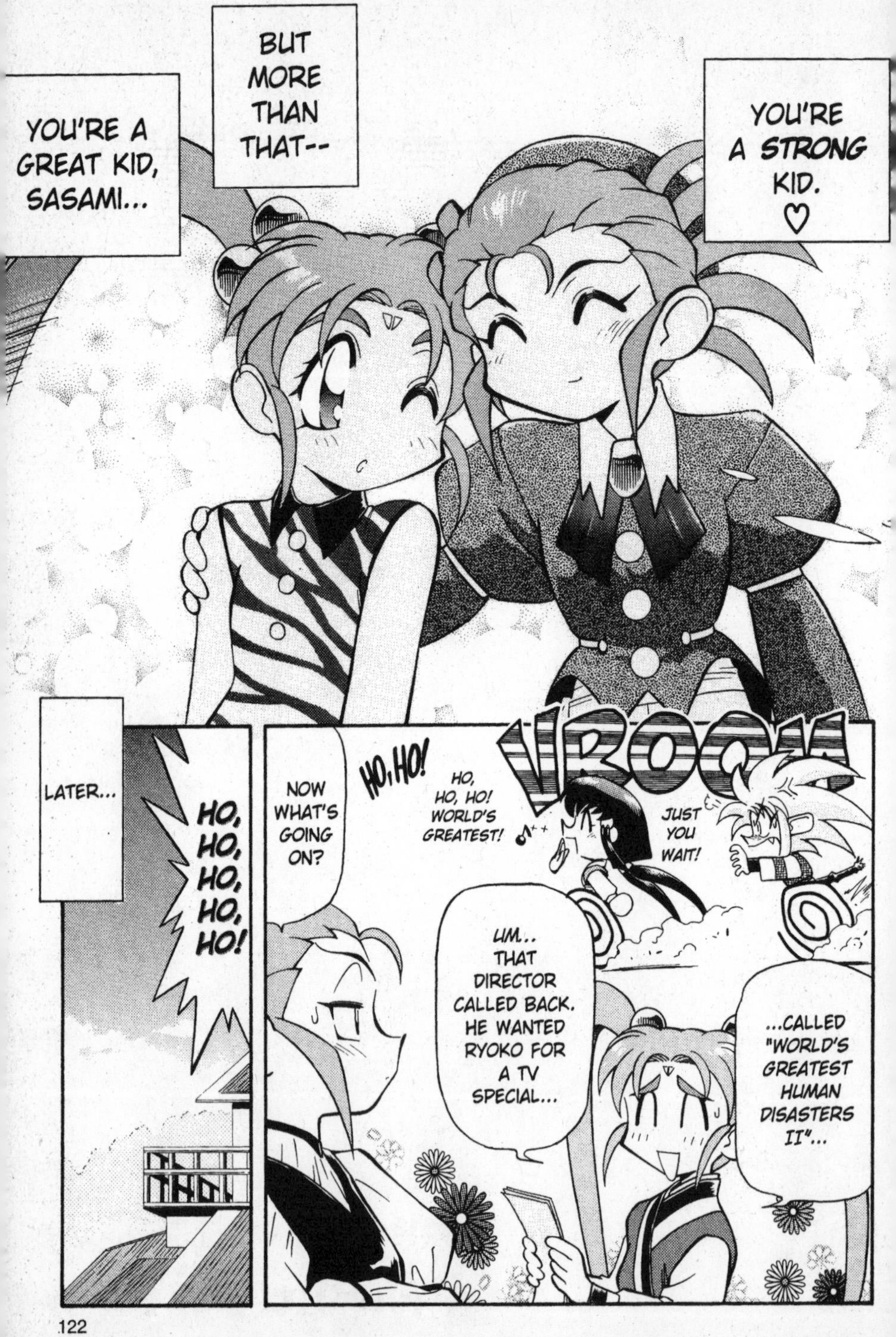

YOU'RE A GREAT KID, SASAMI...
BUT MORE THAN THAT--
YOU'RE A STRONG KID. ♡
LATER...
HO, HO, HO, HO, HO!
NOW WHAT'S GOING ON?
HO, HO!
HO, HO, HO! WORLD'S GREATEST!
VROOM
JUST YOU WAIT!
UM.. THAT DIRECTOR CALLED BACK. HE WANTED RYOKO FOR A TV SPECIAL...
...CALLED "WORLD'S GREATEST HUMAN DISASTERS II"...

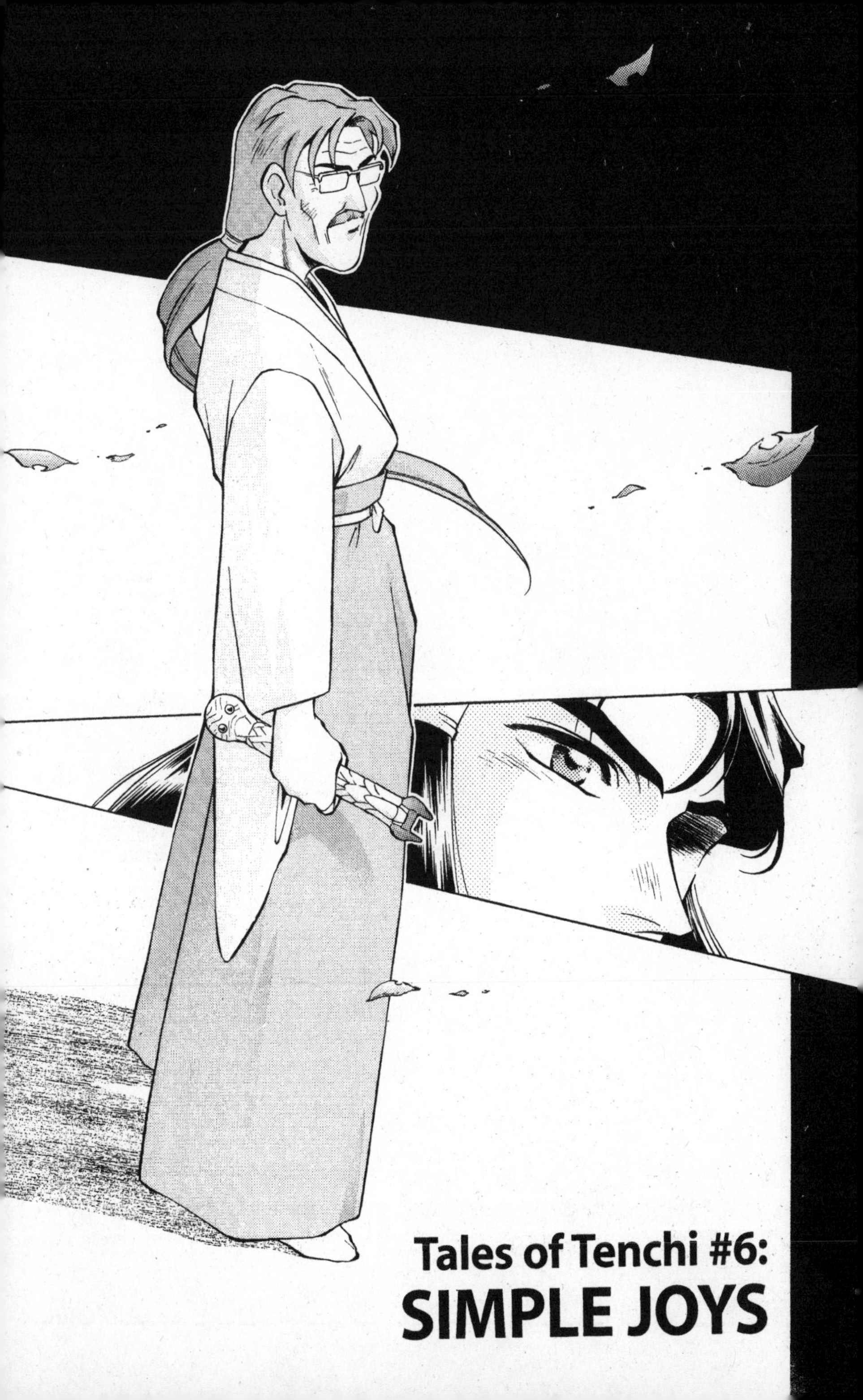

Tales of Tenchi #6:
SIMPLE JOYS

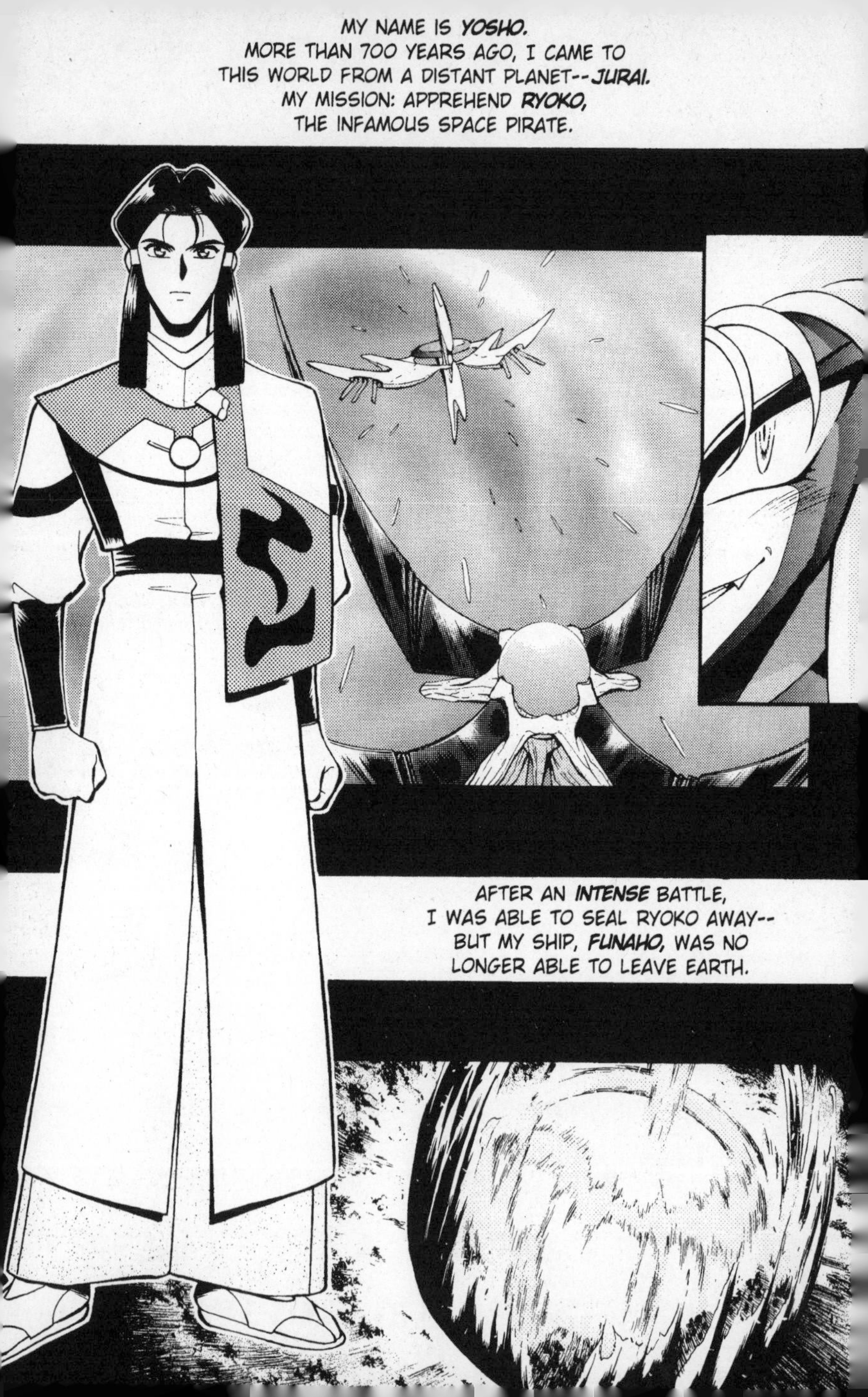
MY NAME IS YOSHO. MORE THAN 700 YEARS AGO, I CAME TO THIS WORLD FROM A DISTANT PLANET--JURAI. MY MISSION: APPREHEND RYOKO, THE INFAMOUS SPACE PIRATE.
AFTER AN INTENSE BATTLE, I WAS ABLE TO SEAL RYOKO AWAY-- BUT MY SHIP, FUNAHO, WAS NO LONGER ABLE TO LEAVE EARTH.

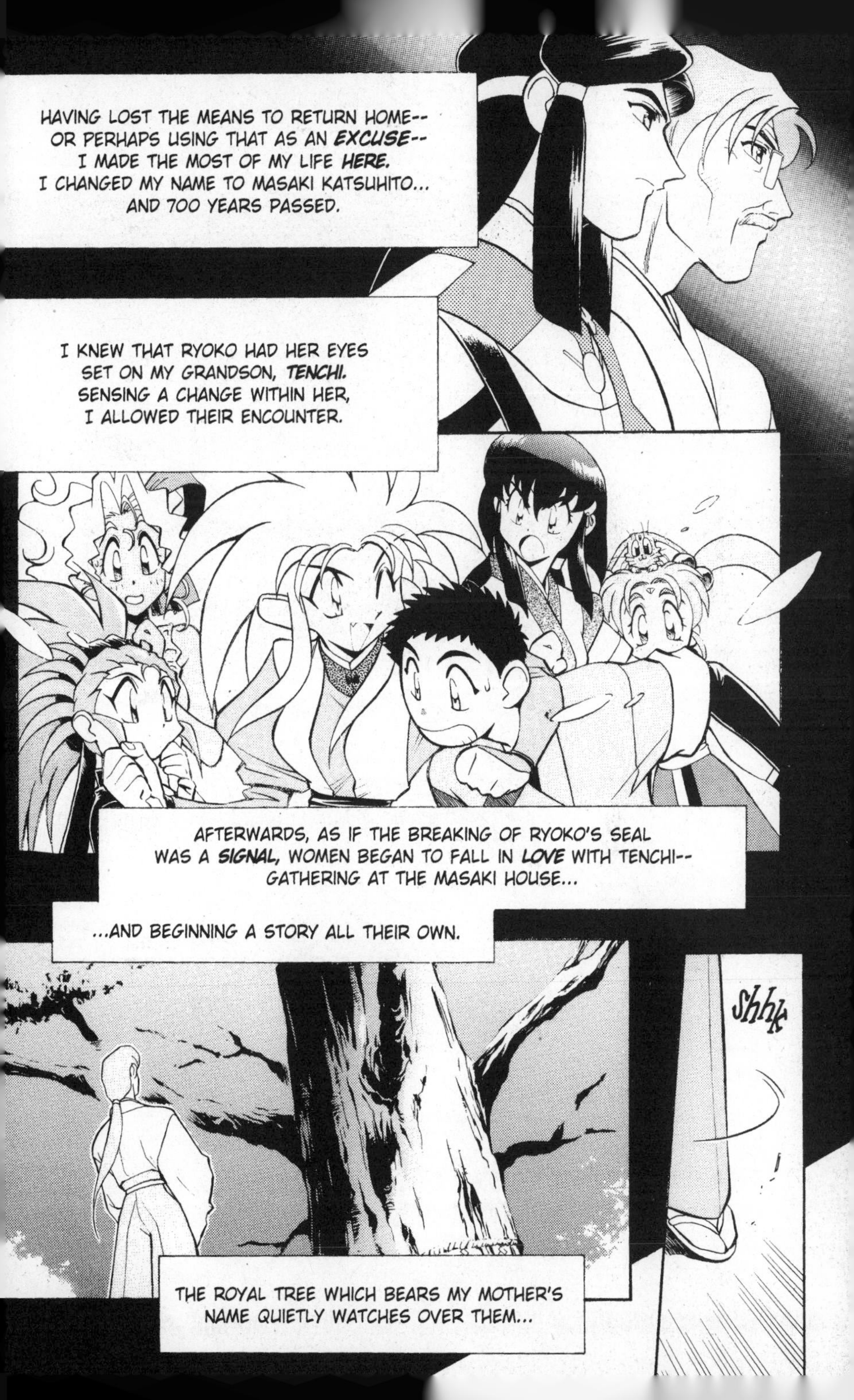
HAVING LOST THE MEANS TO RETURN HOME-- OR PERHAPS USING THAT AS AN EXCUSE-- I MADE THE MOST OF MY LIFE HERE. I CHANGED MY NAME TO MASAKI KATSUHITO... AND 700 YEARS PASSED.
I KNEW THAT RYOKO HAD HER EYES SET ON MY GRANDSON, TENCHI. SENSING A CHANGE WITHIN HER, I ALLOWED THEIR ENCOUNTER.
AFTERWARDS, AS IF THE BREAKING OF RYOKO'S SEAL WAS A SIGNAL, WOMEN BEGAN TO FALL IN LOVE WITH TENCHI-- GATHERING AT THE MASAKI HOUSE...
...AND BEGINNING A STORY ALL THEIR OWN.
THE ROYAL TREE WHICH BEARS MY MOTHER'S NAME QUIETLY WATCHES OVER THEM...
Shhk

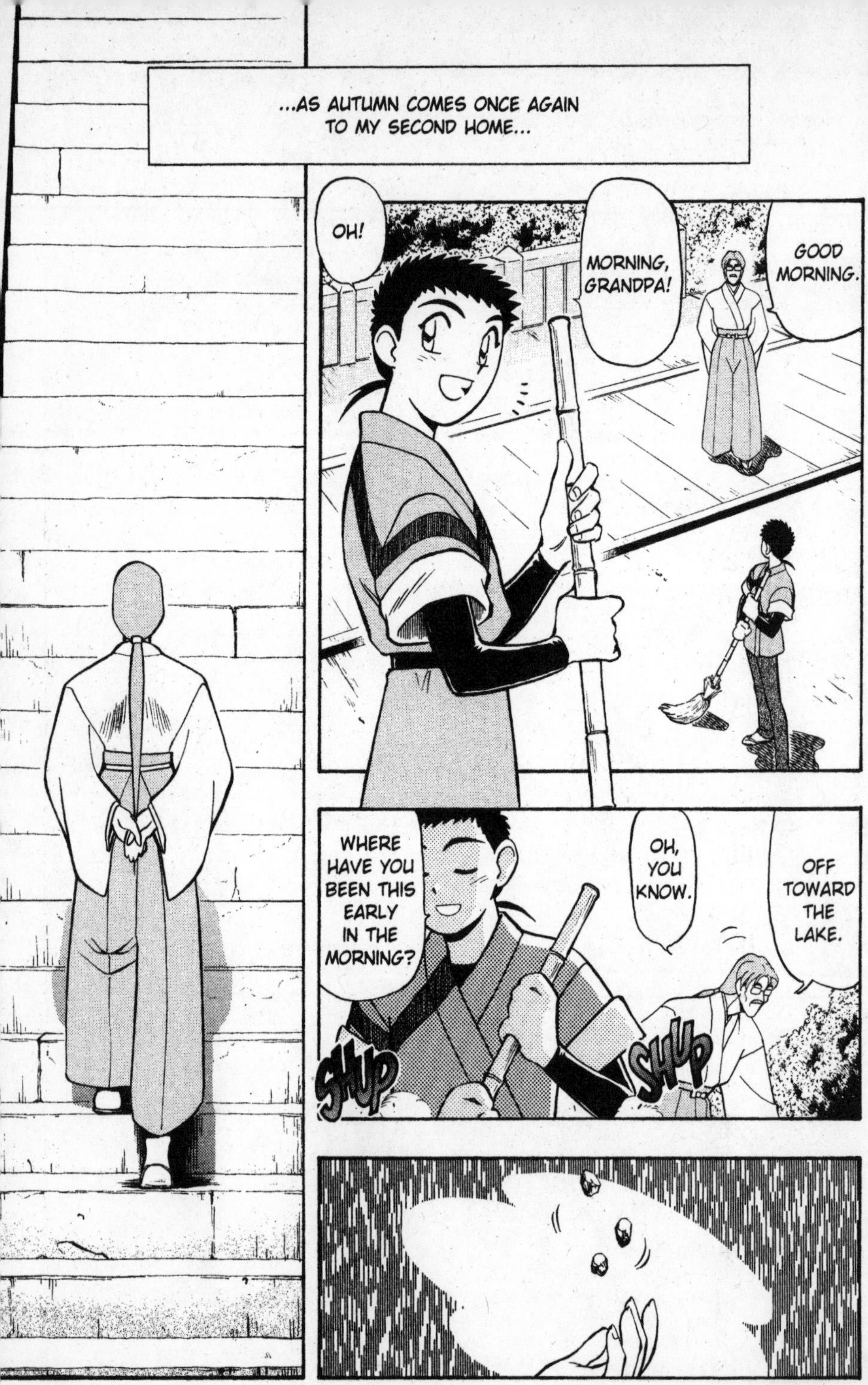
...AS AUTUMN COMES ONCE AGAIN TO MY SECOND HOME...
OH!
MORNING, GRANDPA!
GOOD MORNING.
WHERE HAVE YOU BEEN THIS EARLY IN THE MORNING?
OH, YOU KNOW.
OFF TOWARD THE LAKE.
SHUP
SHUP

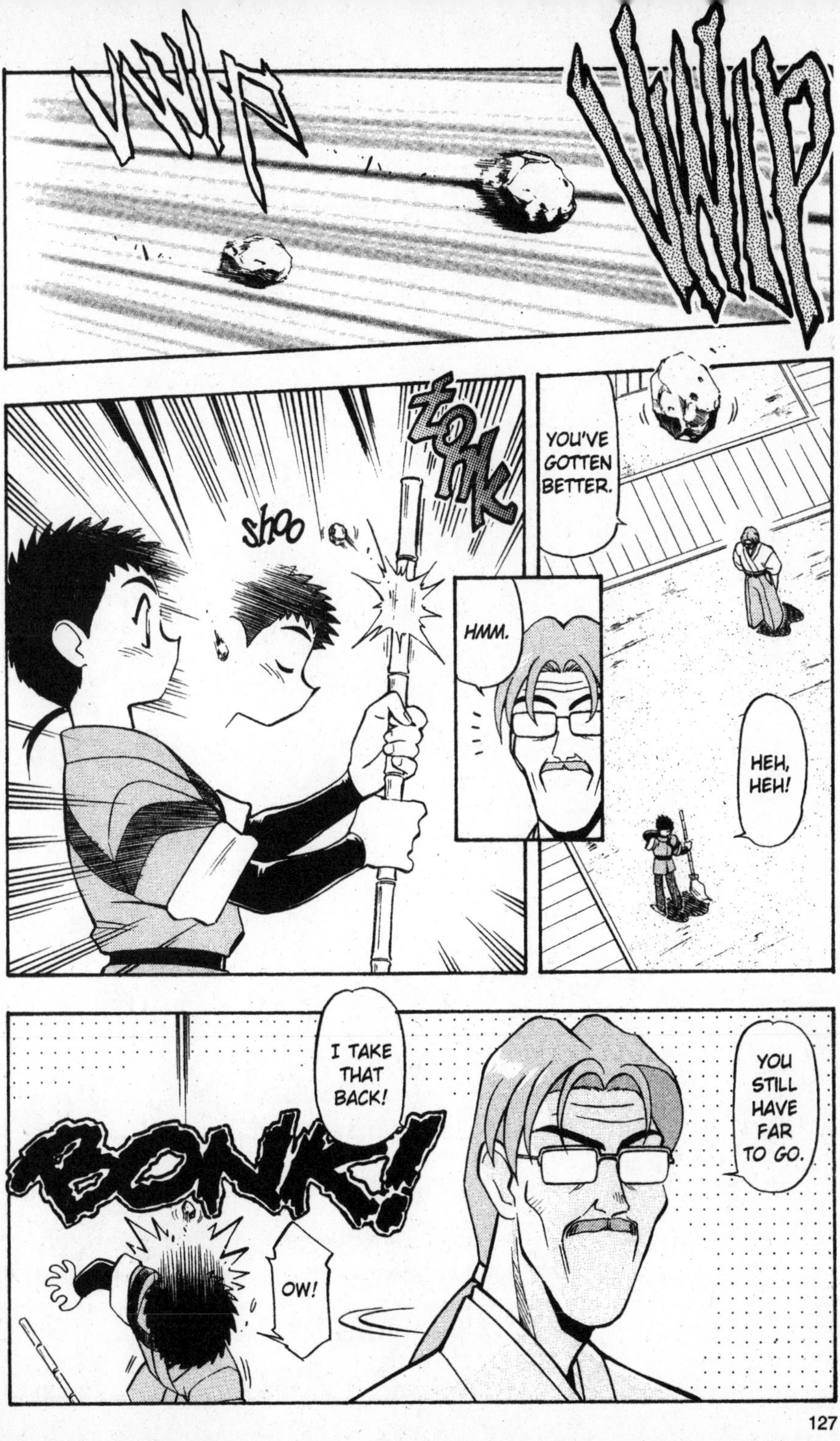
WHIP
WHIP
TONK
shoo
YOU'VE GOTTEN BETTER.
HMM.
HEH, HEH!
BONK!
I TAKE THAT BACK!
OW!
YOU STILL HAVE FAR TO GO.

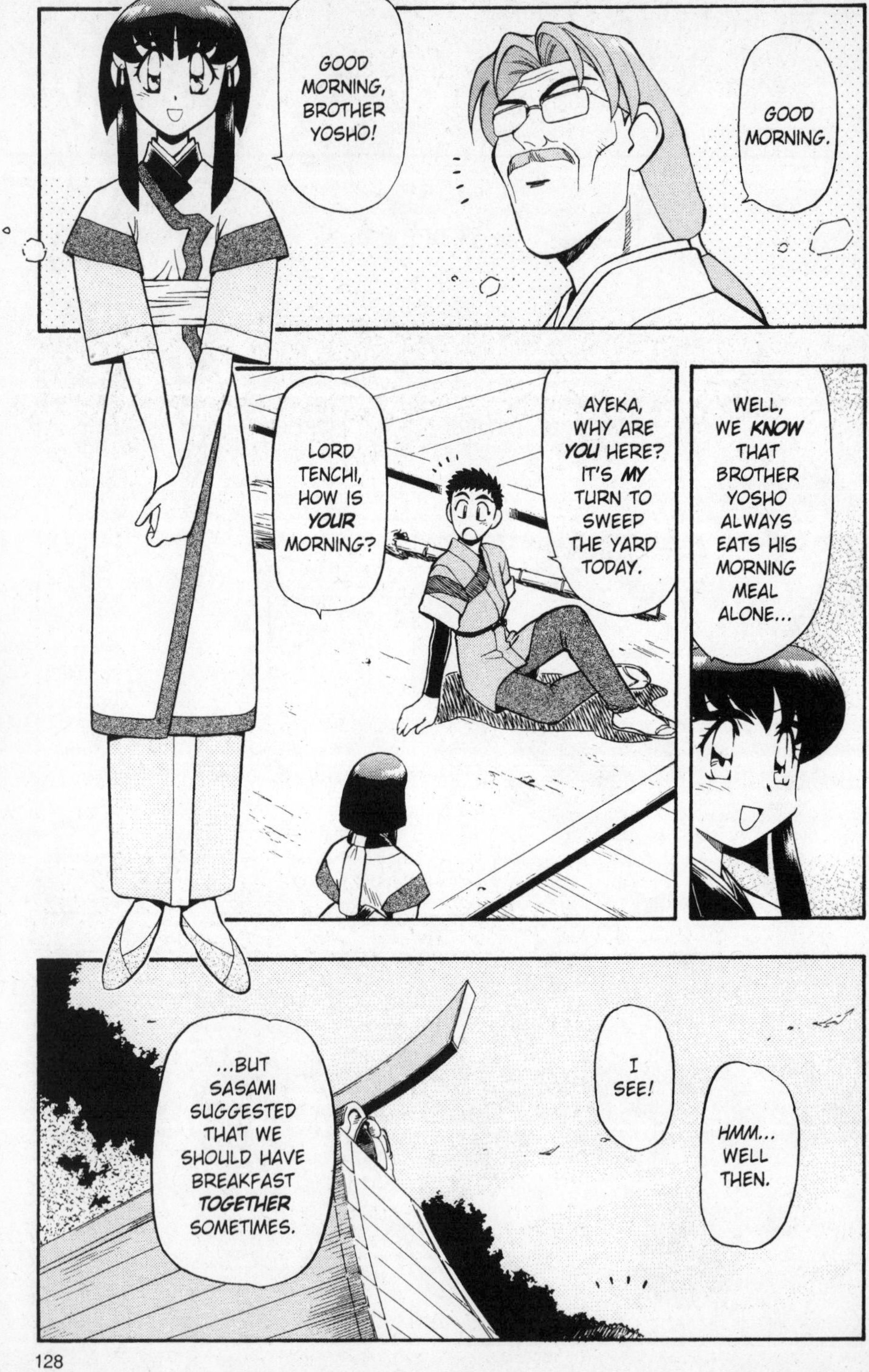
GOOD MORNING, BROTHER YOSHO!
GOOD MORNING.
LORD TENCHI, HOW IS YOUR MORNING?
AYEKA, WHY ARE YOU HERE? IT'S MY TURN TO SWEEP THE YARD TODAY.
WELL, WE KNOW THAT BROTHER YOSHO ALWAYS EATS HIS MORNING MEAL ALONE...
...BUT SASAMI SUGGESTED THAT WE SHOULD HAVE BREAKFAST TOGETHER SOMETIMES.
I SEE!
HMM... WELL THEN.

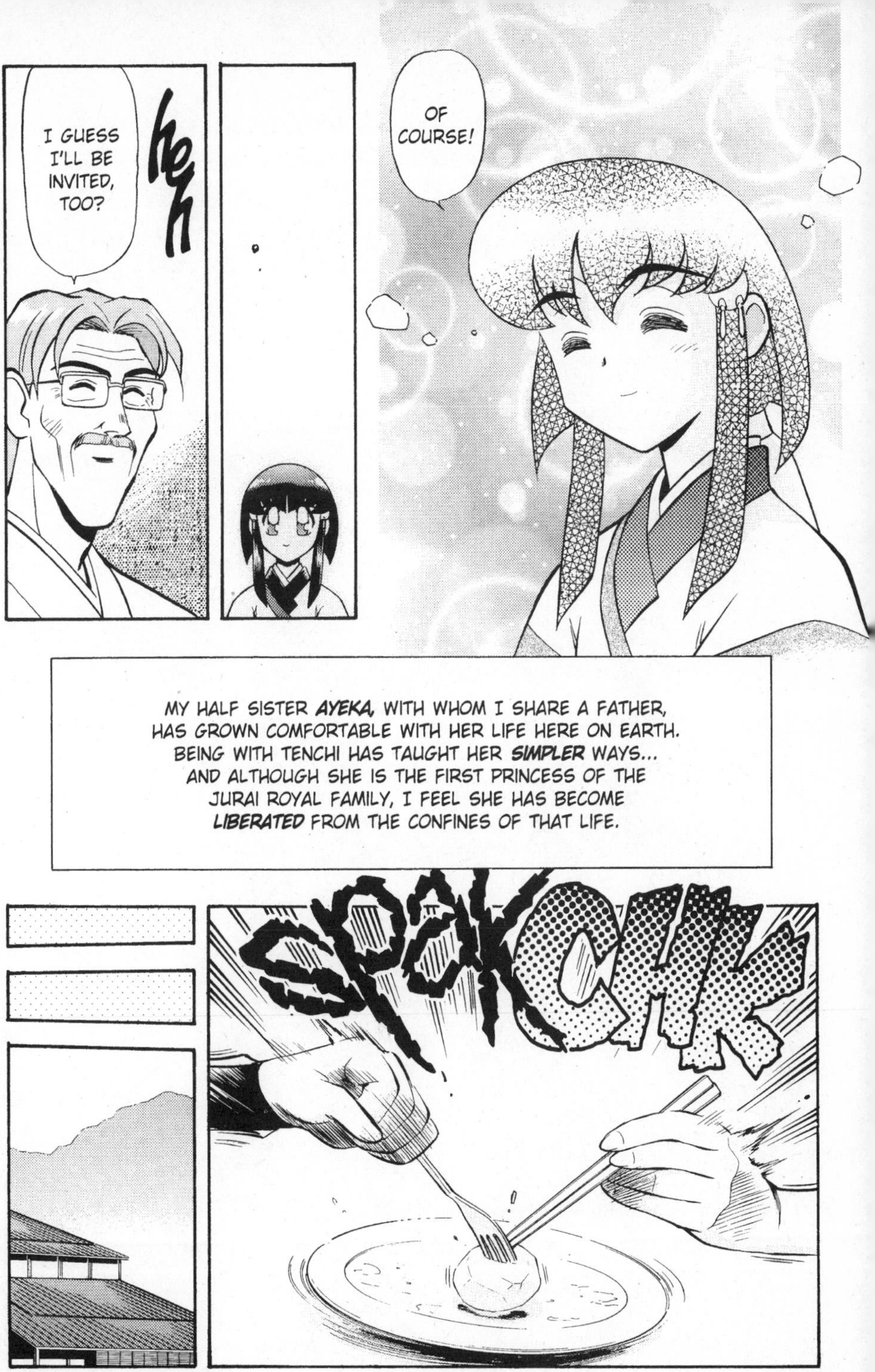
I GUESS I'LL BE INVITED, TOO?
heh
OF COURSE!
MY HALF SISTER AYEKA, WITH WHOM I SHARE A FATHER, HAS GROWN COMFORTABLE WITH HER LIFE HERE ON EARTH. BEING WITH TENCHI HAS TAUGHT HER SIMPLER WAYS... AND ALTHOUGH SHE IS THE FIRST PRINCESS OF THE JURAI ROYAL FAMILY, I FEEL SHE HAS BECOME LIBERATED FROM THE CONFINES OF THAT LIFE.
SPAKCHIK

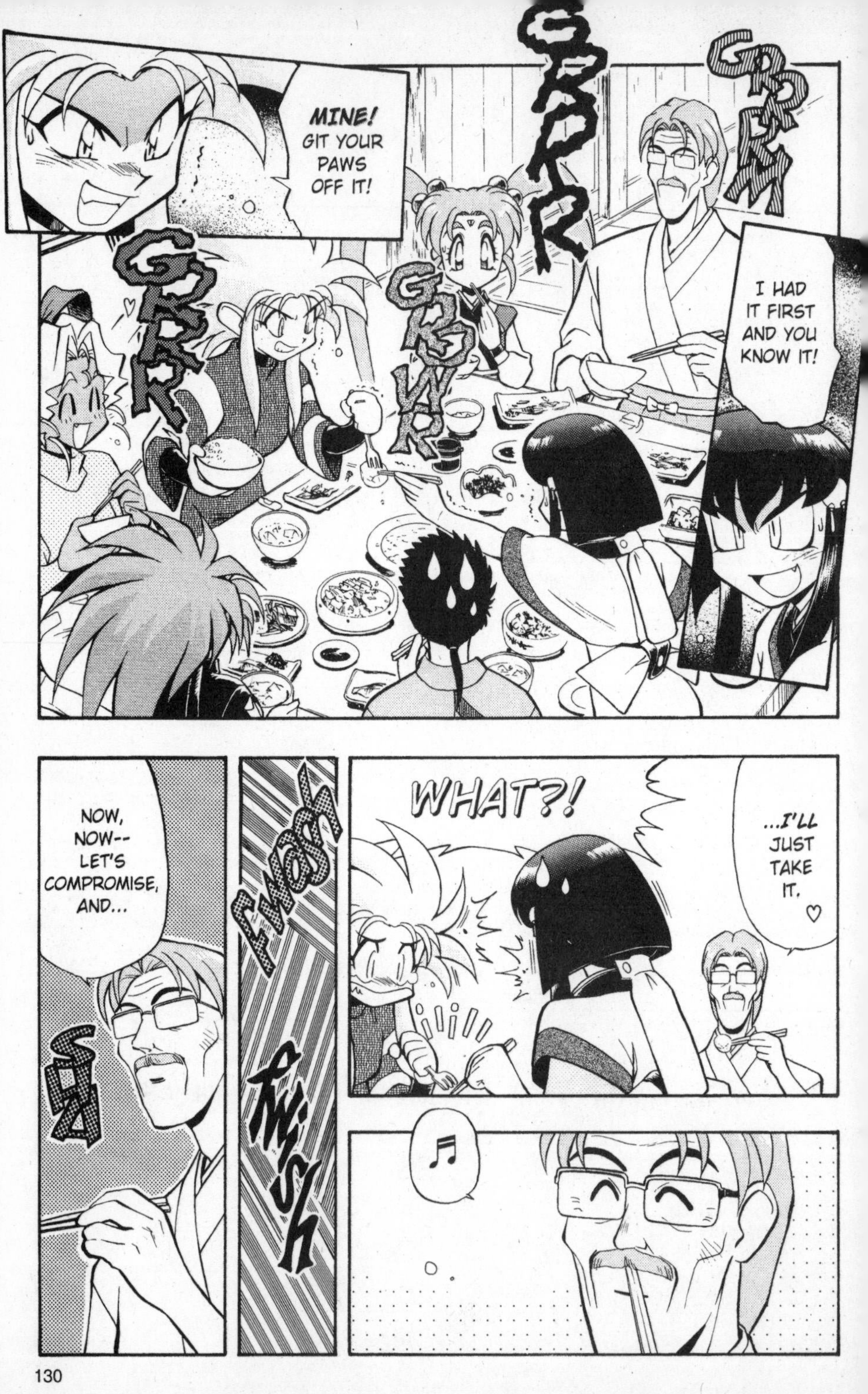
MINE! GIT YOUR PAWS OFF IT!
I HAD IT FIRST AND YOU KNOW IT!
NOW, NOW-- LET'S COMPROMISE, AND...
WHAT?!
...I'LL JUST TAKE IT. ♡
♬

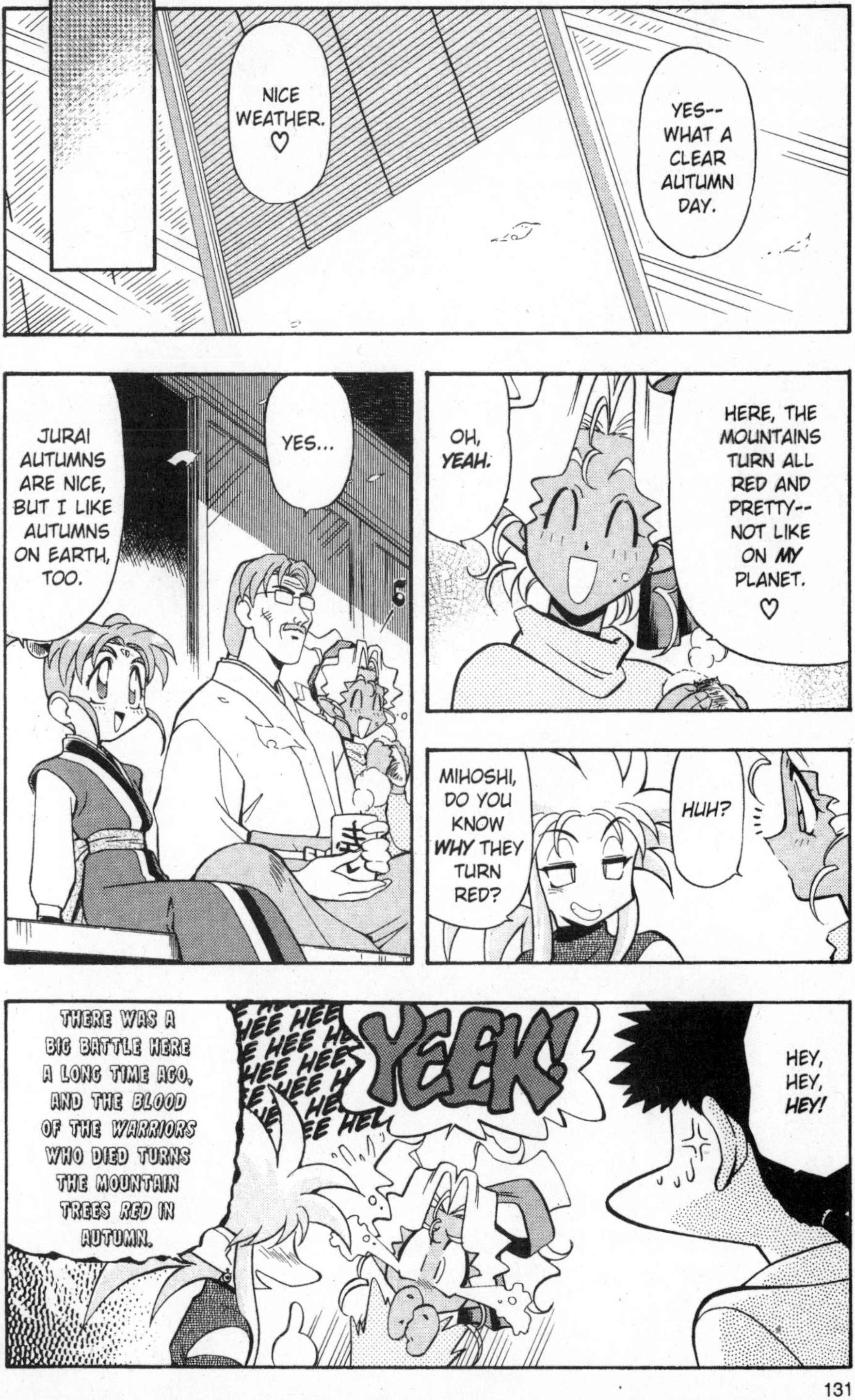
NICE WEATHER. ♡
YES-- WHAT A CLEAR AUTUMN DAY.
JURAI AUTUMNS ARE NICE, BUT I LIKE AUTUMNS ON EARTH, TOO.
YES...
OH, *YEAH.*
HERE, THE MOUNTAINS TURN ALL RED AND PRETTY-- NOT LIKE ON *MY* PLANET. ♡
MIHOSHI, DO YOU KNOW *WHY* THEY TURN RED?
HUH?
THERE WAS A BIG BATTLE HERE A LONG TIME AGO, AND THE *BLOOD* OF THE *WARRIORS* WHO DIED TURNS THE MOUNTAIN TREES *RED* IN AUTUMN.
HEE HEE HEE HEE
YEEK!
HEY, HEY, *HEY!*

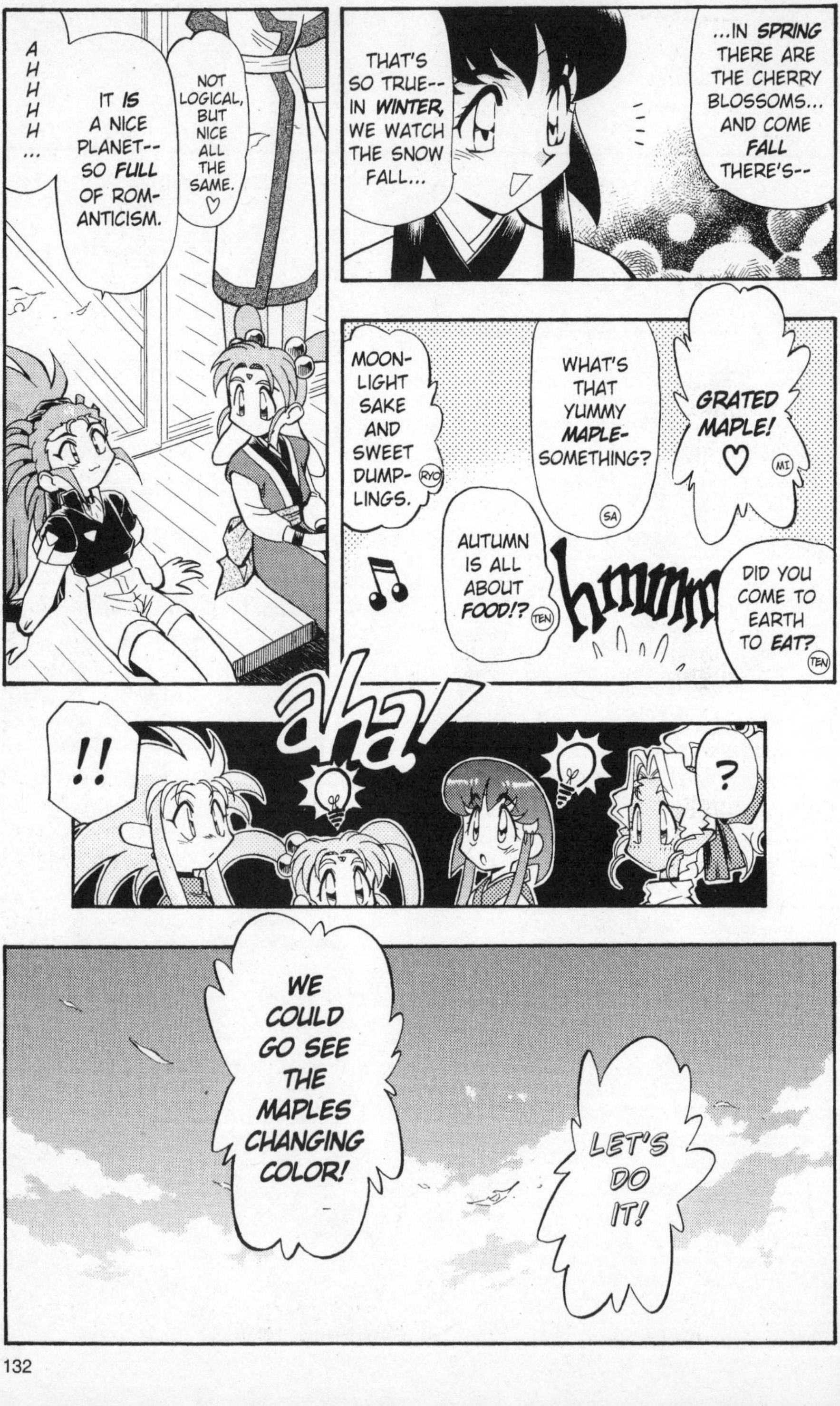
AHHHH...
IT IS A NICE PLANET-- SO FULL OF ROMANTICISM.
NOT LOGICAL, BUT NICE ALL THE SAME. ♡
THAT'S SO TRUE-- IN WINTER, WE WATCH THE SNOW FALL...
...IN SPRING THERE ARE THE CHERRY BLOSSOMS... AND COME FALL THERE'S--
MOON-LIGHT SAKE AND SWEET DUMP-LINGS.
RYO
WHAT'S THAT YUMMY MAPLE-SOMETHING?
SA
GRATED MAPLE! ♡
MI
AUTUMN IS ALL ABOUT FOOD!?
TEN
hmmm
DID YOU COME TO EARTH TO EAT?
TEN
!!
aha!
?
WE COULD GO SEE THE MAPLES CHANGING COLOR!
LET'S DO IT!

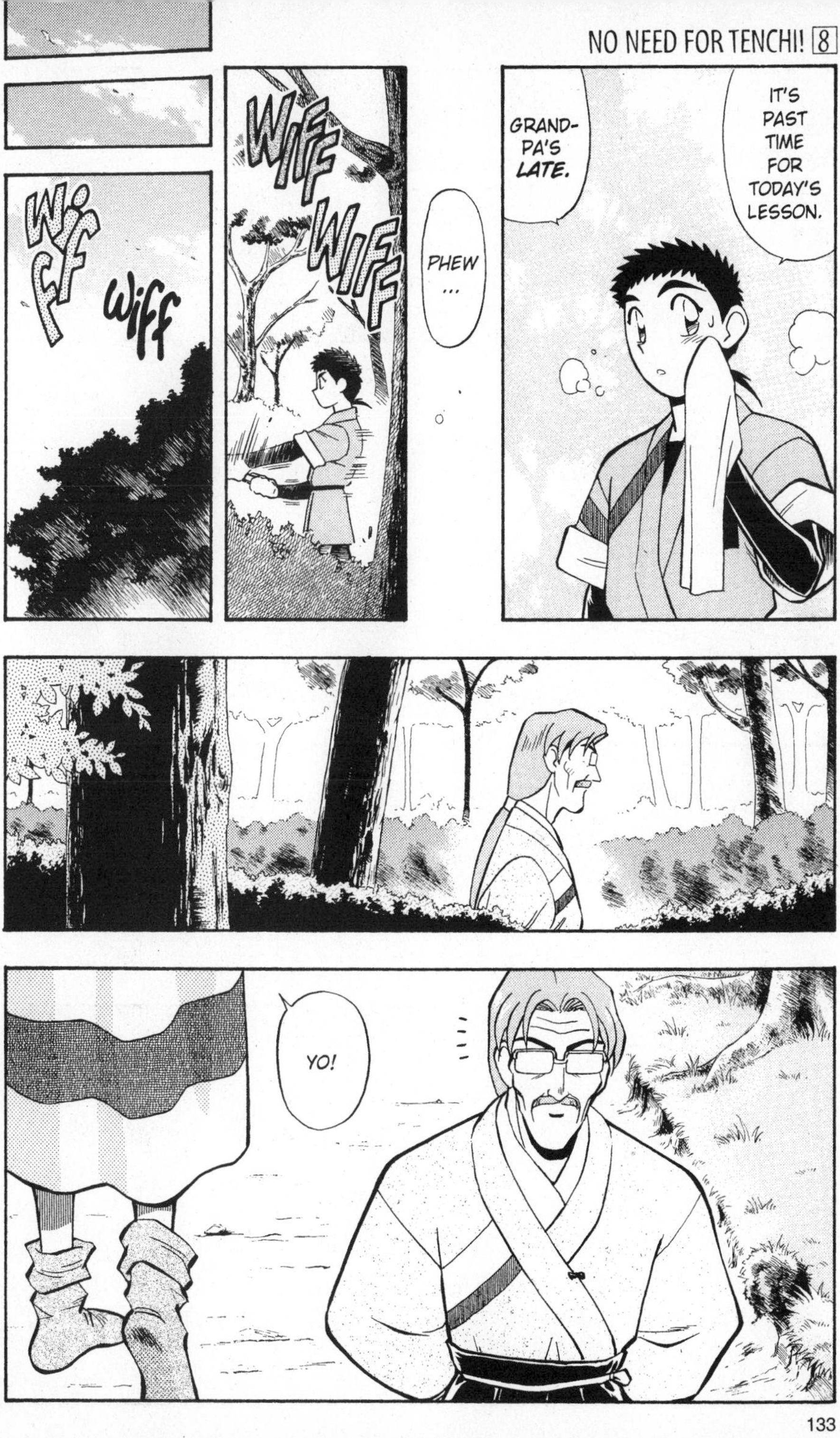
Wiff
wiff
WIFF
WIFF
PHEW ...
GRAND-PA'S LATE.
IT'S PAST TIME FOR TODAY'S LESSON.
YO!

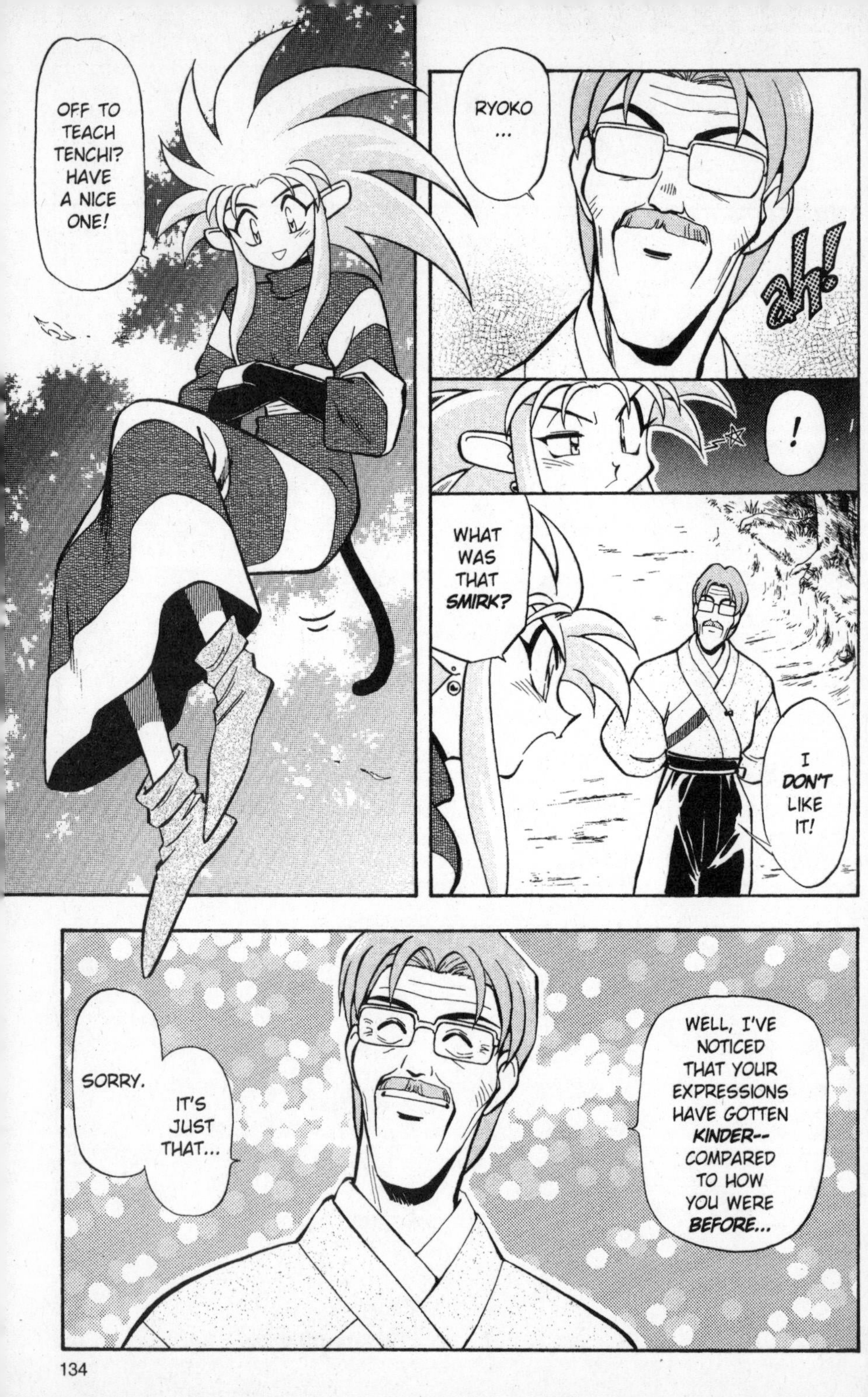
OFF TO TEACH TENCHI? HAVE A NICE ONE!
RYOKO ...
ah!
!
WHAT WAS THAT SMIRK?
I DON'T LIKE IT!
SORRY.
IT'S JUST THAT...
WELL, I'VE NOTICED THAT YOUR EXPRESSIONS HAVE GOTTEN KINDER-- COMPARED TO HOW YOU WERE BEFORE...

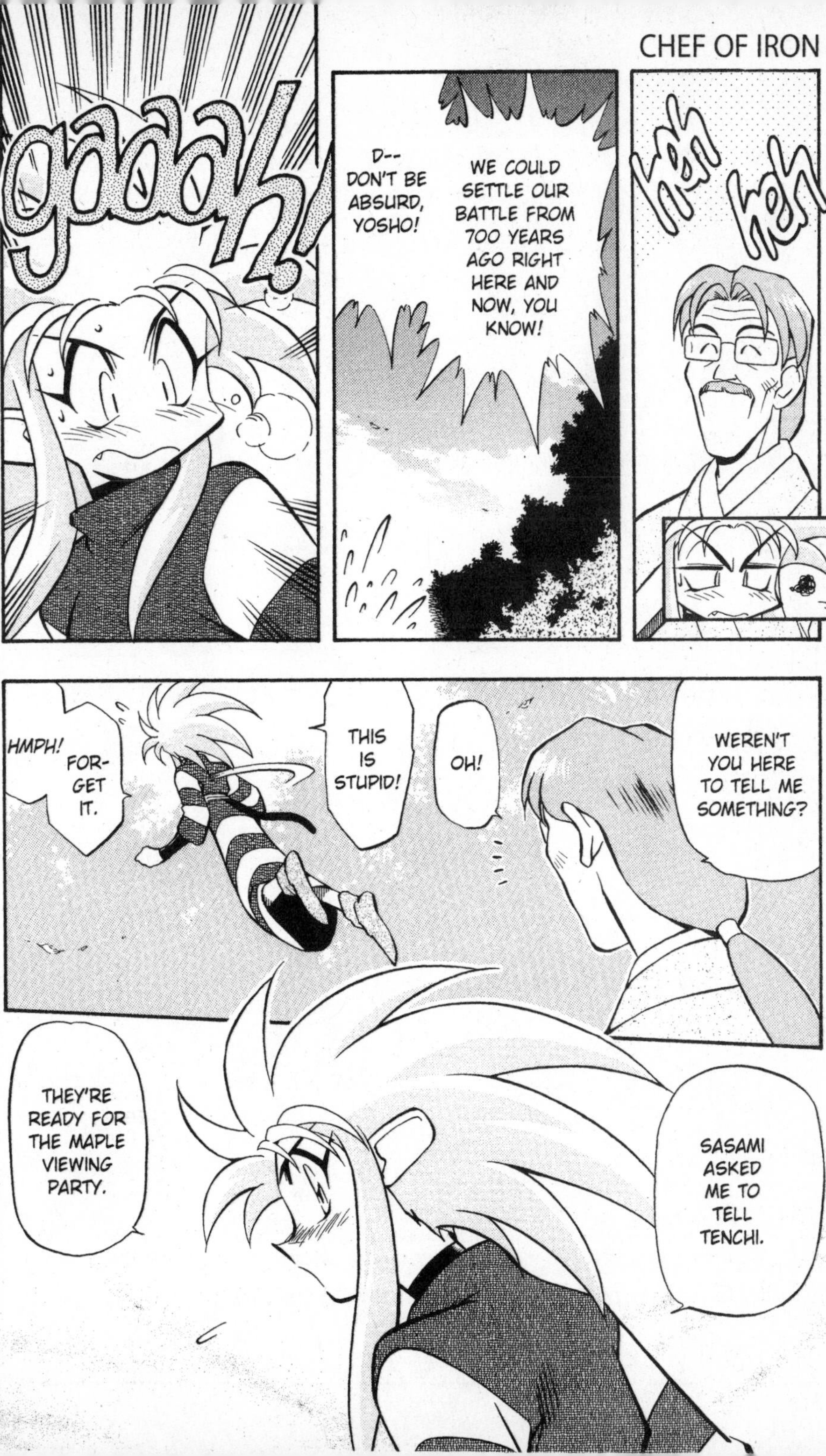
gaaah!
D-- DON'T BE ABSURD, YOSHO!
WE COULD SETTLE OUR BATTLE FROM 700 YEARS AGO RIGHT HERE AND NOW, YOU KNOW!
heh heh
HMPH!
FOR-GET IT.
THIS IS STUPID!
OH!
WEREN'T YOU HERE TO TELL ME SOMETHING?
THEY'RE READY FOR THE MAPLE VIEWING PARTY.
SASAMI ASKED ME TO TELL TENCHI.

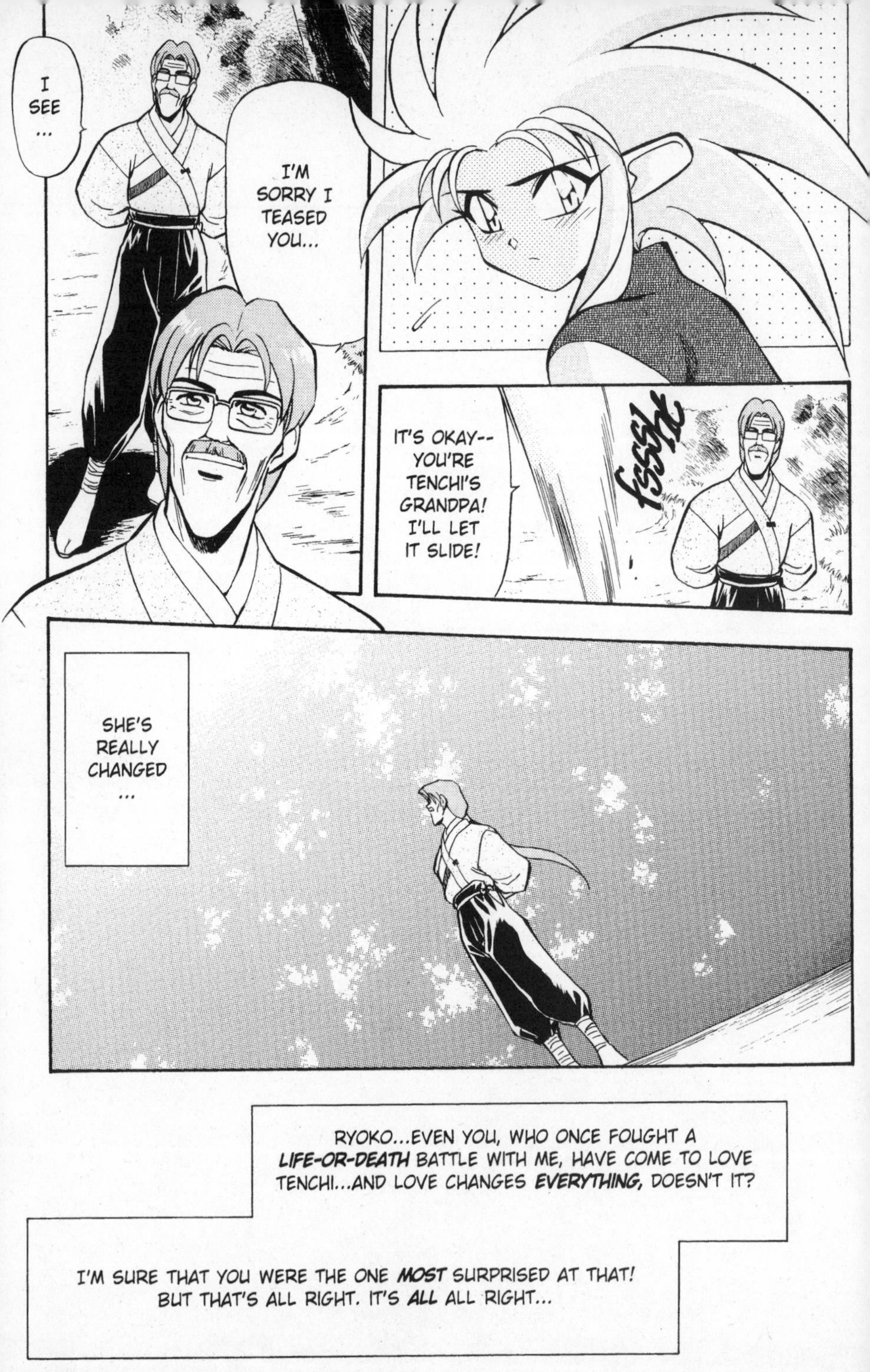
I SEE ...
I'M SORRY I TEASED YOU...
IT'S OKAY-- YOU'RE TENCHI'S GRANDPA! I'LL LET IT SLIDE!
fsssht
SHE'S REALLY CHANGED ...
RYOKO...EVEN YOU, WHO ONCE FOUGHT A **LIFE-OR-DEATH** BATTLE WITH ME, HAVE COME TO LOVE TENCHI...AND LOVE CHANGES **EVERYTHING,** DOESN'T IT?
I'M SURE THAT YOU WERE THE ONE **MOST** SURPRISED AT THAT! BUT THAT'S ALL RIGHT. IT'S **ALL** ALL RIGHT...

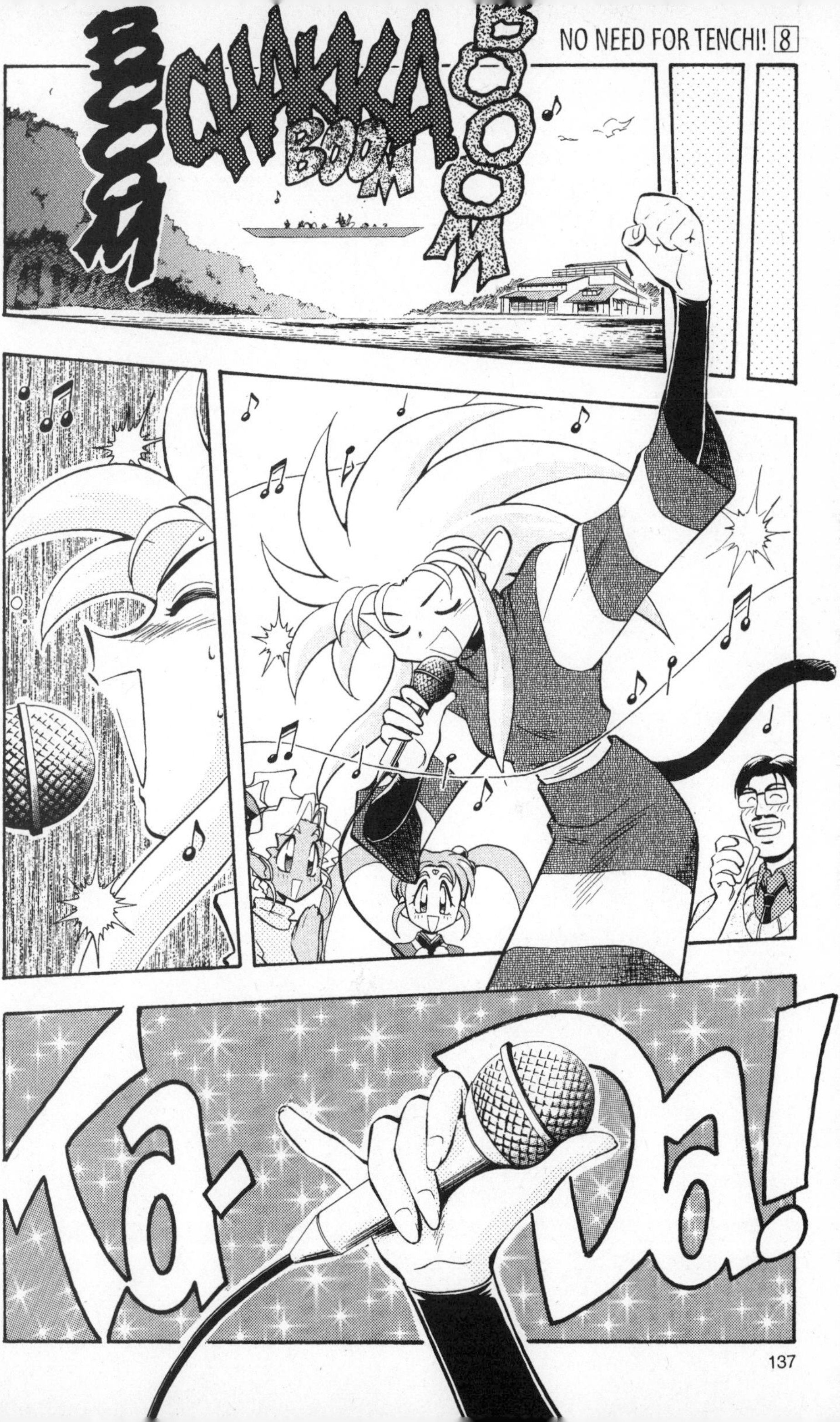
CHAKKA
BOOM
BOOOM
Ta-Da!

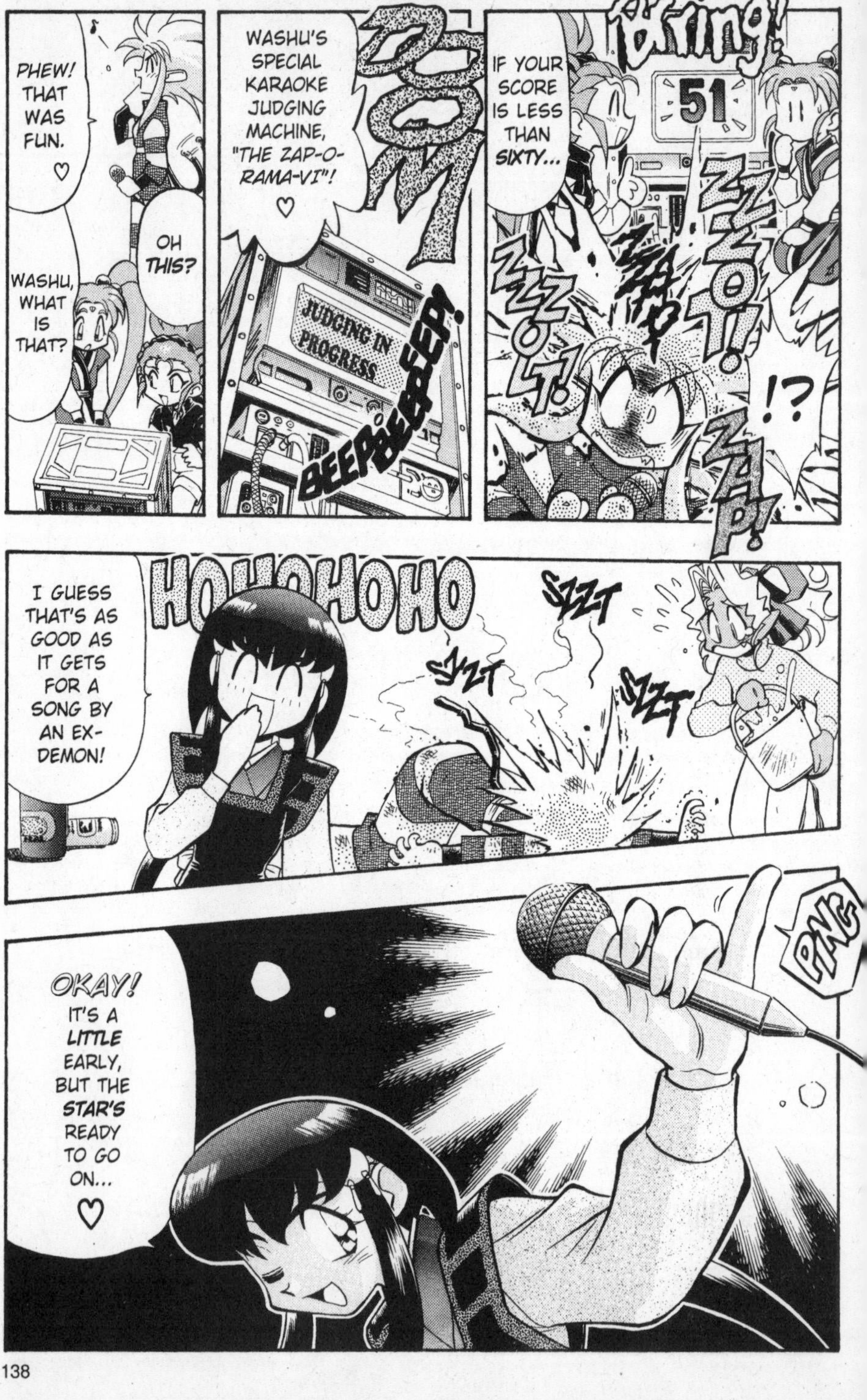
PHEW! THAT WAS FUN. ♡
OH THIS?
WASHU, WHAT IS THAT?
DOOM
WASHU'S SPECIAL KARAOKE JUDGING MACHINE, "THE ZAP-O-RAMA-VI"! ♡
JUDGING IN PROGRESS
BEEP BEEEP
BRING!
51
IF YOUR SCORE IS LESS THAN SIXTY...
ZZZOLT!
ZZZOT!
!?
ZAP!
HOHOHOHOHO
I GUESS THAT'S AS GOOD AS IT GETS FOR A SONG BY AN EX-DEMON!
SZZT
SZZT
SZZT
PING
OKAY! IT'S A LITTLE EARLY, BUT THE STAR'S READY TO GO ON... ♡

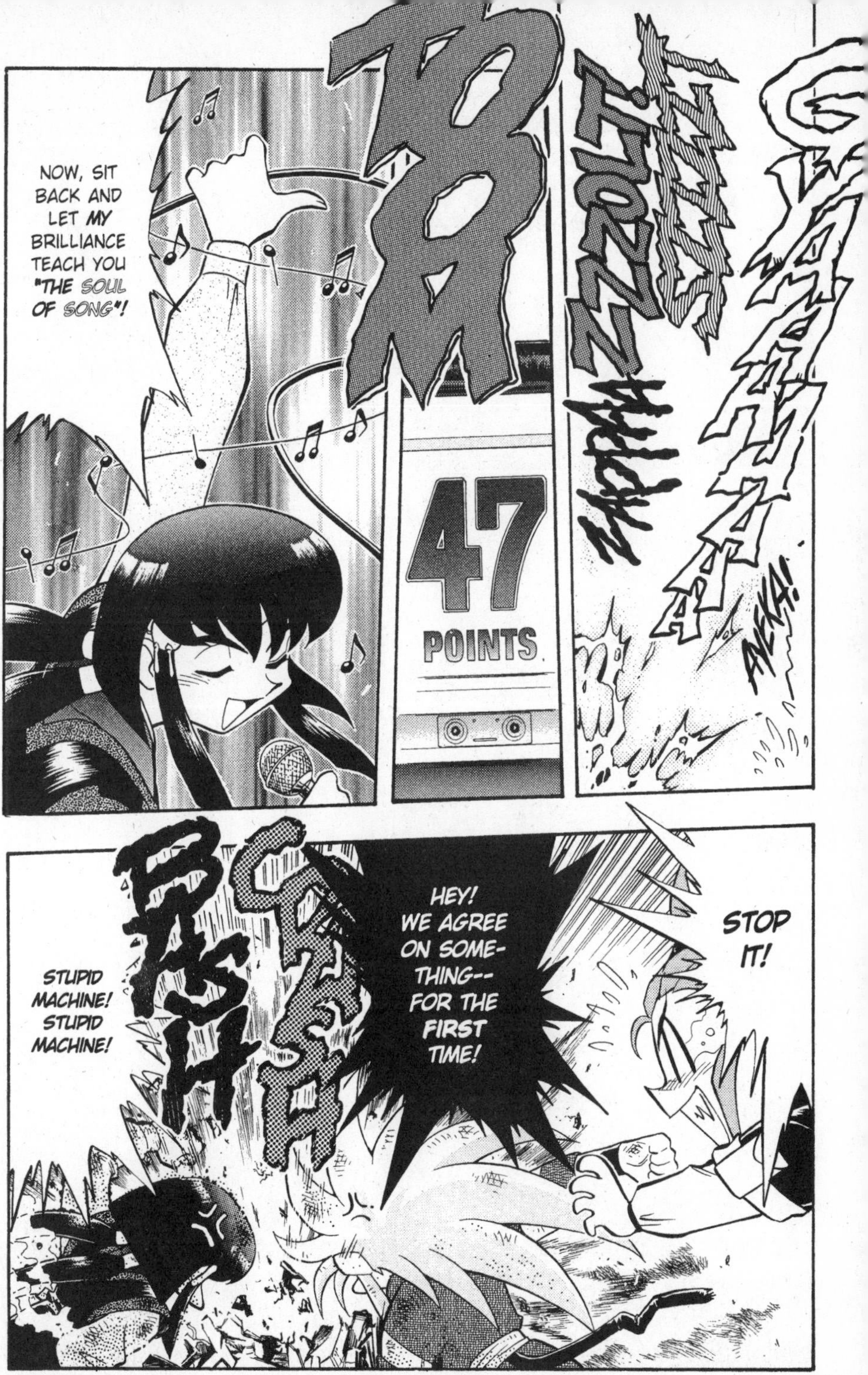
NOW, SIT BACK AND LET MY BRILLIANCE TEACH YOU "THE SOUL OF SONG"!
47
POINTS
AYEKA!
STUPID MACHINE! STUPID MACHINE!
HEY! WE AGREE ON SOME-THING-- FOR THE FIRST TIME!
STOP IT!

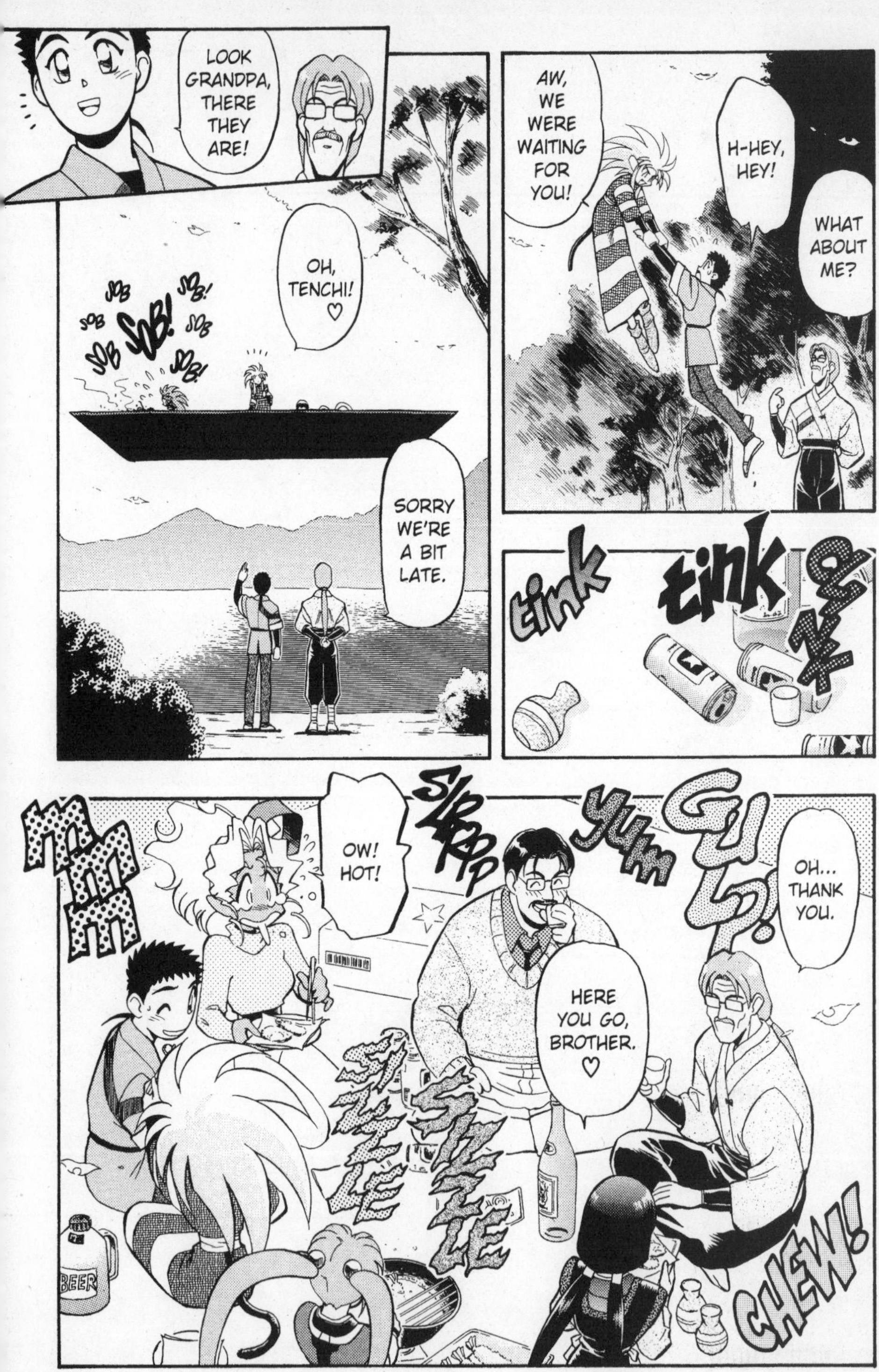

LOOK GRANDPA, THERE THEY ARE!
OH, TENCHI! ♡
SOB SOB SOB! SOB SOB SOB!
SORRY WE'RE A BIT LATE.
AW, WE WERE WAITING FOR YOU!
H-HEY, HEY!
WHAT ABOUT ME?
tink
tink
OW! HOT!
SLURRP
YUM
GULP!
OH... THANK YOU.
HERE YOU GO, BROTHER. ♡
SIZZLE SIZZLE
BEER
CHEW!

HMM... FRIED MAPLE LEAVES-- A NICE TOUCH!

THE RED COLOR OF THE LEAVES MAKES YOU CONSCIOUS OF THE SEASON.

SURE.

HAVE A DRINK, DAD.

HMM! I NEVER THOUGHT ABOUT IT, BUT THE *SACRED TREE* DOESN'T TURN COLOR! HOW ODD.

EVEN IF IT *HAS* TAKEN ROOT ON EARTH, FUNAHO STILL HAS THE SPECIAL POWERS OF A *ROYAL TREE*.

SO IT'S NOT ODD AT ALL.

.....

FUNAHO...

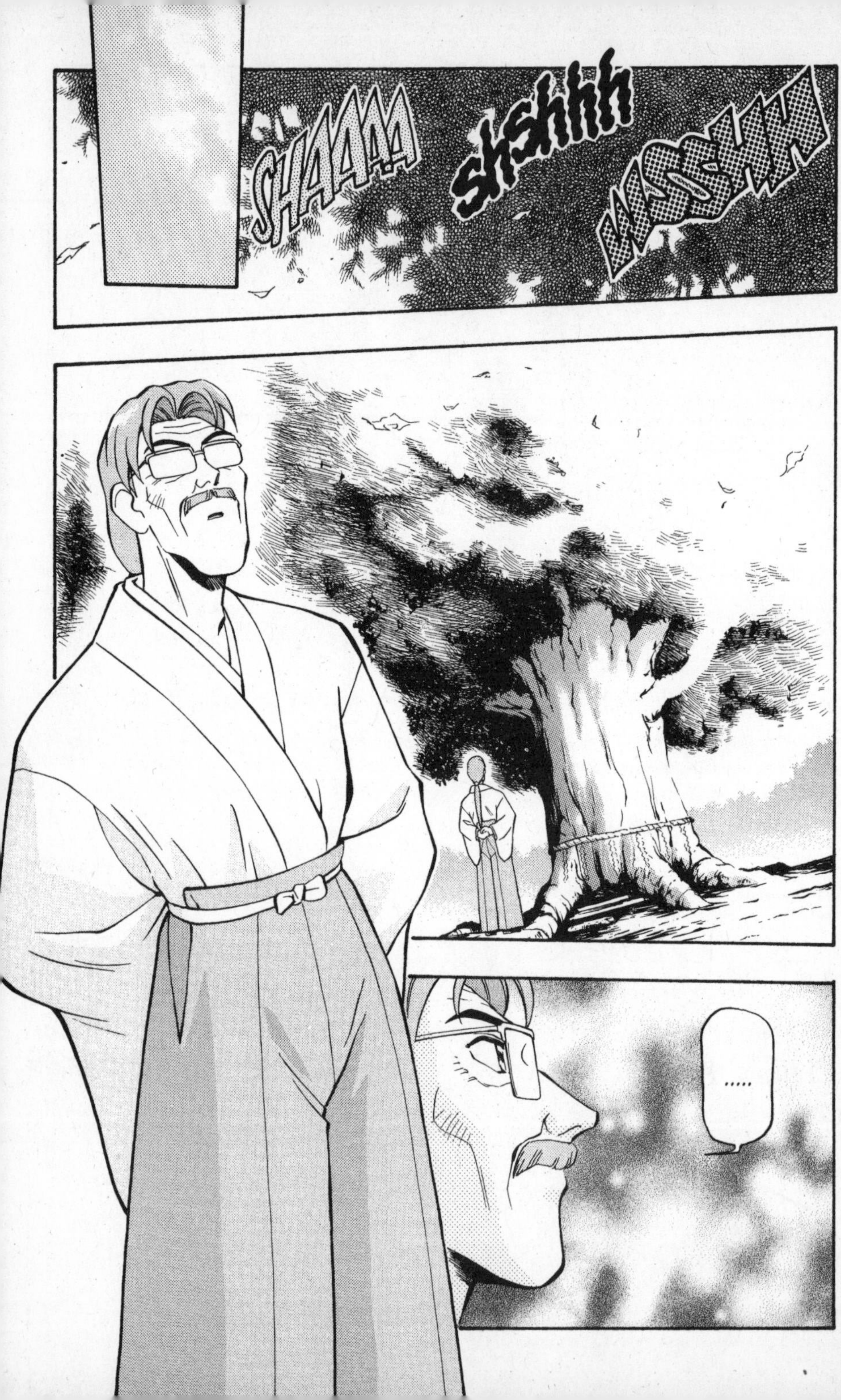
SHAAAA
shshhh
WSSHH
......

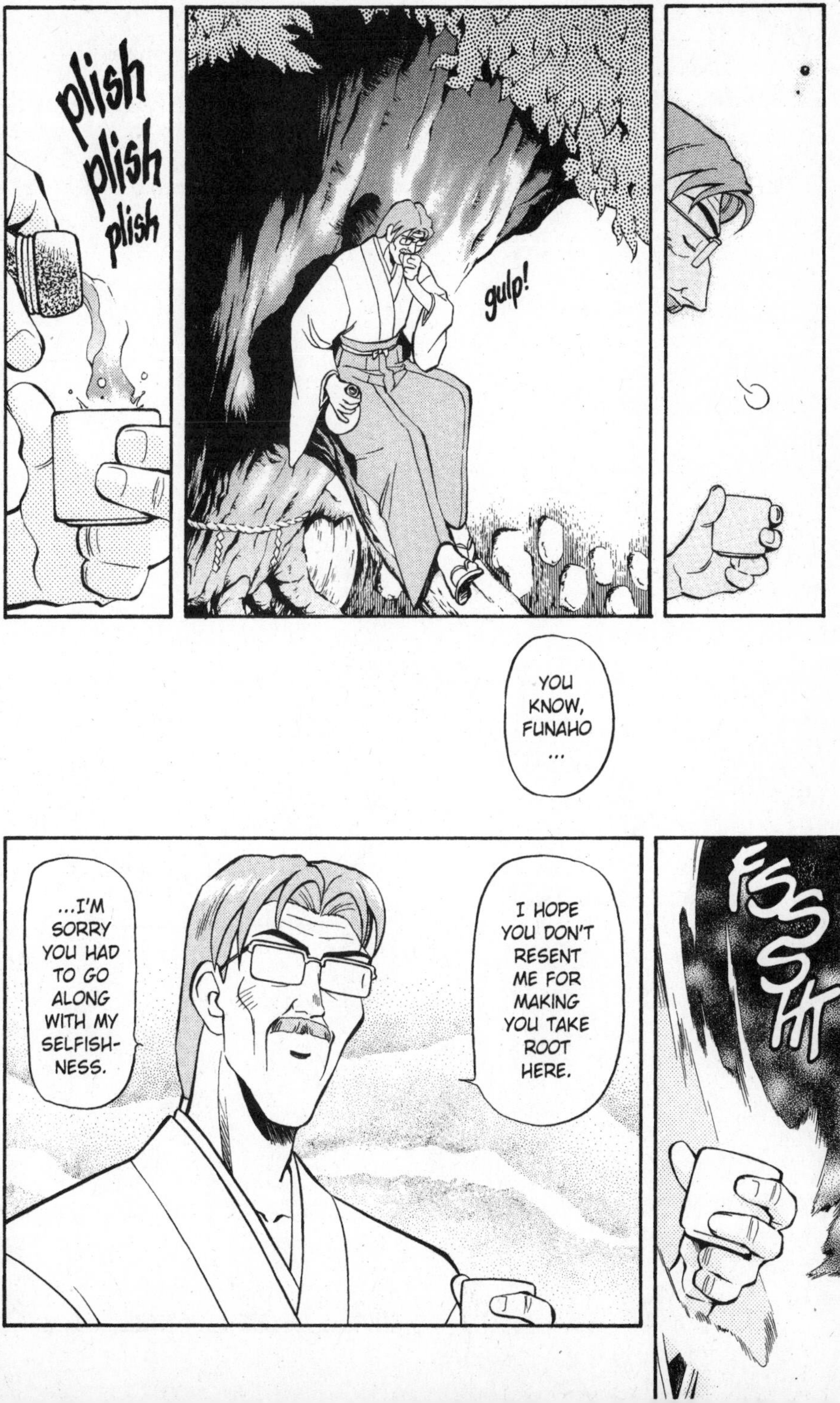
plish
plish
plish
gulp!
YOU KNOW, FUNAHO ...
...I'M SORRY YOU HAD TO GO ALONG WITH MY SELFISH-NESS.
I HOPE YOU DON'T RESENT ME FOR MAKING YOU TAKE ROOT HERE.
FSSSH

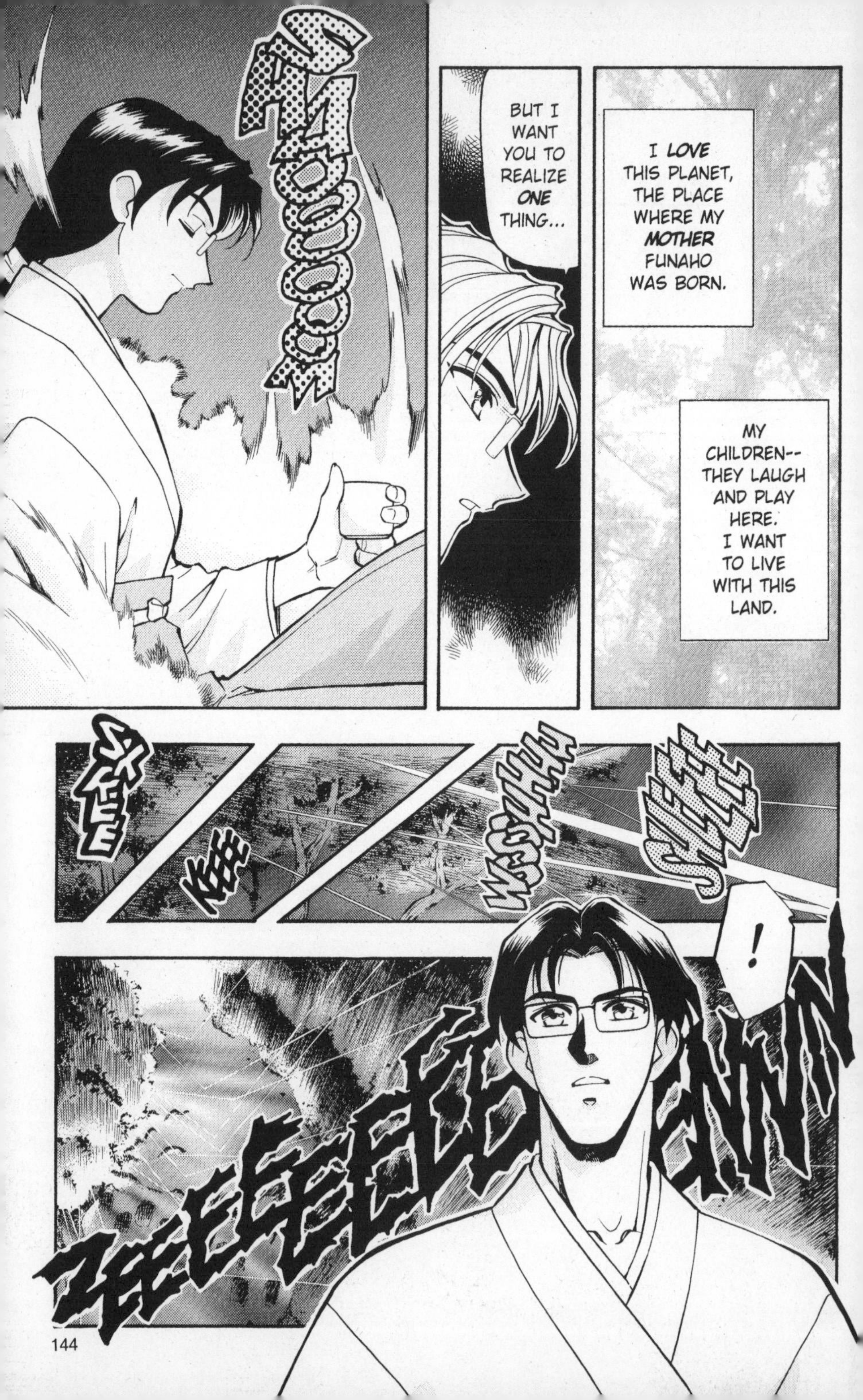
BUT I WANT YOU TO REALIZE ***ONE*** THING...
I ***LOVE*** THIS PLANET, THE PLACE WHERE MY ***MOTHER*** FUNAHO WAS BORN.
MY CHILDREN-- THEY LAUGH AND PLAY HERE. I WANT TO LIVE WITH THIS LAND.
SKREE
KEEEE
!

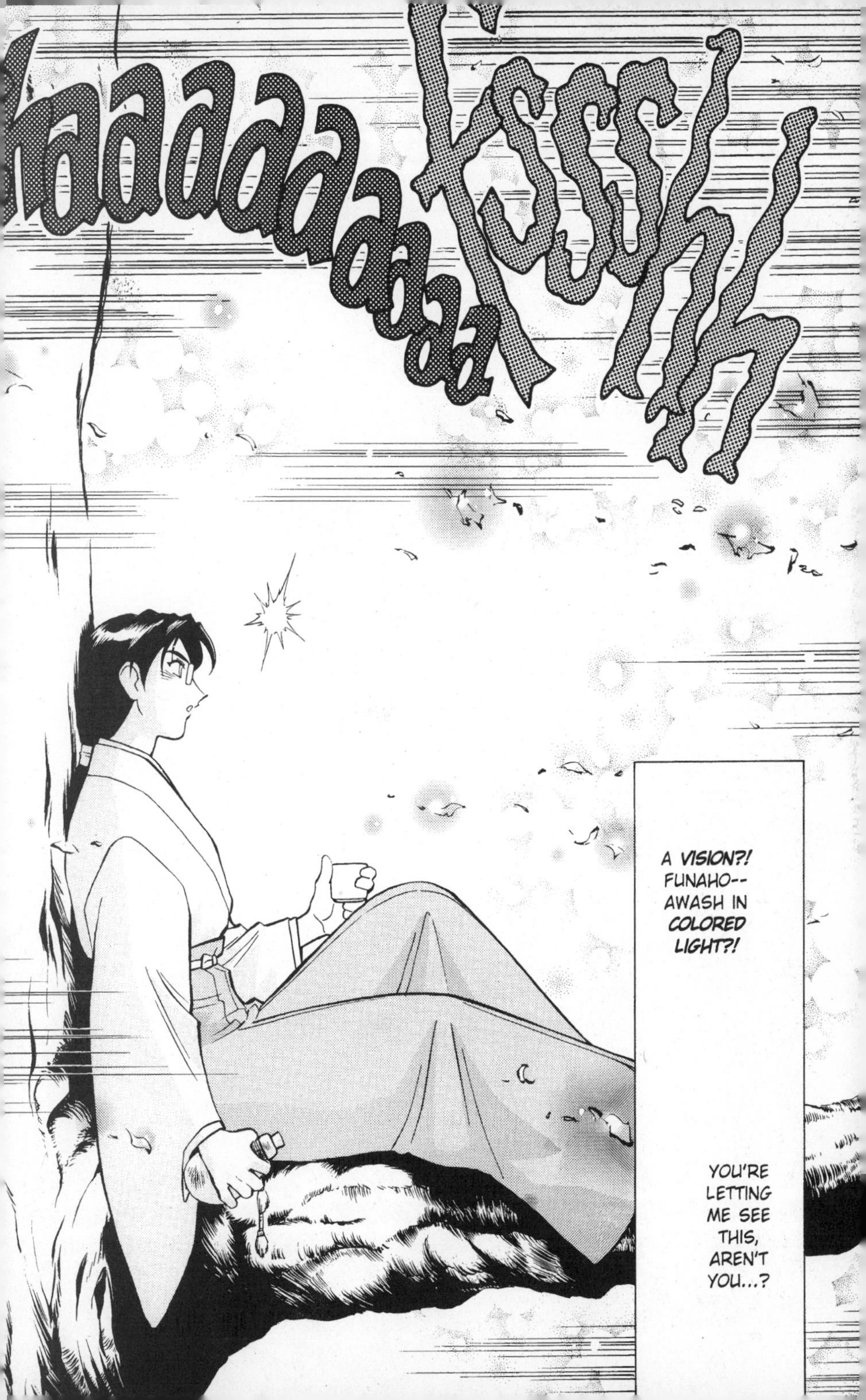
haaaaaaaaaaaaa
kssshh
A **VISION?!** FUNAHO--AWASH IN **COLORED** **LIGHT?!**
YOU'RE LETTING ME SEE THIS, AREN'T YOU...?

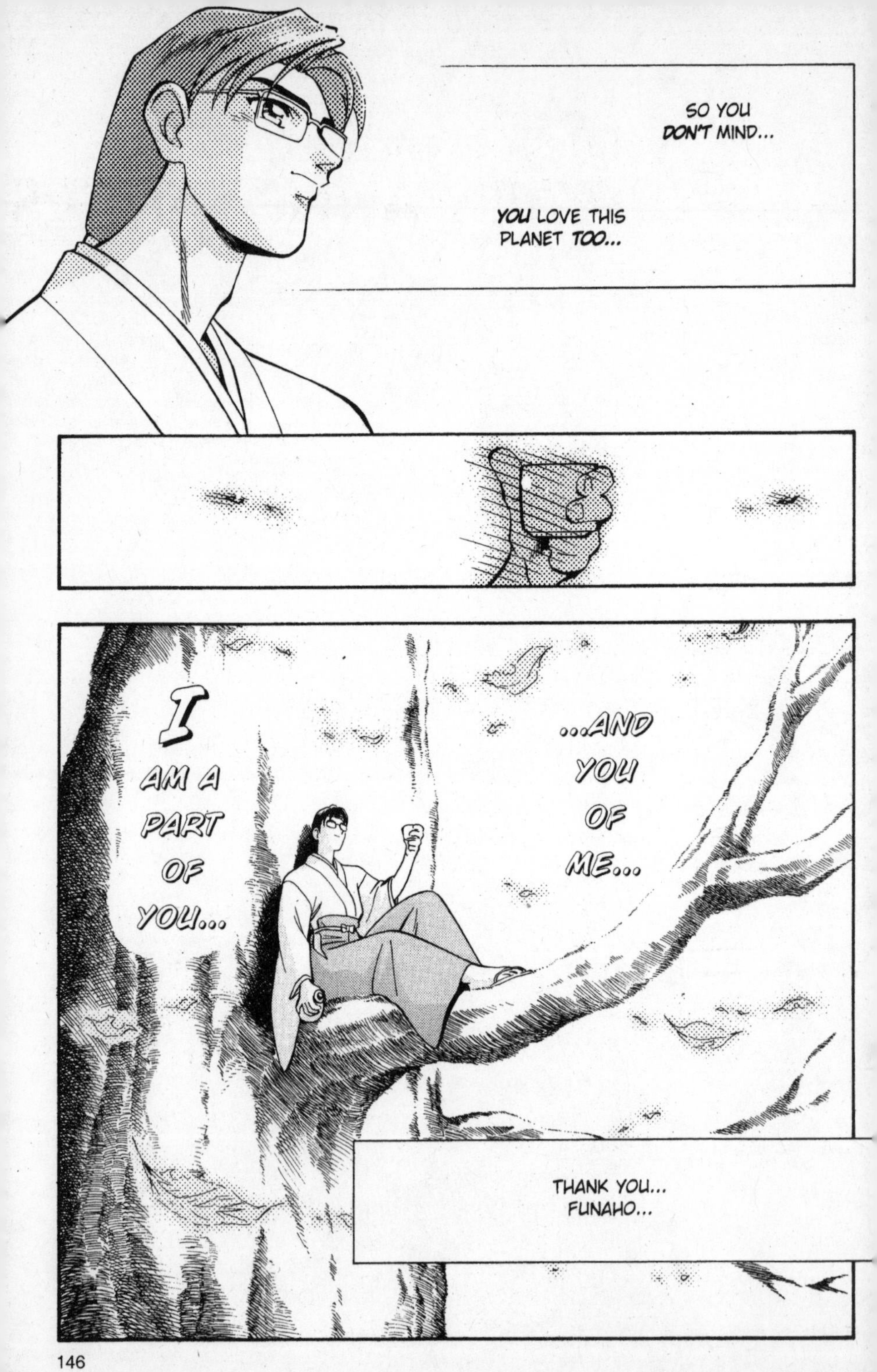
SO YOU DON'T MIND...
YOU LOVE THIS PLANET TOO...
I AM A PART OF YOU...
...AND YOU OF ME...
THANK YOU... FUNAHO...

Tales of Tenchi #7:
PETTY ANNOYANCES

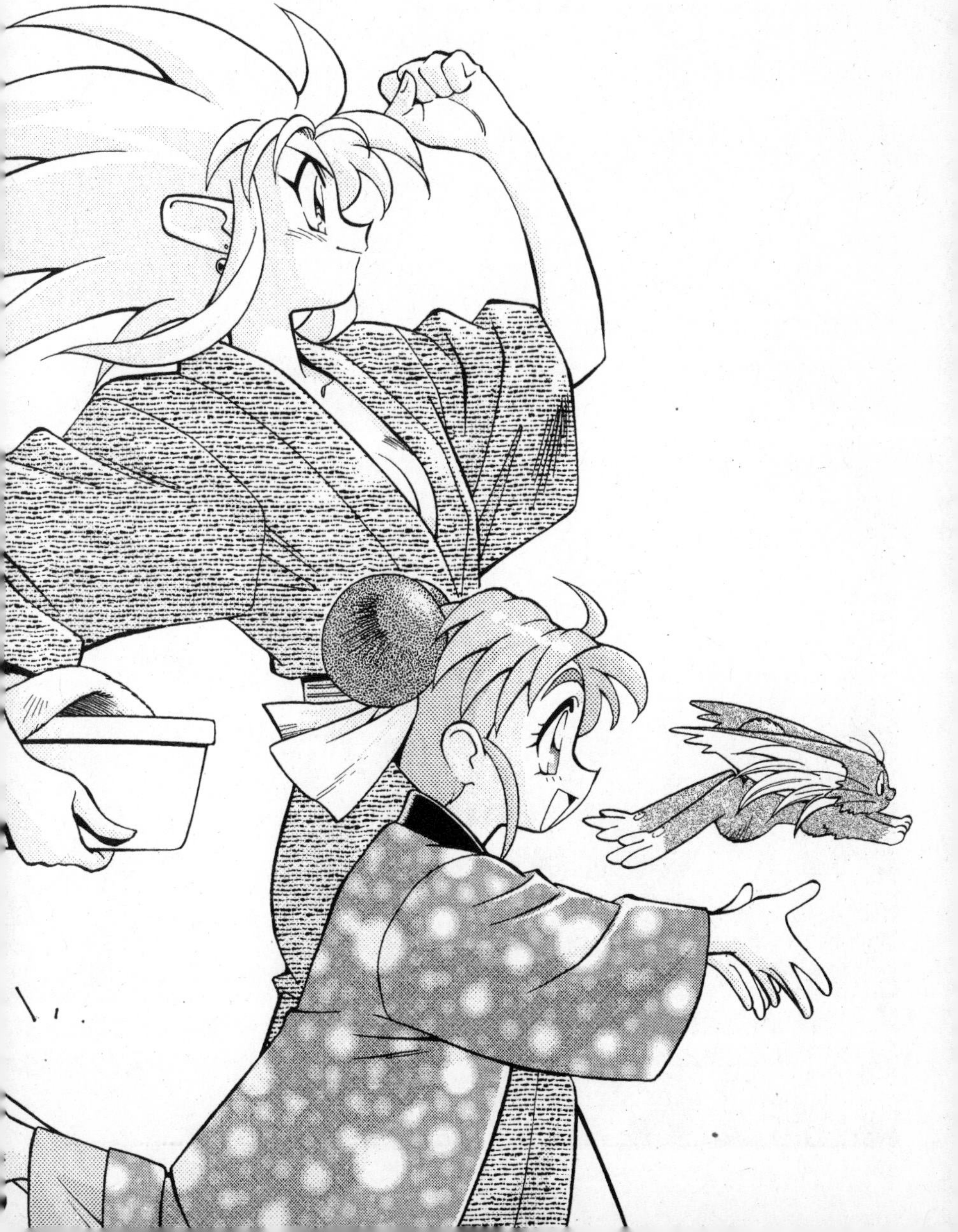

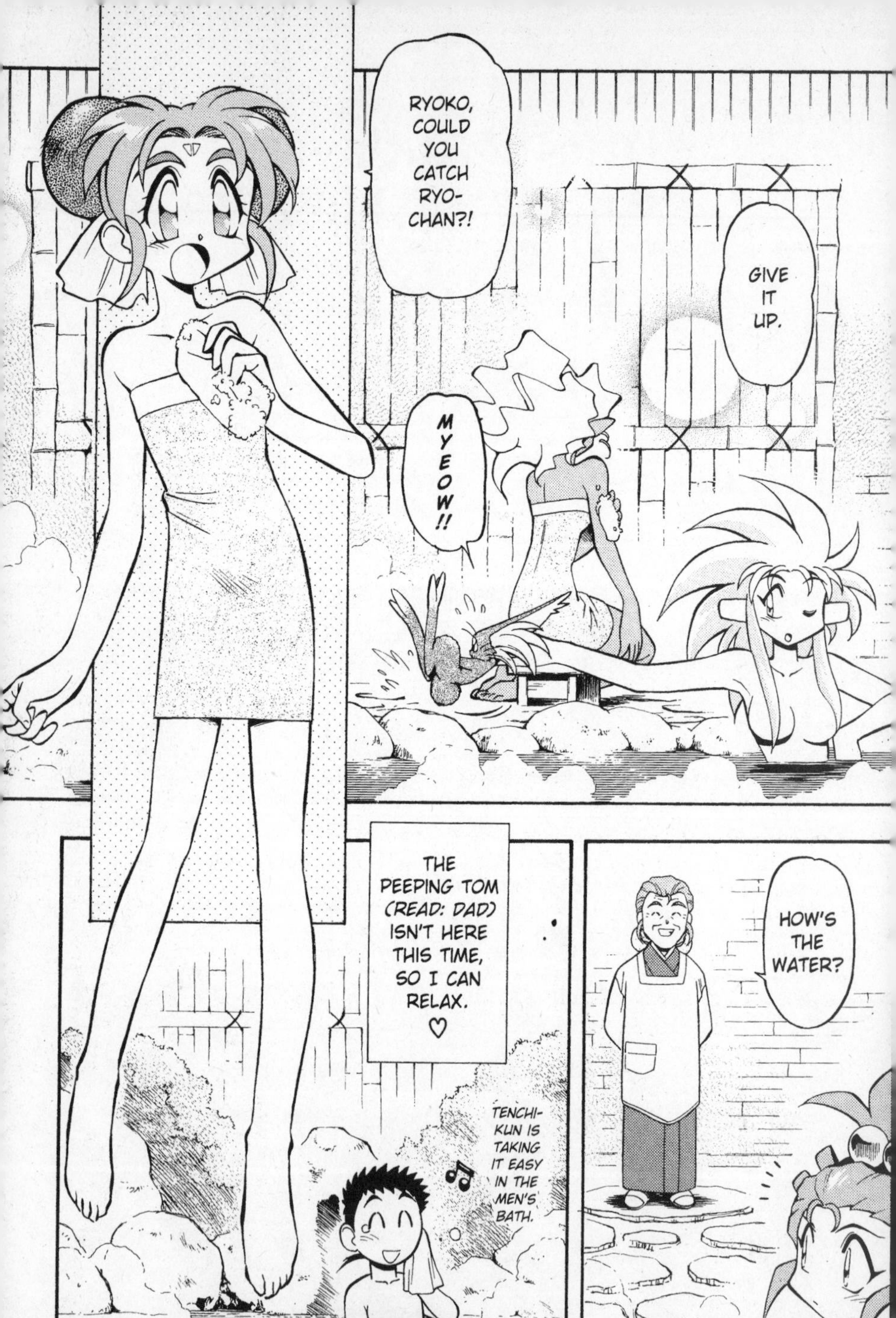
RYOKO, COULD YOU CATCH RYO-CHAN?!
MYEOW!!
GIVE IT UP.
THE PEEPING TOM (READ: DAD) ISN'T HERE THIS TIME, SO I CAN RELAX. ♡
TENCHI-KUN IS TAKING IT EASY IN THE MEN'S BATH.
HOW'S THE WATER?

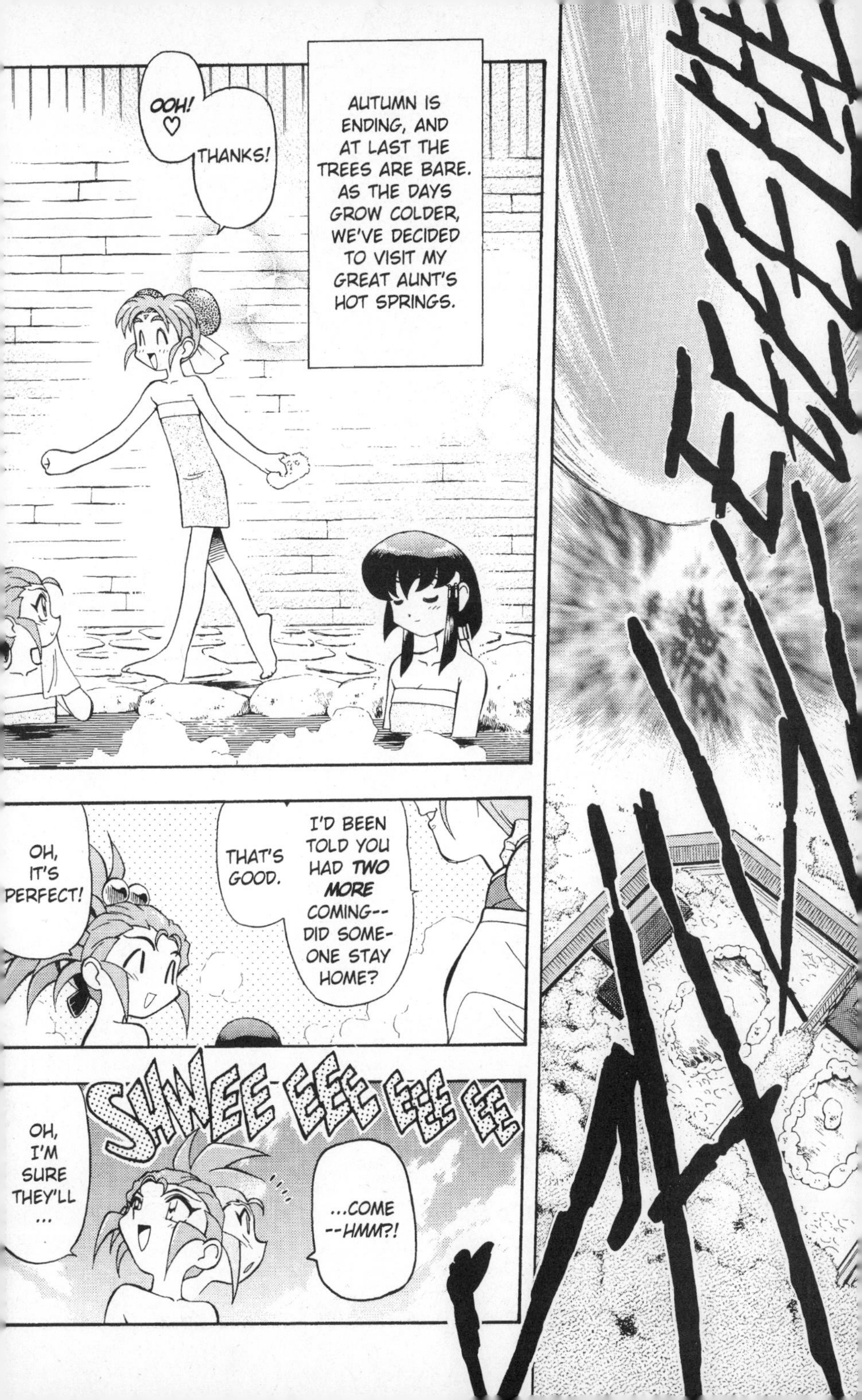

OOH! ♡ THANKS!
AUTUMN IS ENDING, AND AT LAST THE TREES ARE BARE. AS THE DAYS GROW COLDER, WE'VE DECIDED TO VISIT MY GREAT AUNT'S HOT SPRINGS.
OH, IT'S PERFECT!
THAT'S GOOD.
I'D BEEN TOLD YOU HAD **TWO MORE** COMING--DID SOME-ONE STAY HOME?
SHWEE EEE EEE EE
OH, I'M SURE THEY'LL ...
...COME --HMM?!

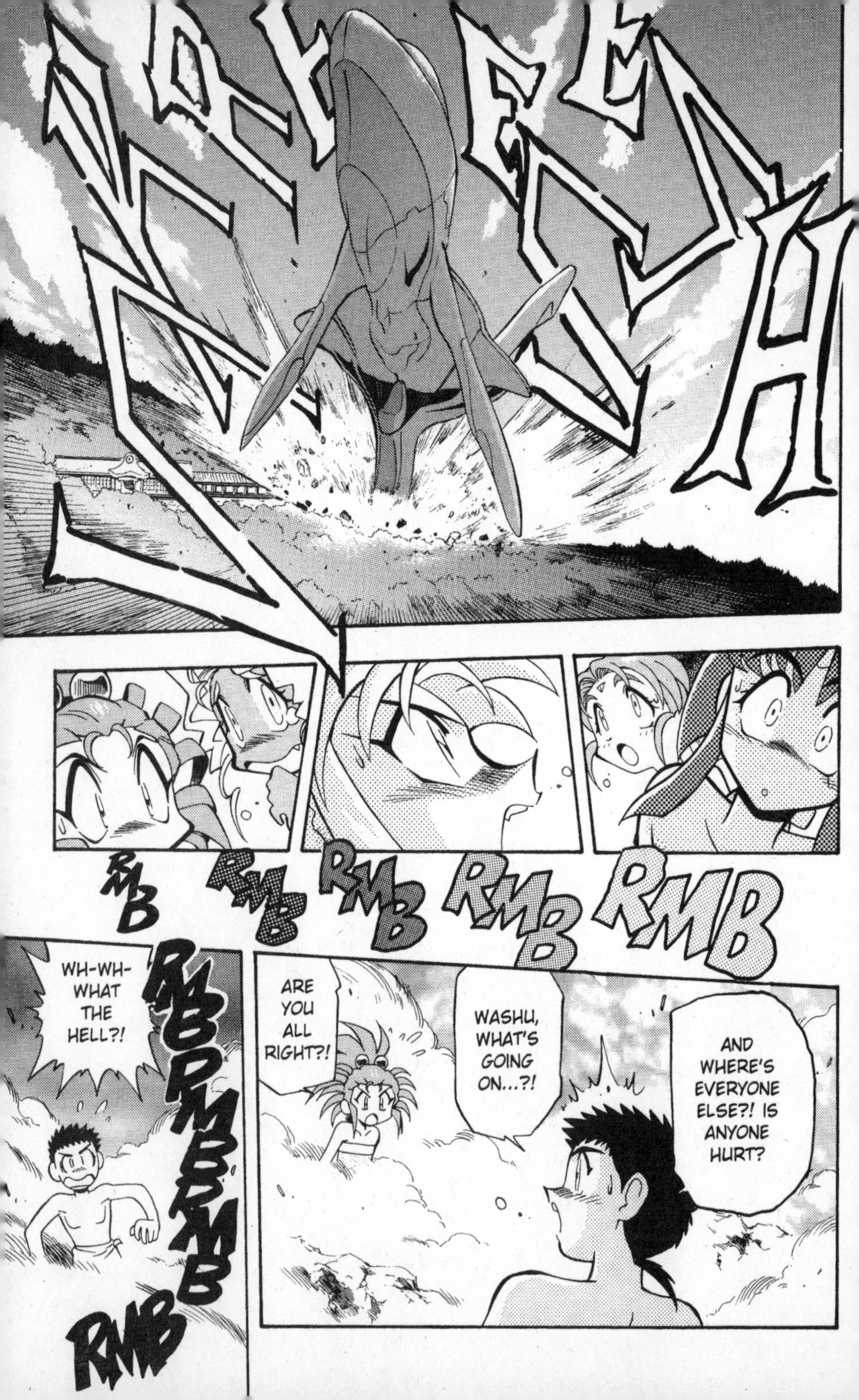
RMB RMB RMB RMB RMB
WH-WH-WHAT THE HELL?!
RMBRMBRMBRMB
RMB
ARE YOU ALL RIGHT?!
WASHU, WHAT'S GOING ON...?!
AND WHERE'S EVERYONE ELSE?! IS ANYONE HURT?

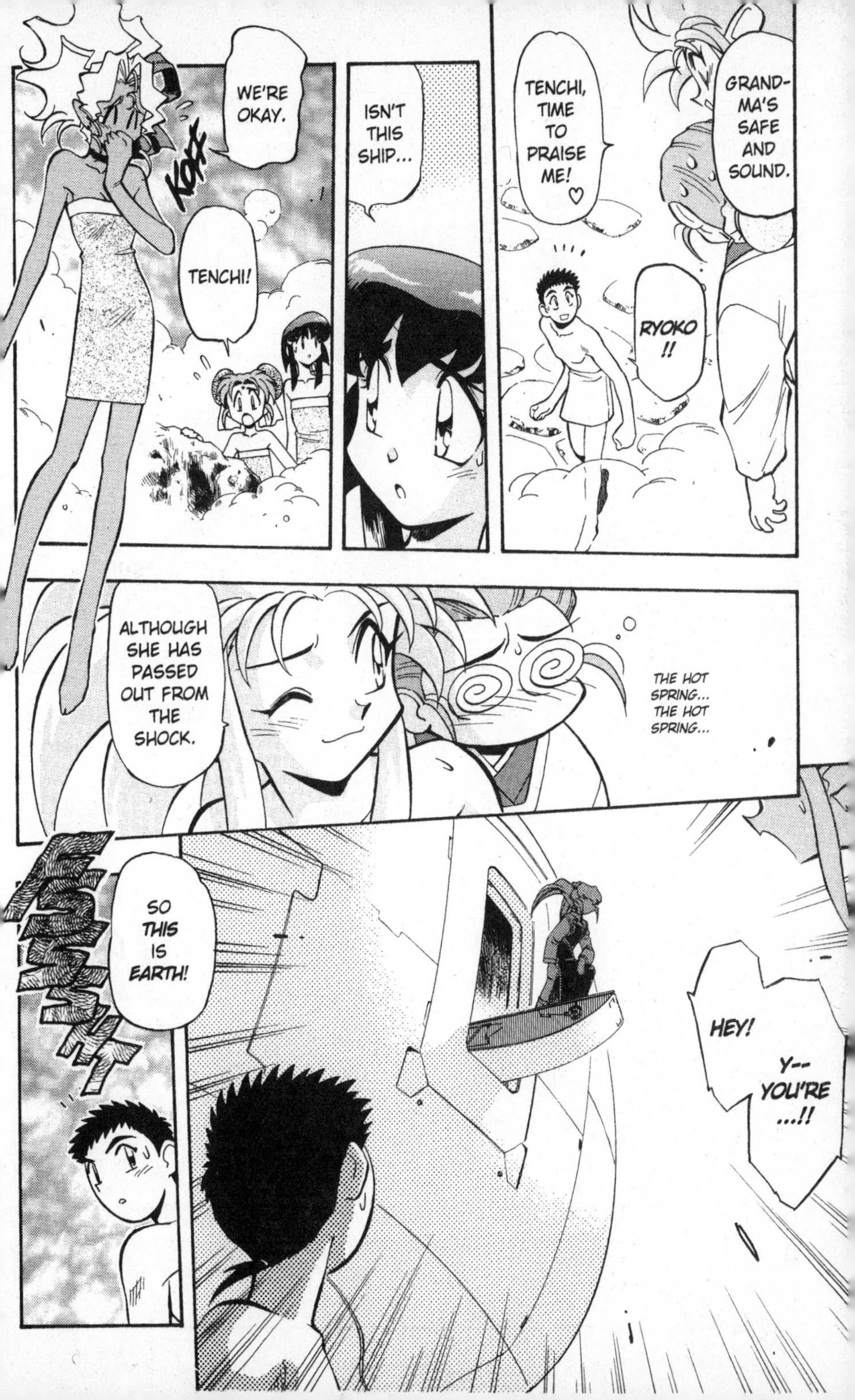
WE'RE OKAY.
KOFF
TENCHI!
ISN'T THIS SHIP...
TENCHI, TIME TO PRAISE ME! ♡
RYOKO !!
GRAND-MA'S SAFE AND SOUND.
ALTHOUGH SHE HAS PASSED OUT FROM THE SHOCK.
THE HOT SPRING... THE HOT SPRING...
SO THIS IS EARTH!
HEY!
Y-- YOU'RE ...!!

YUME!

WHOA! GRANDMA!

HMM?

WELL, WELL-- IT'S WASHU'S DAUGHTER.

WHY THE HELL ARE *YOU* HERE?

I CAME ALL THIS WAY BECAUSE WASHU *TOLD* ME TO! "THERE'S AN INTERESTING EVENT--YOU SHOULD COME," SHE SAID.

THAT'S SOME WAY TO SAY "HI"!

LADY WASHU! *SHE'S* THE VERY PERSON WHO CAUSED AN *UNPRECEDENTED* CRISIS IN THIS GALAXY!

NOW, NOW-- DON'T BE SO UPTIGHT.

HOW COULD YOU!

JUST KEEP IN MIND...

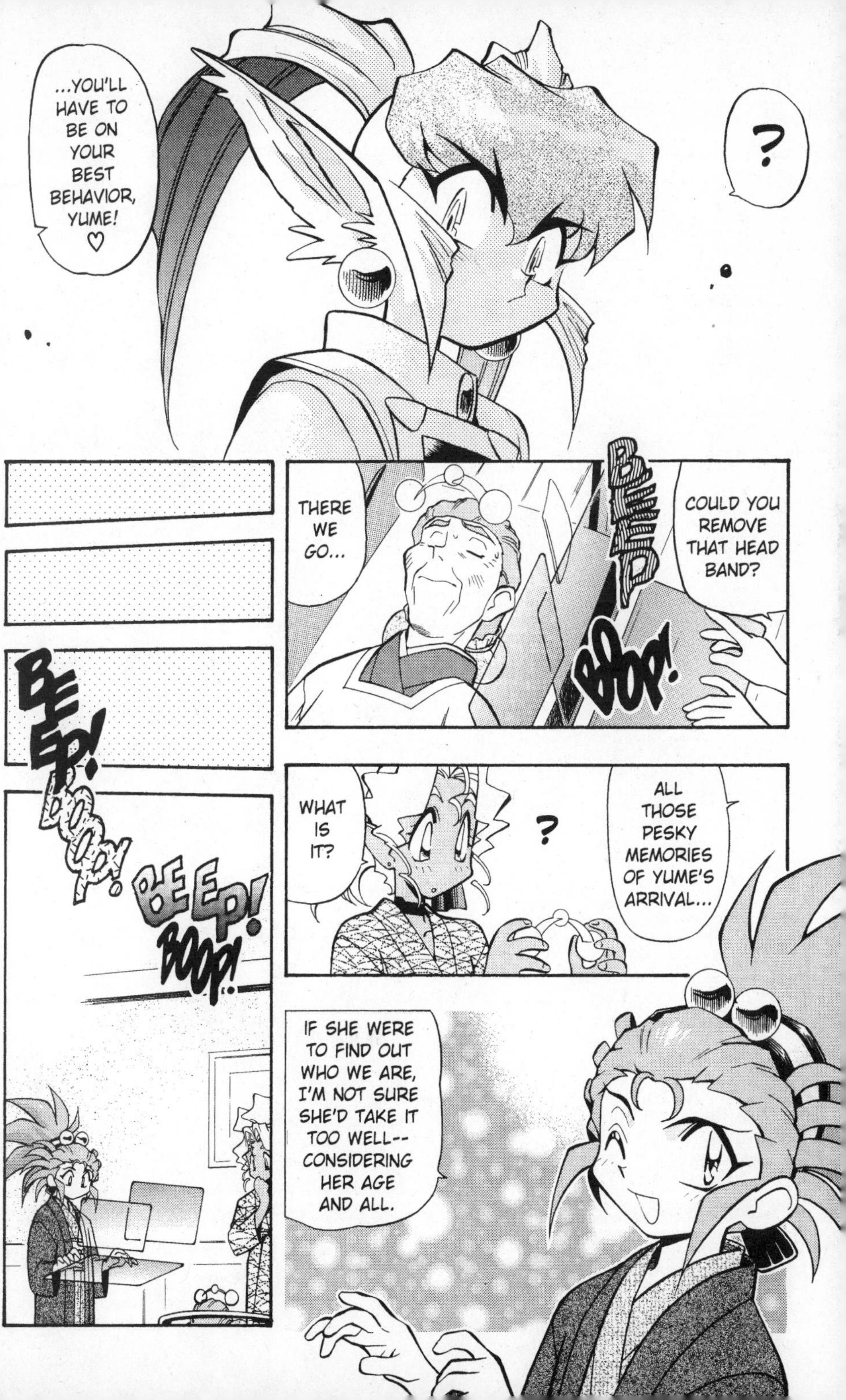

...YOU'LL HAVE TO BE ON YOUR BEST BEHAVIOR, YUME! ♡
?
BEEP! BOOOP!
BEEP! BOOP!
THERE WE GO...
BEEP! BOOP!
COULD YOU REMOVE THAT HEAD BAND?
WHAT IS IT?
?
ALL THOSE PESKY MEMORIES OF YUME'S ARRIVAL...
IF SHE WERE TO FIND OUT WHO WE ARE, I'M NOT SURE SHE'D TAKE IT TOO WELL-- CONSIDERING HER AGE AND ALL.

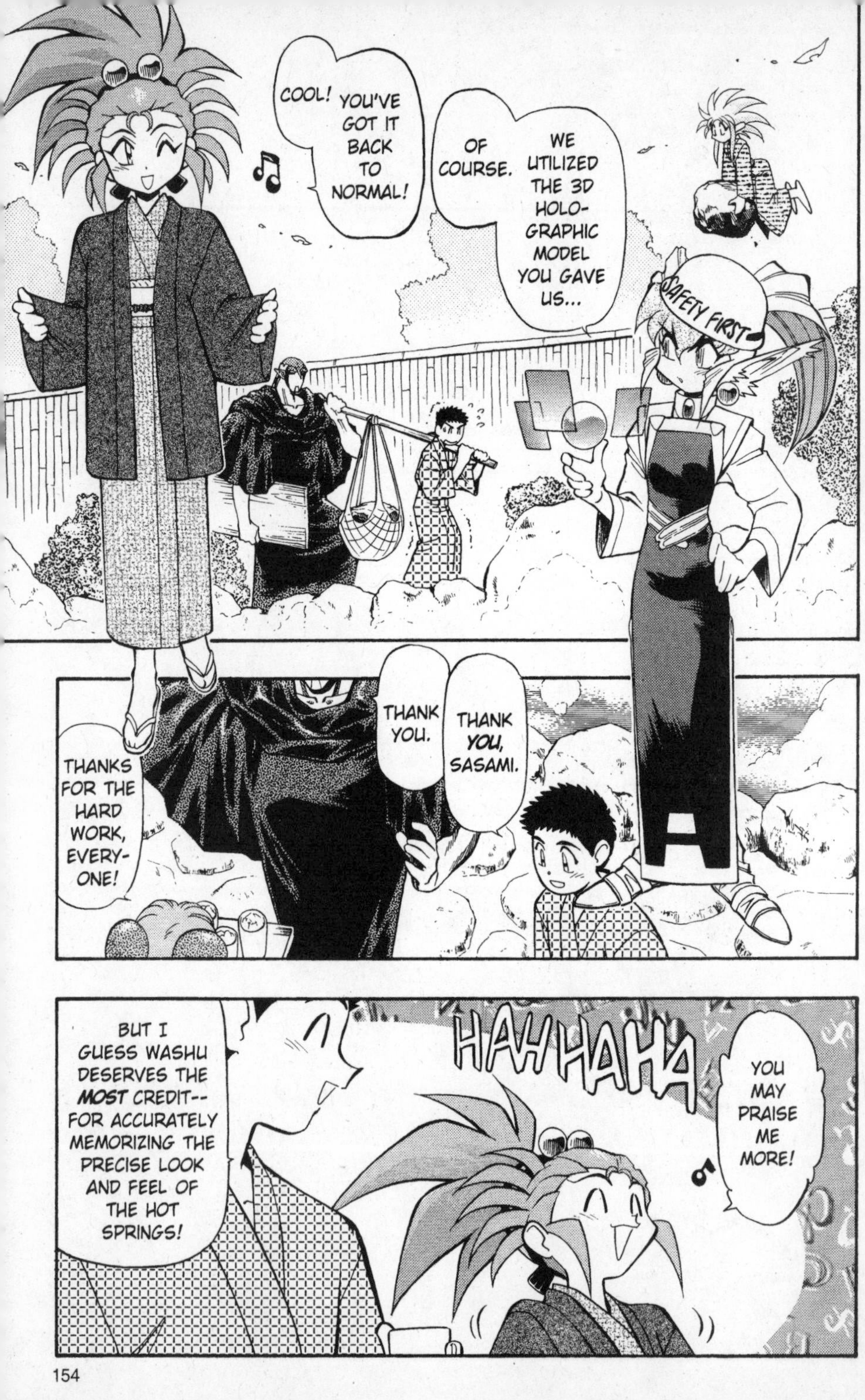
COOL! YOU'VE GOT IT BACK TO NORMAL!
OF COURSE.
WE UTILIZED THE 3D HOLOGRAPHIC MODEL YOU GAVE US...
SAFETY FIRST
THANKS FOR THE HARD WORK, EVERYONE!
THANK YOU.
THANK *YOU*, SASAMI.
BUT I GUESS WASHU DESERVES THE ***MOST*** CREDIT--FOR ACCURATELY MEMORIZING THE PRECISE LOOK AND FEEL OF THE HOT SPRINGS!
HAHHAHA
YOU MAY PRAISE ME MORE!

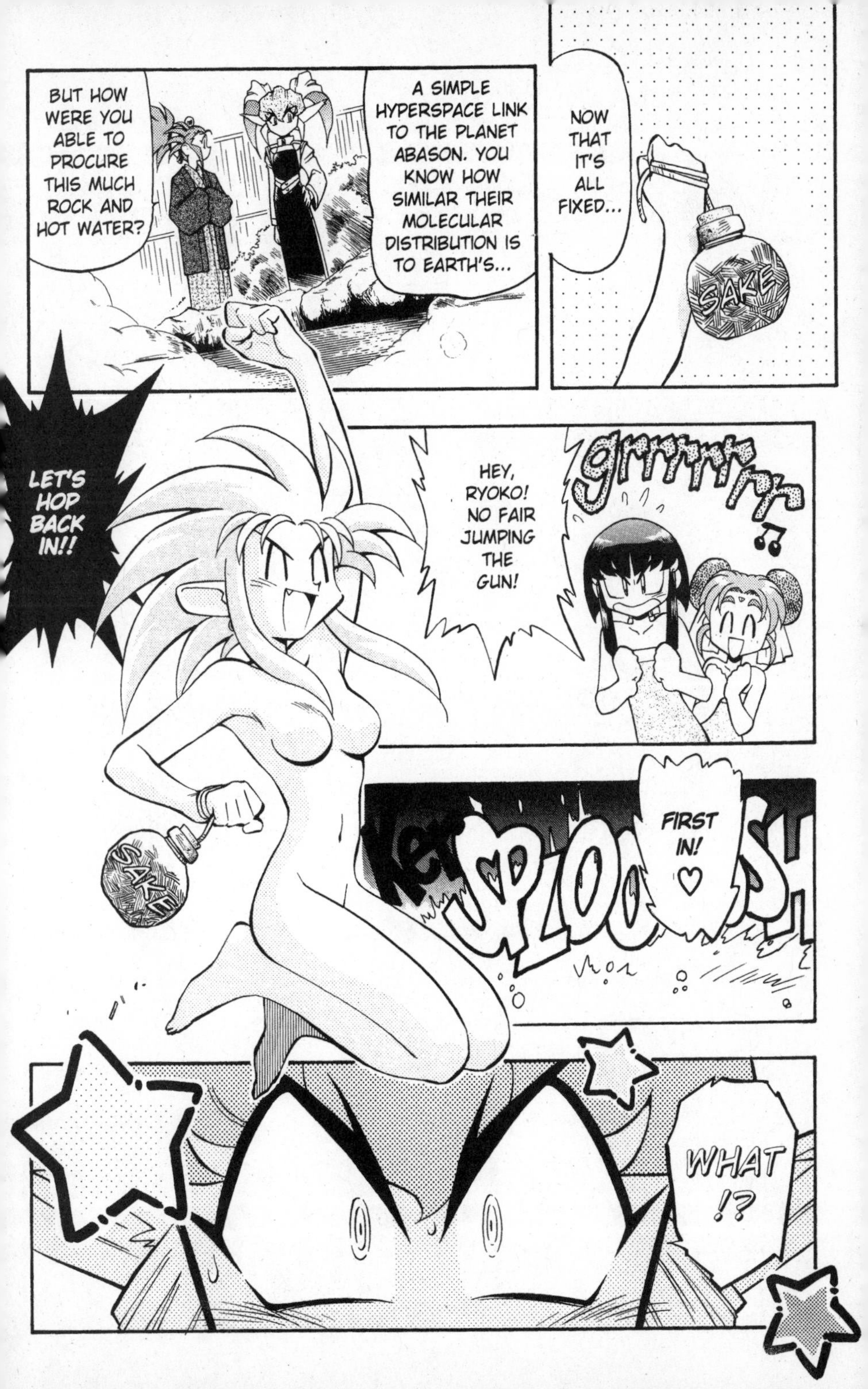

BUT HOW WERE YOU ABLE TO PROCURE THIS MUCH ROCK AND HOT WATER?
A SIMPLE HYPERSPACE LINK TO THE PLANET ABASON. YOU KNOW HOW SIMILAR THEIR MOLECULAR DISTRIBUTION IS TO EARTH'S...
NOW THAT IT'S ALL FIXED...
SAKE
LET'S HOP BACK IN!!
SAKE
HEY, RYOKO! NO FAIR JUMPING THE GUN!
FIRST IN! ♡
WHAT !?

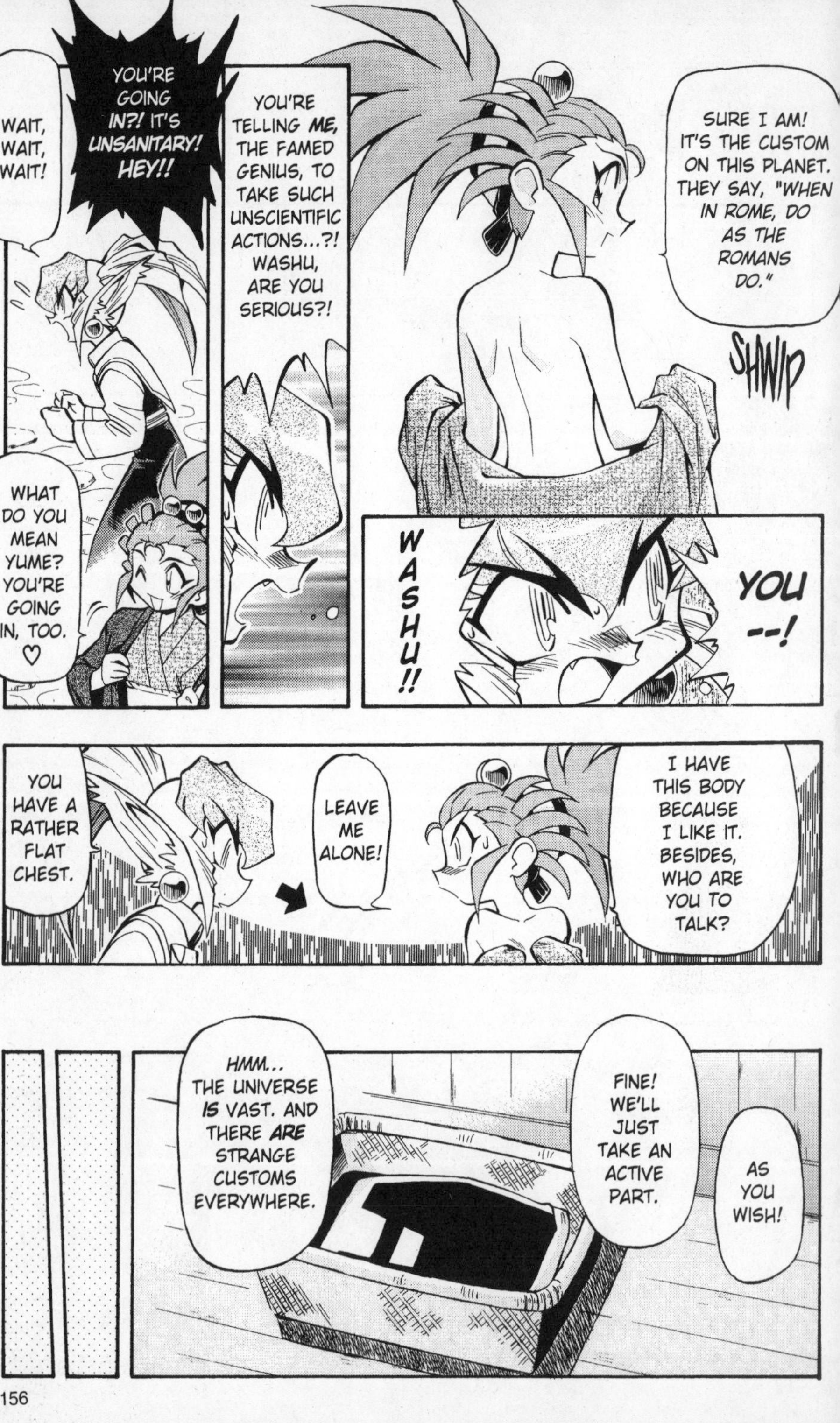
WAIT, WAIT, WAIT!
YOU'RE GOING IN?! IT'S UNSANITARY! HEY!!
WHAT DO YOU MEAN YUME? YOU'RE GOING IN, TOO. ♡
YOU'RE TELLING ME, THE FAMED GENIUS, TO TAKE SUCH UNSCIENTIFIC ACTIONS...?! WASHU, ARE YOU SERIOUS?!
SURE I AM! IT'S THE CUSTOM ON THIS PLANET. THEY SAY, "WHEN IN ROME, DO AS THE ROMANS DO."
SHWIP
WASHU!!
YOU--!
YOU HAVE A RATHER FLAT CHEST.
LEAVE ME ALONE!
I HAVE THIS BODY BECAUSE I LIKE IT. BESIDES, WHO ARE YOU TO TALK?
HMM... THE UNIVERSE IS VAST. AND THERE ARE STRANGE CUSTOMS EVERYWHERE.
FINE! WE'LL JUST TAKE AN ACTIVE PART.
AS YOU WISH!

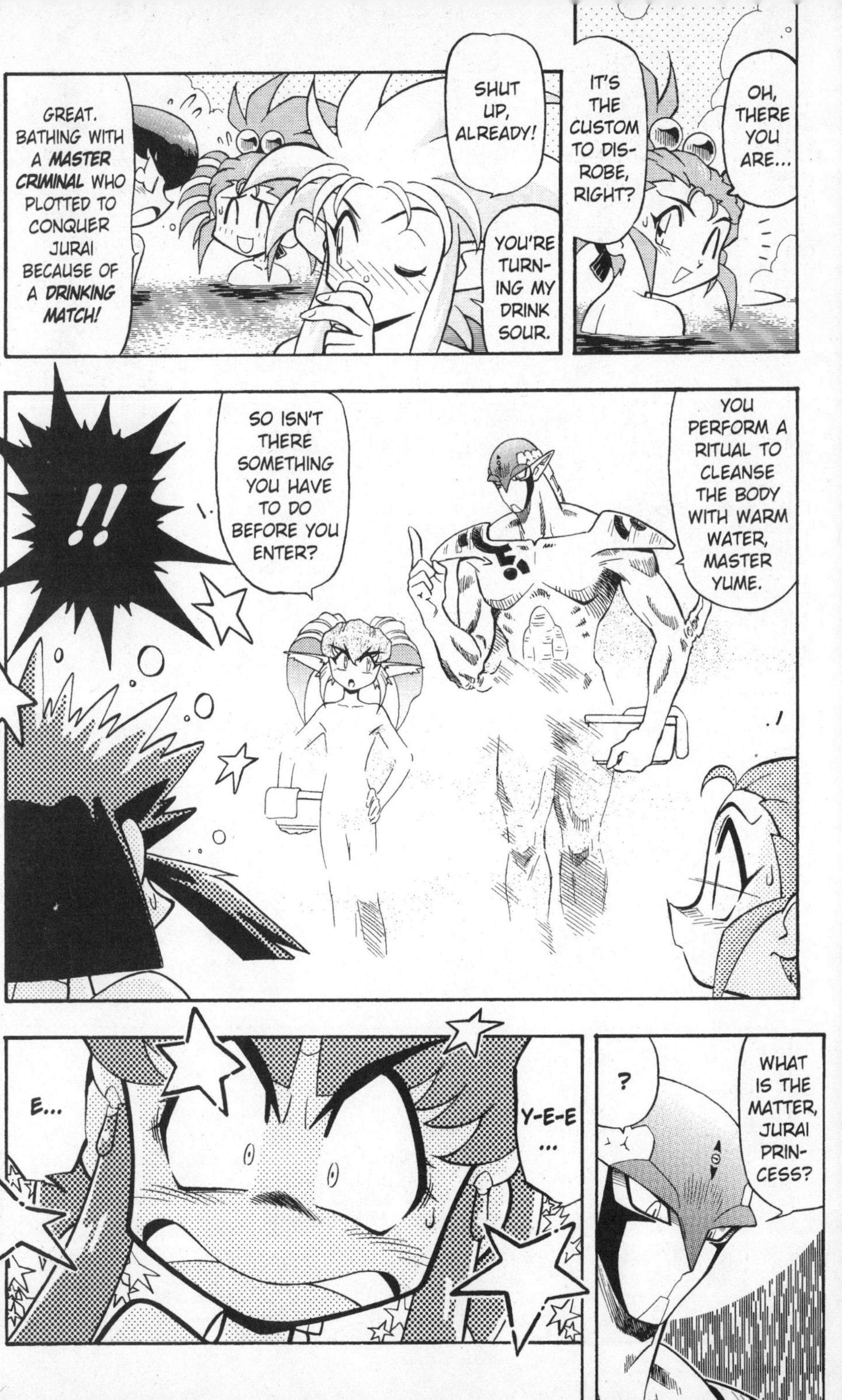
GREAT. BATHING WITH A **MASTER CRIMINAL** WHO PLOTTED TO CONQUER JURAI BECAUSE OF A **DRINKING MATCH!**
SHUT UP, ALREADY!
YOU'RE TURNING MY DRINK SOUR.
IT'S THE CUSTOM TO DIS-ROBE, RIGHT?
OH, THERE YOU ARE...
!!
SO ISN'T THERE SOMETHING YOU HAVE TO DO BEFORE YOU ENTER?
YOU PERFORM A RITUAL TO CLEANSE THE BODY WITH WARM WATER, MASTER YUME.
E...
Y-E-E ...
?
WHAT IS THE MATTER, JURAI PRIN-CESS?

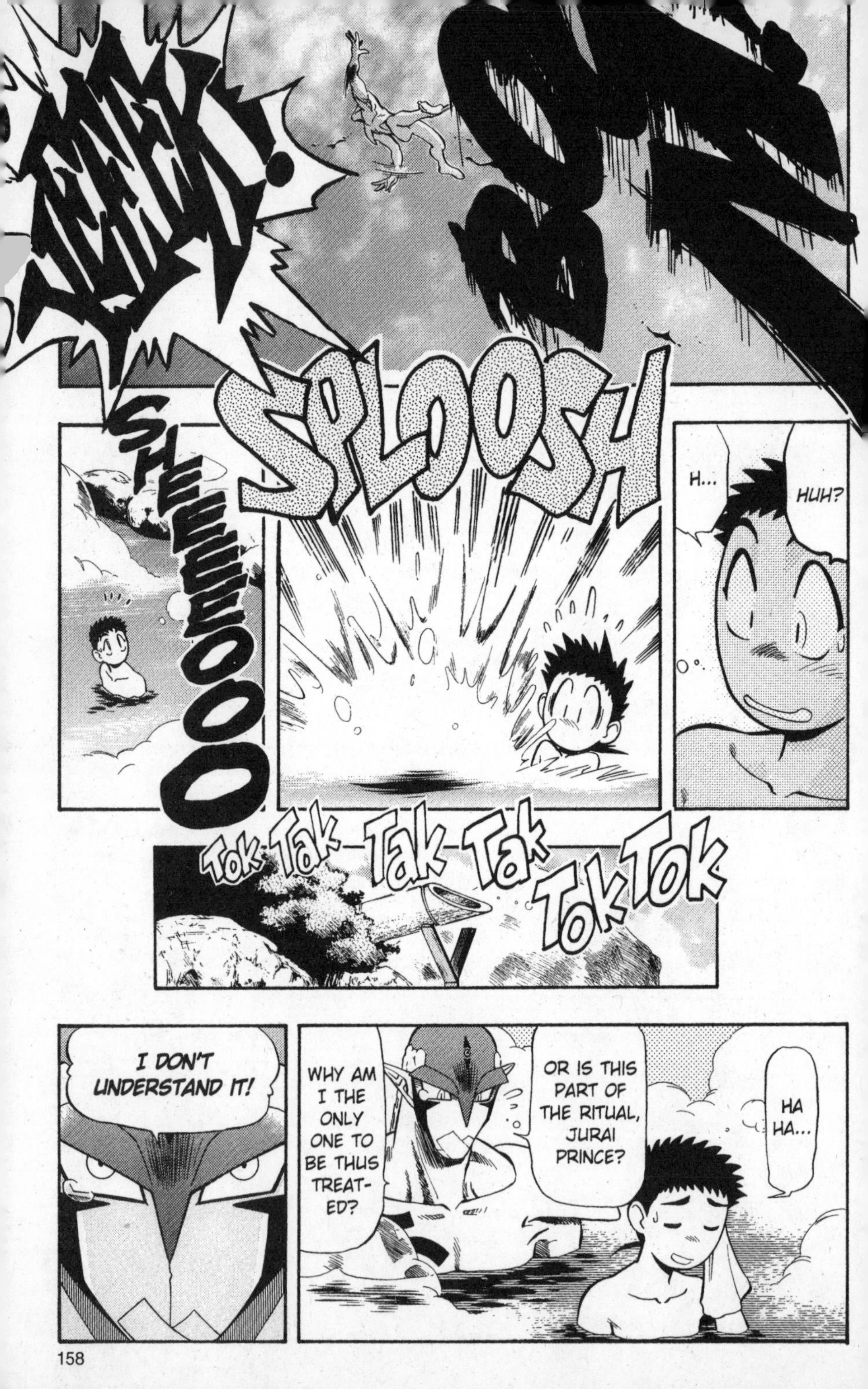
SHEEEEEOOOO
SPLOOSH
H...
HUH?
Tok Tak Tak Tak Tok Tok
I DON'T UNDERSTAND IT!
WHY AM I THE ONLY ONE TO BE THUS TREATED?
OR IS THIS PART OF THE RITUAL, JURAI PRINCE?
HA HA...

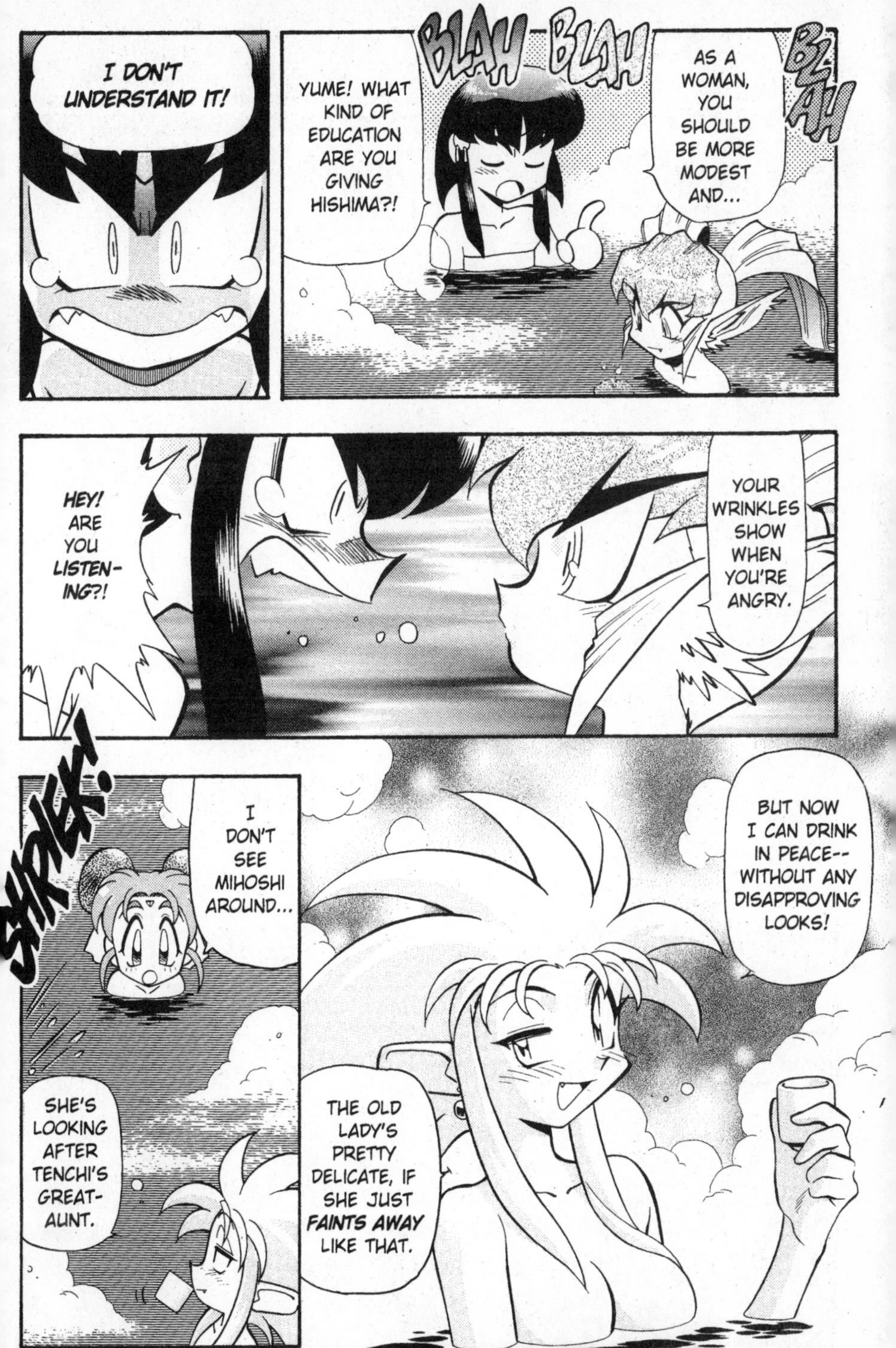
I DON'T UNDERSTAND IT!
BLAH BLAH
YUME! WHAT KIND OF EDUCATION ARE YOU GIVING HISHIMA?!
AS A WOMAN, YOU SHOULD BE MORE MODEST AND...
BLAH
HEY! ARE YOU LISTENING?!
YOUR WRINKLES SHOW WHEN YOU'RE ANGRY.
SHRIEK!
I DON'T SEE MIHOSHI AROUND...
SHE'S LOOKING AFTER TENCHI'S GREAT-AUNT.
THE OLD LADY'S PRETTY DELICATE, IF SHE JUST FAINTS AWAY LIKE THAT.
BUT NOW I CAN DRINK IN PEACE--WITHOUT ANY DISAPPROVING LOOKS!

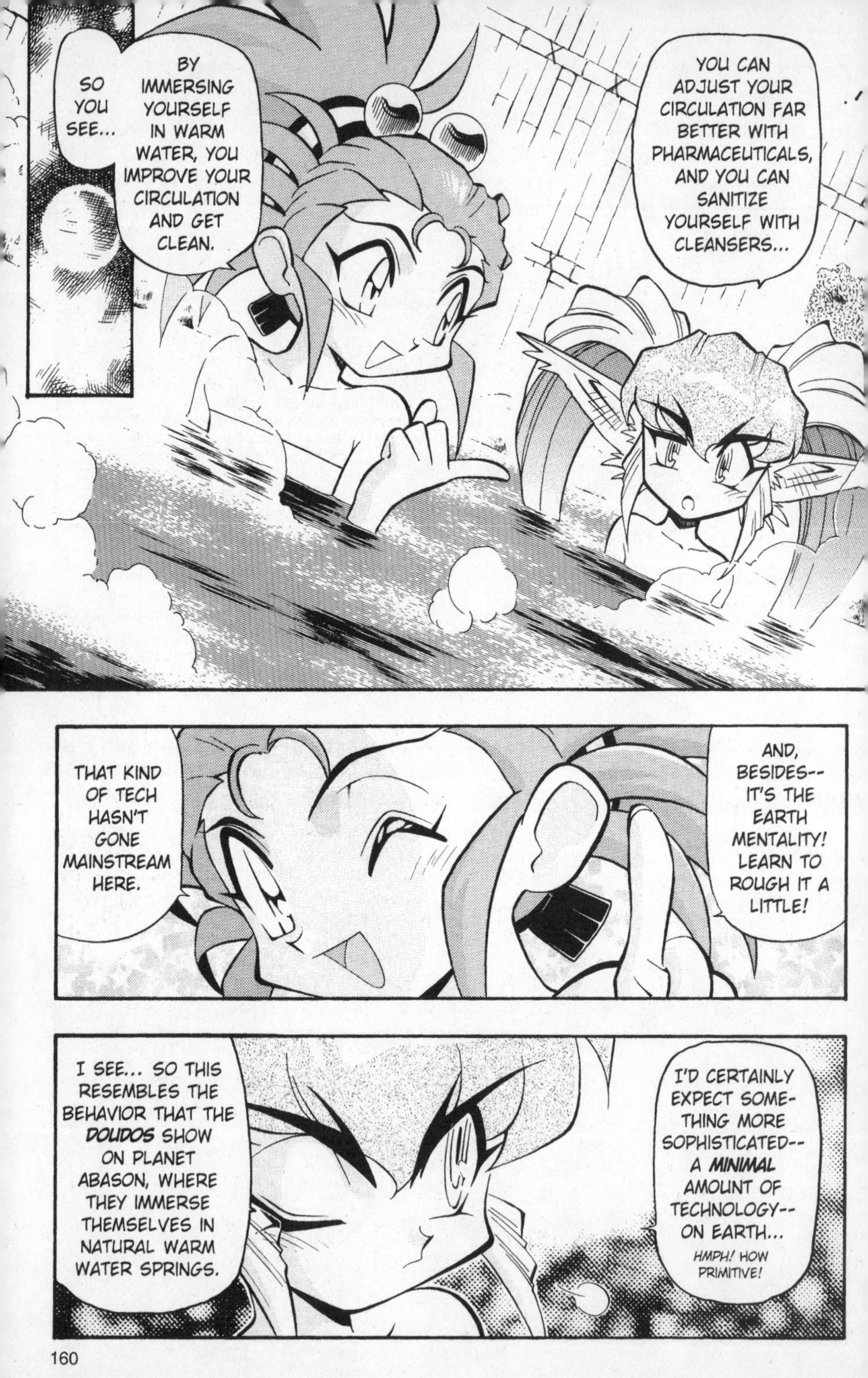
SO YOU SEE...
BY IMMERSING YOURSELF IN WARM WATER, YOU IMPROVE YOUR CIRCULATION AND GET CLEAN.
YOU CAN ADJUST YOUR CIRCULATION FAR BETTER WITH PHARMACEUTICALS, AND YOU CAN SANITIZE YOURSELF WITH CLEANSERS...
THAT KIND OF TECH HASN'T GONE MAINSTREAM HERE.
AND, BESIDES-- IT'S THE EARTH MENTALITY! LEARN TO ROUGH IT A LITTLE!
I SEE... SO THIS RESEMBLES THE BEHAVIOR THAT THE **DOUDOS** SHOW ON PLANET ABASON, WHERE THEY IMMERSE THEMSELVES IN NATURAL WARM WATER SPRINGS.
I'D CERTAINLY EXPECT SOME-THING MORE SOPHISTICATED-- A **MINIMAL** AMOUNT OF TECHNOLOGY-- ON EARTH...
HMPH! HOW PRIMITIVE!

HEY, RYOKO! YOU'RE NOT SUPPOSED TO SWIM IN THE BATH!
fsssh
FOOL! IT'S MORE FUN WHEN IT'S NOT ALLOWED! ♡
TIME FOR A DIVE!
I WISH I COULD DO THAT...
YOU MUSTN'T BECOME STEEPED IN VICE!
BLUB! BLUB!
HIC... HUH?
WAS THERE SUCH A DEEP SPOT BEFORE?
!
WHAT'S THAT?
DANGER
DANGER
Don't Touch!

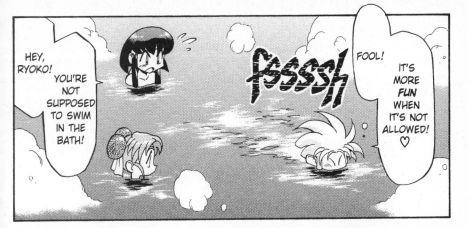

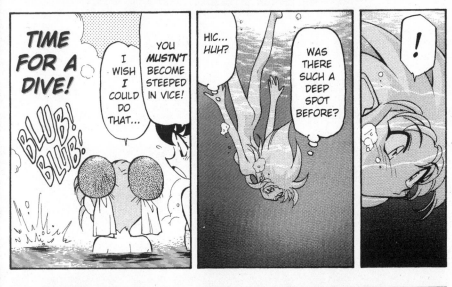

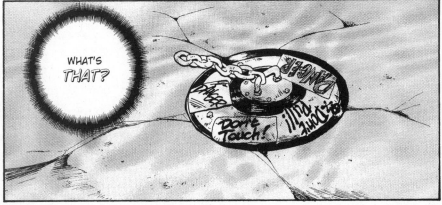

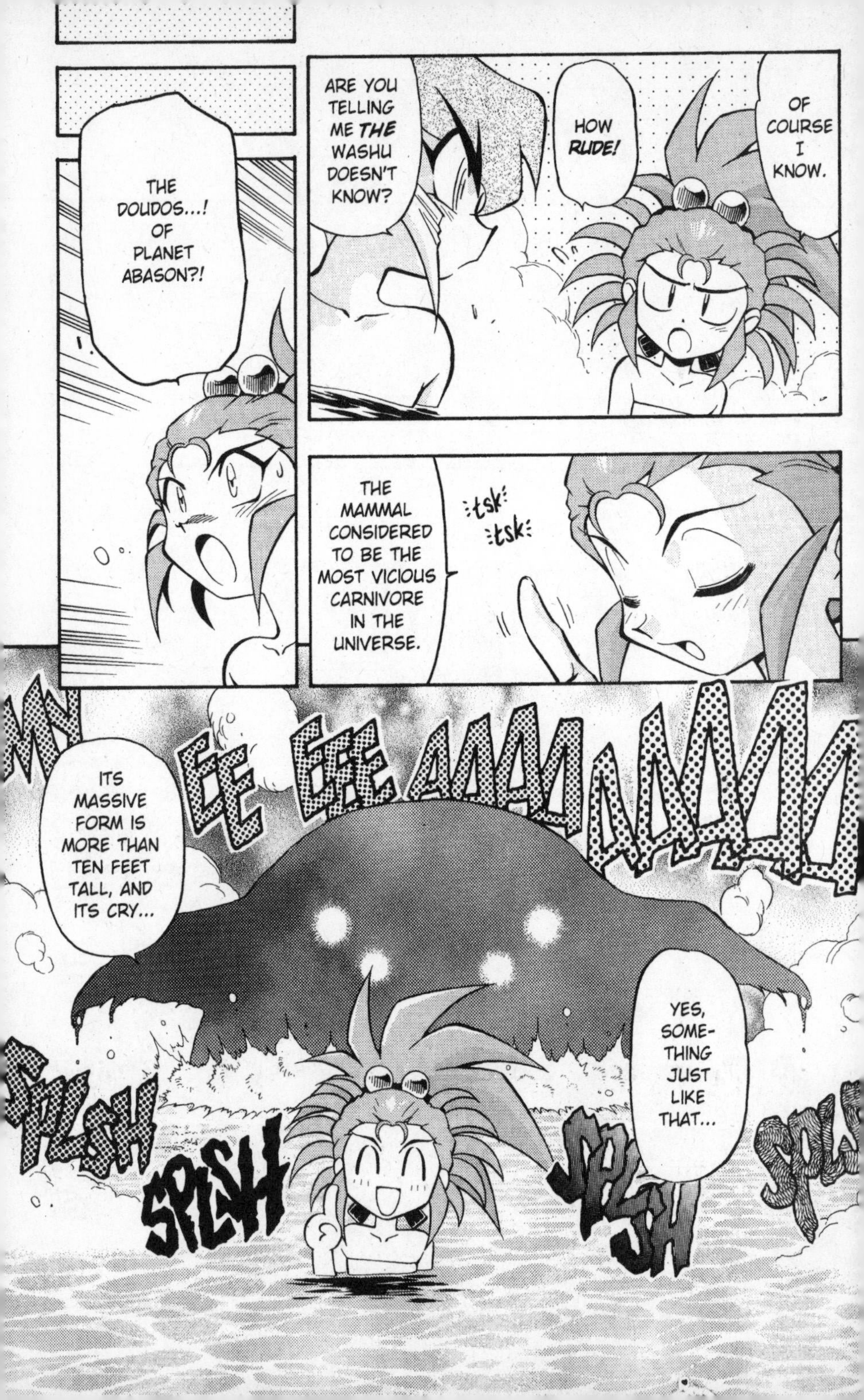
THE DOUDOS...! OF PLANET ABASON?!
ARE YOU TELLING ME ***THE*** WASHU DOESN'T KNOW?
HOW ***RUDE!***
OF COURSE I KNOW.
THE MAMMAL CONSIDERED TO BE THE MOST VICIOUS CARNIVORE IN THE UNIVERSE.
tsk
tsk
EEE EEE AAAAAAAA
ITS MASSIVE FORM IS MORE THAN TEN FEET TALL, AND ITS CRY...
SPLSH
SPLSH
YES, SOME-THING JUST LIKE THAT...
SPLSH
SPLS

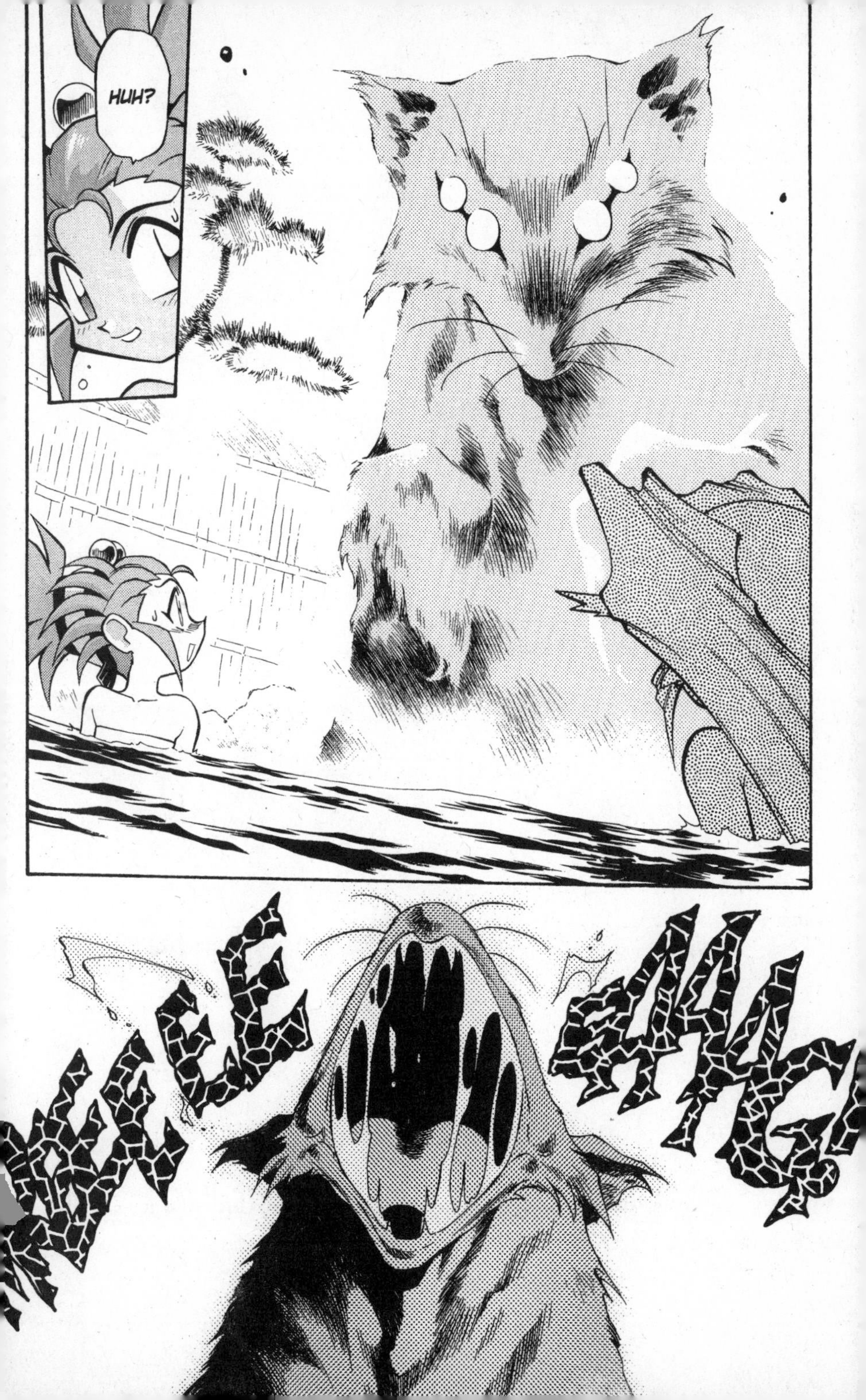
HUH?

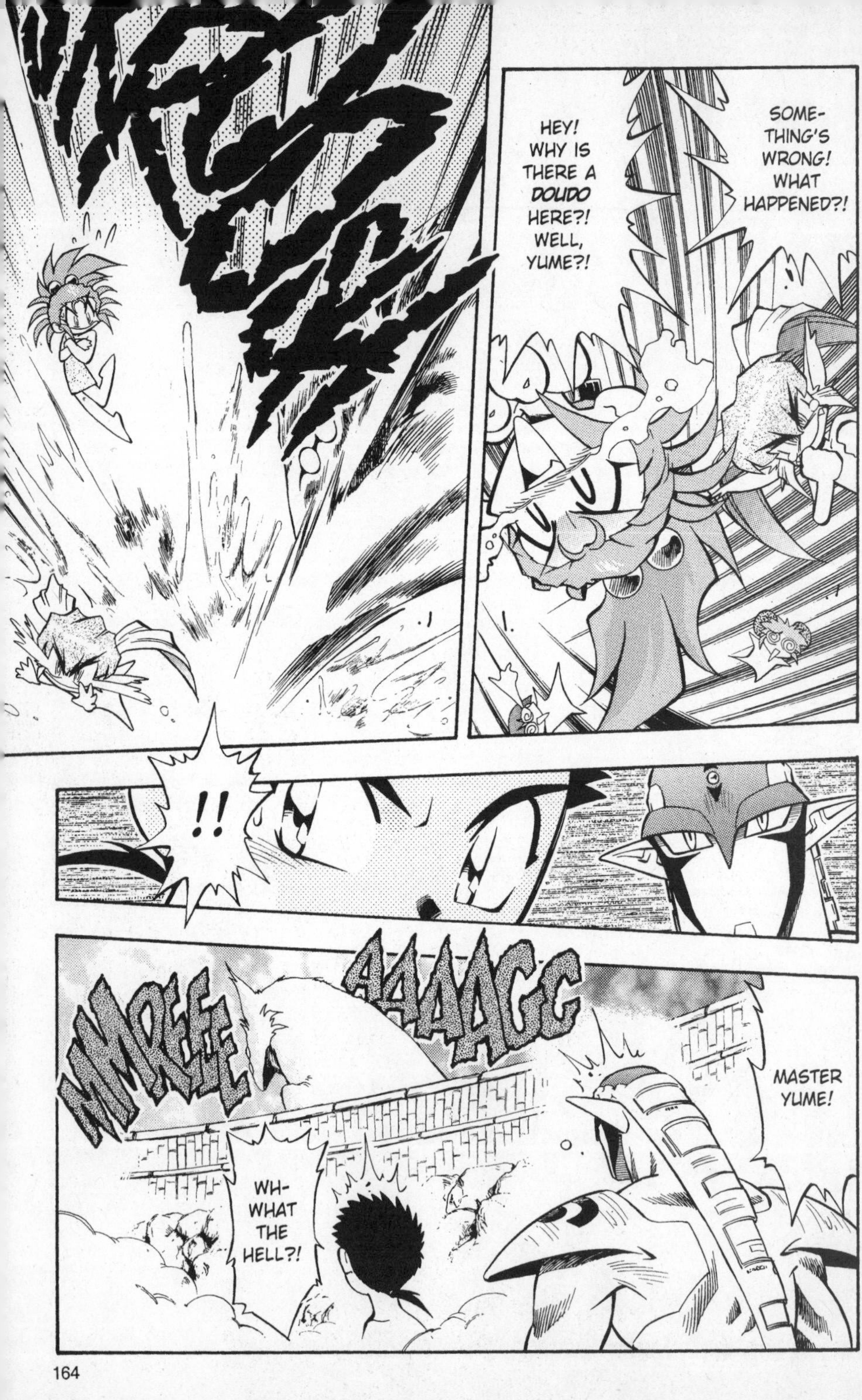
HEY! WHY IS THERE A DOUDO HERE?! WELL, YUME?!
SOME-THING'S WRONG! WHAT HAPPENED?!
!!
WH-WHAT THE HELL?!
MASTER YUME!

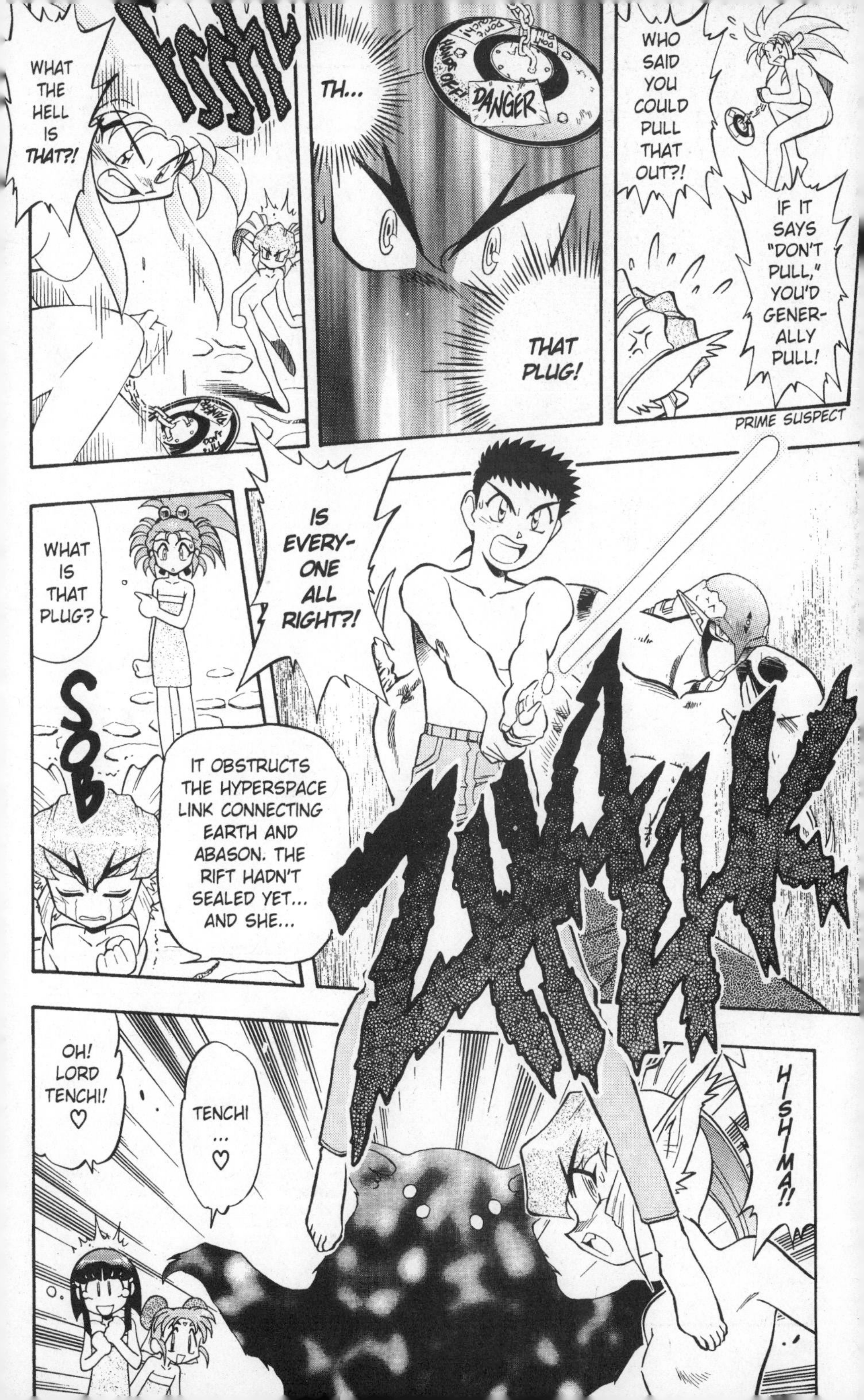
WHAT THE HELL IS THAT?!
TH...
DANGER
THAT PLUG!
WHO SAID YOU COULD PULL THAT OUT?!
IF IT SAYS "DON'T PULL," YOU'D GENERALLY PULL!
PRIME SUSPECT
WHAT IS THAT PLUG?
IS EVERYONE ALL RIGHT?!
SOB
IT OBSTRUCTS THE HYPERSPACE LINK CONNECTING EARTH AND ABASON. THE RIFT HADN'T SEALED YET... AND SHE...
OH! LORD TENCHI! ♡
TENCHI ... ♡
HISHIMA!!

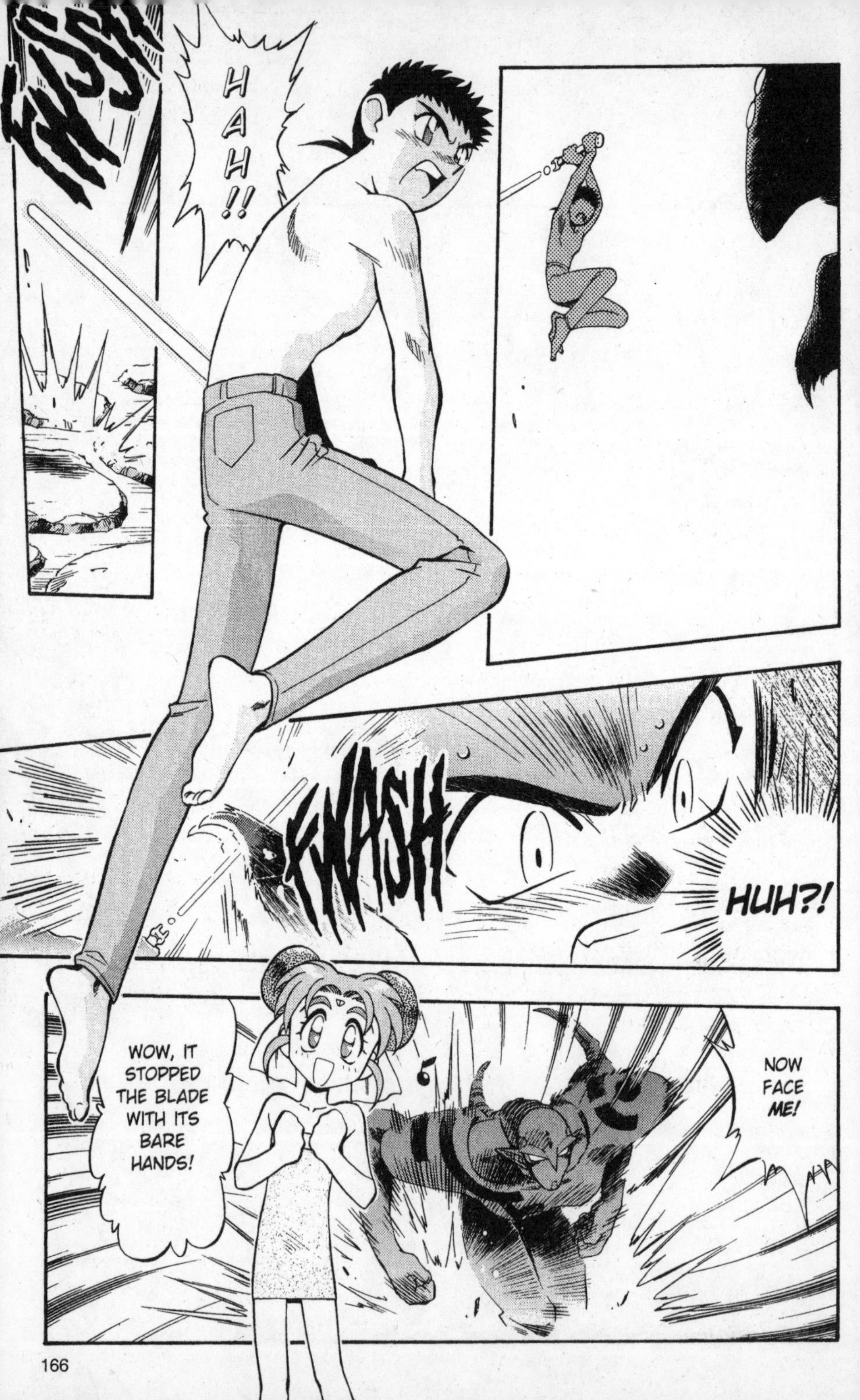
FWSH
HAH!!
FWASH
HUH?!
WOW, IT STOPPED THE BLADE WITH ITS BARE HANDS!
NOW FACE *ME!*

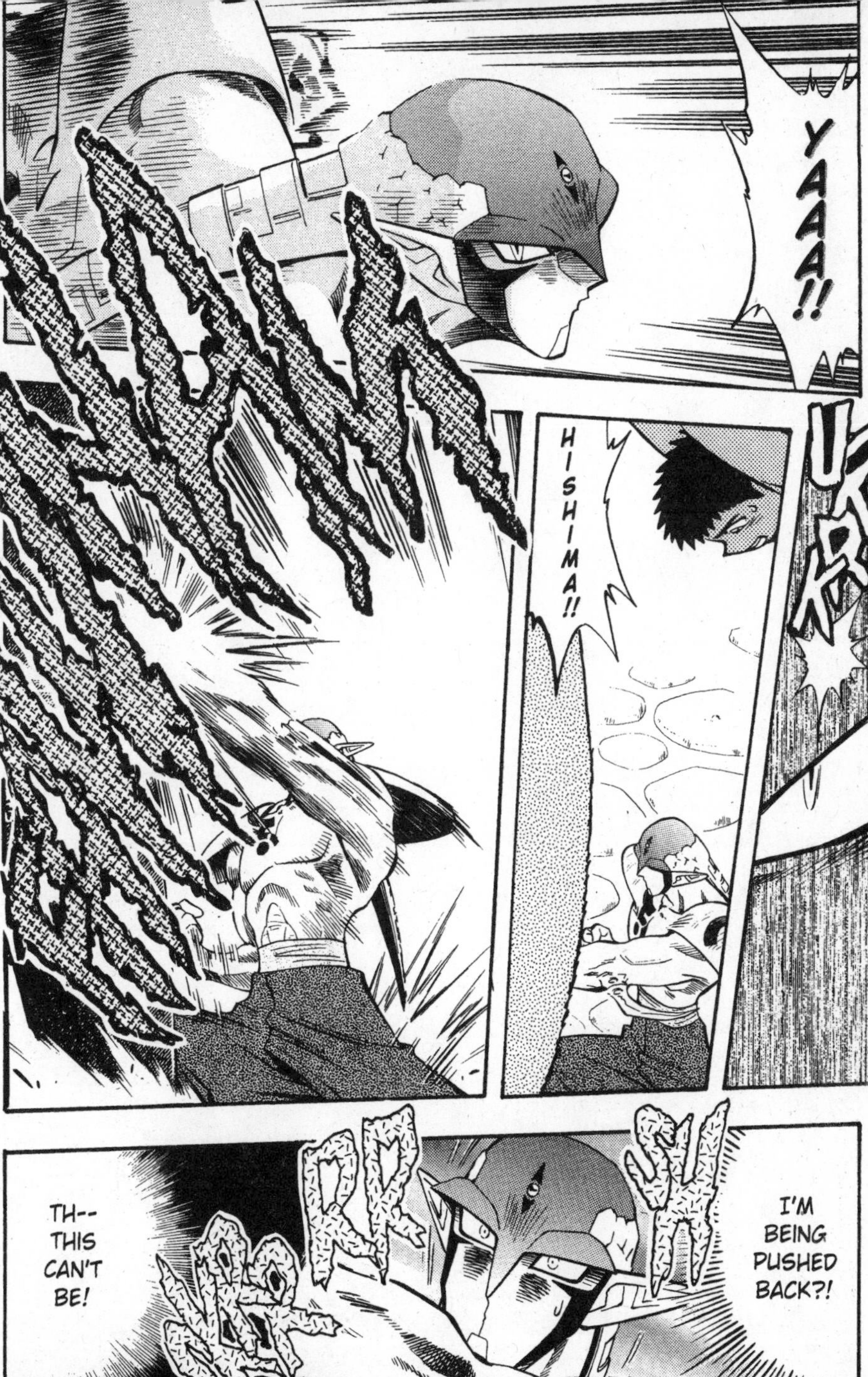
YAAAA!!
HISHIMA!!
TH-- THIS CAN'T BE!
I'M BEING PUSHED BACK?!

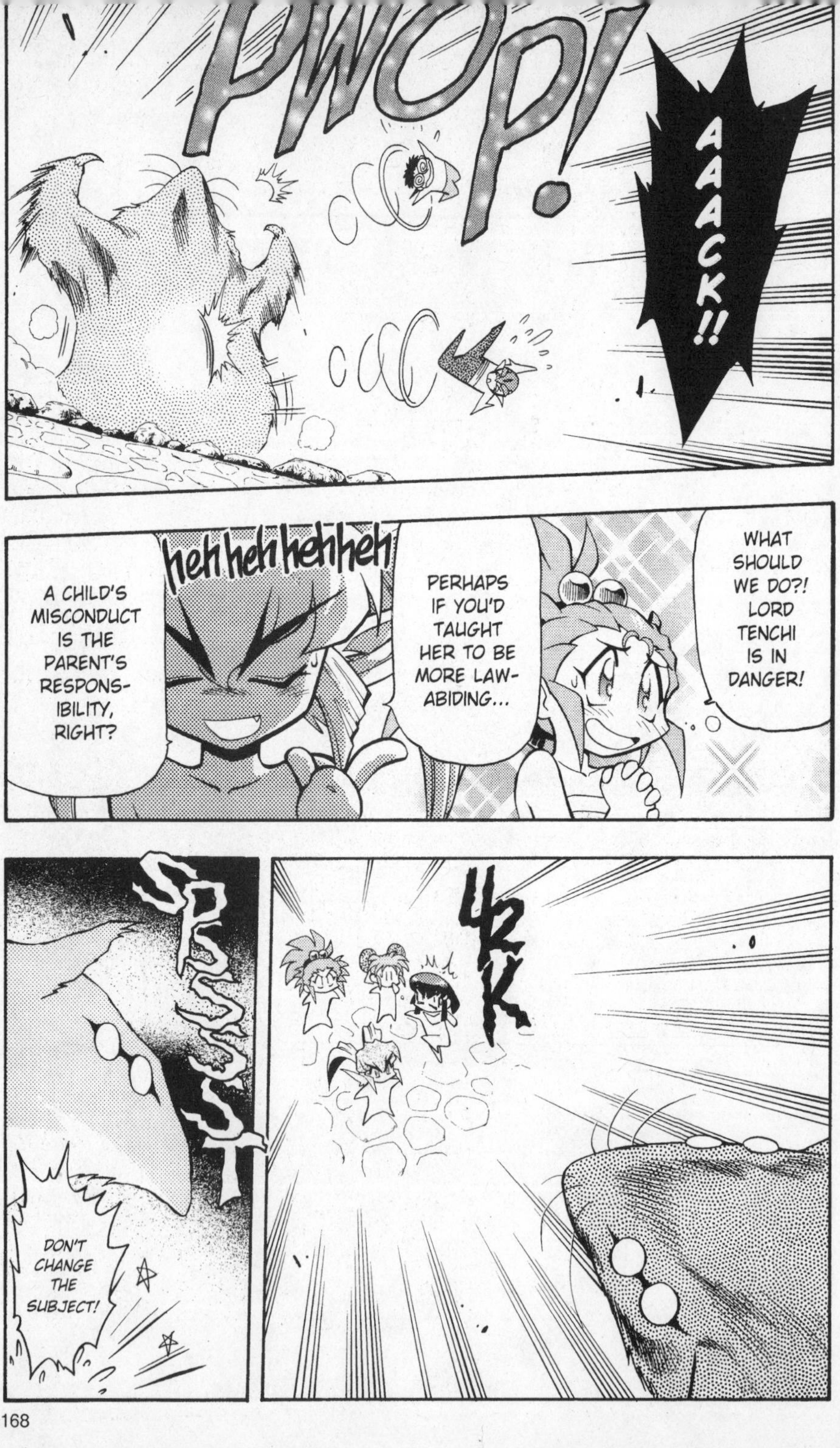
PWOP!
AAACK!!
A CHILD'S MISCONDUCT IS THE PARENT'S RESPONSIBILITY, RIGHT?
heh heh hehheh
PERHAPS IF YOU'D TAUGHT HER TO BE MORE LAW-ABIDING...
WHAT SHOULD WE DO?! LORD TENCHI IS IN DANGER!
SPSSST
DON'T CHANGE THE SUBJECT!
UK

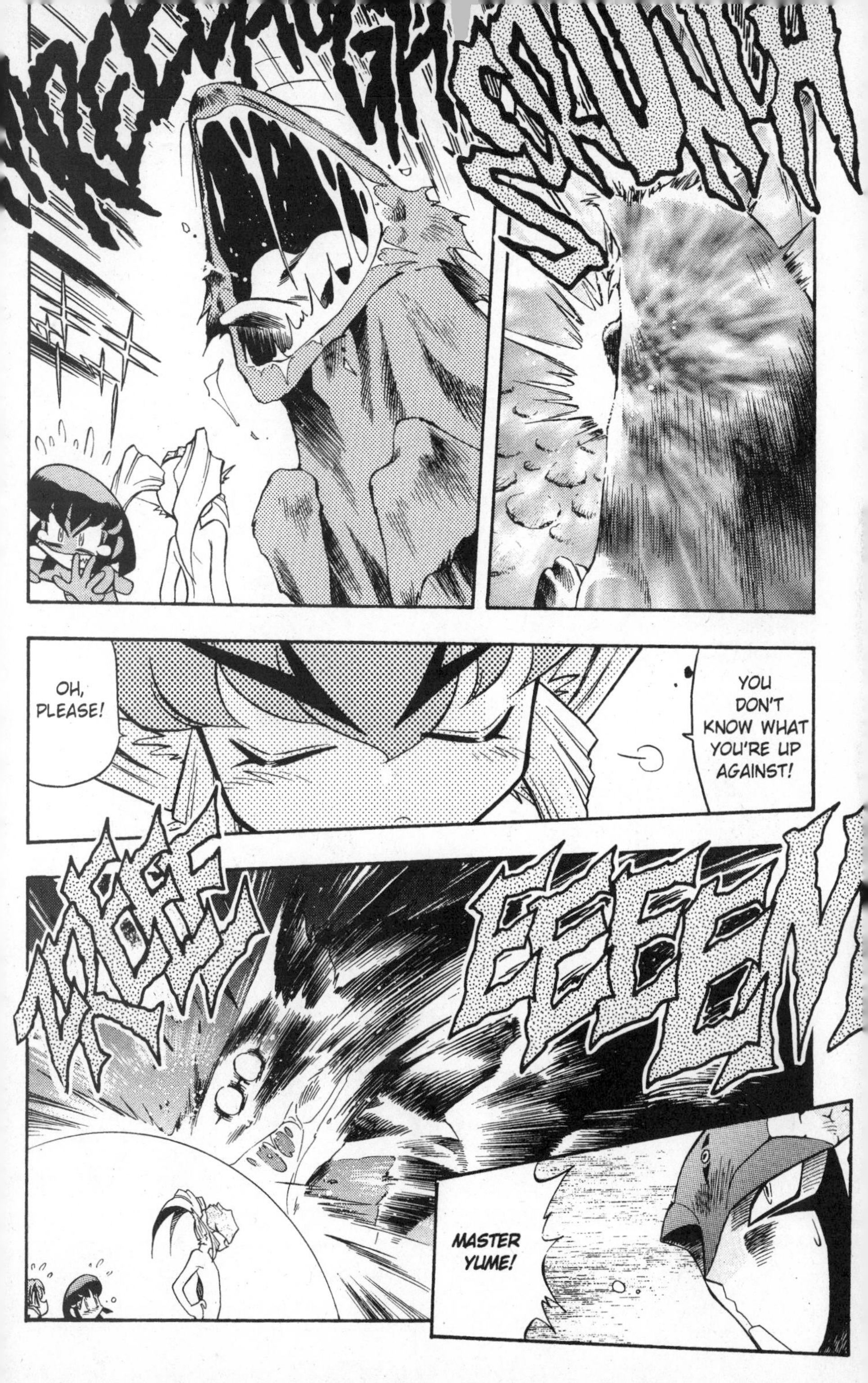
OH, PLEASE!
YOU DON'T KNOW WHAT YOU'RE UP AGAINST!
MASTER YUME!

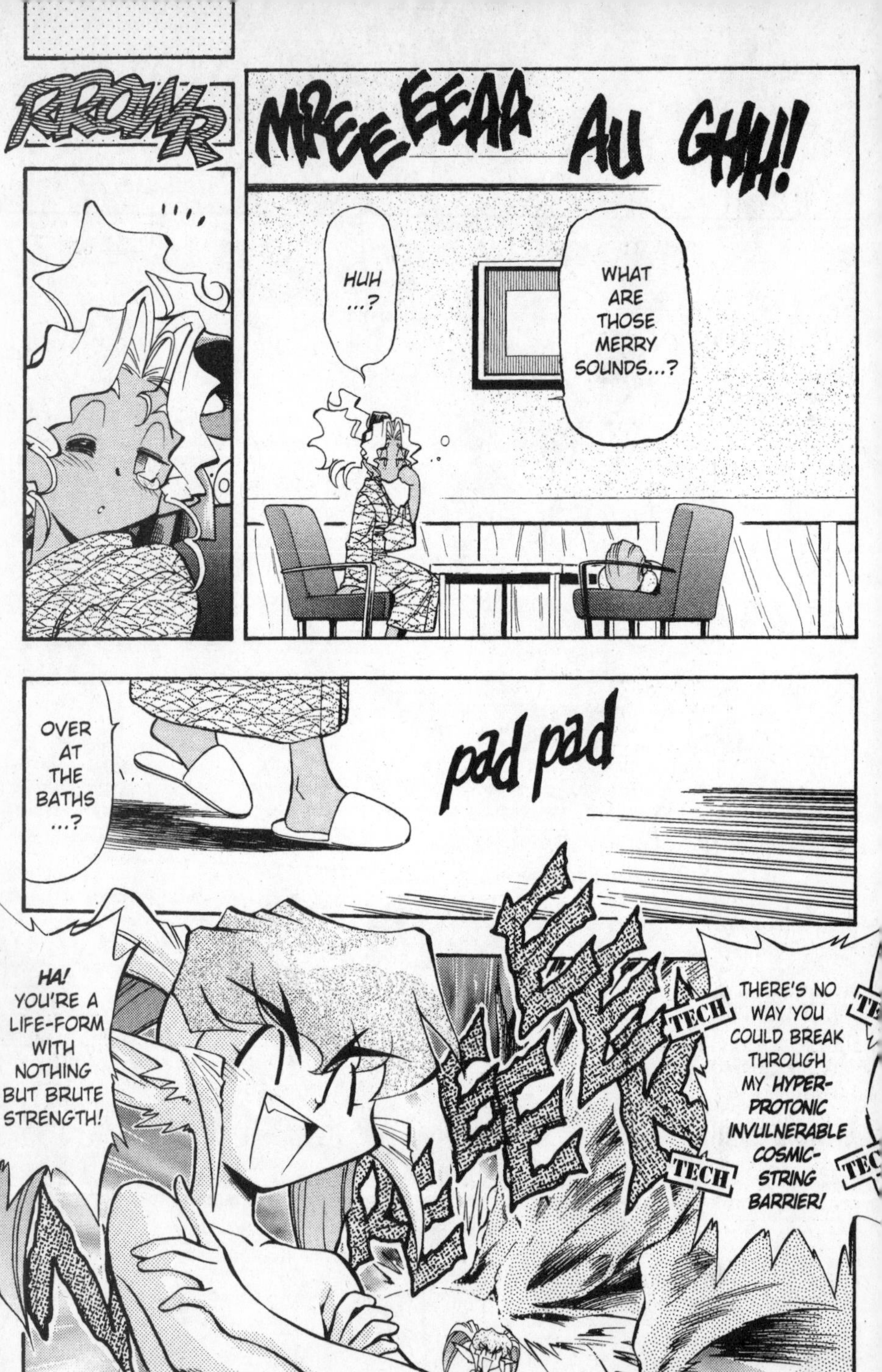
KRROWR
MREE EEAA AU GHH!
HUH ...?
WHAT ARE THOSE MERRY SOUNDS...?
OVER AT THE BATHS ...?
pad pad
HA! YOU'RE A LIFE-FORM WITH NOTHING BUT BRUTE STRENGTH!
TECH
TECH
THERE'S NO WAY YOU COULD BREAK THROUGH MY HYPER-PROTONIC INVULNERABLE COSMIC-STRING BARRIER!
TECH
TECH

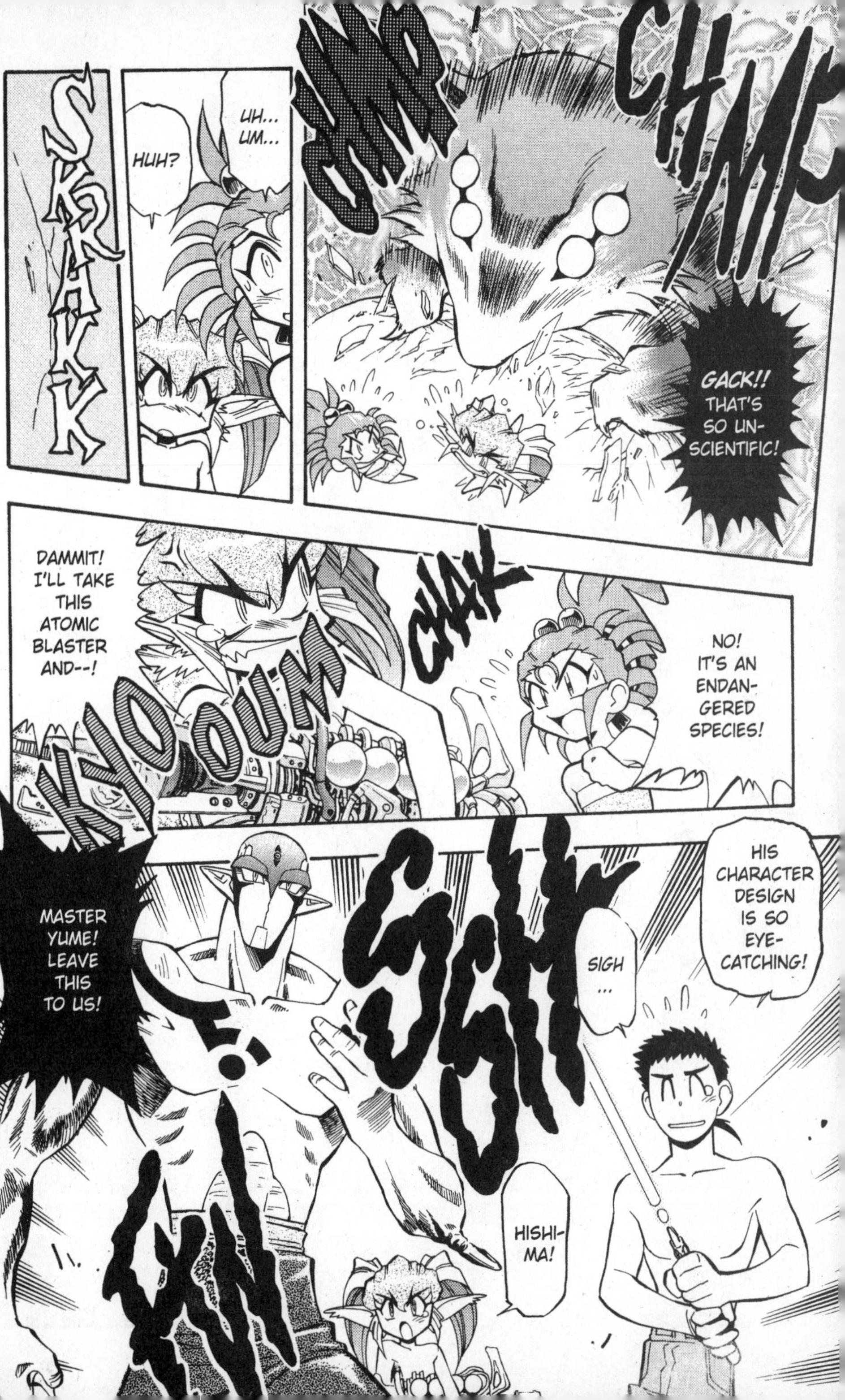
SKRAKK
UH... UM...
HUH?
CHOMP
CHOMP
GACK!! THAT'S SO UN-SCIENTIFIC!
DAMMIT! I'LL TAKE THIS ATOMIC BLASTER AND--!
KYOOUM
CHAK
NO! IT'S AN ENDANGERED SPECIES!
MASTER YUME! LEAVE THIS TO US!
SIGH
SIGH ...
HIS CHARACTER DESIGN IS SO EYE-CATCHING!
HISHIMA!

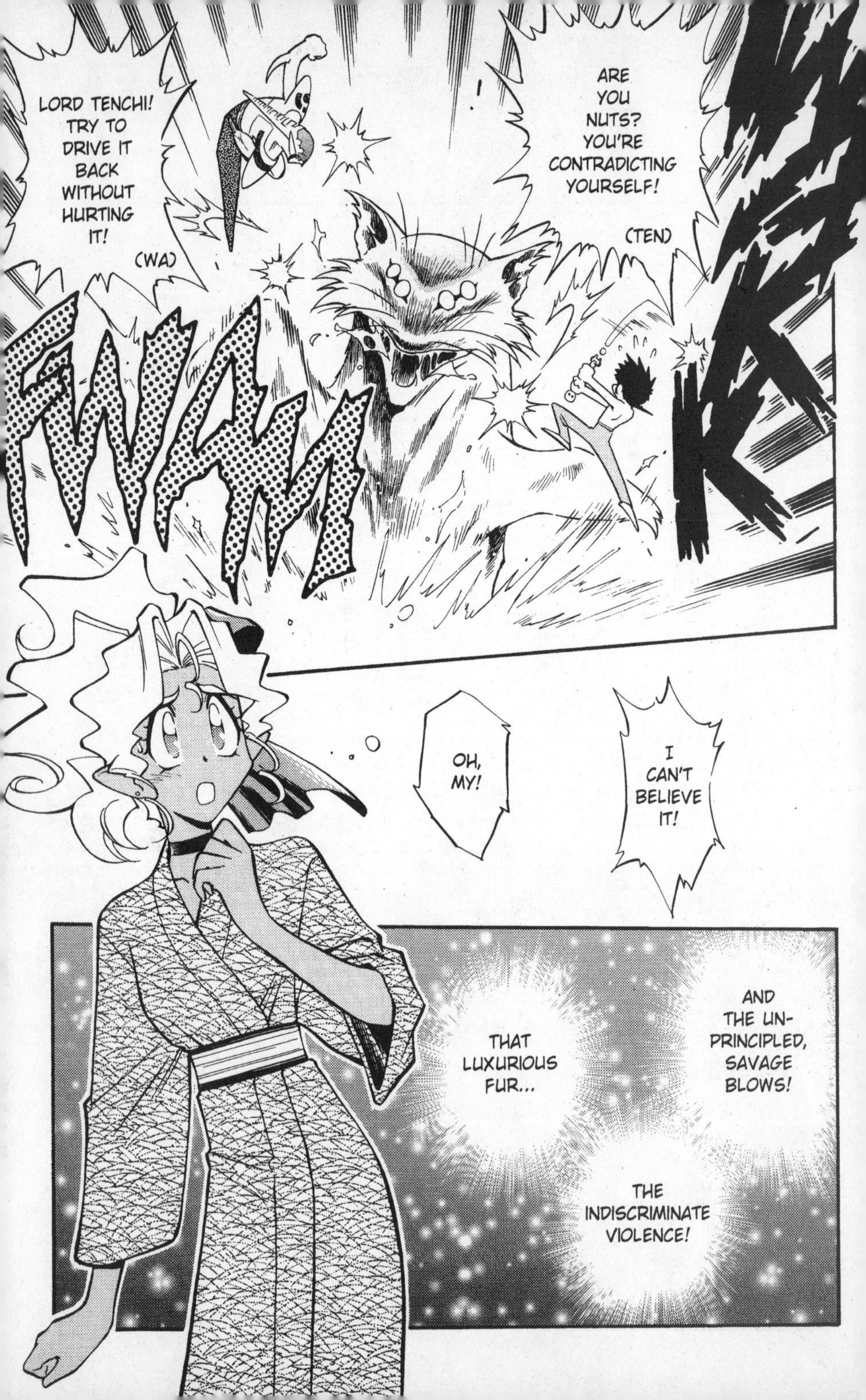
LORD TENCHI! TRY TO DRIVE IT BACK WITHOUT HURTING IT!
(WA)
!
ARE YOU NUTS? YOU'RE CONTRADICTING YOURSELF!
(TEN)
FWAM
K
OH, MY!
I CAN'T BELIEVE IT!
THAT LUXURIOUS FUR...
AND THE UN-PRINCIPLED, SAVAGE BLOWS!
THE INDISCRIMINATE VIOLENCE!

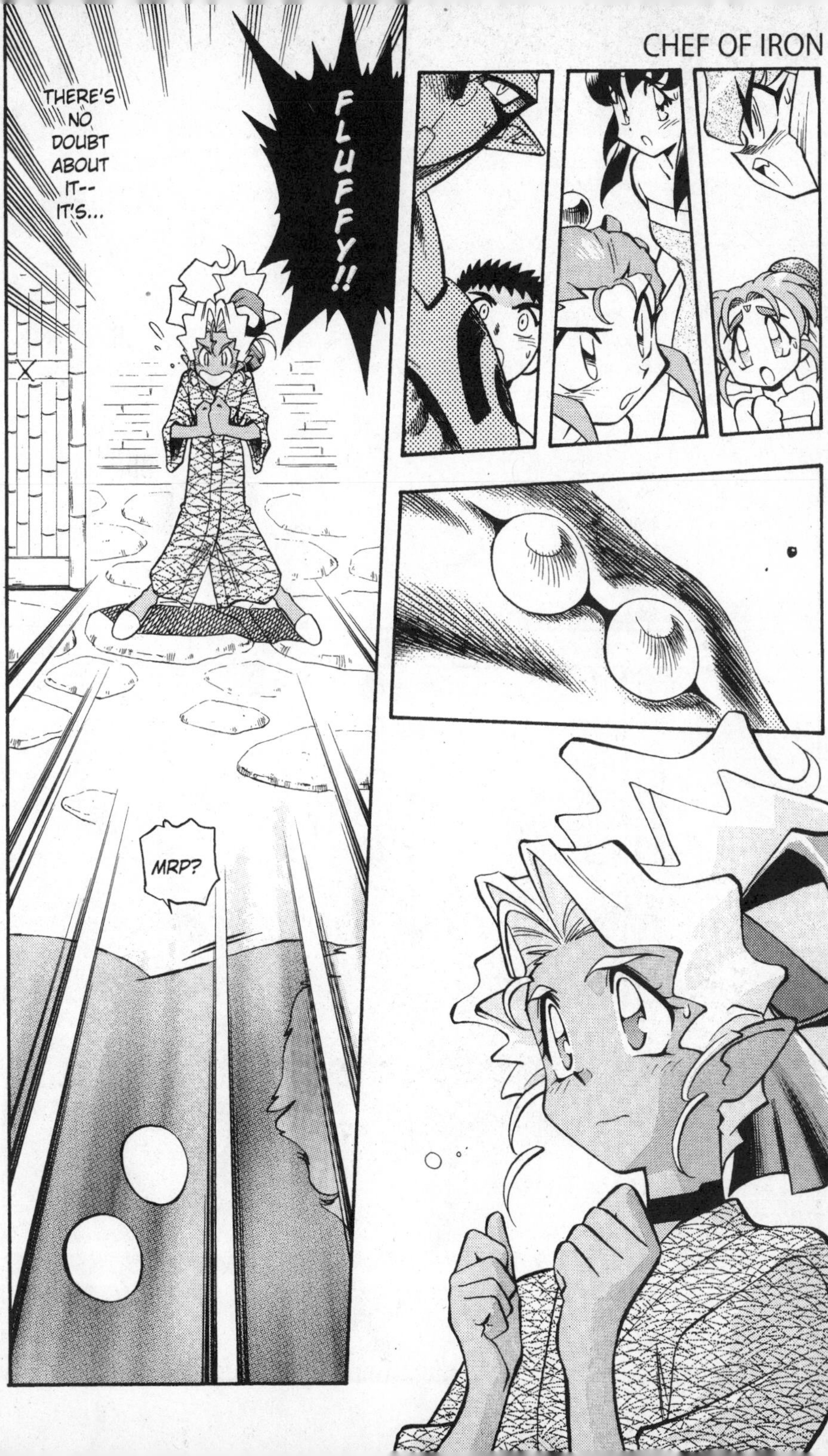
THERE'S NO DOUBT ABOUT IT-- IT'S...
FLUFFY!!
MRP?

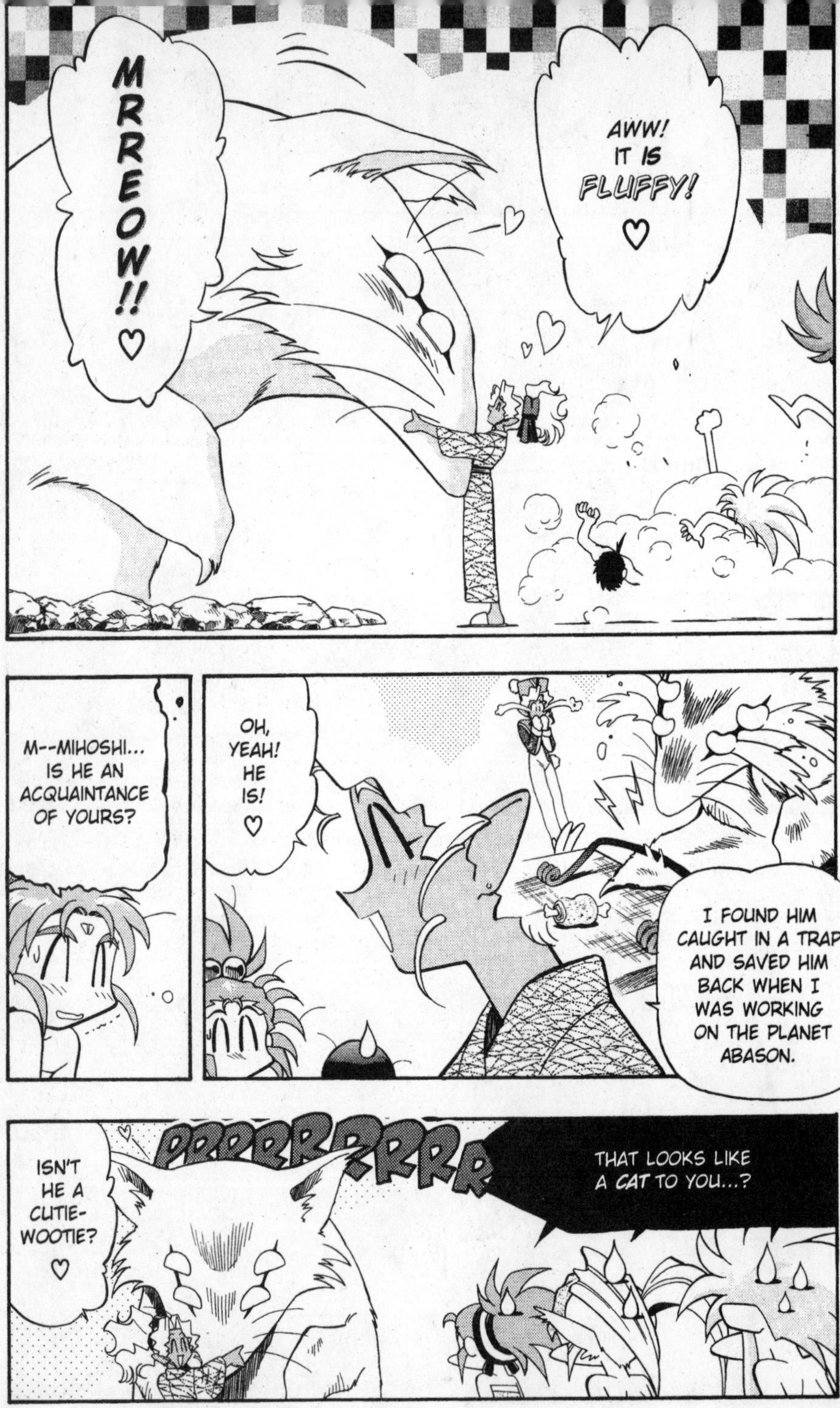
MRREOW!! ♡
AWW! IT IS FLUFFY! ♡
M--MIHOSHI... IS HE AN ACQUAINTANCE OF YOURS?
OH, YEAH! HE IS! ♡
I FOUND HIM CAUGHT IN A TRAP AND SAVED HIM BACK WHEN I WAS WORKING ON THE PLANET ABASON.
ISN'T HE A CUTIE-WOOTIE? ♡
PRRRRRRRRR
THAT LOOKS LIKE A CAT TO YOU...?

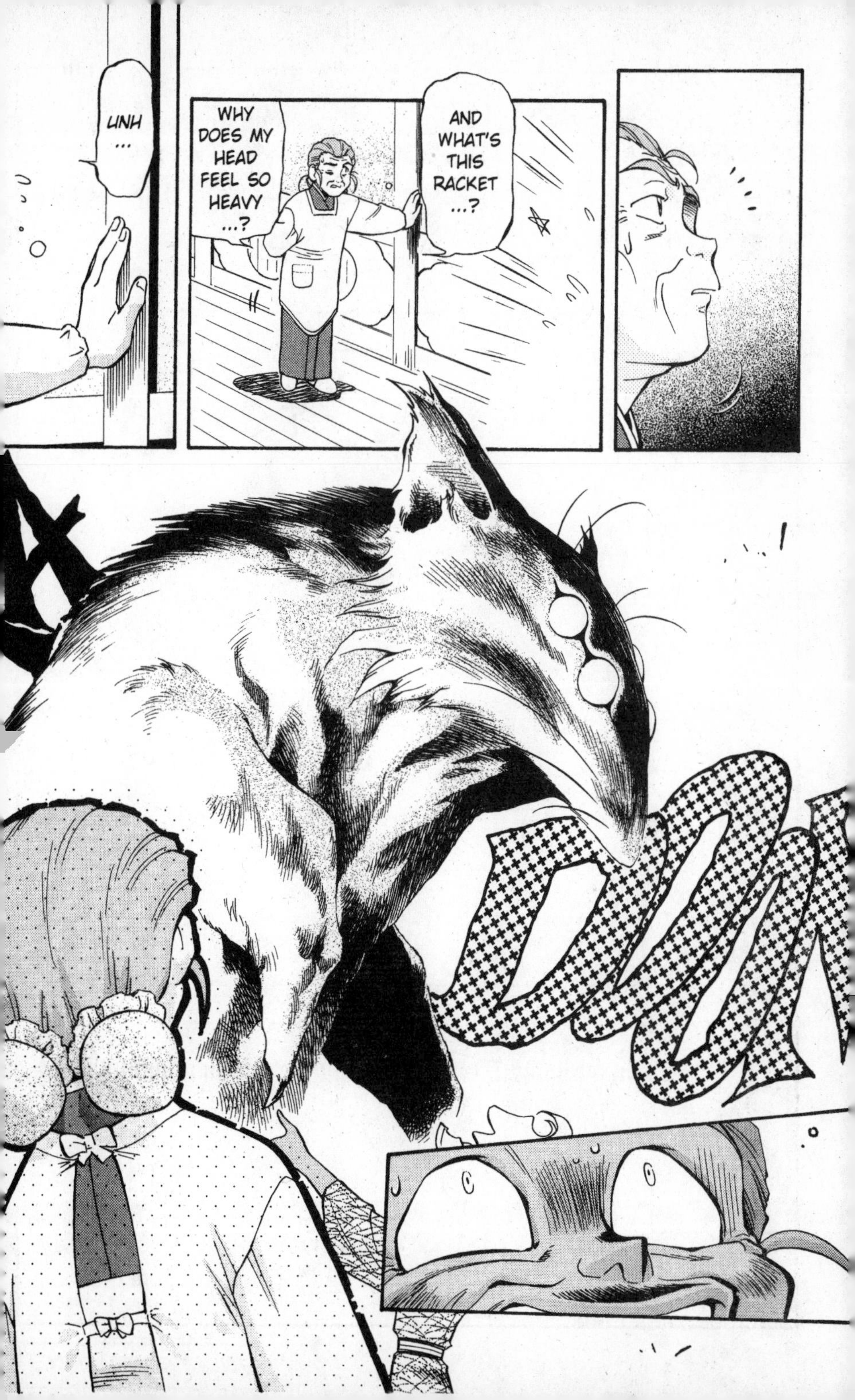
UNH ...
WHY DOES MY HEAD FEEL SO HEAVY ...?
AND WHAT'S THIS RACKET ...?
...!

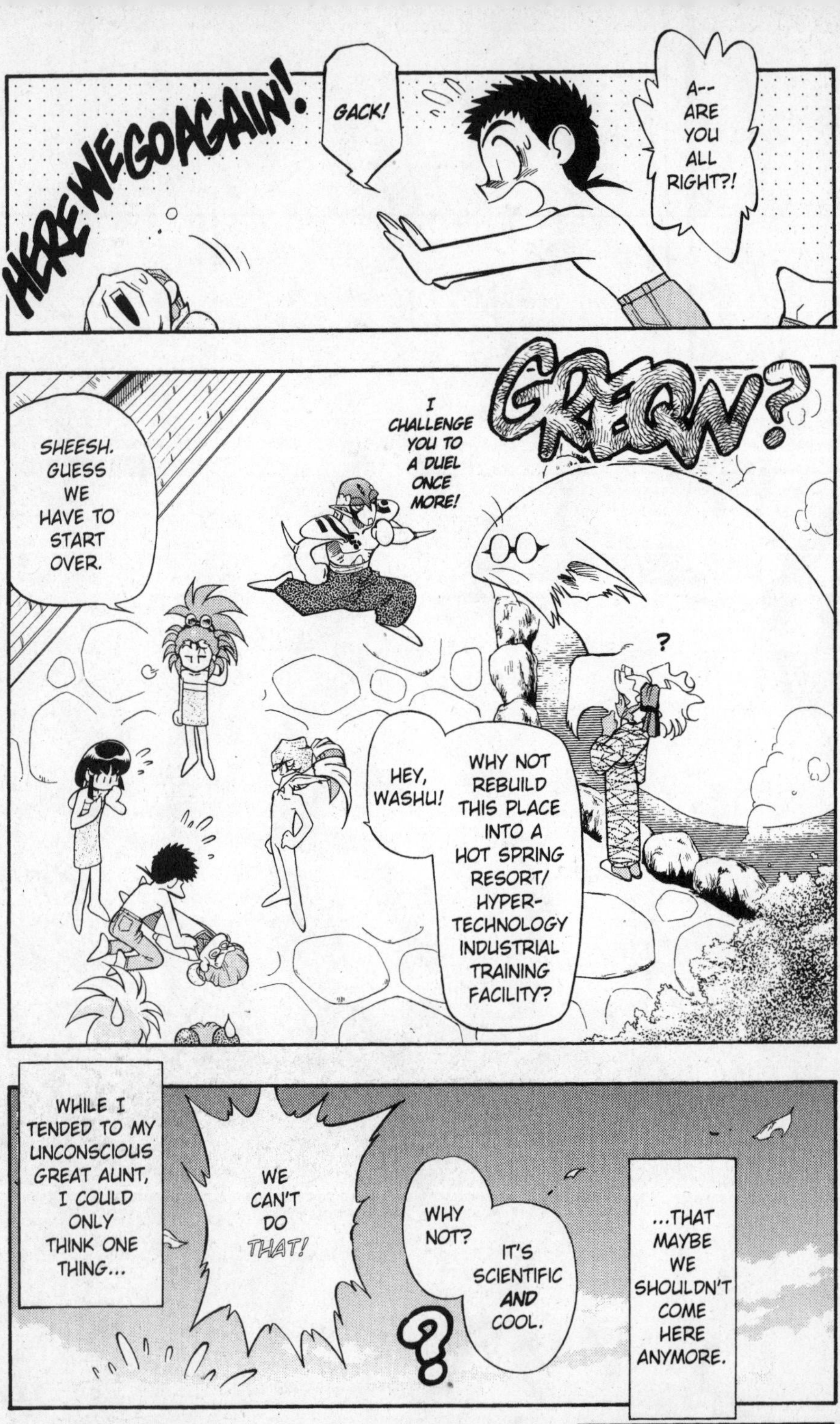
HERE WE GO AGAIN!
GACK!
A-- ARE YOU ALL RIGHT?!
SHEESH. GUESS WE HAVE TO START OVER.
I CHALLENGE YOU TO A DUEL ONCE MORE!
GREOW?
?
HEY, WASHU!
WHY NOT REBUILD THIS PLACE INTO A HOT SPRING RESORT/ HYPER-TECHNOLOGY INDUSTRIAL TRAINING FACILITY?
WHILE I TENDED TO MY UNCONSCIOUS GREAT AUNT, I COULD ONLY THINK ONE THING...
WE CAN'T DO *THAT!*
WHY NOT?
IT'S SCIENTIFIC **AND** COOL.
?
...THAT MAYBE WE SHOULDN'T COME HERE ANYMORE.

TO BE CONTINUED...